BRITAIN'S RAILWAY LIVERIES

Colours Crests and Linings

By the same Author:

THE MODEL RAILWAY ENCYCLOPAEDIA

THE RAILWAY ENCYCLOPÆDIA

BRITAIN'S RAILWAY LIVERIES

Colours Crests and Linings
1825—1948

ERNEST F. CARTER

LIMITED

First published (by Burke Publishing Company Limited) 1952
Second edition October 1963
Third edition January 1980

To "Bob" Mitchell

ISBN 0 287 66989 0

Harold Starke Limited
Pegasus House, 116–120 *Golden Lane, London* EC1Y 0TL

Printed in Great Britain
at the University Press, Oxford
by Eric Buckley
Printer to the University

ACKNOWLEDGEMENTS

IT is a pleasure to acknowledge the valuable assistance the Publishers and I have received from many kind friends, without whose co-operation this book would not have been so comprehensive or accurate; and our sincerest thanks are due to V. Boyd-Carpenter, S.M.E.E., and H. Leslie Overend for so kindly reading the proofs of many of the sections; to John N. Maskelyne, A.I.Loco.E., President, Stephenson Locomotive Society, for scrutinising the proofs of the Great Western section and the pre-group companies comprised in the Southern Railway; and to A. B. McLeod, M.I. Loco.E., for carrying out the same important task with the railways of Scotland.

I would also mention with gratitude the great assistance given by G. F. Westcott, B.Sc., curator of the Land Transport Section of the Science Museum, South Kensington, London, who was so good as to allow me free access to the original Stephenson records, some very early Great Western coloured drawings, goodly portions of the celebrated Philimore and Dendy Marshall collections, and for reading the proofs. My thanks also to Mr. Westcott's able assistant, Mr. Eastwood, who opened the glass cases of many historical models to allow me to effect contact colour matchings.

During my stay at York, Mr. Goaten, who is in charge of the Queen Street (larger exhibits) section of the Railway Museum, gave me every conceivable assistance and facility to enable me to obtain perfect contact colour-matchings on some of the most inaccessible parts of the locomotives under his immediate care; and to him my very best thanks are tendered, for without his help, almost all the detailed and keyed colour and livery descriptions of the engines and other rolling-stock in the Museum would have been impossible.

In my search through nearly a hundred volumes of *The Engineer* at the Tate Library, Brixton, London, Mr. Callender, the Chief Librarian, not only gave me every possible facility for research, but also arranged for permission to reproduce facsimile copies of locomotive number-plates.

At the Croydon Reference Library a similar "freedom of the Library" was readily given by my old friend and librarian, Kenneth

Ryde, who piloted me through several score of volumes of *Engineering* and the *Railway Magazine* from its first volume; whilst at H.M. Patent Office Library all the assistants were extremely helpful, and lightened what was very literally an extraordinarily heavy task!

Lastly, but by no means least, I wish particularly to thank my son, Kenneth E. Carter, for the patience and care he has taken in the skilful preparation of the coloured plates which help to illustrate this book and enhance its value as a historical record.

1952. E. F. C.

The Author and Publishers wish to thank the following for permission to reproduce photographs: British Railways, The Locomotive Publishing Co. Ltd., *The Engineer*, and The Science Museum, South Kensington, (the "Alexandra" locomotive, 1851; from a Crown Copyright model).

CONTENTS

PART I
Pre-Group Liveries, 1825–1922

PART II
Group Liveries 1923–1948

ILLUSTRATIONS

COLOUR PLATES

MONOCHROME PLATES

LININGS AND DIAGRAMS

Crests and Coats-of-Arms
throughout

PREFACE

In the early days of railways, when one line was perhaps in Durham, another in Cornwall, and a third in Lancashire, there was obviously no need for any distinguishing colours for the rolling-stock and there was no attempt at standardisation, locomotives being painted in different colours for the *same* railway. Again, early railways bought their locomotives from independent makers who probably had special standard colours and decorative methods. It was not until the 1840's, when two or more different railways met in the same district, that some form of distinction became imperative.

When "grouping" took place at the beginning of the year 1923, about forty large companies and twice as many smaller railways lost their identity in the "Big Four" (which comprised the Great Western Railway, the London, Midland and Scottish Railway, the London and North Eastern Railway, and the Southern Railway); and at the same time the characteristic colour-schemes of their locomotives and rolling-stock, as well as their crests and heraldic devices disappeared, and their places were taken by the well-known "amalgamation" colour-schemes, which persisted until nationalisation in the year 1948.

The railways of Britain being thus merged into one vast concern, the liveries and heraldry of the group and pre-grouping companies are in very real danger of passing into complete oblivion; and this book—the only one ever to be written on the subject—is the result of a sincere effort to present in an integrated form as much available information as possible on this intensely interesting side of railway history—the rolling-stock colours and liveries. This knowledge has been gathered from many hundreds of widely scattered literary and factual sources; and it represents the culmination of many years of intensive research, enquiry and travel.

It will be readily appreciated that, as it is impossible for even a very elderly person to remember details with any accuracy for much more than about fifty years, the writer has been forced therefore to rely entirely upon the written word in almost all cases dating prior to approximately the beginning of this century.

In every possible case, the sources of information have been cross-checked, and in some cases conflicting references have been recorded for the sake of completeness.

In no single instance has the writer's personal knowledge, opinion, or bias modified or amplified the material collected; but in rare cases, where incorrect descriptions have been noted, these have been referred to the specialist authorities, with a view to checking their accuracy. Where confirmed, such errors have been corrected.

To assure the accurate identification of those of the colours the author could actually check against rolling-stock as well as those of more subtle shade and tint, these colours have been keyed into the text numerically, so that reference may be made to the *actual paint* colour-chart which is included in this book.

The locomotive colour plates, as distinct from the paint colour-chart, are definitely not intended to be used as colour guides, as they are subject, like all other colour reproductions, to the vagaries and variations of four-colour process reproduction. The reproductions, produced with highest technical skill will, however, give the reader an accurate picture of the liveries of some of the early engines of the railways of Britain.

It is sincerely hoped that this volume will not only form a permanent record of and guide to the colour-schemes and liveries of Britain's railways, and, through the medium of the colour-chart, provide a "common meeting-place" for future colour matching, but that it will also find a ready use among those railway lovers and modellers who have made their speciality "old-time" rolling-stock and locomotives.

ERNEST F. CARTER.

WARLINGHAM, Surrey.
October, 1952.

INTRODUCTION

It is generally known that a normal individual perceives six colours or hues in the solar spectrum, *viz*. red, orange, yellow, green, blue, and violet; but it is not so widely known that rarely do two people see a given colour as precisely the same tint. For example, a certain green may appear bluer to one individual, and yellower to another; and the only criterion of an accuracy of match becomes thus dependent upon a general consensus of opinion on the part of any number of viewers.

Optical experts declare that no less than one out of every five persons has some form of diminished colour-perception, and that about 3½ per cent suffer from some form of colour-blindness. Some, however, with little or no art training, are naturally gifted with a very fine sense of colour-perception, and can "carry" a colour in "their mind's eye", and effect a perfect match at a later date without the need for a "matched pattern".

Colour is an abstract, intangible quality which can only be understood and appreciated by the sense of sight; mere verbal or written description being utterly useless for matching purposes. Any record—if such it can truly be called—of a definite shade or tint of a colour, carried *only* by word of mouth or by writing, must inevitably be seriously liable to grave error; this risk being due in part to possible optical disability and in part to personal bias or prejudice.

The same holds good for such abstract qualities as perfumes, flavours, and sounds; each of which is incapable of accurate description for matching purposes, either by the written word or by verbal communication. They can only be truly matched by actual imitation, using the senses of smell, taste and hearing, respectively, for the purpose.

In the writer's confirmed experience, the whole question of the matching of the colours of older railway rolling-stock is one of the most contentious of all the many debatable railway subjects; and it is very obvious that our present-day conception of the colours of rolling-stock now no longer in existence, and of which no authentic *actual colour* records remain, must perforce be purely hypothetical;

being arrived at by a complicated process of verbal communication and that most fallible of all methods of transfer of knowledge—"common acceptance".

A great many attempts have been made to standardise colour classification by a numerical system, but the task is almost impossible because the texture of the material which has been coloured, and the medium used to mix the pigment, both tend to modify the final tonal value of the colour under review. Similarly, the number of varnish coats applied to a painted panel will alter its colour-tone, turning a "cool" green into quite a "warm" one. The effects of weathering are too well known to railway students to need mentioning.

A colour is said to be "tinted" when white has been added to it, and is "shaded" when mixed with black—or in any other way darkened. A colour is said to be "cold" or "warm" according as to whether its "cold" or "warm" constituents predominate; blue and violet being termed "cold" colours, and red and yellow "warm". Thus a green is said to be "cold" if it tends towards blue, or "warm" if it contains a high proportion of yellow.

It is not generally known that colours appear to be lighter in tint when observed in large expanses, such as the side of an engine or tender, and even if accurately matched, and reproduced on a small area, the reproduction will—although of precisely the same shade as the original—appear much too dark. As an illustration it may be mentioned that the "dark" Caledonian Railway engine blue appears almost black even when seen on a crest-panel of four square feet area! Such difficulties of colour-matching are only too well known to railway stores officials, who are aware that colour shades and tints vary greatly according to the manufacturer of the paint, and with each individual batch purchased.

Needless to say it is absolutely hopeless to effect a true colour match from a locomotive boiler, or to reconcile the colour of the latter with that of—say—the tender-side panel; for the continual effects of internal heat and top-surface weathering play havoc with the best of paints and often completely alter their shade.

Another point often overlooked is that the colour of nearby objects—such as the upper panel of a coach in juxtaposition to a darker lower panel, will greatly influence the apparent colour tone of a neighbouring object being matched "by eye". Even the brightness or dullness of the day has a profound effect on a colour, as the writer found when at York Railway Museum; when nearly two hours were spent before the subtle "Scotch" green of the L.B. & S.C.R. "Gladstone" locomotive could be accurately determined and matched.

The risk of bad lining-position errors and omissions, attendant upon the study of monochromatic prints made from old photographic negatives, may or may not already be known. The danger lies in the fact that the earlier negatives were made before the days of panchromatic emulsions, and thus, being approximately orthochromatic in their actinic characteristics, they gave an entirely false monochromatic rendering of the colours of the object photographed. On prints from older negatives, for example, a red line may appear black or very dark grey; being often entirely invisible if the background was not orthochromatically contrasting. Similarly, blues normally appeared as very light greys or white. On prints from modern panchromatic negatives, however, red appears as a medium grey; and is usually easily traceable together with the other shades and tints of colours which are more equably translated into monochrome—both on the negative and on the print.

All these matters must not be overlooked when an attempt is being made to match a given colour or to derive lining sequence from a photographic print; and extreme accuracy can only at times reasonably be assured by careful research and comparison, using as many independent sources as possible.

Bearing in mind the well-nigh insuperable limitations of written colour description, colour-chart codings have therefore *only* been given in the text in the following cases :—(*a*) actual existing locomotives painted in their pre-group liveries, (*b*) authentic railway companies' colour-crest panels, (*c*) models built and painted contemporaneously with their prototypes, and (*d*) *oil* * paintings executed at the time when the subject of the picture was in existence. In each of these four conditions the colours have been accurately matched by *actual contact and comparison* with over four hundred various paint shades of "railway" reds, greens, browns, blues, and ochres; and from them the fifty colours in the chart were eventually chosen.

In these pages no attempt has been made to give any specific

* Old *framed* water-colour pictures, like that of "Jenny Lind" in York Railway Museum, have faded badly; greens becoming bluer, and reds, yellower. They are thus unreliable.

indication of tints or shades of colours in those instances where they are *only known* by written or verbal description. In such cases, all the available written colour-information has been collected and arranged chronologically under the appropriate railway company, the colour descriptions appearing in the text.

In the earlier written descriptions of rolling-stock liveries, the words "red", "blue", and "green", were very loosely applied; "red" being often broadly descriptive of any shade or tint of that colour ranging from vermilion to maroon, progressing through many tones of crimson, purple, chocolate, Indian red, and brick red. Such vagueness is very misleading, and often applies to greens, and in a lesser degree to blues as well; and great care is again needed to ensure that a correct interpretation is made by the close study of as many independent descriptions as possible of other contemporaneous rolling-stock of the same railway company. It may also be mentioned that, in the earlier livery descriptions, the term "bordering" was often used synonymously with "edging", and similarly "picking-out" meant what we should nowadays term "lining".

Where possible a semi-standardised system of colour-description and lining terminology has been used, and the reader is invited to study the key diagrams on pages 6, 18 and 29, and Appendix D, which will clearly show the general methods of nomenclature used throughout the book.

E. F. C.

NORTH EASTERN RAILWAY LOCOMOTIVE CLASS "901" BUILT AT GATESHEAD IN 1875 (P. 173)

PART I

PRE-GROUP LIVERIES

1825 — 1922

BARRY RAILWAY

THIS Welsh railway, which owned 47 route miles of track and leased or worked nearly 21 route miles more, was incorporated in 1884 and opened in 1889. It was the first company in Great Britain to adopt locomotives of the 0–8–0 type as main-line engines.

It was absorbed into the Great Western group, together with the Rhymney, Cardiff and four other constituent companies in 1922.

Little seems to have been placed on record as to the liveries of the rolling-stock during the first decade of the railway's existence, but it would appear that the details given here for 1897 would also apply to stock built before that date.

Mr. S. J. Hosgood was the Locomotive Engineer of the Barry Railway from 1890 to 1910, and Mr. J. Auld from 1910 until the line lost its identity in 1922.

1897 Locomotives were a dark lake with black borders and yellow lining, with broad black bands between yellow lines round the tank sides, etc. Buffer-beams were vermilion with a border of black, with a white line between; also the letters "BR" appeared thereon in gold shaded with blue. The engine numbers were painted on the back of the bunkers in yellow, and also appeared in brass figures on the front of the chimney; whilst the side number-plates had polished brass figures and letters on a black background. (Fig. 22, p. 34.) There was a monogram surrounded by a garter on the tank sides.

Passenger locomotives had brass chimney tops and dome casings, as well as brass beadings round the splashers. They had also brass figures at the back of the bunker and an ornamental monogram in the centre of the tender-panels. Coupling-rods were left bright steel. Coaches were a dark lake shade, with black borders round the panels and gold lining. Lettering was in gold shaded with red, and a similar monogram to that appearing on the locomotives was placed centrally on the lower panels. Ironwork and underframes were black. Goods wagons were dark red, as were goods brakes, the ends of the latter being vermilion. Lettering was white, shaded black, and all ironwork was black.

1897 Locomotives were a dark lake with black bands and fine vermilion* lining. Dome covers and chimney tops were bright brass. The tanks had an oval number plate in the centre, with the number (*e.g.* "88") between the word "BARRY" above and "RAILWAY" below. Another smaller plate appeared on the bunker-sides.

1900 Goods brakes were brown, with vermilion ends and black ironwork. "BARRY CO." appeared in white letters. Weight-plates were black with white letters, and were placed (thus) between "No." (*plate*) "47".

1903 The 2–4–2T locomotives (No. 90, etc.) had brass domes and copper tops to chimneys. They were painted dark brown. The engine number appeared in brass figures on the front of the chimney and on the tank sides, where the number was enclosed in an oval frame around which were the words "BARRY RAILWAY". Building plates were placed on the bunker sides.

1907 Coaches were almost indistinguishable from the South Eastern Railway coaches of the period (before amalgamation with the London, Chatham and Dover Railway). They were of a reddish shade. Goods stock. Covered wagons were lettered "BARRY CO" not "Railway".

1914 Locomotives were (27), described in sources as dark red, with polished brass domes and copper-topped chimneys. Coaches were red.

1918 Locomotives were (27), described in sources as a red-lake or red-brown colour, with black bands and yellow and vermilion lines. Engine numbers were in brass figures on the chimney fronts, except in the case of Nos. 139–148, where they were in white metal figures fixed to the smoke-box door. Brass dome-covers and safety-valve bases were used as well as copper-topped chimneys. Goods locomotives were not so elaborately lined out as the passenger types. Coaches were a red-brown shade.

1923 Locomotives were (27), described in sources as a dark crimson

* Some authorities say orange, others vermilion.

lake, with fine scarlet lining. Chimneys were copper-topped, and domes were often of polished brass. The company's crest ("coat-of-arms")* was somewhat similar to that of the Taff Vale in that it contained the "Welsh" dragon.

BARRY RAILWAY CREST

* See footnote on p. 32.

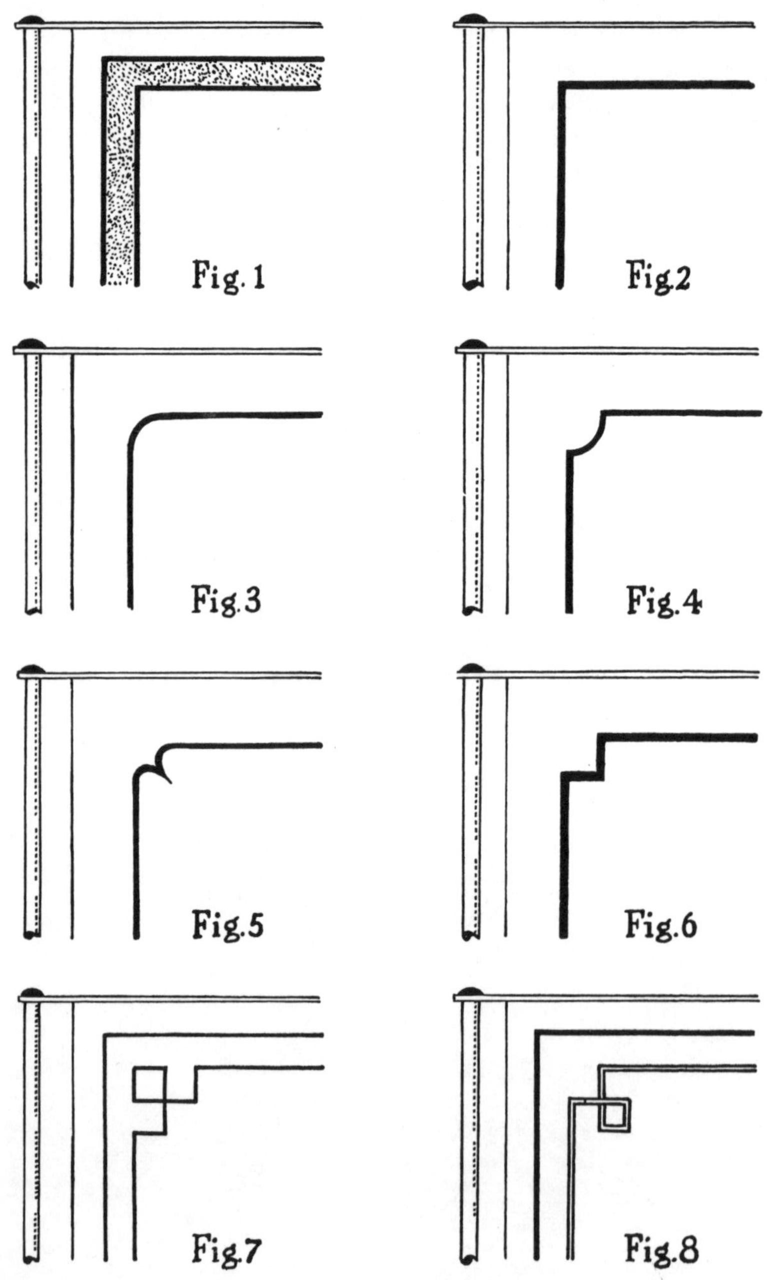

See Appendix D

BRECON AND MERTHYR RAILWAY

AUTHORISED in 1859 and opened in 1863, the Brecon and Merthyr Railway extended, at the height of its career, to a length of 60 route miles, its full title being the Brecon and Merthyr Tydfil Junction Railway. It was absorbed into the Great Western Railway as a subsidiary company as from 1st July 1922.

No records can be traced of the liveries of this line before the end of the last century, and though photographs of both locomotives and coaches are in existence, these do not give any clues to colour identification.

In the year 1918, Mr. J. Dunbar was Locomotive Superintendent and he remained in office until 1922.

1897 Locomotives were (37), described in sources as brick-red, with black borders and bands edged with yellow lines and fine vermilion inner lining. Buffer-beams were vermilion with black borders, upon which most engines had numbers in yellow figures, shaded with black. Coupling-rods were finished bright steel. Number-plates were of brass, with the figures in relief on a vermilion background. Dome-casings were polished brass.

Coaches were a dark purple, with gold lines edged with vermilion and having a fine inner pair of white lines. Lettering was in gold, shaded with red. Most vehicles had the company's monogram and crest on the panels below the waist-line.

Wagons were a light slate colour, with white lettering which was, in some cases, shaded with black. Goods brakes were the same colour, but had vermilion ends. All ironwork was painted black.

1899 The 0-6-2ST locomotives were painted lake colour with oval number-plates of brass in which the number (e.g. 23) was enclosed in a double-lined oval, between which lines the words "BRECON & MERTHYR" appeared above the number, and "RAILWAY" below it.

1908 Coaches were (39), described in sources as a very poorly-painted chocolate, and the tank locomotives (37) (all), described as red, with brass dome covers.

1909 The six-coupled saddle tanks which appeared were painted a bright shade of red. Some locomotives had brass-cased domes and safety-valve covers, whilst others were painted a darker shade of red, without brass domes and safety-valve covers.

Coaches had large class numerals in gold, shaded with red.

1915 Coaches (39) were described in sources as a dark shade of chocolate; engines (37) as a red-brown or lake colour.

1917 Under Mr. J. Dunbar's superintendency the number-plates were slightly altered to a double-lined raised oval plate in which the engine number (e.g. 46) appeared in larger serif figures, with "BRECON & MERTHYR" above, and "RAILWAY COMPANY" below, between the two concentric ovals.

GREAT NORTH OF SCOTLAND CREST (*page 50*)

CALEDONIAN RAILWAY

OPENED on October 11th 1845, this vital Scottish railway worked lines from Carlisle to Glasgow, Edinburgh, Aberdeen and Oban, with a concentration between the first two Cities and branches down the Clyde coast. From 1867 it gradually developed from a purely local undertaking into a large national system with a very intense traffic and an interesting locomotive history; the celebrated "Dunalastair" series of locomotives being among the most beautifully-proportioned machines in Great Britain.

The history of the Caledonian is a record of amalgamations, absorptions and extensions, most of which took place during a limited period of time; and a study of the way in which the original lines gradually coalesced to form the "Caley"—as it was lovingly known by its admirers—will be found extremely interesting.

Locomotive Engineers

1847–1856	Robert Sinclair	1890	Hugh Smellie
1856–1876	Benjamin Connor	1890–1895	John Lambie
1876–1882	George Brittain	1895–1914	John F. McIntosh
1882–1890	Dugald Drummond	1914–1922	William Pickersgill

The Caledonian Railway (incorporated in 1845) was composed of:

1 The Scottish North-Eastern Railway (1856), which was itself composed of:

Arbroath and Forfar Railway
Aberdeen Railway
Newtyle and Glamis Railway
Newtyle and Coupar Angus Railway
Scottish Midland Railway (opened in 1854)

2 The Scottish Central Railway (1866), which was itself composed of:

Dundee and Newtyle Railway

Dundee and Perth Railway (absorbed 1863)
Scottish Central Railway (opened in 1845)
Crieff Junction Railway
Dunblane, Doune and Callander Railway

3 The above major lines, together with the following smaller ones were also absorbed into the Caledonian Railway:

Wishaw and Coltness Railway (opened 1833, absorbed 1848)
Garnkirk and Glasgow Railway (opened 1826, absorbed 1846)
Glasgow, Ayr and Kilmarnock Railway
Glasgow, Paisley and Greenock Railway (absorbed 1847)
Perth and Methven Railway (absorbed 1866)
Alyth Railway
Dundee and Forfar Railway
Dundee and Arbroath Railway
(absorbed in 1866)
Crieff and Methven Railway
Solway Junction Railway
Busby Railway
Alloa Railway
Glasgow Central Railway
Moffat Railway
Wemyss Bay Railway
Forfar and Brechin Railway
Crieff and Comrie Railway (absorbed in 1898)
Paisley and Barrhead Railway

4 The Caledonian Railway also partially owned:

Callander and Oban Railway
Killin Railway
Cathcart Circle Railway
Lanarkshire and Ayrshire Railway
Lanarkshire and Dumbartonshire Railway
Dumbarton and Balloch Junction Railway
Brechin and Edzell Railway
Kilsyth and Bonnybridge Railway

5 The Caledonian Railway also worked jointly with the Glasgow and South-Western Railway the following lines:

Glasgow and Paisley Railway
Glasgow, Barrhead and Kilmarnock Railway
Glasgow and Renfrew Railway

6 Also jointly with the North British Railway, the following:
Dundee and Arbroath Railway (see above)
Dumbarton and Balloch Railway

7 And jointly with the L.N.W.R., Midland, and G. and S.W.R.:
The Portpatrick and Wigtownshire Railway

8 Also jointly with the North British and G. and S.W.R.:
Prince's Dock Railway

1856 onwards The cylinders on the blue locomotives were painted the same light crimson lake as the foot-plate edges, and were panelled out with a black band edged on each side with a white line.

1880 (c) The old 4 and 6-wheeled coaches were (30), described in sources as a very dark purple, not lake.

1880 (c) Passenger stock painted (30), described in sources as a dark purple lake, with yellow lining, with a fine vermilion line on one side.

1891 onwards The Company's initials appeared in gold on either side of one full-stop on all the tenders, thus dividing the side-sheets into four parts. In the case of the 4–4–0's the crest was placed on the driving-wheel splashers, whilst in the case of the 4–4–0T engines the crest appeared between the "C" and the "R" on the tank sides.

The number on these locomotives also appeared in gold shaded red and white to left in the centre of either the tender or bunker back panels in smaller letters than those of the Company's initials on the sides.

1894 TWO LOCOMOTIVE STYLES. Locomotives running in passenger service and goods locomotives fitted with Westinghouse brakes were painted (25),* described in sources as dark blue. The term "dark blue" indicates that the true "Caledonian" blue was, according to specification, ultramarine blue; which is much nearer to "Great Eastern" blue than is generally imagined. Ultramarine blue, being a rather weak pigment, required many coats before the correct dark shade could be obtained. It was later mixed with white paint in the proportion of two parts to one of white, by which the blue shade was lightened from "light Great Eastern"

* The Caledonian Railway "Dark" Blue (25), and the London, Brighton and South Coast Railway "Marsh Umber" are both shown as slightly lighter tints of their respective colours than those shown on the companies' panels. If these latter shades had been shown, they would have appeared almost black by reason of the small area of colour available for observation on the chart.

blue to (22), the bright and well-known "Caledonian" or "Royal" blue.

Locomotives built outside were, however, delivered in (25), described as the darker shade which, though officially correct, was unofficially wrong! Thus it was that a few passenger locomotives were to be seen at the end of the last century in a much darker blue livery than the rest of the locomotives. Goods locomotives were black all over.

1895 onwards Locomotives (of 0–6–0, 4–4–0T, 4–4–0, and 0–6–0) were painted (22), described in sources as a lighter shade of blue than that used by Mr. D. Drummond on his engines. The boilers, upper frames, cab, boiler mountings and tender-sheeting were blue, lined out with black bands edged on both sides with a white line. Boiler-banding: (see Fig. 17, p. 29). The wheels were blue, with black axle ends and wheel tyres. A single white line was painted at the bottom and top of the tender coal flare; though the lining was continuous around the back and sides of this vehicle. The Westinghouse pump was blue with white-edged black bands around. The footplate valances were painted (28), described as a slightly lighter shade of crimson lake than that used for the lower panels of the coaching stock; the locomotive steps and tender underframes being also painted this colour. The edging of the crimson lake was black, with a fine white line between the black and the lake. The springs of the tender, as well as its axle-boxes were black, with a small crimson lake panel edged with white on each spring buckle. The roof of the cab was black, but its back roof angle face was painted vermilion; the safety-valve levers being also this colour. This was the passenger locomotive livery.

1895 onwards The buffer-beams of the blue locomotives—fore and aft—were crimson-lake, with a black edging surrounding the lake and a white line forming a large panel which was vermilion coloured, and upon which (in the case of the front buffer-beam) appeared the engine number in gold figures of a small size. "C.R." on the left of the coupling-hook and the number on the right. The casing of the buffers was (22), described in sources as crimson lake, with a black band edged with a white line on either side.

1895–1914 In Mr. McIntosh's time, engine number-plates were brass castings with raised borders, and letters and figures which were polished. The background was red up to 1906, then blue.

This type of plate was fitted only to locomotives built at St. Rollox works, and those engines built by outside firms had polished brass plates with sunken lettering and numerals which were filled with black wax; the word "CALEDONIAN" being above the number and "RAILWAY" below.

1895 The locomotives of the "19" class (0–4–4T) were originally painted passenger blue, but were afterwards repainted with red and white lining.

1895 onwards The goods locomotives were painted black all over; the boiler bands being formed by a red line flanked by a white line on either side with the background of black showing between the red and the white lines. The splashers, cabs and tenders were panelled out in red and white lines, the red being outside the white. The tender coal flares had red and white lines at the top and bottom, thus forming a panel which passed round sides and back of the vehicle. The wheels were in all cases unlined black. Some McIntosh and Pickersgill goods locomotives had white lines on tyres and wheel bosses. The crest was also placed on the tender panels between the "C" and the "R" instead of a full-stop.

The foot-plate valances, steps and tender underframes were black, edged with a red line and a white line inside it. The Westinghouse pumps were black, lined red inside and white outside. The cylinders on all black engines were also painted black and were panelled with white and red lining.

The cab roofs were black, with a vermilion back roof-angle face and safety-valve lever. The tender axle-boxes were black, as were the springs; the spring-buckles being lined out in red and white.

Buffer-beams were vermilion, with a black edging and an inside white line forming a panel upon which the letters "C.R." appeared on the front buffer-beams only, on the left of the hook, and the number on the right in gilt with a black shading. Buffer casings were black, with a white and red line around the shank; the white being nearest to the buffer-beam. This was the goods locomotive livery.

1895 onwards Cab interiors were painted a light shade of buff, and the insides of the frames, axles and cranks were vermilion. Roof, black outside and buff inside.

Date-plates were small and oval in shape, being fixed to either the splashers or sand-box according to the locomotive class. All steelwork was polished, and in some cases the coupling-rods were painted vermilion.

This style of livery for passenger and goods locomotives was carried on right up to grouping days in 1923, with the slight modification of the shade of blue used. White lining was added to the wheel centres and tyres on the 1919 black or blue locomotives as they left the shops after overhaul.

The class 4–4–0T locomotives lasted until 1929 in L.M.S. red with yellow lining with the L.M.S. crest on the tank sides, and though later repainted black with red lining in 1928, the crest was still retained.

1895–1911 Locomotives were (25), described in sources as a Prussian blue. Some express locomotives were (22), described as a lighter shade. Chimney, underframes and smoke-box were black. Boiler mountings, upperframes and tender side-sheets were blue, lined out black, edged on both sides with a white line.

1897 The "92" class 0–4–4T locomotives Nos. 92–103 were painted blue, later, black—the goods colour.

1897 Locomotive No. 97 was experimentally painted black, with tanks, bunker sheeting and splashers lined out with a white line on either side of the red, but was later relined in the standard goods colours.

1897 Locomotives Nos. 723 and 724 (4–4–0 "Dunalastair" I) were painted (22), described in sources as royal blue, and lined out in gold and royal purple for the Diamond Jubilee of Queen Victoria.

1897 The first "scrolls" appeared on locomotive No. 766 (a "Dunalastair II") which when named in 1898 was painted a lighter shade of blue (22) with gold scrolls on each side of the crest on the tender. These scrolls continued to appear on all 8-wheeled tenders subsequently produced.

1898 Locomotives Nos. 766–771 and 773–774 were (25), described in sources as the usual dark blue; as were Nos. 721, 723, 724, 775 and 780 (although No. 766, when named, was the lighter shade).

1899 Locomotive "Dunalastair II" had the name in gilt block letters on the front driving-wheel splasher, with "2nd" beneath, with a scroll on either side of the figure. The letters "CR" appeared in gold, shaded red on the tender side-sheets with the crest between the initials. The number-plates were bright brass with raised figures and letters against a red background. Underframes were lake-coloured, and wheel centres blue with white rims and black tyres, and two white lines round the wheel boss.

1899–1900 "92" class locomotives Nos. 879–886 and 437–438 were goods black.

1900 (c) Coaches painted with lower panels (30), described in sources as crimson-lake, but the upper panels were painted white, with lines in yellow, and a fine white edge line. In both the 1880 and 1900 stock the lettering was in gold, shaded with red and black, with the company's crest on the lower centre panels.

1900 (c) The ends of all passenger brake-vans were vermilion. Horse-boxes were painted similarly to the 1880 passenger rolling-stock, but had plain yellow lines only. Goods wagons were (37), described in sources as brick-red, with white letters and wheel-tyres and black ironwork. Number-plates were of cast iron with white letters on a black background. At times no background was used.

Goods brake-vans were red oxide, and had ends (37), described in sources as vermilion.

Pre 1901 Coaches were (30), described in sources as red-brown.

1903 McIntosh régime locomotives Nos. 49 and 50 ("Sir James Thompson" class) had the initials C.R. on the tender-sides in letters half as large again as normal. The crest between the letters was enclosed in a wreath of gilt thistles and leaves instead of in the normal scrolls which appeared on other passenger locomotives.

1905 Coaches. Grampian Express stock was white upper panels, crimson-lake lower panels, underframe black, roof white, with lettering in gilt serif capitals.

Up to 1906 Locomotives were painted (25), described in sources as Prussian blue, with vermilion backgrounds to their number-plates. "Cardean" was the first engine to be painted with (22), described as the lighter blue, and to have the same blue used as a background to number-plates.

1906 The red number-plate (see Figs. 50 and 60, pp. 114 and 209) backgrounds went with the red safety-valve levers, but this liaison was not entirely universal, being tried for a period and then discarded about the year 1909.

1906 The blue varied in shade on locomotives, becoming darker towards 1900. Perth locomotives were finished a lighter blue than those from St. Rollox. Sky blue was re-introduced with the **4–6–0** class for the best passenger locomotives.

1908 Coach roofs were painted white.

1910 (c) Backgrounds of number-plates were painted blue instead of red in the case of passenger engines, and black for goods. Some of the St. Rollox-built locomotives had sunk letters, filled with black wax. It appears that the sunk plates were Mr. Drummond's idea, and formed his standard, which continued until the "Dunalastair II" period; after which Mr. McIntosh's raised number-plates came into prominence.

1913 Carriage trucks were (30), described in sources as chocolate-brown, with black ironwork. The Mansell wheels had red-brown centres, black rims and white tyres. The lettering was in medium chrome yellow, with the initials "CR" shaded to the left and below in vermilion.

1914 Carriages were (30), described in sources as a redder-brown than those of the North British, with white upper panels. Goods stock was a red-brown. Passenger locomotives had a lined-out vermilion panel on a red-brown ground for the buffer-beams. Buffer-shanks were also red-brown.

1915 Coaches were dark lake with white upper panels and locomotives blue.

1917 Fish open wagons were coach-chocolate colour, with black ironwork and medium chrome yellow lettering. The wheels had white tyres.

1917 Coach weights appeared in large white figures on each end of the vehicle, half-way up between the platform level and the coach carline.

1919 One only "29" class goods locomotive (0–6–0T) after repair by the Yorkshire Engine Co., was returned painted in (22), described in sources as "passenger" blue.

McIntosh locomotives repaired by the Perth Works were repainted a lighter shade of blue.

1920 Brake vans were painted (37), described in sources as red oxide, with ends regal red. Ironwork was black and lettering white.

1920 The 20-ton rail wagons built by Messrs. Cravens of Sheffield for the company were coloured brick-red. Lettering was white, and ironwork below the solebars (with the exception of the springs) was black. The name-plate was lozenge-shaped, with the lettering and number in raised white letters and figures against a sunken black background. The vehicle number was also painted in white figures on each end of the body.

GREAT EASTERN RAILWAY "W" CLASS LOCOMOTIVE NO. 51 AS REBUILT IN 1873 IN THE "CANARY" LIVERY (P. 38)

1920 Goods stock was painted red-brown (oxide) and lettered in white block initials.

1922 On the Glasgow, Barrhead and Kilmarnock Joint section (which was opened in 1873), the two six-wheeled coaches (one a 1st–3rd composite, and the other a 1st–3rd brake composite), were painted in the old Caledonian livery, which was used up to 1922 on the "Cathcart Circle" trains in Glasgow. The coaches are, however, lettered "G.B. & K.", and numbered 1 and 2.

1922 Passenger locomotives were blue, and goods types black. Main line coaches were lake and white, and local coaches, lake.

CALEDONIAN RAILWAY CREST

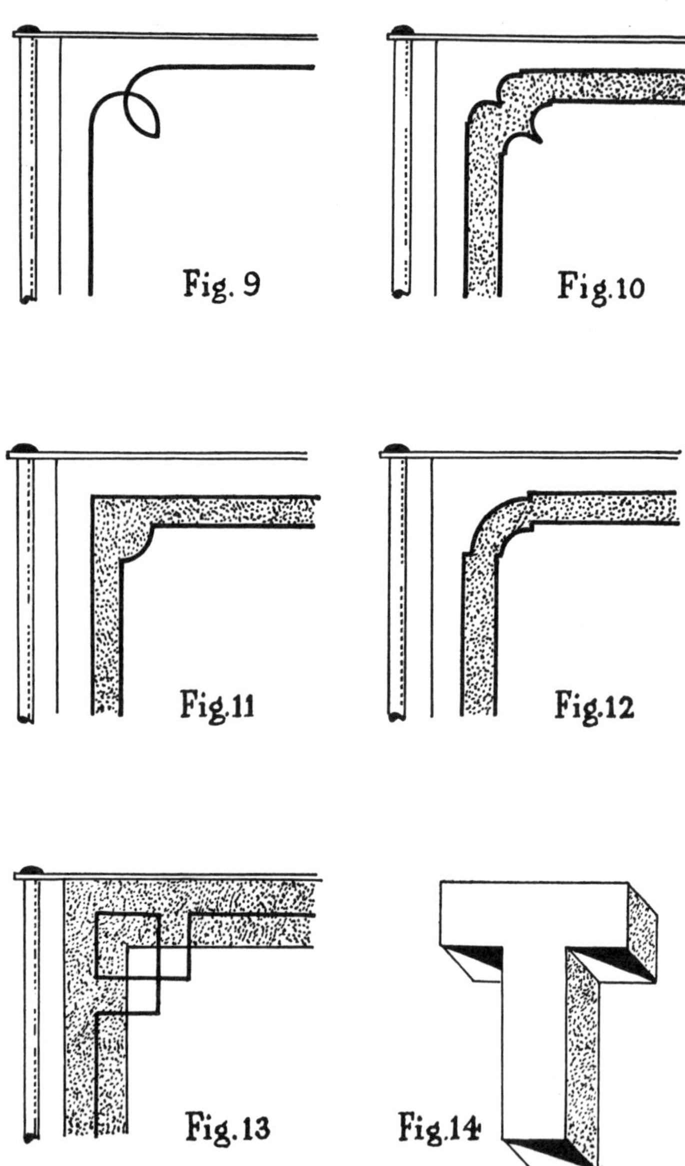

Fig. 9 Fig. 10 Fig. 11 Fig. 12 Fig. 13 Fig. 14

CAMBRIAN RAILWAYS

STANDING alone, without any physical connection with other railways for the first decade of its life, this Welsh line might well be called a railway "system" in the truest sense of the word.

It was quite an important railway, boasting over 295 route miles of owned, leased or worked track when amalgamated with the Great Western group in 1922; its working association with that railway and with the London and North Western Railway had always been extremely close.

The constitution of the Cambrian Railways was as follows:

1864 Incorporated, being composed of the following railways:
Oswestry and Newtown Railway (opened 1860)
Llanidloes and Newtown Railway (opened 1859)
Newtown and Machynlleth Railway (opened 1863)
Oswestry, Ellesmere and Whitchurch Railway (opened 1863)

1865 Aberystwyth and Welsh Coast Railway (opened 1863)

1895 Wrexham and Ellesmere Railway

1904 Mid-Wales Railway (opened 1864)

1913 Vale of Rheidol Railway (opened 1902)

1921 Tanat Valley Light Railway (opened 1904)

*Van Railway (6¾ miles long) (opened 1871)

*Welshpool and Llanfair Light Railway (opened 1903)

*Mawddwy Light Railway (6¾ miles long) (opened 1865)

Very little seems to be on record as to the liveries of its early rolling-stock, and the first definite accounts begin to appear at the commencement of the present century, wherein rather vague references only are made as to the colour and decorative details of "earlier" engines.

The following were Locomotive Engineers to the Cambrian Railways:

* The last three railways were worked by the Cambrian.

1864–1882	Alexander Walker	1900–1918	Herbert E. Jones
1882–1899	W. Aston	1918–1923	G. C. McDonald

1866 2–4–0T Locomotive No. 59 carried rectangular name-plates, with "Gladys" in raised brass letters.

1893 Locomotive No. 59 (2–4–0T) ex–"Gladys", rebuilt by Mr. Aston and renamed "Seaham" in raised letters on a rectangular plate at front end of tanks. Number-plate oval at rear end of tanks.

1894 Locomotive No. 74 (Neilson, 0–6–0 tender), was black, boiler-banded with broad yellow, flanked with fine red lines which again had fine yellow lines on their outer sides. Panelling consisted of a narrow red line flanked by fine yellow lines; all panelling having rounded corners. (See Fig. 3, p. 6.)*

Number-plates were of brass with raised numerals on a red background, and the Cambrian crest appeared on the centre driving-wheel splasher, the lining of which was parted into two panels to embrace it. The date-plate was similar to the number-plate, but smaller, being mounted on the front sand-box. A single yellow line ran round the driving-wheel hubs and crank-pin bosses. Wheel tyres were black, with a fine yellow line within.

The earlier 4–4–0 tender engines, as well as the 0–4–4T locomotives sometimes had their numbers in cut-out brass numerals mounted on the rear splashers, or on the bunker-sides. There were single brass bands round the splashers of 4–4–0 No. 20, and round the front driving-wheel splashers of 0–4–4T No. 5.

The 0–6–0 tender engine No. 90 had the orthodox oval number-plates of raised brass on a vermilion background mounted on the cab side-sheets, and had all splashers brass-beaded, with the company's crest on the centre splasher and the building date-plate on the forward one.

The earlier 0–6–0 tender engines had brass bands between the smoke-box and the boiler and between the latter and the fire-box.

1899 Locomotive No. 19 (4–4–0) appeared in a somewhat altered style of livery. The body colour remained black, but the lining consisted of a broad gold band around the panelling and boiler bands. The tender-sides bore the words "CAMBRIAN RAILWAYS" in shaded gold letters, with the Prince of Wales' feathers between the words.

Pre 1900 Coaches were green, with white upper panels.

* References to rounded corners are as in Fig. 3 throughout.

1900 Locomotives were black, with panelling formed on tender-sides and cabs by two vermilion lines with a blue-grey stripe between them. Wheels were unlined black on older locomotives running at that date, but the then new locomotives had frames and wheels lined out in vermilion. Buffer-beams were vermilion, and the number appeared thereon in gold, shaded with black.

All passenger locomotives and some of the goods ones had the company's crest on the leading splasher, around which was a polished brass beading. The underneath of all engines was painted a very dark grey. Building plates were placed on the coupling-rod splashers over the port driving wheel.

Some of the very early locomotives then carrying name-plates had their numbers on the cab-sides.

1900 Passenger stock was dark green below the waist, with white panelling above. Black edging and gold lining was used, and the lettering and numbers were in gold with blue shading.

Horse-boxes and other passenger stock were painted a slightly brighter green than the lower panels of the passenger coaches, numbering and lettering being in unshaded gold. Underframes were black.

Goods stock was dark grey with white lettering, and the ends of goods brake-vans were painted vermilion. Underframes and all ironwork were black.

1901 Locomotives were black, lined with yellow and red. Coaches were bronze-green with white upper panels, being lined out in black and gold, with very fine red picking out.

1903 The new design of goods brakes were painted as follows:

No 2

CAM ( ) RYS

In shaded white, the Prince of Wales' feathers being between the letter groups. The brake number also appeared in white on the arches of the end roofs.

1905 Coaches were (4), described in sources as a bronze-green, below the waist and white above it.

1908 Locomotives were black, with a broad yellow panel band edged with vermilion. The Prince of Wales' feathers appeared in the tank centres, and the engine numbers in raised brass figures on the bunker sides.

1909 The upper panels of coaches ceased to be painted cream colour, being instead painted in the same colour (4), described as bronze-green, as the lower portion of the bodies; being lined out with black and gold and a very fine red line.

1914 Coaches had white upper panels.

1914 Locomotives were black, lined out in yellow and red. No. 51 had brass-beading round the leading driving-wheel splashers, together with black underframes and bogie-wheel splashers; these, together with the foot-plate valances being lined with red only. Safety-valve base was polished brass, and the spring and lever was painted vermilion. The company's crest was displayed on the forward driving-wheel splasher, and beneath the same coupling-rod splasher was the oval date-plate with raised brass lettering on a red background. The number-plates on the cab side-sheets were also in raised brass figures on a red ground. The Prince of Wales' feathers appeared in the centre of the tender-side panels, with "CAMBRIAN" to the left and "RAILWAYS" to the right of it. Locomotive and tender wheels were lined out in red round their rims, and engine wheels were also double lined in red round the hubs. The turned-out sides of the tender top were lined in red only.

1915 Coaches were (4), described in sources as green. Locomotives were green.

1918 (c) Grey replaced the yellow lining on engines.

1922 Locomotives were black, lined out in grey. Coaches were bronze-green lined out in yellow.

CAMBRIAN RAILWAY CREST

FURNESS RAILWAY

ORIGINATING as a small mineral railway from Barrow and Piel Pier to Kirkby Quarries and Dalton Mines, which was incorporated in 1844 and opened in 1846, the Furness Railway eventually owned over 115 route miles of track of its own, and had a working share in a further 43 miles.

It included the Ulverston and Lancaster Railway, which was incorporated in 1851 and absorbed in 1862, there being no locomotive stock on this line. The Whitehaven and Furness Junction Railway (see p. 257) was acquired in 1866, and the Coniston Railway (incorporated in 1857—without any engines) in 1862.

The Furness Railway owned and worked the Whitehaven, Cleator and Egremont Railway (see p. 257) jointly with the London and North Western Railway, also part of the Cleator and Workington Railway, which was opened in 1879. (See p. 219.)

The first locomotive superintendent was Sir James Ramsden, who took office in 1846. Richard Mason was locomotive superintendent for nearly fifty years—down to 1896, being followed by W. F. Pettigrew, who was locomotive, carriage and wagon superintendent until 1920. He was succeeded by Mr. D. L. Rutherford, who was engineer and locomotive superintendent.

Mr. Meikle was the first locomotive engineer of the Whitehaven and Furness Junction Railway, and Mr. A. Robson occupied the same post on the Whitehaven, Cleator and Egremont Railway.

1846 Locomotive 0–4–0 ("Old Coppernob") built in 1846, had an Indian red (29) boiler lined out in black with a fine red line on each side of the black. Between the smoke-box and the boiler was a polished brass ring, and the splashers over both wheels and along the foot-plate between them was also polished brass. The fire-box was polished copper, and the safety-valve casings were polished brass. Panelling was black-lined, with a fine red line on each side. The locomotive number was in raised figures on an oval plate of brass on the boiler; the figures being on a black background. On the tender sole-bars was placed a small oval cast-iron plate, upon which the engine number appeared in grey on a black background. The locomotive axle ends were painted yellow, and the coupling-rods were bright steel. The buffer-beams were chocolate-coloured.

1866 Locomotives Nos. 27 and 28 (0–4–0's) were painted dead black and lined out in vermilion, in the same style as the "C–1" 0–4–0's and the Manning Wardle 0–6–0 dock tanks.

All other engines ("A1", "A2", "A3" and "A4" classes) were painted (29), described as standard dark red in sources, and lined out in black and vermilion. All brass and steel banding was kept polished.

(N.B.—"Midland red" was *not* the colour employed on the Furness engines, the colour used being of a definite Indian red, and not of the pronounced chocolate shade of the Midland.)

Pre 1890 Engine No. 71 (2–4–0 tender, by Sharp, Stewart and Co.) was (29), described as Indian red in sources, and had panelling blocked and lined with wide lines of vermilion. Number-plates were oval with raised figures and letters, being curved to fit the boiler, where they were mounted between the chimney and the dome. There were brass bands between the smoke-box and the boiler, and between the latter and the fire-box. Safety-valve casings were bright brass, and a double brass banding was fitted round the front driving-wheel splashers; a narrow inner band and a wider outer one. The tender was panelled into two by lining with squared corners. (See Fig. 2, p. 6.)*

Engine No. 37 (2–2–2T, by Sharp, Stewart and Co.) was finished in the same style as No. 71, but did not have any brass band between the smoke-box and the boiler. The date-plate was mounted on the bunker-side.

Locomotive No. 27 (Sharp, Stewart and Co., 0–4–0 tender) was lined and panelled as No. 71, but with single brass-beadings round each driving-wheel splasher.

Engine No. 8 (0–6–0 tender, by Nasmyth) had a new style of lining, with number-plates fitted to the cab-sides. These plates were smaller than the earlier ones, and had raised block figures

* References to squared corners are as in Fig. 2 throughout.

and letters, "FURNESS", appearing curved round the plate above the number, and "RAILWAY" similarly curved, below it.

1890 (c) The larger (old-type) number-plates ceased to be used.

1897 Locomotives were (29), described as dark red in sources (which persisted until grouping) with black bands having fine vermilion lines on either side forming the boiler-bands. Similar striping formed panels round the splashers, cabs and tender-sides. Buffer-beams were vermilion, with brass figures screwed thereon. The number-plates on the sides of the boilers were of brass, with a black background. On the newer 4–4–0 locomotives of this period the company's crest (see Fig. 86, p. 258) appeared on the front driving-wheel splashers, and the initials "F.R." in gold on the tender side-panels, shaded in light blue to left and below.

On the 0–6–2T locomotives (No. 110, etc.) the crest was placed on the front splasher and the date-plate over the central pair of wheels. The letters "F.R." were on the tank sides in the same style of letters. On the 0–6–0 tender goods engines these positions were reversed.

All types of engines—goods, passenger, tender, and tanks—were similarly decorated.

1897 New compo-brake bogie coaches were painted similarly to L.N.W.R., but with dark blue lower panels instead of chocolate. Underframes were dark blue with white lines instead of the gold lines of the bodies.

1898 Four-wheeled coaches were dark blue lower panels, with underframes of blue with white lining instead of gold as on the bodywork.

1900 Mr. Aslett, the General Manager, introduced coaches of pure white and ultramarine blue.

1900 (c) Coaches appeared with their lower panels dark blue and their upper portion a very light blue—almost white. Framing was in dark blue, with gold stripes round the windows, etc. All lettering and figures were in gold with very fine blue lines round each figure and letter. Horse-boxes and other passenger train vehicles were dark blue with white lining.

Goods stock was finished light grey, with white lettering and figures, whilst the ironwork was painted black.

1901 Locomotive No. 36 (Manson 4–4–0) had the number-plate mounted centrally on the boiler under the dome and brass-beading round the driving-wheel splashers.

1901 For many years locomotives were painted a rich dark crimson.* The Midland Railway adopted it some 16 years previously.

Coaches. Bodies ultramarine blue with white upper panels.

1914 Coaches. Dark blue, with white upper panels and blue mouldings. Locomotives. Red-brown.

1915 (c) The upper white panels on coaches were abolished.

Pre 1918 Coaches. Blue-lake with white upper panels.

1919 Coaches were all blue, with chrome yellow lining.

LANCASHIRE AND YORKSHIRE RAILWAY CREST (*page 86*)

*This obviously refers to (29).

GLASGOW AND SOUTH WESTERN RAILWAY

THIS important Scotch railway, which was opened on 12th August, 1840, under its original designation of the Glasgow, Paisley, Kilmarnock and Ayr Railway, did not assume its well-known title until 1850, when it absorbed the Glasgow, Dumfries and Carlisle Railway (opened 1850).

As the G. & S.W.R. it later acquired the oldest railway in Scotland—the Kilmarnock and Troon (opened 1811), as well as the Greenock and Ayrshire Railway and the Ardrossan and Kilwinning Railway.

The chief mechanical engineers of the G. & S.W. were as follows:

1853–1866	Patrick Stirling	1890–1912	James Manson
1866–1877	James Stirling	1912–1918	Peter Drummond
1877–1890	Hugh Smellie	1918–1923	R. H. Whitelegg

1860 Locomotives maintained the dark green colour from 1860–70 and were thus almost the only railway which survived the various colour-changes of locomotive stock. (For the light greens of the later N.E.R. locomotives and G.C.R. engines eventually became quite different shades from those originally used in 1900.)

1876–86 Midland Scottish Joint stock coaches were lettered "M.S.J.S."

1880 Coaches were (up to *circa* 1885) a dark green.

1890 Coaches were similar to Midland coaches in colour.

1897 Coach underframes and running-gear were dark red.

1898 Twelve-wheeled vestibuled dining cars were painted the standard lake shade with black bands, picked out with red and gold lining.

1897 Joint stock coaches were lettered "M & GSW" and "M & NB"; this lettering persisting until 1915.

1900 Locomotives were painted (13), described in sources as green, somewhat paler than the Highland railway engines. Lining was black, edged on each side with white, and a fine white line ran along the foot-plate valance and round the edges of the foot-steps. Frames were a (29) claret colour. Wheels were green, with black tyres, edged with white. The cylinders of outside-cylindered engines were chocolate-coloured. Numbers were painted on the bunker- or cab-sides in plain gold block letters, being shaded to the left and below with pale yellow and white; and to the right with black. The tanks or tender-sides carried the initials "G. & S.W.R." in serif capital letters, which matched the numbers in both size and colour. The buffer-beams were red, the locomotive number being painted upon them in yellow letters and figures thus: No. 67.

Coaches were (28), described in sources as lake, matching that of the North British, Midland, Great North of Scotland and South Eastern Railways in general shade. They were lined round in yellow in a single line, and lettered G & SW on the waist panels. Roofs were white, coach ends—lake, and the underframes and running gear black.

1900 Goods stock was a medium grey, and lettered G & S.W. in white. The ironwork and running gear was painted black, and the tare weights appeared at the lower left-hand corner. The wagon-numbers were not shown on the sides of the vehicle, but appeared on a number-plate. These plates were rectangular in shape, with the number and "G. & S.W.R." in raised white letters and figures.

1901 Locomotives were dark green with black bands and white lines on each side. Underframes were chocolate, lined white. Safety-valve spring and levers were red. Whistle was polished brass. Brass band round boiler immediately to rear of smoke-box. Wheels green, lined with white. G. & S.W.R. on tender in gold letters shaded red.

The date-plates were mounted on the leading driving-wheel splashers on the Manson 4–4–0's.

1901 Locomotives green. Coaches a crimson-lake.

1903 Locomotives green, lined black bands and white lines.

1904 The Manson railcar (with an 0–4–0 locomotive with Walschaert's valve gear) numbered "1", was painted in crimson-lake (as M.R. stock, and lined out in black and yellow).

1905 Two other similar railcars (Nos. 2 and 3) were built and similarly painted. (They were all built at Kilmarnock, and scrapped in 1922.)

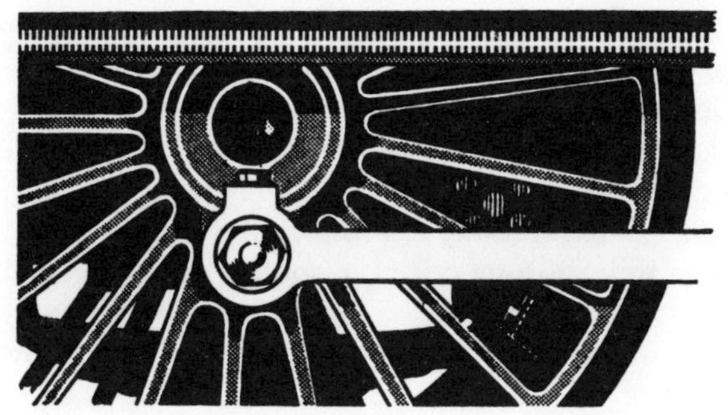

Fig. 15

Fig. 16

Fig. 17

Fig. 18

Fig. 19

1905 Vestibuled dining-cars were crimson-lake with black bands picked out with red and gold.

1907 (Dec.) A large number of engines left the shops after repairs painted green, without lining; a style of painting similar to that adopted by the Highland Railway at this period.

1910 Locomotives were (13), described in sources as green, lined black and white.

1913 Goods stock was a very light grey, which had a faint yellow tinge in it. Ironwork was black, and lettering and roofs, white.

1915 Locomotives green. Coaches crimson-lake.

1915 Baltic tank locomotives designed by Mr. Whitelegg had the unusual feature of blued planished-steel boiler clothing which was left unpainted. The cylinder lagging and dome was also similarly finished.

1918 The "Drummond" red-shaded lettering on locomotives was altered to blue shading.

1920 Coach mouldings were black.

1922 Engines were green. Coaches were crimson-lake.

GLASGOW AND SOUTH WESTERN RAILWAY CREST

GREAT CENTRAL RAILWAY

THE actual commencement of the Great Central Railway system was when the Sheffield, Ashton-under-Lyne and Manchester Railway was incorporated in 1837, from which date it grew by means of various acquisitions—under the title of the Manchester, Sheffield and Lincolnshire Railway (see p. 236), until it became renamed the Great Central Railway in 1897. The more important details of its constitutional history are appended.

The Manchester, Sheffield and Lincolnshire Railway was formed in 1847, and included the following lines:—

- Sheffield, Ashton-under-Lyne and Manchester Railway (first section opened in 1841)
- Barnsley Junction Railway, absorbed in 1845 by S.A. & M. Railway
- Sheffield and Lincolnshire Railway
- Sheffield and Lincolnshire Extension Railway
- Manchester and Lincoln Union Railway
- Great Grimsby and Sheffield Junction Railway
- South Yorkshire Railway, opened 1849, amalgamated 1864

After the Great Central Railway was formed in 1897, the following Railways were added:—

- North Wales and Liverpool Railway, in 1905
- Wigan Junction Railway, in 1906
- Wrexham, Mold and Connah's Quay Railway (see p. 259), in 1905
- Liverpool, St. Helens and South Lancashire Railway, in 1906
- Lancashire, Derbyshire and East Coast Railway (opened 1892) absorbed in 1907 (see p. 230)

The locomotive superintendents of the Manchester, Sheffield and Lincolnshire Railway were as follows:—

1847–1854	Robert Peacock	1859–1886	Charles Sacré
1854–1859	W. G. Craig	1886–1893	Thomas Parker

1894–1900 Harry Pollitt, who also served with the Great Central Railway

1900–1922 John G. Robinson (Chief Mechanical Engineer as from 1902)

The locomotive superintendents of the L.D. & E.C.R. were, successively: Messrs. C. T. Broxup, T. B. Grierson, W. Greenhalgh, J. Connor, J. W. Dow and R. Thom; probably a record number for a line which enjoyed only fourteen years' independent existence.

(*See also Manchester, Sheffield and Lincolnshire Railway, p.* 236)

1897 Locomotive No. 268 was painted grey, with the new coat-of-arms on the driving-wheel splasher with "FORWARD" below.

1897 Several 6-wheeled coaches were painted a medium brown for the lower portion and a light greenish grey with gold lining in the upper panels. Underframes were black edged with yellow lines.

1897 to 1899 Coaches of the new main line corridor built by Parker (dining-cars, etc.) were French grey in upper panels, and lower panels brown, picked out with fine gold lines. The panels were emblazoned with the company's coat-of-arms.

Immediately after the "MS and L" changed to "GCR", the coaches were painted light grey in the upper panels with chocolate-coloured lower panels, being picked out with gold lines.

1898 On formation of the Great Central Railway, the company's coat-of-arms was registered at the Royal College of Heralds, London; its heraldic description being as follows:—

Argent on a cross gules, voided of the field between two wings in chief sable and as many daggers erect in base of the second a pale of the first, thereon eight arrows saltirewise banded also of the third between on the dexter side three bendlets enhanced and on the sinister a fleur-de-lis or. Crest: on a wreath of the colours a representation of a locomotive proper between two wings or. (*Granted at College of Arms 25th February*, 1898.)*

1899 Coaches were brown, with French grey upper panels, but this livery was later changed to cream, and then to teak colour.

* The College of Arms substantiate that most railway coats-of-arms are known officially as bogus arms, and that the companies using them had no right to incorporate City and other coats-of-arms into any other so-called "coats-of-arms".

1899 Locomotive No. 499 (a 6-coupled radial tank), also 494 and 495, were painted standard green and lined.

1900 Locomotive No. 969* was painted a darker green than usual, and lining was varied to wide black bands with fine white lines on either side. The number was shown on a brass plate with red background instead of being painted on direct, as previously. (See Figs. 94 and 95, p. 280).

Locomotive No. 919 was also fitted with a cast number-plate, and was painted black, lined red and white. The words "GREAT CENTRAL" on the side were lettered much smaller than on former locomotives.

1900 The single locomotive (No. 969*) and engine No. 619 were painted green, with black panelling edged with a thin white line with a broad black line inside. This black line was edged with a fine white line on each side. Frames were chocolate-coloured and lined out vermilion. Number-plates were brass with the figures on a vermilion background. Some goods engines were black.

1901 Goods locomotives began to be painted black.

1903 The 1873-built Sacré double-framed, 6-coupled goods engines had raised fire-boxes with polished brass copings. When rebuilt in 1903, they were fitted with cast-iron chimneys and were painted black, with red lining instead of the original green with red and white lines.

1903 Several of the smaller standard 0–6–0 goods locomotives were, when they appeared, painted in the new style, with white lines in place of the previous yellow ones.

Engine No. 17 (an old single-framed locomotive) was rebuilt as a shunting tank; being painted black, with broad red lining, and the words "GREAT CENTRAL" upon the driving-wheel splashers.

1903 Rebuilt Sacré 0–6–0's (Nos. 1067–1072) unlike other locomotives were painted black and lined red instead of the previous green with white lining; as also were the 0–8–0 goods engines (Nos. 1052–1054).

1903–4 Bogie coaches (compo-slips) were brown in the lower panels, with cream upper panels, the mouldings being picked out in gold. Panels were lettered and emblazoned with the company's coat-of-arms. The revised locomotive colours were green for passenger, and black with red lining for goods.

* References to the livery of locomotive No. 969 are from different sources, and are partially conflicting.

Fig. 20

Fig. 21

Fig. 22

Fig. 23

Fig. 24

Fig. 25

Fig. 26

Fig. 27

1904 The American-built Mogul No. 952 came out of the shops black, but Moguls generally were originally standard locomotive green.

1904 The new standard colours were similar to those previously used by the M.S. and L. Railway. (See p. 236.)

1906 Locomotive No. 1097 ("Immingham") had its name-plate over the driving-wheel splasher as on Great Western locomotives.

1908 Goods locomotives (4–6–0 Robinson, No. 1113) were painted black, boiler bands being twin red lines. The cab was lined in red, with a fine white line within. Splashers were brass-beaded, with a red line within the beading. Engine valances were outlined with red, the lining continuous round the steps. Cylinders were black, with red and white lining fore and aft. Tender-underframes and steps were continuously lined out in red, whilst the axle-box tie-rods and spring buckles were also lined round. The buffer socket-plates were lined out in red. The engine number appeared in raised figures on a raised brass plate, both figures and oval being polished; the background being black.

1909 Coaches returned to the plain teak colour.

1910 Goods stock was lead grey.

1910 Coaches: colours returned again to plain varnished teak of the Manchester, Sheffield and Lincoln Railway.

1910 Passenger locomotive green, with brown frames and splashers. Goods locomotives black with red lining.

1914 Coaches reverted to plain varnished teak, after years with brown lower panels and cream-white upper panels. On the opening of the London extension, the coaches had grey upper panels and brown lower, but were later changed to light-brown varnished wood.

1914 Engines were (15),* described in sources as green, lined out black-white-black. There were brass beadings to splashers and spectacle windows, and brass safety-valve casings. Underframes chocolate, edged with a thin red line. Number-plates were oval brass on cab side-sheets. Brass rectangular name-plates over the company's coat-of-arms on the driving-wheel splashers.

* The Great Central Railway locomotive green (15) as shown is lighter than that shown on the company's panel, and has been shown because it agrees with a consensus of opinion on the part of several well-known and competent observers who were well acquainted with this Company's engines. The Company's panel colour is a slightly darker shade of the green shown in (12) and lies between this colour and (4).

Buffer-beams and guard-irons were vermilion. Engine number in gold on the buffer-beams thus: "No (*hook*) 44" in black, shaded to right and below. The words "GREAT CENTRAL" appeared on the tender-sides with the coat-of-arms between the words.

1914 Passenger engines were (15), described in sources as dark green, with black and white lining. Underframes, and sometimes splashers and cylinders were dark red with vermilion lining. Goods engines were black, with a red—or a red and white—line.

Coaches were of varnished teak, some with gold lettering and figures.

1922 Passenger engines were (15), described in sources as green, lined with back and white. Underframes were brown, with red and black lining. Goods types were black, lined out in red and white. Coaches were varnished teak.

GREAT CENTRAL RAILWAY COAT-OF-ARMS

GREAT EASTERN RAILWAY

ORIGINALLY incorporated in 1836, and opened in 1840 as the Eastern Counties Railway, which was itself formed of the Eastern Union Railway, the Ipswich and Bury Railway and the original Eastern Counties Railway.

In the year 1862 the name was changed to Great Eastern Railway, which then absorbed the Norfolk Railway, the East Anglian Railway, the East Suffolk Railway, the Northern and Eastern Railway (opened in 1836), the Harwich Railway, and the Newmarket Railway.

The chief engineers or locomotive superintendents of the railway were as follows :—

1839–1843 John Braithwaite
1843–1845 William Fernihough
1845–1846 W. F. Scott
(autumn) 1846–1850 John Hunter
August, 1850–1856 J. V. Gooch
December, 1856–1865 Robert Sinclair
December, 1865–June, 1866 W. Kitson
1866–1873 S. W. Johnson (later of Midland Railway)
1873–1878 W. Adams (later of L. & S.W.R.)
1878–1881 Massey Bromley
1881 Malcolm Gillies
1882–1885 T. W. Worsdell
July, 1885–1907 J. Holden
1908–1912 S. D. Holden
1912–1922 A. J. Hill (who was styled C.M.E. as from 1915)

1856–65 Under Mr. Sinclair's régime locomotives were painted a light shade of green, with black banding and fine white lining. Engine framing was chocolate-coloured.

1856–75 Sinclair locomotive livery: pea green, black bands with red lines. Number painted on the boiler barrel except in the "140" class, where it was on the space between the coupled-wheel splashers. Buffer-beams were green, and cab side-sheets, cylinders and tender side-panels were panelled out.

1863 Some engines appeared painted a pea-green with black banding and red lining The engine numbers were painted on the buffer-beams, except in the "140" class, where it appeared on the space between the coupled-wheel splashers. Cylinders were panelled out.

On March 10th this year, locomotive No. 284 (a Sinclair 2–2–2 tender type) was specially painted a cream colour and was garlanded with roses, for hauling the train carrying Princess Alexandra when she was married to Albert Edward, Prince of Wales. The engine was garlanded round the base of the chimney and dome, the garlanding being twisted three times round the stack. Along the foot-plate valance of both engine and tender and on the cab side-sheets were also floral decorations. There were three hanging drapes on the tender-sides and there were five bands around the boiler. Splasher beadings were painted violet, as also were the connecting-rod splasher beadings. The front and rear beading round the cylinder-cum-smoke-box unit was also painted violet. The side eaves of the cab and the corner beadings down to the fenders were violet, as also were the tender foot-plate edging and the cab side-sheet lower edge down to the foot-plating. The safety-valve casings were brass, and feed-pipes, copper. Boiler-bands were vermilion, and tender foot-boards, grey. The body colour was ivory-cream.

1866–73 Under Mr. S. W. Johnson's régime engines were painted a darker green with green buffer-beams. There were three express engines (Nos. 51, 60 and 291—"W" class) which were painted a bright chrome yellow. These were rebuilds by Mr. Johnson of Sinclair locomotives, and they appeared in the yellow livery about the year 1873. (See plate facing p. 16.)

1871 The 0–4–2 tank engines Nos. 81, 82 and 83 were painted a vivid yellow*, with black bands and fine white lines. They were nicknamed "Canaries". Passenger stock was plain varnished teak.

1872–82 Passenger engines were painted black, with fine red lining, whilst the goods locomotives were black, but devoid of lining.

1872–3 The 0–4–4T locomotives later known as the "133" class (Nos. 134–39, 162–65, 186–89, 166–70 and 190–99) were painted a dark moss green, lined out with white, with incurved corners when originally delivered.

1873–75 Under Mr. Adams' régime locomotives were painted black, with red lining. This colour-scheme continued up to 1882.

* Termed "Canary" yellow by one authority.

1875 (c) Passenger coaching stock was painted a pale brown umber as it was redecorated, yellow lining being carried out round the windows and round the beading which did duty as panelling. Coach buffer-casings were either deep green or black, as was all the ironwork. Lettering was in gold, shaded with light brown.

1878–81 During Mr. Bromley's régime as locomotive superintendent very little alteration was made in the style of engine livery. The black paint introduced by his predecessor was continued, but the width of the red lining was increased. Large oval number-plates with raised figures were introduced in place of the previous rectangular ones. The buffer-beams had the engine number painted on them in 8 in. yellow figures.

1882 Locomotive No. 189 (later No. 0189), an 0–4–4T was the first Great Eastern engine to be painted in the well-known blue livery, this being done for the occasion of the opening of Epping Forest to the public on 6th May, by Queen Victoria, when the engine drew train of Great Western stock and created quite a furore.

1882 The first blue engines began to appear, a medium shade of that colour first being used. There was a broad black band or border round the cabs, tanks, splashers and tenders, with a bright blue line inside it. The number-plates had raised polished brass numerals on a vermilion background. Buffer-beams were also vermilion, with the engine-number thereon in yellow figures shaded with light brown. Coupling-rods were painted vermilion and the engine frames were grey. The interior of the cab was light brown, and the tenders or tanks had the company's initials (G.E.R.) on them in gold, shaded with red and light brown. Goods engines were painted plain black, with vermilion coupling-rods and buffer-beams.

1882–1914 Locomotive livery for all engines fitted for passenger working was (24), described in sources as Royal blue, panelled out with black, with vermilion lining. The "Royal Clauds" had additional white lines. Wheels were blue, and coupling-rods were vermilion. On outside-cylindered engines, the connecting-rods were also vermilion. Buffer-beams and buffer-casings (except on the "tram-engines") were vermilion, edged with white. Cab fronts were black, and the inside of framings yellow.

Tank and goods engines not fitted for passenger working were (with few exceptions) black, lined out in vermilion, other parts and fittings being painted as on passenger engines.

1883 Engines had black boiler-banding flanked with red lines. The common driving-wheel splashers were blocked round outside with black only, as were the coupling-rod splashers. The tender was also similarly treated.

There were very large oval number-plates on the splashers with raised polished brass figures, the words "GREAT EASTERN" above the numerals and "STRATFORD WORKS. 1883" below. There was a polished brass band between the smoke-box and the boiler.

The locomotive "Petrolea" (No. 760) had a brass band between the smoke-box and the boiler, brass-beads round the driving-wheel and coupling-rod splashers, and the main-frames black edged only. The front spring-buckles were of polished bronze.

Engine No. 529 had the standard red lining, blocked with black, the cab side being in one panel. The front and rear driving-wheel splashers were panelled as one with the front sand-box, and bordered with a flat brass beading; this being lined within with red and black.

1884 The Great Eastern Railway was the first company to place photographs in its coach compartments, the introduction taking place this year.

1885 Sinclair's "Canaries" were painted black, and some of them were in later years painted the "standard" G.E.R. blue.

1885 The "G–16" compound engines had additional brass plates on the coupling-rod splashers inscribed—"PATENT COMPOUND ENGINE—WORSDELL AND VON BORRIES' SYSTEM". During Mr. Worsdell's time, engines were painted a dark blue with a black border and vermilion lining. The initials "G.E.R." appeared on the tank or tender-sides, and a new type of cast brass number-plate with raised numerals and letters on a vermilion background was used (see Fig. 24, p. 34). Coupling-rods were painted vermilion, and the yellow numbers on the buffer-beams introduced by Mr. Worsdell's predecessor were retained, "No." being added to them.

1886 Locomotive No. 275 (0–6–0T, James Holden) was painted a medium shade of grey, edged with a black border; these colours being separated by a fine white line. This livery was used for photographic purposes; the running colour was black, with red lining.

No. 377 (also an 0–6–0T), was a passenger engine, and was

painted (24), described in sources as standard blue; coupling-rods were red. The body blue was edged with black from which it was separated by a fine red line. Lettering was in gold, shaded to the left and below. Number-plates were brass with numbers on a vermilion background. (See Fig. 25, p. 34.)

Locomotive No. 275 (in running livery) had polished brass spectacle window-frames, an ornamental rim to the safety-valve casing, and a curved brass cover over the boiler front angle-iron.

1897 The saddle-tank engines Nos. 1,201 to 1,210 differed from previous saddle-tank locomotives in having their safety-valves fitted with painted covers. There was not any brass beading round the splashers.

Engine No. 95 also had a painted safety-valve cover. The additional decoration of the Company's crest was confined to the single-driver engines Nos. 421, 455, 718, 725 and 750.

1900 (c) Some engines were painted a lighter shade of blue than the majority. These engines were painted at Cambridge and shedded there. The idea was to give a "Cambridge blue" tint by the addition of white to the "standard" blue. This "standard" blue (24) has been variously described as "Royal", "Prussian" and "Ultramarine".

The tram engines of the Y–6 class were painted in the same shade of brown as that of the coaching stock.

Engines Nos. 1870 and 1871 were specially painted for the coronation of King Edward VII, a white line being included in the boiler lining, also round the framing, cab and wheels.

1900 Locomotive "Claud Hamilton" was originally painted a *slightly* lighter shade of blue than the standard colour (24).

1900 Goods wagons were painted dark grey with white lettering. Permanent-way wagons and vans were red, and break-down cranes green; whilst goods brakes had vermilion buffer-beams.

All 0–6–0 shunting tank engines were painted plain black.

1901 The engine "Claud Hamilton" (No. 1900) was painted Royal blue, and had brass safety-valve covers and a brass band round the boiler immediately to the rear of the smoke-box. There were also brass beadings round the cab windows and round the rear bogie-wheel splashers. The Company's crest appeared in the centre of the leading driving-wheel splashers and brass beadings were round all driving-wheel splashers. The number-plate was of cast brass, with raised figures on a vermilion background

(Fig. 26, p. 34). The letters "GER" appeared on the tender sides in gold, shaded with red. Coupling-rods were painted vermilion. The main body-colour was (24), described in sources as Royal blue, with a black border, and lined vermilion inside. Wheel-spokes were Royal blue, with vermilion axle-ends, and a thin vermilion dividing line between the rims and the tyres; the latter being painted black (see also Figs. 26 and 27, p. 34). The spectacle-plate and cab front were also black.

1901 There were in use at this time two types of passenger train destination boards. The "main-line" type, with gold lettering on a vermilion background; and the "suburban" type, with black lettering on a vermilion background.

1902 The 6-wheeled T.P.O. vans had a teak finish with the letters "ROYAL MAIL", the van-numbers and crests being made of metal and screwed to the van sides.

The later vehicles were further decorated with lining bands along the lines of the panel fixing-screws, a gold line also appearing on either side of the band.

1902 Suburban and main-line coaching stock was at times lettered "G.E." instead of the more usual "G.E.R."

1903 Gunpowder vans had bodies painted vermilion, with chocolate underframes. Lettering was white, and the rectangular panel on the body was chocolate-coloured with the words "GUNPOWDER VAN" in white block letters on it.

The new steel-framed 10-ton goods wagons carried the letters "G.E.R." (one plank high) in the left-hand panel and the number (e.g. 29866) in the same sized figures. The tare weight (5–3–0), "G.E.R." and the number also appeared on the sole-bars in 2 in. letters.

1906 The original "Gooch" tank engines (Nos. 250–259), when first built, did not have a safety-valve on the middle of the boiler. The safety-valve casings were of polished brass, unlike those of the earlier types of these engines, which were painted over—except No. 20. When engines Nos. 250–259 began to haul "Tilbury" trains, the brass safety-valve covers were unpainted and polished; but subsequently they were painted over, like engines Nos. 4–12, 21–25, and the express engines Nos. 27, 94, and 274–279. All engines later received the Sinclair valve-casing, which eventually replaced the "Gooch" type.

1906 Locomotives Nos. 1848 and 1849 were set apart for working

"Royal special" trains, being lined out with broad scarlet vermilion bands, edged with white.

1908 Coaches, when new, were varnished teak finish; but as they became older, they were painted a shade of chocolate very similar to the then new Great Western Railway coaches.

1908 The 4–4–0 tender engine No. 1830 was experimentally painted black, unlined.

A characteristic feature of suburban trains, as well as some of the main-line ones, was the use of very large numerals on the carriage doors to denote the class. These outside figures were in gold, and they were repeated in smaller black figures on the inside of the doors.

1913 The 4–6–0 (main-line) engines were painted (24), described in sources as Royal blue, with black bands and vermilion lining on either side of the bands. Chimneys were brass-capped, and a polished brass band was placed round the boiler-smoke-box joint. The feed-pipes to the boiler and brake-pump were of polished copper, and the whistle was of polished brass. Brass beading surrounded the cab windows, and also the driving-wheel splashers. There was also a brass beading round the openings in the coupling-rod splashers (Fig. 17, p. 29). The engine number-plates were oval in shape, with raised polished brass numerals on a vermilion background (Fig. 26, p. 34). All wheels were painted Royal blue, lined with vermilion. Axle-ends and tyres were also lined out with vermilion. Coupling-rods were vermilion with polished steel end-bosses. Smoke-box doors were polished steel. Track-guards were vermilion, as were buffer-beams and buffer-shanks. Underframes were Royal blue, lined out in vermilion.

Coaches were plain varnished teak.

1914 The crest on passenger engines was made of cast-iron, and was fitted on the driving-wheel splashers. It was painted out in full colours. The letters "GER" on the tenders were in gold, blocked in red.

Goods engines were painted black, with vermilion lining and vermilion coupling-rods.

Coaches were varnished teak, and goods wagons painted lead grey.

1914–23 The 1882–1914 liveries were discontinued, except for the vermilion coupling-rods; and "shop grey" was first used instead. Some engines were kept in (24), described in sources as Royal blue with yellow figures and letters, until 1924.

Engine No. 1121 was repainted in the blue livery during this period.

Engines Nos. 1541–1560 (Beardmore, 4–6–0 type) were delivered painted a greyish green with black panels and white lining, the coupling-rods being vermilion. In this case the lettering was in gilt, shaded with red and white, though this was discontinued and replaced by large yellow numerals, in 1921.

1915 Engines of the "1001" class (0–6–2T) had all piping painted black, as also were the guard-irons. Safety-valve balance, whistle and snifting-valves were polished brass.

1915 (c) Engines appeared in a temporary livery of grey, with vermilion coupling-rods.

1919 Coaches were changed to crimson-lake, lined out in gold.

1922 Some engines were painted grey with buffer-beams and coupling-rods vermilion. Lettering was yellow, shaded black on the buffer-beams only.

Coaches were painted crimson-lake, lettered and lined in gold.

GREAT EASTERN RAILWAY CREST

GREAT NORTHERN RAILWAY

THE London and York Railway, and the Direct Northern Railway, both of which were founded in 1844, finally merged in 1846; and when the main line of the Great Northern Railway—which was the resulting company—was opened in 1850, it ranked, and continues to rank, as one of the main trunk lines to the North of England.

The Great Northern Railway was the southernmost partner in the trinity of companies constituting the "East Coast Route" to Scotland, the other two being the North Eastern and the North British Railways.

The locomotive engineers of the Railway were as follows :—

1850–1866	Archibald Sturrock	1895–1911	H. A. Ivatt
1866–1895	Patrick Stirling	1911–1922	H. N. (later Sir Nigel) Gresley

1867 2–4–0 tender locomotives of the "280" class (built in 1867) had no brass-beadings round the splashers; whereas the "280's" built between 1874 and 1883 had beadings to splashers and safety-valve covers.

1870 Locomotive No. 1 (single) had number on front buffer-beam in small sans-serif figures and letters above the coupling-hooks. There was a square full-stop after the "1". This small type of lettering on buffer-beams continued up to 1909 (minus the full-stop) and appeared on "Atlantic" No. 273. (See also Fig. 23, p. 34.)

Early 1886 Locomotives had always been green of one shade or another. A number of suburban tank locomotives were experimentally painted black, lined out in red. Goods engines were black, as standard.

Post 1886 All engines and tenders were painted a bright, almost grass green, panelled with a darker shade of the same colour; with a broad black band with a white line on either side outlining the panels on tenders or tanks. A black edging of about the same width, with a white line inside it edged the cabs and splashers. Buffer-beams were painted vermilion, with the locomotive number in gold block-figures, shaded in red; and figures denoting the bore and stroke of the cylinders also appeared on the buffer-beams towards the left-hand side. Locomotive framing was chocolate coloured, edged with black with a vermilion line between these colours. Inside the frames was painted vermilion. Cab interiors were green, and the numbers on the cab side-sheets (Fig. 21, p. 34), as well as the letters GNR on the tender were in gold, shaded with red.

1886 One engine, an 0–4–4T by Stirling, was experimentally painted black, with vermilion lining. It was exhibited at King's Cross Metropolitan station.

1898 The Ivatt "Atlantic" locomotive No. 990 was painted green, with black bands round the boiler, with a white line on each side of the black. The tender was panelled round with black, and a white line between the black and the green body colour. The corners of the panel were "scalloped" (incurved) (Fig. 4, p. 6).* There was no lining on the cab side-sheets, but there was a brass beading round the driving-wheel splashers. The underframes were painted maroon, lined red. The engine number was in block figures of yellow, shaded red to right and below. The letters "GNR" appeared on the tender sides in block yellow letters shaded in red.

1898 Larger letters and figures were adopted on the tanks and bunkers of locomotives Nos. 761 and 934.

1899 The covered goods wagons built during this year were painted vermilion red. They ran in pairs, and had the words "EXPRESS GOODS" in large white letters spread across the two wagons.

1900 Scotch Express destination boards had white letters on a blue ground.

1900 Coaches were not painted, but were natural teak, varnished, the shading of this finish being remarkably uniform, never varying from a light yellow to a dark brown, as was noticeable on some of the other companies' stock using the same finish. Lining and lettering was in gold, shaded and edged with blue.

1900–7 East Coast Joint Stock was similarly decorated in every way, excepting that the shading and lining of the letters (E.C.J.S.) which were shaded in green. All passenger stock underframes were of natural wood-colour, and the iron-work was painted a bronze green.

* References to incurved corners are as in Fig. 4 throughout.

Workmen's trains were painted a dark umber brown, with yellow letters, shaded blue; and on this stock, as well as ordinary suburban stock, the class designation was in large block figures on the doors.

Carriage trucks, milk vans, horse-boxes and all other passenger train stock was painted a light umber brown with yellow lettering and blue shading.

Goods stock was finished in chocolate brown, with white lettering; the ironwork being black.

1904 Goods stock was lettered "G. NORTHERN R."

1905 Locomotives of "251" class had the brass bands round the driving splashers done away with, and a black rim, edged inside with a fine white line substituted; similar to that which adorned Mr. Stirling's 4-coupled engines in 1867–8.

1906 G.N.R. "Atlantic" model in South Kensington Museum, is (10), described in sources as light grass-green. Underframes are (30), described as purple-brown.

1906 A novelty in the outside finish of the two new vestibuled trains turned out at Doncaster in August was the large letters and figures along the sides. The name of the railway was given in full "GREAT NORTHERN". The doors were designated thus:—"1st" and "3rd", which was quite an innovation on main line G.N. stock.

The new vestibuled corridor trains had high elliptical roofs instead of the clerestory roof which had been a feature of G.N.R. stock since 1896.

1908 Coach class numerals were repeated on the insides of the doors, as was done on the Great Eastern Railway.

1908 Goods stock was lettered in very large letters.

1910 (c) The lettering on the engine "Henry Oakley" (No. 990), now in the York Railway Museum, is in gold, shaded to the right and below in dark rose and back-shaded in black; with white lining between the gold and the rose. Main lining on the body is in white, and the bordering is black. Boiler-banding consists of a 2 in. wide black band flanked by $\frac{3}{16}$ in. wide white lines. Body green is (10) and underframes (3), lined red. Buffer-sockets are chocolate (30) with black ends and a vermilion line between.

The lettering on the buffer-beams is in gold block letters and numerals, these not being shaded as those on the cab side-sheets. They are shaded with chocolate to right and below, back-shaded in black; with a white line between the gold and the chocolate.

Engine No. 1 now in York Railway Museum, has the front buffer-beam number in gold block letters shaded to the right with crimson and below in black; with white angles and parting line between the gold and crimson. Wheel-hubs are lined with black only and axle-ends are black. Spokes are lined black, as are the crank-bosses. The big-ends are conspicuously of brass. Bogie-wheels are green and are lined as are the drivers. Bogie-splashers are green, edged with black and lined white; whilst round their edges is a 2 in. wide brass-bead. The body-colour is a slightly yellower green than that used on "Henry Oakley". The inverted splashers between the bogie-wheels are decorated as follows, commencing at the lower edge:—First, a 2 in. wide brass bead, then a fine white line, next a wide band of body green which is followed by another fine white line. Next comes a wide black band and another 2 in. wide brass bead, this being followed by a wide black band with a fine vermilion line next to it. Within all the above is the underframe colour (30), described as chocolate-maroon. The ends of the buffer-beams are maroon, edged with black and lined vermilion with incurved corners. The injector wheels and their axles (through the foot-plate on the left-hand side of the engine), as well as the injector body are vermilion red.

1910 East Coast Joint Stock 1st class sleeping-cars were teak finished, with gold panelling and mouldings. Roofs were buff colour. Coach numbers, appeared in gold letters on the end doors. "E.C.J.S. SLEEPING CARRIAGE" was inscribed on three long panels immediately under the windows, and the English and Scottish coats-of-arms appeared near each end of the coach at the waist-line, with the E.C.J.S. emblem between them at the centre of the coach. Destination boards were red with white letters.

1912 Goods engines were grey, lined white.

1913 (c) Engines had a round metal disc on the centre of the outside edge of the cab top-sheeting which bore a number corresponding with the district to which the engine was attached. The numbers represented sheds as follows :—

1. Doncaster
2. Peterborough
3. London
4. Nottingham
5. Leeds
6. Bradford
7. Grantham
8. Lincoln
9. Retford
10. York (G.N.)
11. March (G.N.)

(During the 1914–18 war, Bradford shed was amalgamated with Leeds, and Grantham became shed No. 6. Lincoln was amalgamated with Peterborough, and Retford and York with Doncaster. March became No. 7. The system was discontinued in 1923.)

1914 Passenger engines were (10), described in sources as bright green, lined out in black and white. There was a darker green edging on tenders and tanks. Underframes were (30), described in sources as red-brown, lined vermilion. Cylinder casings were black.

Coaches were varnished teak. Goods stock was red-brown.

1914 Locomotives were (10), described in sources as green, with black and white lining. The underframes were (30), described as chocolate-coloured, lined out in red. The date-plate was placed on the leading driving-wheel splasher. Buffer-beams were vermilion, and the locomotive number appeared thereon in gold figures, unshaded. Main-frame extensions were (30), described as chocolate-coloured, lined in red.

1914 (c) Locomotive head-lamp tops indicated the engine home district by the colour. Thus red indicated Peterborough, yellow Nottingham; and black, London, the latter district including the sub-sheds at Hornsey, Hitchin, Hatfield and Cambridge. The colours brown, green and blue were also used.

Lamps also bore the locomotive number, driver's name, and shed, *e.g.*:—T. Ingleton, Grantham, 1432.

1914–18 Goods engines were painted grey, with white lining. The letters "G.N.R." appeared in white shaded black on the tenders, which were devoid of lining.

Passenger locomotives were grey, except those built by contractors, which were green.

1922 Engines were (10) described in sources as bright green. Goods types were grey. Coaches varnished teak.

Great Northern Railway crest on p. 72.

GREAT NORTH OF SCOTLAND RAILWAY

INCORPORATED in 1846, for a railway from Aberdeen to Inverness, the Great North of Scotland Railway was far in advance of other Scottish railways in adopting the electric telegraph from the start.

The Inverurie and Old Meldrum Railway, the Aberdeen Junction Railway (opened 1858), and the Banffshire and Morayshire Railway were amalgamated with the G.N.S.R. in 1865; the Deeside Railway (opened in 1846) in 1875, and the Aberdeen and Turriff Railway in 1866.

Other railways amalgamated included the Alford Valley Railway, the Formartine and Buchan Railway, the Macduff and Turriff Extension Railway, the Keith and Dufftown Railway, and the Strathspey Railway, all of which were amalgamated in 1866.

The locomotive engineers of the G.N.S.R. were as follows :—

1853–1855	D. K. Clark	1883–1890	James Manson
1855–1857	J. F. Ruthven	1890–1894	James Johnson
1857–1883	William Cowan	1894–1914	W. Pickersgill
1914–1922	T. E. Heywood		

1857–83 Engines were grass-green, lined out in red with black bands. Domes were polished brass, and chimneys were copper-topped. Number-plates were of brass with sunk lettering, wax-filled. Buffer-beams and lamps were vermilion.

1870 Coaches were painted (40), described in sources as a dark lake, panelled in black with two yellow lines and a very fine red line edging.

1870 Old type wagons were dark red, with black ironwork.

1885–93 The engines were (3), described in sources as green, with black bands, and white lining, with a darker green border. Lettering was gilt, with red and black shading; with white highlights.

1898 Locomotives were (3), described in sources as bright green, cab and tender having a border of a darker shade of the same colour. Bands and panel lines were black with vermilion edges. Framing and wheels were green, having a black margin with a vermilion line. Buffer-beams were vermilion with a black border edged with white; and the engine number was painted on it in gold, shaded with French grey and black. The number-plates were of brass (see Fig. 63, p. 209), with black lettering, and the initials GNSR appeared on the tender sides in gold letters shaded black.

1899 Locomotive No. 118 (Neilson, 4–4–0) had panelling with a dark green border round a body colour of (3), described in sources as bright green. Within the border was a vermilion line with square corners, and within this again another vermilion line with incurved corners. The boiler-bands were black, flanked with vermilion, and there was a brass band between the smoke-box and the boiler. The number-plate was oval, being of brass with sunk letters (Fig. 63, p. 209), being mounted on the cab sides, which latter were lined round with black and vermilion. The date-plate was fixed to the leading driving-wheel splasher, and had sunk lettering; being lined round black and vermilion (Fig. 64, p. 209).

Axle-ends were black, lined vermilion, with a wide black line round the boss. Tyres were black, and buffer-shank ends ringed with black and vermilion lines.

1899 Horse-boxes were (40), described in sources as dark claret, with no lining, and gold lettering, shaded red and black.

1899 Wagons were dark slate with black ironwork and cast-iron number-plates with white letters on black. Brake vans were painted dark red with vermilion ends.

1899 to 1910 Pickersgill introduced new stock with creamish-white upper panels and (28), described in sources as dark claret, lower; but the latter colour was more of a red-brown (40), in 1901, and more deep purple or maroon in 1914. The coach lining was yellow, with a fine red line on either side. Lettering was in gold, shaded red and black.

1913 Horse-boxes were (28), described in sources as lake, with roofs and wheel tyres white. Lettering was yellow, shaded red, and ironwork was black.

Locomotive green (3) almost matched North Eastern Railway locomotive green. Lining was black, with a red line on either side. Buffer-beams were vermilion, and carried the engine number in gold figures. Tank or tender sides bore the initials "G.N.S.R."

in gold, shaded with red. Locomotive number-plates were oval, and solid brass, carrying the words "GREAT NORTH OF" curved above the engine number, and "SCOTLAND RAILWAY" below; the number being in the centre of the plate. The characters were recessed and wax-filled.

Coaches were painted (28), described in sources as dark claret colour, below the waist-line and creamish-white above it; being lettered "GNSR" on the waist-panel in gold, the letters being shaded red. Coach roofs were white, and their ends, underframes and running gear, black. Coaching stock such as horse-boxes, etc., was (38), described in sources as chocolate-coloured, and unlined, though it was lettered in plain block ochre-coloured letters.

Goods stock was a dark grey of a similar shade to that of the L.N.E.R. goods stock, the ironwork being usually black, though occasionally dark grey. Roofs of vans were white. Stock was lettered "GNS" in white. Goods stock number-plates were of a similar design to those of the engines, but were rectangular in shape instead of elliptical; and having raised white letters and figures.

1915 Coaches were cream upper and purple-lake lower panels. Locomotives were green.

1916 At the end of 1914–18 war all locomotives were painted black, being picked out with red and yellow lines and lettered in the older style.

1920 The lower panels of coaches were the same (28), described in sources as crimson, as the N.B.R., but a *very* slightly darker shade. The top panels were cream, a one inch wide vermilion line being painted between the crimson and the cream. Lining was in yellow ochre, both against the vermilion and the cream; but there was an extremely fine vermilion line inside the ochre in the case of the upper panels only. The raised mouldings were not picked out, so that the distant effect was that of a coach with an all cream top panelling. Destination boards were crimson with a vermilion edge, lettering appearing in white. The corners of the boards were rounded.

Coaches were numbered thus : "No. 67" (not just the numerals alone).

1922 Engines were (3), described in sources as black, lined out in red and yellow, and coaches green below the waist and white above, until L.N.E.R. livery was adopted.

For Great North of Scotland crest, see p. 8.

GREAT WESTERN RAILWAY

THIS company's incorporated existence dates from 31st August, 1835, when the Act authorising its construction received Royal Assent. The first section of line was opened to the public in 1838, and the story of the company's continued growth over a period of almost a hundred years is almost too well-known to need repetition. An abridged chronological list of the acquisitions, amalgamations and extensions which took place after its incorporation is appended, and shows in concise form how well over 100 minor railways became consolidated—by 1911—into the Great Western Railway; which, by further amalgamation added yet almost another fifty large and small companies, to become the Great Western Railway Group.

COMPANIES ABSORBED BY GREAT WESTERN RAILWAY UP TO GROUPING IN 1923

1835 Great Western Railway incorporated

1838 Great Western Railway opened

1843 Cheltenham and Western Union Railway (1841)

1844 Oxford Railway (1844)

1846 Oxford and Rugby Railway (1850)
Berkshire and Hampshire Railway (1847)

1847 Great Western and Uxbridge Railway (1856)

1848 Birmingham and Oxford Junction Railway (1852)
Birmingham, Wolverhampton and Dudley Railway (1854)

1851 Wilts. Somerset and Weymouth Railway (1848)

1854 Shrewsbury and Birmingham Railway (1849)
Shrewsbury and Chester Railway, which itself was composed of Shrewsbury, Oswestry and Chester Junction Railway (1848), and North Wales Mineral Railway (1846)

1862 Hereford, Ross and Gloucester Railway (1853)

1863 South Wales Railway (1850), which itself was composed of Bullo Pill Railway (1812), and the Forest of Dean Railway (incorporated 1826)
West Midland Railway (incorporated 1860), which was composed of Stratford and Moreton Railway (1826), Oxford, Worcester and Wolverhampton Railway (1850), Worcester and Hereford Railway (1859), Newport, Abergavenny and Hereford Railway (1854)

1865 Aberdare Valley Railway, which was composed of Swansea and Neath Railway, 1863; Vale of Neath Railway (1851)

1866 Wellington and Drayton Railway, (1867)

1867 Wycombe Railway (1854)

1868 Bristol and South Wales Union Railway (1863)

1869 Tenbury and Bewdley Railway (1864)

1870 Stourbridge Railway (1863)
Severn Valley Railway (1862)

1871 Wrexham and Minera Railway (1862)
Great Western and Brentford Railway (1859)

1872 Wallingford and Watlington Railway (1866)

1873 Briton Ferry Dock and Railway (1861)

1874 East Somerset Railway (1858)
Gloucester and Forest of Dean Railway (1851)
Bourton-on-Water Railway (1862)

1876 Pontypool, Caerleon and Newport Railway (1874)
Bristol and Exeter Railway (1841), which itself absorbed Chard and Taunton Railway (incorporated 1861) in 1863; Cheddar Valley and Yatton Railway (incorporated 1864) in 1865; and Exe Valley Railway (incorporated 1874) in 1875

1877 Bala and Dolgelly Railway (1868)

1878 West Cornwall Railway (opened 1852). Originally Hayle Railway (1838)

1880 Monmouthshire Railway and Canal (1798)
Ely and Clydach Valleys Railway (1878)
Mitcheldean Road and Forest of Dean Junction Railway (1885)
Culm Valley Light Railway (1876)
Malmesbury Railway (1877)

1881 Carmarthen and Cardigan Railway (1860)

1882 Berks and Hants Extension Railway (1860)
Swindon and Highworth Railway (incorporated 1870)

1883 Torbay and Brixham Railway (1868)
Watlington and Princes Risborough Railway (1872)
Stratford-on-Avon Railway (1860)
Alcester Railway (1876)
Cardiff and Ogmore Valley Railway (1876), which was composed of Llynvi and Ogmore Railway (incorporated 1866); Ogmore Valley Railway (1865); Ely Valley Extension Railway (1865); Llynvi Valley Railway (1861); Duffryn, Llynvi and Porthcawl Railway (1829)

1884 Coleford Railway (1883)
Bristol and North Somerset Railway (1873)
Bristol and Portishead Pier Railway (1867)

1886 Faringdon Railway (1864)

1887 Coleforth, Monmouth, Usk and Pontypool Railway (1856)

1888 Leominster and Bromyard Railway (1884).
Worcester, Bromyard and Leominster Railway (1874)
Kingsbridge and Salcombe Railway (incorporated 1882)

1889 Cornwall Railway (1859)
Llanelly Railway and Dock (1833)

1890 Whitland and Cardigan Railway (1873)
Witney Railway (1861)
East Gloucestershire Railway (1873)

1892 Wellington and Severn Junction Railway (1857)
Calne Railway (1863)
Ross and Ledbury Railway (1885)
Newent Railway (1885)
East Usk Railway (incorporated 1885)

1894 Oldbury Railway (1884)
Tiverton and North Devon Railway (1884)

1896 Lostwithiel and Fowey Railway (1869)
Cornwall Minerals Railway (incorporated 1873), which was itself composed of Newquay and Cornwall Junction Railway (1874), and Treffry Tramroad (1842)
Wenlock Railway (1864)
Llangollen and Corwen Railway (1865)
Abbotsbury Railway (1885)
Vale of Llangollen Railway (1861)

Much Wenlock and Severn Junction Railway (1862)
Milford Railway (1863)
Marlborough Railway (1864)
Corwen and Bala Railway (1866)

1897 Great Marlow Railway (1873)
Nantwich and Market Drayton Railway (1867)
Banbury and Cheltenham Direct Railway (1881)
Woodstock Railway (1890)
Kington and Eardisley Railway (1874)
Pembroke and Tenby Railway (1863)
Buckfastleigh, Totnes and South Devon Railway (1872)
Minehead Railway (1874)

1898 Leominster and Kingston Railway (1857)
Helston Railway (1887)
Rosebush and Fishguard Railway (later North Pembrokeshire and Fishguard Railway) (incorporated 1878)
Narborth Road Railway (1876)

1899 Golden Valley Railway (1881)

1900 Birmingham and Henley-in-Arden Railway (1894)
Staines and West Drayton Railway (1884)
Birmingham, North Warwickshire and Stratford-on-Avon Railway (incorporated 1894)

1901 Devon and Somerset Railway (1871)
Bridport Railway (1857)

1903 Ely Valley Railway (1860)

1904 Abingdon Railway (1856)

1905 Wye Valley Railway (1876)
Lambourn Valley Railway (1898)

1909 Liskeard and Caradon Railway (1846)

1910 Bala and Ffestiniog Railway (1882)
Festiniog and Blaenau Railway (1868)

1911 Manchester and Milford Railway (1866)

The chief mechanical engineers of the railway from its commencement were as follows:—

At Swindon:—

1837–1864	Daniel Gooch	1877–1902	William Dean
1864–1877	Joseph Armstrong	1902–1921	George Churchward
1921–1922	Charles B. Collett*		

*Mr. Collett continued in office with the amalgamated company of the Western Group in 1923 until his retirement in 1941.

At Wolverhampton:—

1854–1864 Joseph Armstrong 1864–* ? George Armstrong
? –1877 William Dean

1840 I. K. Brunel selected a deep chocolate for passenger rolling-stock (see entry for 1903).

1846 There were no copper tops to chimneys, and no thin red lines on either side of the black boiler-bands of locomotives.

1849 The locomotive "Gorgon" (built in 1840–42 by Messrs. Fenton, Murray and Jackson, of Leeds) had a bluish-green† boiler and fire-box sides, the crown and corners of the latter being polished brass; as was the safety-valve casing. The smoke-box and chimney were black. Splashers had wide brass beadings, and the wheels were painted green. The frames were dark umber edged with deep crimson, this lining being carried out round all frame piercings. Axle-boxes were dark grey, lined out in deep crimson, and wheel tyres were also dark grey. Buffer-beam ends were dark umber, being square-panelled out in deep crimson. Handrails were brass-covered, and their stanchions were painted green. Track guard-irons were steel, and all piping polished copper.

The maker's date-plate was rectangular in shape with incurved corners, and was mounted over the rear wheel axle-box on the main-frames. The name "GORGON" was on a rectangular plate in cut-out brass letters on a grey background, the plate being mounted on the frames over the driving wheel axle-box. The oval brass "GREAT WESTERN" plate containing the words "GREAT October WESTERN 1841 RAILWAY" in that order from top to bottom in black inset letters, was mounted over the leading axle-box on the frames.

1849 The engine "Behemoth" (0–6–0 "Pyracmon" class—2nd series), built by the G.W.R. 1847–8, had a blue-green boiler and fire-box. Smoke-box and chimney were black, and the sand-boxes and track guard-irons steel. The fire-box was banded front and rear with wide brass bands. Handrails were brass covered, and their stanchions bright steel. The safety-valve casing was polished brass and its lever bright steel. The two whistles were also brass. Buffer-beam ends were painted umber, and the buffers

* The exact date of the change at Stafford Road between George Armstrong and William Dean cannot be verified.

† Probably this colour was deep Brunswick green, but faded. (Twining).

mahogany-coloured.* The faces of the splashers were painted ochre with brass beadings. Underframes were a dark shade of chocolate, and the feed-piping polished copper. The portion of the fire-box below foot-plate level was iron grey. The name-plates carried lettering of brass, raised and polished, the letters being on a grey background. There was a brass surround to the plate which was again enclosed in a wide bright vermilion line.

1849 The locomotive "Queen" (2–2–2 of the "Elk" class, built by G.W.R. in 1847) had the boiler painted a blue-green, with chocolate-coloured boiler-bands. The smoke-box and chimney were black. The crown of the fire-box was polished brass, but the lower portion was wood lagged and painted blue-green. The fire-box safety-valve casing and spring cover was polished brass, whilst the front and rear of the lower fire-box was brass-banded. Hand-rails were brass-covered, but their stanchions were left bright steel. The outside of the frames were a cold shade of chocolate, and the foot-plate valances had a thin brown line along their upper edge, with their lower portion brass (or painted to represent brass). Wheels were blue-green and springs were dark grey (probably bare steel). Sand-pipes were brass, track guard-irons grey, and the portion of the fire-box below the foot-plate level, iron grey.

Buffer-beam ends were a light chocolate shade (possibly bare varnished oak), and the buffers themselves dark brown. All piping was polished copper. The name-plates had raised, polished brass letters in a raised brass rectangular frame, the latter being surrounded by a polished mahogany framing. The plates were mounted on the centre-line of the boiler. (See Fig. 28, p. 82.)

1850 The engine "Lord of the Isles" was finished with the boiler, tender, and cab side-sheets green of a lighter shade than that of later years. The smoke-box was black, and all below the running-plate level, Venetian red† edged with a fine yellow line. Boiler-bands were lined black, with a red line on either side. The tender was lined with a thin black line with yellow lines on either side—two panels to each tender side. Later a copper top was fitted to the chimney and a brass case to the safety-valve. Hand-rails were of polished steel. Buffer-shanks were red, as were the buffer-beams. The spokes of the wheels and springs were Venetian red, and the sanding-pipes vermilion. The guard's shelter at the back of

* *i.e.* Natural brown leather.

† Indian red darkened by addition of burnt umber.

the tender was painted grey. Name-plates were raised figures of brass on a black background (see Fig. 35, p. 82).

1851 "Lord of the Isles" had all splashers, safety-valve casings, and the large rounded corners to the front and back of the fire-box, as well as boiler-bands, of polished brass.

1851 When the "Lord of the Isles" was exhibited at the Great Exhibition, it had an iron chimney and small sand-boxes over the leading wheels.

1855 It became the practice to paint the numbers on engines of standard gauge.

1855 Engine "Ivanhoe" and four-coupled types had iron chimneys.

1855 Engine "Ivanhoe" had polished brass corners to the front and rear of the fire-box, as well as brass-beaded angles below the foot-plating, which latter formed the faces of the splashers. The boiler lagging-bands were of painted iron.

1855–6 Copper-topped chimneys were introduced.

1856 A photograph of "Lord of the Isles" shows a copper-topped chimney and large sand-boxes against the driving-wheels as well as the smaller ones.

1856 First class coaches were painted yellow, second class brown, and third class, green.

1858 The small sand-boxes were removed from "Lord of the Isles".

1860–1908 Coaches (which were originally chocolate all over) had cream upper panels.

1864 Coach roofs were painted white, which on varnishing became a cream shade.

1866 At Wolverhampton, a deeper and bluish-green was used for engines, with black panels and bordering. Boiler-bands were also black, with a fine vermilion line on either side. Outside framing was nut-brown, lined out with red and black. Buffer-beams were painted vermilion and were not lined.

1866 The engine boiler colour was a dark holly green, the boiler-bands being black, edged with white lines. The wheels were of the same colour, with black tyres. Buffer-beams were painted vermilion with a black border lined out with white, and the outside-frames were umber brown with a black border and a vermilion line. Main panelling was carried out with one inch wide light green banding, bordered below and to the left with a black line with a fine vermilion line edging, and above and to the right with a fine white line.

1868 (May and June) 2–4–0's (six, Nos. 439–444) of the "Bicycle" class had no splashers. Dome-covers were painted green, and safety-valve covers were brass.

1869 2–4–0T ("Metro" class) had the number painted on the side-tanks.

Standard gauge locomotives had painted numbers.

1870 (c) –1880 Broad yellow bands on engine tanks and tender panels, fine lined both sides in black. (Twining).

1875 The engine "Prince Christian" (No. 1118, 2–2–2, built at Swindon, 1875) had orthodox number-plates on cab-sides, brass beadings to driving-wheel splashers, and a curved brass name-plate with sunken black letters mounted on the face of, and not above, the splasher; with the gartered crest below it on the splasher face. The locomotive was almost devoid of lining except for boiler-bands.

1876 Cast engine number-plates were introduced in two differing styles, *viz.* (*a*) The present-day type, and (*b*) a type which had characters very different from those to be seen on modern number-plates (see Figs. 31, 32, 34 and 37, p. 82).

1879 Dean's 7 ft. singles (Nos. 157–166) had the driving-wheel splashers and safety-valve casing only of brass, with copper-topped chimneys. Until some time after they came out, these engines (and all other types) were picked out with black, fine-lined in yellow. But the tanks and tenders were elaborately panelled with brilliant grass-green bands, fine-lined on the upper edge with yellow, and on the under edge with black.

1880 At Wolverhampton a blue-green was used as the body-colour for engines. Boiler-bands, panels and bordering were black with fine cream-white lining. Outside frames were painted brown, with black edging and vermilion lining. Wheels were brown, but their bosses were lined out in black with a vermilion line on either side. This livery was similar to that of the older Oxford, Worcester and Wolverhampton Railway engines. Side tanks were lined into two panels with the number-plate in the rear panel.

1878–80 Broad gauge engines "Raven", "Jay" and "Lark", which were 0–4–0ST and "Crow" and "Rook", which were narrow gauge machines, were dark green.

1881 Mr. Dean altered the colour of wheels and splashers.

1881 Engines were painted in a yellower shade of green, and the black boiler-bands commenced to be edged with orange. Outside frames were painted (31), dark Indian red, with black borders lined out with orange, and buffer-beams were vermilion lined black and orange. Wheels were green with black tyres. Splashers and sand-boxes were painted the same shade as the frames and were, in some cases, brass-beaded with black bordering and orange lining.

1883 (c) A lighter green was substituted for the darker shade on engines.

1885 "Bicycle" class rebuilds had a stamped brass crest mounted on the splashers.

1885 Engine coupling-rods ceased to be painted to match the frames, *i.e.* with their bosses of polished steel.

1885 Engine wheels began to be painted Indian red.

1887 Engine No. 3227 (2–4–0) had rectangularly shaped number-plates with the numerals slightly smaller than those in use to-day, with "WOLVERHAMPTON WORKS, 1887" in small lettering below, but within the border of the plate, which was of brass with raised numerals and letters.

Locomotive No. 823 had number-plates of raised polished figures, within a curved square-ended plate, and the company's crest was placed on the front driving-wheel splasher. The building date-plate was mounted on the foot-plate valance between the splashers.

1888 The panelling of tender-sides into three, instead of the previous two, became the style of painting at Swindon.

1889 Locomotive No. 3224 (2–4–0) had brass-beadings to all splashers, and the numerals 3224 were cut-out brass, mounted centrally on the rear splasher face. The gartered "**Q**" crest appeared on the front driving-wheel splasher. The underframes were devoid of lining, as also was the tender, but the G.W.R. monogram (Fig. 38, p. 82) appeared on the centre of the tender side-sheets. The chimney was copper-topped, and the dome and safety-valve casing were polished brass.

1889 At Swindon, tenders were panelled into three, with the script monogram in the centre of the middle panel, which became standard (Fig. 38, p. 82).

1890 (c) Locomotives painted a relatively light shade of green, with red oxide frames and splashers. These colours continued until about 1903–4, when the frames were painted black, and the splashers green. All engines were fully lined with black and fine orange lines. This style continued until the commencement of the 1914–18 war, when lining was dispensed with and engines began to be painted a khaki green and black without any lining.

1890 Mr. Dean's 0–4–4T locomotives (Nos. 34 and 35) were painted the standard green for the boilers, cabs and bunkers, being lined out in black and orange. Splashers, outside framing and wheels were (31), described in sources as Indian red, with black edging and orange lining. Chimney-tops were polished copper, and the domes, safety-valve casings, and break between fire-box and boiler were polished brass; as also were the rims of the cab windows. The smoke-box door handles, hinges and rims were polished steel. Buffer-beams were vermilion, edged black with orange lining. Tool-boxes were green and sand-boxes Indian red.

1893 The practice of naming express engines was instituted, raised brass letters on a curved black painted strip fixed on the splashers being used.

1893 The name-plates on the first of the 2–2–2 class (No. 3001) were of bright steel with letters fretted out of brass. Later the steel backgrounds were painted black, some having a yellow line around the black; the raised brass letters remaining polished.

1894 The "3001" class had the transferred crest on the driving-wheel splashers replaced by a cast-brass one in relief; the crests of London and Bristol appearing on either side of it. (See Figs. 29 and 30, p. 82.) A lighter green colour, which persisted through later years, was adopted about this time for express engines, instead of the older and darker green; the first locomotive to be so painted being No. 3031, "Achilles" (4–2–2).

1894 Wolverhampton abandoned the 1880 livery and fell into line with that in use at Swindon. The old livery could, however, be seen as late as 1900.

1894 For some time after this date there were two locomotive greens in use, one described in sources as "deep holly",* used at Wolverhampton, and very similar to the previous "Swindon" green (20); and the other (19),† described as "middle chrome green", used at Swindon. This latter shade was introduced on the 7 ft. 8 in., 4–2–2 engine No. 3031, "Achilles"; and was eventually adopted as standard right up to 1951.

* Exactly as (19) (E. W. Twining).
† As No. (15) (E. W. Twining).

1894 The panelling of tender-sides into three, instead of the previous two, became the style of painting at Wolverhampton.

1894–5 "River" class engines as rebuilt into 2–4–0's were painted (19), described as the standard green, lined out with black striping and fine orange lines. Frames, coupling-rod bosses and wheels, together with splashers and sand-boxes were all painted deep Indian red. The edges of the frames and slots within them were outlined with a narrow black stripe, having a fine orange line on its inner edge. The springs were Indian red, except the top leaf of each, which was black. The wheels had black tyres. The heads of the spring-hanger bolts were polished steel. The domes, safety-valve casings, cab window-frames and all beading was of polished brass; and between the boiler barrel and the smoke-box was a brass fillet. Buffer-beams were vermilion, outlined in black with orange lining. The engine number was later painted in yellow figures shaded in black on the front buffer-beam. The chimney-tops were of polished copper, whilst all hand-rails, tie-bars, buffer-heads, safety-valve levers and coupling-rods were of steel, kept brightly polished.

1894 The locomotive body-colour was changed to (19), the present shade of green, the engine "Achilles" being the first to be so treated.

1896 Locomotives were (19), described in sources as chrome green, the shades varying slightly according to whether they were built at Swindon or Wolverhampton. Express engines from Swindon works were of a slightly lighter shade than the tank and goods locomotives from the same works. Wolverhampton engines were painted quite a blue shade of green, and their lining differed also. Swindon engines had a medium-width black band with a very fine orange line on each side, whereas Wolverhampton engines had a fine cream line in place of the yellow. (White may mean pale yellow, and yellow orange. Varnish and fading produced such an effect.)

All engines had their framing and splashers a dark red-brown, edged with a narrow black border with a fine yellow line inside it.

Domes and safety-valve casings were bright brass. Swindon engines had a "bell" copper top, and Wolverhampton ones a rolled copper top. Buffer-beams were vermilion, edged with black and a fine yellow line. Cab interiors were vermilion to the height of the splashers, then green above, edged round with black, and a fine yellow line.

1894 The very imposing splashers of the "3001" class had the crests of the G.W.R. emblazoned on them, surrounded with a garter cast in relief and painted up in the multi-coloured heraldic fashion. On either side of these arms were the arms of London and Bristol in relief.

On most other passenger express engines the crest was transferred on the driving-wheel splashers. Number-plates were of brass with raised figures, the background being black, with a fine yellow line round inside (Fig. 34, p.82).

1896 Coaches were light brown umber on the lower panels, a yellow line running round the edge. Upper panels were cream, with a fine brown line inside. Lettering on the lower panels and doors was in yellow, shaded black, whilst the numbers appearing along the upper portion were in yellow shaded with brown. Underframes were black. Horse-boxes, carriage trucks, etc., were light brown umber all over, lettering being in yellow shaded with black.

Wagon stock was a light red colour with white lettering.

Goods brakes were dark grey.

1897 Engine No. 3006 (4–2–2 "Courier") was experimentally fitted with a cast-iron chimney, which she carried for only a few months.

1898 The engine "Earl Cawdor" had green boiler and cab side-sheets with black and orange lining. Frames and splashers, as well as the sand-boxes, were a deep "mahogany" red with black edging and yellow lining. The raised projections of the inside frames were black on their outer faces and vermilion within.

Wheels were "mahogany" red with black tyres. A bright brass fillet surrounded the joint between the smoke-box and the boiler-barrel. The chimney had a polished copper top, and the dome and safety-valve cover were bright brass. There were brass-beadings round both driving and bogie-wheel splashers, and the cab spectacles were also brass-beaded. The smoke-box door fittings and the coupling-rods were bright steel.

1898 "Badminton" class engines were fitted with a curved name-plate which was fixed to the boiler immediately above the driving-wheel splashers.

Pre 1899 Copper-capped chimneys were standard.

1899 On the engines "Atbara" and "Bulldog", combined name and number-plates were used, there being two varieties of plates. In the earlier variety used on "Atbara" the company's crest was

LONDON AND NORTH WESTERN RAILWAY LOCOMOTIVE NO. 375 (EXTRA "LARGE BLOOMER" CLASS) BUILT IN 1861 IN SOUTHERN DIVISION LIVERY (P. 121)

included in the middle of the plate, replacing the "3375" shown in Fig. 32, p. 82. Beneath the crest, in the centre of the lower part of the outer oval appeared the engine number; to the left of this was the word "SWINDON", with the works number below it; and to the right the words "AUGUST–1899".

1899 The "3292" class had large oval name-plates on the cab sides, with the Swindon number and date in the centre, the name above, and the number below. All other locomotives in this class had standard name-plates over the splashers.

1899 The plain cast-iron chimneys were introduced with the "Camel" class 4–4–0's.

1899 Engine boiler-bands were double-lined with orange, two lines of this colour, spaced ½ in. apart, appearing on either side of the black band.

1899 Engines of the 4–2–2 ("Lorna Doone") class had boilers, fire-boxes, tender and cab sides painted the standard G.W. green being lined in black and orange chrome yellow. The splashers, outside frames and sand-boxes were (29), described in sources as deep Indian red, being also lined in deep orange chrome. The springs were Indian red, as well as the hangers and buckles, the latter being edged with black and lined with yellow. The top plates of the springs were black. Wheels were painted (29), described as Indian red, and the tyres either black or bright steel.

The driving-wheel splashers were decorated with three heraldic devices, of which the centre one was a circular cast brass plaque 12 ins. in diameter, containing the coats-of-arms of the cities of London and Bristol; the arms being surrounded by a garter, with buckle and clasp. The company's title was emblazoned on the garter. To the left of this centrepiece was a crest (see Fig. 41, p. 82) formed of the griffin's wing of London, and to the right a crest formed of the crossed arms holding the serpent and scales of Bristol City. All three devices were of cast brass, being painted in the true heraldic colour scheme. The sides of the tender were divided into three rectangular panels, each of which were formed by a one inch wide black stripe with a fine orange line on each side of it. The centre panel contained an elaborate monogram of the letters "GWR" (Fig. 38, p. 82), which were in gold, relieved and shaded in black and burnt sienna. The Swindon date-plate was placed immediately above the driving-wheel outside axle-box on the frames. The axle-box was bright polished brass. The number-plates were on rectangular plates in the modern type of figures. The engine name was on a curved plate placed on the driving-wheel splasher.

1900 "Camel" class engines had no number-plate on the smoke-box, but the number painted in yellow on the buffer-beams. "Camel" herself had the number on the smoke-box.

1900 Relief line trains carried green tail-lamps.

1900 The practice of painting the engine number on the buffer-beams was commenced.

1900–4 The old suburban four-wheeled first-class coaches had their lower and waist panels, as well as their ends brown. The upper panels were cream, with a fine black line inside the mouldings; the latter being black, with a $\frac{3}{8}$ in. yellow edge. The roofs were white above the rain-strip and brown below. Ironwork was black, and wheel-centres brown.

1901 The coach destination boards on the Birkenhead to Bournemouth expresses were red with gold lettering.

1903 Some coaches were being experimentally painted all chocolate colour.

1903 When the Great Western Railway fell into line with the other companies by providing 2nd and 3rd class dining-cars on the London and Cardiff trains, the destination boards fitted thereon extended the whole length of the coach; being placed in front of the clerestory windows. The boards bore the words "LONDON . NEWPORT . CARDIFF . DINING CAR" in large gold decorated block letters on a vermilion background.

1903 On the later combined name and number-plate as used on "Bulldog", the crest was omitted, and the number was placed in the centre of the plate, as shown in Fig. 32, p. 82. In the blank space shown in the figure, the words "SWINDON WORKS–JANUARY, 1903," appeared in two lines of lettering.

1903 Experiments were made with warmer and deeper shades of the standard colours originally chosen by Brunel in 1840, and coaches were painted a rich chocolate shade with upper panels ivory white.

1903 A train was experimentally painted a dark lake shade.

1903 Engine splashers commenced to be painted green, to match the bodywork.

1903 The engine "La France" originally ran in a black livery with red lining, but the two later de Glehn compounds were run from the outset in standard green.

1904 The engine "La France" had a standard Great Western number-plate which was placed above the name-plate in the position previously occupied by the maker's works plate (i.e. on the cab side-sheets). The works plate was transferred to the trailing driving-wheel splasher, whilst the leading splasher carried the standard cast-brass G.W.R. crest. Locomotive and tender were painted black, being lined out with fine vermilion lines. Number-plates of cast-brass with polished letters and figures were fitted, the background being black. The bosses of both four-coupled and trailing wheels were left bright steel.

1904 Locomotive splasher colour altered to green, but otherwise the general style remained unchanged.

1904 Goods guard's vans had "G.W." in large white letters painted on each end of the vans, in place of "GWR" on an iron plate on the lower part of the van, as previously.

1904 (c) A few coaches and vans were painted all brown, with yellow lining, different shades being used. After many experiments, a deeper cream shade and a rich chocolate brown colour were adopted which lasted until about 1911.

1904 Engines had their boiler-banding modified from what it had been previously, in that instead of the orange lines flanking the black, and in contact with it, a space of $\frac{1}{2}$ in. was left through which the green body colour could be seen.

1904 During this year, and leading up to the later "GREAT '**Q**' WESTERN" (garter) standardization of tender livery, some tenders were seen with "G.W.R.", one letter in each panel. At times the three letters were all placed in the centre of the middle panel, whilst the garter crest alone in the centre panel appeared on a few tenders.

1905 Coaches were running painted wholly brown, relieved only by gold lining.

1905 Most locomotives did not boast domes, and had black chimneys without copper tops. The old Great Western monogram was changed to "GREAT WESTERN". Those engines which had domes had them painted green instead of the previous polished brass.

The 4-4-0 (No. 3310, "Waterford") had its driving-wheel splasher painted green, instead of the chocolate frame colour previously used.

1905 Some of the engines used on auto-trains were painted chocolate with black underframes and wheels, but this special livery was abolished during the first World War.

1905 There were engines running painted in six different styles of livery. (*a*) Those without lettering, crest or monogram; which were the old six-wheeled goods locomotives. (*b*) Those which had the monogram in the centre panel of the tender, which was the standard until 1905. (*c*) Those which had G.W.R. in large block letters on the centre panel of the tender. (*d*) Those which had G.W.R. spaced one letter in each of the three tender-panels. (*e*) Those which had the Company's crest only on the centre tender-panel, and (*f*) those which had the name "GREAT WESTERN" painted in full in block letters with red shading, the crest appearing between the two words. (See Figs. 14 and 16, pp. 18 and 29.)

Pre 1906 Locomotives had underframes painted red-brown, as also were their splashers and cylinder-covers. Tenders were either two- or three-panelled, the three-panelled type having the letters "GWR" in copper-plate script, instead of the "GREAT WESTERN", later adopted.

1906 On tank engines, the number-plates were removed from the side tanks and placed on the bunkers; but on the smaller locomotives, the plates were simply moved to the rear panel of the tanks.

1906 The new livery was first introduced on engines, and the wheels and underframes were at first painted black, with orange lining.

1906 Tank engines commenced to be decorated with the familiar "GREAT **'Q'** WESTERN" on the side tanks, though at first the garter was omitted.

1906 The custom of painting engine frames and wheels a reddish-brown was abandoned, and black substituted.

1906 All locomotives had their numbers painted in yellow on the front buffer-beams as they passed through the shops.

1906 Trains on the "Middle Circle" had "1st", "2nd" and "3rd" on the doors of coaches.

"Duke of Cornwall" class engines (Nos. 3252–3291) originally had names on horizontal plates on the boiler, and Nos. 3313–3331 similar plates on the fire-box.

1906 All name-plates were placed over driving-wheel splashers on curved plates for uniformity. (See Figs. 39 and 40, p. 82.)

1906 "County" tanks of this date (2221–2229) (Dec.) had "GREAT

WESTERN" on the tank sides, and number-plates removed to the bunker sides.

1906 0–4–2T engines on motor-trains were painted a reddish-brown.

1906 The painting of wheels and frames a reddish-brown was abandoned.

1907 All goods stock began to be marked "GW" in plain style, instead of with the "GWR" monogram. This lettering was also employed on carriage-trucks, fruit-vans, horse-boxes and milk-vans.

1907 "La France" was repainted green above the running-plate and black below, being fully lined out in the practice of the time. The tender was, at first, divided into the usual three panels, the middle one of which carried the company's crest instead of the old monogram. This was altered soon after to a single panel with the words "GREAT WESTERN", having the crest between them in the standard style.

1907 The practice of painting the engine numbers in gold figures on the front buffer-beams (which was first adopted in the case of No. 3352, "Camel" class, which made her appearance at the end of 1900), was now generally adopted.

1908 Cream upper panels for coaches were discarded, and stock began to be painted a chocolate shade all over; the colour being very similar to that used by the Great Eastern Railway for repainting their teak stock when it became old.

"Flower" class engines began to be fitted with copper-topped chimneys, which style was, prior to 1899, the standard, and had been so for many years.

1908 Locomotive No. 3293 ("Barrington") had a crest similar to those appearing on the driving-wheel splashers of single bogie engines put on each side of the cab above the number-plate. The names were on curved plates fixed to the boiler over the driving-wheel splasher.

1908 Goods stock was lettered "G.W." in "very" large letters.

1908 Engine No. 111 "The Great Bear", the first British "Pacific", had a brass-capped chimney. (See also Fig. 36, p. 82.)

1908 The reinstatement of copper top chimneys was well in hand on all classes of locomotives.

1908 Coaches: cream upper panels were discarded, being a uniform olive-brown; this tint was adopted for the lower panels in 1903.

1908 Coaches were painted chocolate all over once again, which was not changed again until 1912, when crimson-lake was used.

1909 (July) Engine No. 2225 (4–4–2T), was experimentally painted in a shade of crimson-lake, of a somewhat similar shade to that of Midland Railway locomotives, but darker.* Wheels and framing were black. It received a copper cap to its chimney in October, 1909.

1909 Towards the end of July, 4–4–2T engine No. 2225 was put to work on local services in the Swindon and Bristol district, painted in a shade of crimson-lake somewhat similar to the colour adopted for the Midland Railway's engines, but lighter in tint.* The wheels and framing were still painted black. This new colour was considered cheaper then the present (1909) standard colour of "light" green, which was adopted in place of the "dark" green about sixteen years before (*c.* 1893).

1909 During September another engine (No. 14) was painted in the experimental lake colour.

1911 Details of the engine wheel arrangement were stamped on the margins of the brass number-plates, and where the plates were too small, the details were stamped on the actual raised brass figures of the plate.

1911 Coaches were described in sources as being painted a deep crimson-lake all over, with gold lining; this livery remaining in force until 1922.

1911 Works number-plates ceased to be fitted to engines.

1912 The coach colour, described in sources as coach-brown (all over), which was introduced in 1909, was changed to crimson-lake, which colour lasted until 1922; when brown (popularly known as "chocolate") and cream were again made the standard colours of passenger coaching stock.

1912 Coaches were painted crimson-lake all over.

1914 Passenger engines were described in sources as a mid-green, lined out in orange and black. Underframes were black. Dome casings and safety-valve casings were of polished brass. Chimneys had polished copper tops. Goods engines were painted the same green, but devoid of lining.

Passenger coaches were dark red, and wagons dark red and grey.

1914 (c) Coaches: a red chocolate-brown, was substituted for brown lower panels and ivory-white upper panels, as previously.

* *According to two different authorities.*

1915 Engines passing through the shops were painted khaki, with orange buffer-beams and black wheels and underframes. The engines were completely devoid of all lining.

1916 Three distinct colours were being used for engines described in sources as the "standard" green (19), a "khaki" livery, and red-brown for auto-engines. Coaches were also occasionally painted a khaki shade.

1916 (Aug.) As a war measure, many locomotives were painted khaki colour, though the colour did not suggest "khaki" in the generally accepted sense of the word, being of a browner tinge than that olive-green shade used on military vehicles during the 1914–18 war. When the colour was freshly applied it had a very lustrous finish. In this temporary colour scheme, the buffer-beams were painted black. Later engines which were painted khaki colour had the coloured crest between the words "GREAT" and "WESTERN" omitted.

At this time there were three standard colours of locomotives: (*a*) the usual green for the bulk of the stock, (*b*) a "Midland" shade of crimson for auto-train working, and (*c*) the khaki shade referred to above.

1917 Engines appeared painted in unlined green, all brass and copper parts being painted over.

1917 Although many engines were painted a khaki shade, it was decided to discontinue this and to revert to the old dark green above the foot-plate level with black below and red buffer-beams.

1917 Brass-work on engines was painted over green, and brass safety-valve casings continued to be painted over green.

1917 (later) Locomotive copper chimney tops were painted black.

1918 "Red" coaches were discarded in favour of chocolate and cream, and standard green and black for engines was reverted to, without any lining; this style remaining until 1923.

1919 Auto-train engines were painted in unlined crimson-lake.

1922 The original colours of passenger stock were white and brown, but the white became a cream shade when varnished. Lining was yellow. These coach colours were reverted to, but instead of being painted in the traditional methods for coachwork, modern paint and methods were introduced. The 1922 colours persisted until about 1936, when coaches were devoid of lining except black and yellow between the cream and brown. The yellow was subsequently altered to gold, and some trains had a long waist panel with gold and black lines.

1923 Bullion vans were painted chocolate colour and cream, with panelling lined. Ends were black, with a small "23" in white in the upper left-hand corner. The underframes were black and the roofs white. Lettering was in gold, the same as passenger stock.

1923 "Mica B" vans had body, roof and top hand-rails white. Lettering was red, and underframes black.

"Mica A" vans had both bodies and underframes dark grey.

1923 All express passenger engines had their lining restored as they passed through the shops. Other types remained unaltered.

GREAT NORTHERN RAILWAY CREST (*page 45*)

HIGHLAND RAILWAY

THE Highland Railway originated with the Inverness and Nairn Railway, which was incorporated in 1852 and upon which the first train ran on 5th November, 1855. This line was amalgamated with the Nairn and Keith Railway (opened 1858) in 1861, to form the Inverness and Aberdeen Junction Railway; which line was amalgamated in 1865 with the Perth and Dunkeld Railway (opened 1856), and the Inverness and Perth Junction Railway (opened 1863) to form The Highland Railway.

Further acquisitions of the Highland Railway included the Ross-shire Railway (opened 1863), the Sutherland Railway (opened 1868), the Dingwall and Skye Railway (opened 1870), the Sutherland and Caithness Railway (opened 1874), and the Golspie and Helmsdale Railway (opened 1871 as the "Sutherland Railway"). The Highland Railway also worked the Wick and Lybster Railway (opened 1903), and the Dornoch Light Railway (opened in 1902).

The locomotive, carriage and wagon superintendents of the Railway from its inception were as follows:—

1855–1865 William Barclay (of the Inverness and Nairn Rly.)
1866–1869 William Stroudley (later of the L.B. & S.C.Rly.)
1869–1896 David Jones
1896–1912 Peter Drummond
1912–1915 J. Smith (F. G. Smith)
1915–early 1922 C. Cumming
1922–1923 W. Urie

1860 The Inverness and Aberdeen Junction engines were yellow, with numbers painted on the driving-wheel splashers.

Locomotive No. 20, "Birnam", (a 2–4–0 tender type) was at one time painted yellow, like the passenger engines of the period.

1864 Locomotive No. 38 (no name) by Sharp, Stewart and Co., had sharp, but rounded corners to lining, and the cab upper works and side-sheets were panelled separately. This lining applied also to locomotive "Golspie", No. 53.

1864 Engines were dark green with black borders and bands. There was no fine lining. Numbers were painted on the buffer-beams, and they also appeared on the front driving-wheel splashers together with the letters "I & A J Ry."

1865 During Mr. Barclay's régime locomotives were dark green with black borders and bands without lining. Number painted on buffer-beams.

1865–69 Passenger engine livery at Inverness shops was described as golden ochre of the same shade (32) as that Mr. Stroudley originally used on the engines of the L.B.S.C.R. (Goods engines were painted a dark green.)

1868 The passenger locomotives by Dübs of Glasgow were buff-ochre with lake underframes. Goods engines were a dark uniform green.

1869 During Mr. Stroudley's régime* locomotives were painted a yellow with framing dark crimson and very elaborate lining.

Goods engines were dark green. Engine names appeared in gold letters on driving-wheel splashers or tanks. Number-plates were of "Stroudley" (L.B.S.C.R.) pattern, being made of brass with the figures and letters on a vermilion background, instead of blue as on the L.B.S.C.R. (see Figs. 62, 65 and 66, p. 209).

1871 Mr. Jones substituted light olive-green for the "Stroudley" yellow, retaining the dark red underframes and "Stroudley" lining, using white and red lines with a darker green border (see also Figs. 42 and 49, p. 114).

1871–77 Locomotives "Ballindalloch" (No. 3) and "Aldourie" (No. 2) had not any letters on the tender, and carried Stroudley type number-plates (Figs. 62, 65 and 66, p. 209). The front buffer-beams were panelled between the buffers with two concentric white lines.

1874 Locomotive "Nairnshire" (Dübs 4–4–0) had Stroudley type number-plates, which were mounted on the rear driving-wheel splasher. (Also "Strathpeffer", No. 13.)

* The colours of Highland Railway locomotives and coaches under Mr. Stroudley's régime are subject to great differences of opinion. Some authorities firmly insist that the engines—at least—were painted in the famous "Improved Engine Green" (actually 33), as used on Mr. Stroudley's London, Brighton and South Coast Railway engines; whilst others go so far as to state that the Highland Railway coaches in Stroudley's régime were also painted in this colour.

The fact that Mr. Stroudley later experimentally painted a London, Brighton and South Coast close-coupled train in the well-known "ochre" (33), would seem to lend some credence to the latter theory.

Locomotive "Needlefield" (0–4–2 pannier tank) was panelled with a fine white line within a *dark* green outer panel. Tanks, buffer-beam-ends, rear tool-box, tank-saddles, cab sides (front and rear), splashers, steps and valances were thus panelled. A copper-capped chimney and brass dome and safety-valve casings were fitted. The older type of number-plates were fitted, which were longer and narrower than the Stroudley type, and which had sunken letters on polished brass.

The original "Stroudley" Highland livery was the same as the L.B.S.C.R., lined with red outer and white inner lines, with a wider black line between; the outer banding being olive-green. Underframes were painted lake colour, lined out in yellow and vermilion. (No tender lettering appeared in either Stroudley's or Jones' time.)

The "Stroudley" boiler-banding consisted of a wide black band flanked by fine red lines, these again being flanked by fine white lines, set at a distance from the red lines.

The Jones livery was the same as that of Stroudley, but Brunswick green outer banding was used instead of the olive-green (see Fig. 42, p. 114).

1884 Locomotive No. 1 ("Ben-y-Gloe") carried a number-plate with dark sunken letters on cab sides, with the name on driving-wheel splashers (Fig. 61, p. 209). The diamond-shaped maker's plate was placed on the front driving-wheel coupling-rod splasher.

The letters H.R. appeared on the tender with very wide spacing, with a square full-stop between them; being shaded black to the right and below and counter-shaded to left and below with green, white, brown and black

1887–92 The scroll-sided 6-wheeled coaches had white waists and upper panels, with lower panels of light olive-green lined with yellow. A script monogram "HR" was between the coupé and the compartment doors, whilst below the lavatory windows was a garter containing the coach number. The monogram and the garters were in gold. On the waist panel, under the lavatory windows appeared the words "FIRST CLASS" in gold.

1891 Locomotive No. 38 (rebuilt in 1891) had very fine white lining instead of the $\frac{1}{2}$ in. lines. This type refers also to "Cluny", No. 32, and to "Lochgorm", 0–6–0T which latter engine carried a "Stroudley" type number-plate.

1894 The goods engine designed by Mr. Jones (4–6–0) was

painted (18),* described in sources as green with light olive-green panelling, the lining being a red outer line, a black middle, and a white inner one. Boiler-bands were black, flanked first with red lines, then with white. The chimney had a brass cap and safety-valve casings were also brass. Underframes were (27), described as red, lined out vermilion. Cylinders were green, panelled out in red, black and white. The tender coal-flare was lined out red and black at the base. Number-plates were of bright brass with a vermilion background to the numerals. Tender grease-caps were brass and all guard-irons vermilion. Coal-rail was olive-green. Tender springs and horn-plates were black, and the axle-boxes and stretchers (27) red lined out in vermilion.

The buffer-beams were vermilion, panelled out with black and (27) red. The body of the wheels was described as body green, axle-ends were light olive, lined out with red. Hubs were green, lined outside with white. Spokes were body green, with white-lined rims and light olive tyres. Counter-balance weights were lined out white outer and red inner lines.

Big-end liners were bright brass. Spectacle windows were brass-rimmed. Date-plate was brass with a vermilion background.

Tender-spokes were unlined, and there was no lettering on the tender-sides, which were lined out in one panel (see Figs. 42 and 49, p. 114).

1895 Locomotive "Loch Insh" (No. 119, Dübs and Co.) still had number-plates similar to Mr. Stroudley's L.B.S.C.R. design on the rear splasher-cum-cab-side. The background to the lettering and numerals was, however, a vermilion instead of a blue background, as on the L.B.S.C.R. The door between the locomotive and tender was panelled, this and all other panelling having rounded corners. The tool-box at the rear of the tender was also panelled, and the cab sides were lined out in two panels. The sand-box to the front of the leading driving-wheel splasher was fully panelled, as also were the cylinders.

Coaches: Monogram, garter, number and class designation removed and replaced by gold block letters and figures on the waist panels. On each door was the word "FIRST", whilst between each compartment and coupé were the initials H.R., with the number below the lavatory windows. Lettering was shaded with light green and white.

* Or slightly lighter than (18).

Pre 1896 Coaches were a medium shade of sage green with yellow lines and letters in gold shaded with light green and black. Lower panels were dark lake, lined with yellow.

1896 Coaches had a new style of upper panel colouring in which white was used, the lower panels being dark green, with the lining and lettering the same as previously. Coach number-plates were raised yellow letters on a black ground. Wagons were a dark red with white lettering and black ironwork. Wagon number-plates had "H.R." in a monogram above the wagon-number, both the monogram and the number being in red; the monogram was on a yellow background and the number on a white ground. Some goods brakes were painted a dark lake with yellow lettering shaded with red, whilst others were painted similarly to passenger stock, but without lettering.

1896 Locomotives Nos. 28 and 29 (Sharp, Stewart rebuilds) had red coupling-rods, and were the only Highland engines finished in this manner.

1896 The engine No. 119 ("Loch Insh") had the Prince of Wales' feathers and "Ich Dien" painted on the splashers below the name in commemoration of H.R. Highness's trip from Perth to Speyside in the autumn of 1886.

Late 1896 Locomotives were a bright yellowish green, with a border of a darker shade divided by a black band; the marginal lines being vermilion outside and white within.

1896–1903 Coaches were green, with white upper panels.

1897 Both the marginal lines were made white on coaches.

Framing was dark lake with a black border having an outer margin of yellow, and an inner of red. Buffer-beams were painted the same as the framing, but had a vermilion panel with a black border edged with a yellow line.

Early in this year the letters H.R. and the engine number in gold, shaded black was inserted in the vermilion panel.

Number-plates were of brass with raised figures and letters on a vermilion background. Passenger locomotives had their names painted on the driving-wheel splashers in gold, shaded with light green and black.

1897 The Drummond livery consisted of a Brunswick green outer panel, with a wide black line within flanked by two fine white ones. The boiler-banding was a wide black line, flanked by fine white lines, these being flanked by fine white lines set at some distance from the inner white lines. Underframes were painted lake, with a black edge and a single fine white line.

1897 When Mr. Drummond changed the engine colour to green, the coaches were repainted to match, but the style of lettering remained the same.

1897 The "Skye" bogie engines similar to the "No. 70" class, had no copper-top to the chimneys, nor the louvering of the No. 70 class.

1897 There were modifications to locomotives by the new locomotive superintendent (P. Drummond), Nos. 37 and 93 appearing with a narrow white line instead of a red one, whilst the initials "H.R." appeared on the tenders and in conjunction with the engine number on the buffer-beams.

Late 1897 The engine finish included H.R. on the tender in the same colour and shading as that of the name, but in larger letters.

1897–1912 Under Mr. Drummond all new locomotives were fitted with chimneys and number-plates of his type, which was typical. Red lining was abolished on engines, and black boiler and panel-bands were edged with narrow white lines. The initials "H.R." appeared on the tender- and tank-sides, and also (together with the engine number) on the buffer-beams.

1898 Peter Drummond introduced (12), described as olive-green, for engine colour, and up to 1903 it was edged with white and black lines. He retained the Stroudley dark red underframes, and used a vermilion buffer-beam panel similar to Caledonian engines of the period.

1900 When the "Castle" class appeared, the lettering on the tenders became "HIGHLAND RAILWAY".

1901 Locomotives (12), described in sources as green. Coaches: green, with white upper panels. Saloon coaches and sleeping cars bore oval panels in the centre of the side panels below the waist, with "H.R." and "No. 8" inscribed thereon; and there were garters between the number panel and the ends of the coach. Some special saloons and the two "sleepers" were varnished teak at first.

1901 Coaches were a rich green in the lower panels with white upper panels picked out with gold.

1903 Locomotives were (12), described in sources as a dark green, with black bands and white lines. The name of the company was in gold, black-shaded letters.

1903 "Strath" and "Loch" class locomotives were painted a dark green (Jones) with black bands and white lining. The words "THE HIGHLAND RAILWAY." (with full-stop) appeared on the tender-panels in gold block letters, shaded with black.

1903 A complete change took place, engines being painted all over, including the buffer-beams, (11), described in sources as a plain green, of a darker shade than that used before; without any lining whatsoever. Even the smoke-boxes were green. This severe style was adopted for reasons of economy. The initials and numbers on the buffer-beams were retained, and the lettering on the tanks and tender-sides was altered to "THE HIGHLAND RAILWAY". (This applied first to 0–6–0T locomotives Nos. 28 and 29.)

Pre 1906 Locomotives were (12), described in sources as a pale olive-green, with black and white lining.

1906 (c) A change was made to a much darker green which was unrelieved by any lining. Foot-plate edging was green, as were the buffer-beams; the latter bearing the initials HR to the left of the coupling-hook and the engine number to the right of it. The tenders or tanks carried either the initials H.R. or else the full title; the latter being either "HIGHLAND RAILWAY" or "THE HIGHLAND RAILWAY" in gold block letters, which matched those on the buffer-beams, being shaded to the left and below in various shades of green (with white high-lights) and brown, and to the right and below in black.

1906 The engine "Strathpeffer" (No. 40) and "Gordon Lennox" were painted "standard" Highland Railway dark green, and were devoid of lining of any description. The names appeared on the tank sides in gold letters. A new pattern of cast brass number-plates, which appeared at this time were first fitted to these engines.

1907 The new sleeping cars and excursion saloons were finished in varnished teak, the green livery being at first discarded for these vehicles.

1908 Locomotives were painted (11), now described in sources as olive-green, without lining, but the letters "HR" appeared on the tender-sides very widely spaced and in sans-serif letters of gold shaded in black and red. Whistle and safety-valve casings were of polished brass. Smoke-box, chimney, engine and tender under-frames were black, but wheels were green. The number-plate was of large size, being oval, and bearing the number and words "HIGHLAND RAILWAY" in raised polished brass characters on a black background. The engine name was on the leading driving-wheel splasher in the same style of lettering as that on the tender. The building date-plate was placed on the leading coupling-rod splasher. The tender wheels were green.

1910 (12), described in sources as "Drummond" green, was of a slightly greyer shade than that used later by Mr. Cumming.

1910 Locomotives were dark green with green (not red) buffer-beams.

1911 Locomotives were a uniform dark green and devoid of lining. The buffer-beams were dark green (not vermilion).

1912–15 Mr. Smith introduced (12), described in sources as a brighter shade of green, for the engines, and the coaching stock was again finished to match the engines, being also decorated with the Highland Railway crest in the centre of the coach underneath the number; but without any change in the style of lettering. Sometimes coach numbers were very large (as large as the "HR" on locomotive tenders). Coach roofs were always white and iron-work black.

1913 Twin wagons were red oxide with black ironwork and white letters, tyres and figures.

1914 (c) Locomotives green. White upper panels discarded on coaches.

1914–18 Owing to the shortage of brass, all number-plates were melted down as locomotives came into the shops, and large numbers similar to the lettering "H.R." were painted at the top of the cab-sheeting.

1915 Coaches were green. Locomotives were a brighter green, after having being originally olive-green.

1917 Engine number-plates were oval-shaped, containing the words "HIGHLAND" and "RAILWAY" above and below the engine number, respectively. The words "THE HIGHLAND RAILWAY" appeared on the tank sides.

1917–18 Buffer-beams began to be painted red, but this practice had not become universal when "grouping" arrived. Number-plates were either oval and of brass, with the words "HIGHLAND RAILWAY" and the number; or were brass, cast with sunken letters and filled in with red wax.

Coaches and coaching stock were painted (12), a similar green, to match the engines, being lettered in gold, similarly to the locomotive lettering; but coaching stock was lettered in yellow

MIDLAND 2–4–0 LOCOMOTIVE NO. 1305 IN THE PRE-1882–3 LIVERY (P. 154)

ochre or in gilt transfers. Roofs were white and underframes and running-gear black. Coaches were unlined.

Goods stock was red oxide and initialled "H.R." in white. Van roofs were white, and ironwork and running-gear black. Number-plates were oval cast-iron, with the words "HIGHLAND RAILWAY" and the number in relief.

1922 Engines and coaches were green.

HIGHLAND RAILWAY CREST

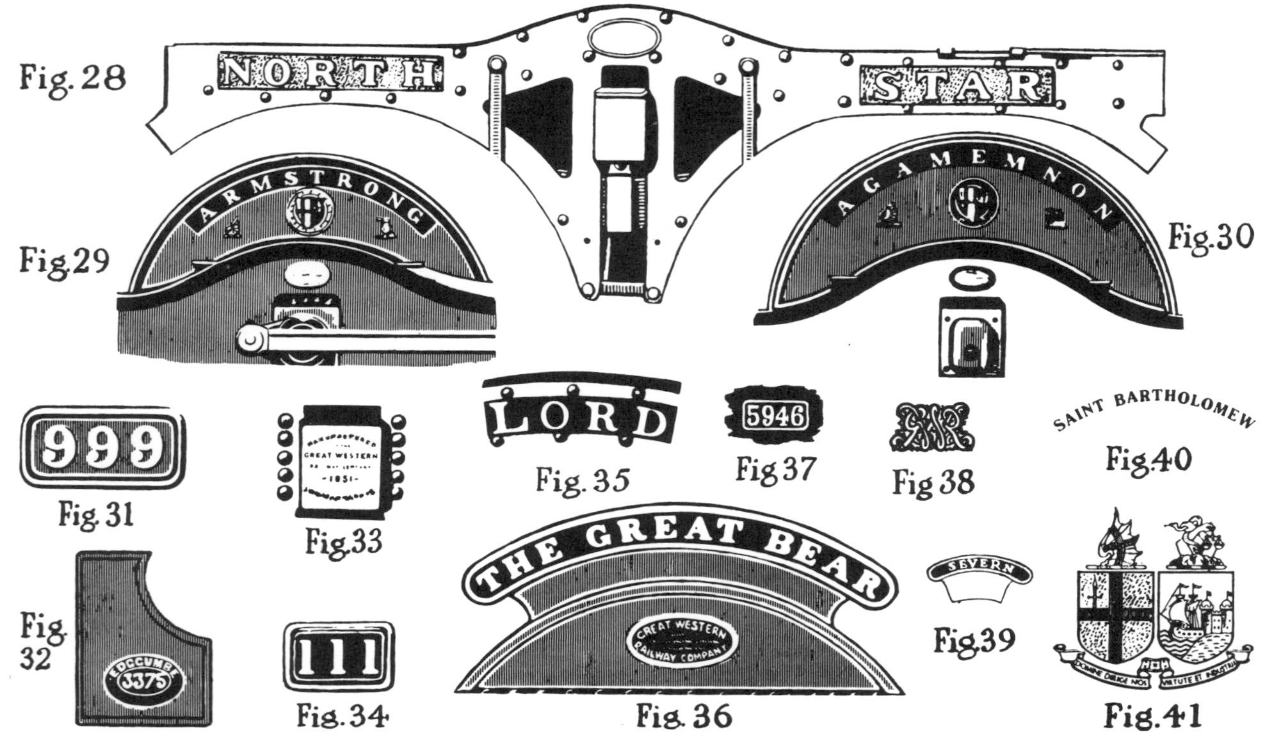

Fig. 28
Fig. 29
Fig. 30
Fig. 31
Fig. 32
Fig. 33
Fig. 34
Fig. 35
Fig. 36
Fig. 37
Fig. 38
Fig. 39
Fig. 40
Fig. 41

HULL AND BARNSLEY RAILWAY

PREVIOUS to 1905 this Railway was known as the Hull, Barnsley and West Riding Junction Railway and Dock Company, which was incorporated in 1880. The South Yorkshire Junction Railway, which was opened in 1894, was worked by the Hull and Barnsley Railway, which was amalgamated with the North Eastern Railway in 1922.

Through the whole of its career the Hull and Barnsley had but one locomotive chief—Matthew Stirling, who held the office from 1885 until the end of the railway's separate existence.

The company owned wholly or jointly, nearly 95 route miles of line, to which can be added the 11 miles comprising the South Yorkshire Junction Railway. In 1922 the company owned 181 locomotives and almost 5,000 other vehicles.

1876 The 0–6–0 tender engine built by the Yorkshire Engine Co., had a very small oval maker's plate (4 ins. across the major axis), mounted on the cab side-sheet. The engine was devoid of number-plates, and the lining had double incurved corners to all panels (as Fig. 4, p. 6, but doubled), the coal-flare on the tender being separately panelled.

1885 The 0–6–0 tender locomotive No. 32 (class G1), had a small monogram in the centre of the tender-side panel—"H.B. & W.R.J.R. & D." (Hull, Barnsley and West Riding Junction Railway and Dock), this being the original title of the company when formed in 1879.

1885 Locomotive No. 32 (Beyer, Peacock, 0–6–0 tender) had similar number-plates to No 12, but they were placed on the cab sides. The middle driving-wheel splashers were double brass beaded, with "BEYER PEACOCK & CO. MANCHESTER, 1885" on a plate between the beadings. All lining was as No. 12.

A script monogram composed of the letters H. B. W. R. J.D.R. appeared in the centre of the single tender panel.

Locomotive No. 42 (Beyer Peacock 2–4–0 tender) was also liveried as No. 32.

1885 Locomotives had cast brass number-plates, but later, transfers of Doncaster type were used.

1885 The Hull, Barnsley and West Riding Junction Railway engine No. 12 (Beyer, Peacock, 0–6–0T) had large oval cast number-plates whereon the words "HULL, BARNSLEY & WEST RIDING" were curved above the serif numerals, and the words "JUNCTION RAILWAY & DOCK CO." below. These plates were fitted on the tank sides. The oval builder's plate was placed on the bunker-sides, and was lettered "BEYER, PEACOCK & CO."—"GORTON FOUNDRY"—"MANCHESTER, 1885".

All lining was with incurved corners, a vermilion broad centre line being flanked by a fine ultramarine blue line at a slight distance each side. Axle ends had a fine white inner circle, then black.

1898 Locomotives were lined with exceptionally wide lines, with incurved corners.

1900 Locomotives were black, picked out with ultramarine and vermilion lines.

Coaches were light teak shade, lined out with gold.

1900 Locomotives were black, with wide panelling and stripes of ultramarine blue, lined on each side with vermilion. Frames were black, with a fine red line, and the buffer-beams were vermilion, with the engine number thereon in gold, shaded black. The cab interiors were light brown, with a black border; with a vermilion dividing line, and a fine yellow line on the side nearest the light brown body-colour. Engine lettering was in gold with red shading, and number-plates were of brass with bright raised figures on a black background.

Coaches were finished in a pale teak, with gold stripes round the mouldings, and the underframes were painted vermilion, picked out in black.

Wagon stock was dark blue, with white shading, and all iron-work was black.

1911 The 4–4–0 Kitson-built engine (No. 33) had the tender lined out with a 2 in. wide blue line in one panel, the corners being incurved. The lower edge of the tender valance had a line of the same colour but only two-thirds of an inch wide. The ends of the buffer-beams were panelled with a blue line of the same width, and a 2 in. wide line panelled the rear of the tender, the corners being incurved. Both the side and rear flair was panelled with a narrow blue line without incurved corners. A very fine yellow line divided the buffer-beams into three panels, the lining being curved round the buffer socket-plates on either side.

The broad blue lining also appeared around the margins of the cab side-sheets up to the level of the roof curve. The maker's number-plate (4700) was of brass, and was placed centrally on the side of the smoke-box saddle.

The letters H. & B.R. appeared in small sans-serif letters of gold with red shading to the left and below in the centres of the tender side-panels.

1913 Coaches were of varnished teak, with lettering in gold, shaded with blue.

1913 Locomotives were painted an "invisible"* green, and lined in blue.

1914 Locomotives were an "invisible" green. Lining was in blue, vermilion and yellow. Safety-valve casings were polished brass. Coaches were varnished teak.

1915 Coaches were light teak, and locomotives black.

1921 Engines were painted an "invisible" green, and coaches varnished teak.

HULL AND BARNSLEY RAILWAY CREST

* Invisible green—i.e. a black, shining as a kind of green in certain lights, as an oil patch on a wet road.

LANCASHIRE AND YORKSHIRE RAILWAY

THE Lancashire and Yorkshire Railway was the title assumed in 1847 by the Manchester and Leeds Railway (opened in 1841), which in the previous year had absorbed the Manchester and Bolton Railway (opened in 1838), the Liverpool and Bury Railway (opened in 1845), and the West Riding Union Railway (opened in 1846).

In 1849 the Lancashire and Yorkshire acquired the Blackburn, Darwen and Bolton Railway (opened in 1846), the Huddersfield and Sheffield Railway, the Wakefield, Pontefract and York Railway, the Blackburn and Clitheroe Railway (opened in 1846); and, in 1897, the West Lancashire Railway (opened in 1878). The Liverpool, Crosby and Southport Railway was amalgamated with the L. & Y. in 1868.

In 1858 the Lancashire and Yorkshire absorbed the Sheffield, Rotherham and Goole Railway (opened in 1849), and, in 1859, the East Lancashire Railway, which had been formed by the previous amalgamation of the Blackburn and Preston Railway (opened in 1844), the Bolton and Preston Railway, and the Liverpool, Ormskirk and Preston Railway. The previous title of the East Lancashire Railway was the Manchester, Bury and Rossendale.

The Lancashire and Yorkshire Railway was, in 1922, amalgamated with the London and North Western Railway, with whom in earlier days it had worked the North Union Railway, the Preston and Wyre Railway, and the Preston and Longridge Railway.

The locomotive superintendents of the railway were as follows:—

1847–1868	William Jenkins (Manchester). Sylvester Lees (Bury).
1868–1876	W. Hurst (Manchester), Joint with William Yates, (c. 1870).
1876–1888	William Barton Wright.
1888–1900	John A. F. (later Sir John) Aspinall (Chief Mechanical Engineer).
1900–1904	H. A. Hoy.
1904–1922	George Hughes.

1847 Engines had cut-out brass numerals affixed to the front buffer-beam, and numbers painted in gold on the rear panel of the tender. Engines were painted dark green and lined out in black and white.

1869 Passenger engines were dark green, with black bands and white lines. Numbers were in large figures of brass on the front buffer-beam, and were also painted on the back panel of tenders.

1870 The engines built by Bury, Curtis and Kennedy, and other early Lancashire and Yorkshire engines had polished copper domes and chimney tops. The numbers appeared on the front buffer-beams in solid figures of brass, and were also painted on the backs of the tenders. The engines were painted a dark green, with black and white lining.

1870 Mr. Hurst's rebuilds of Hawkshaw 0–4–2 goods engines were painted dead black without any lining, with copper domes over raised fire-boxes, and unpierced splashers.

1873 The ten Crewe-built 2–4–0 engines were painted a medium green, which colour they retained for some ten years. They differed from the normal Crewe style only in having L. & Y. chimneys with deep copper bands at the top.

1875 Mr. Hurst removed the brass beadings from locomotive driving-wheel splashers.

Pre 1876 Large brass figures for numbers on front buffer-beams and painted numbers on the back of tender or bunkers. East Lancashire Railway engines were, however, all provided with number-plates, as used by Mr. Wright in later years. Before Mr. Wright's time, engines were painted a dark green with black bands and two white lines.

Coaches were generally of stained wood, but about 1876 there appeared a large number painted a "teak" shade of brown and varnished. Broadly, from 1880 to 1917 coaches were brown-violet.

1876 Number-plates on side panels were not adopted until about this time, all engines being so fitted by 1881.

1876 Goods engines were changed to a dead black, and all dark green engines had disappeared by 1878; when neat number-plates were added on the side panels.

1876 Mr. Wright painted all passenger engines a light green almost the same shade as the old Midland colour (47), and adopted the same green for all his "Ironclad" goods locomotives. All older goods engines and shunting engines, however, were allowed to remain black.

1876 There was apparent a great variety in engine number-plates. Engines built or rebuilt at Miles Platting Works had vermilion plates, some with an outer border of dark brown. Engines built by Sharp, Stewart were dark indigo. Those built by Kitsons were generally blue of an indigo shade, whilst those engines by the Vulcan Foundry had pale blue plates. Neilson-built engines had chocolate-coloured plates, and those from Beyer, Peacock the same green as the locomotive bodies.

1876 Number-plates were fitted to cab side-sheets, all engines being altered by the year 1881.

1876–88 Locomotives which were originally painted dark green were altered to black, lined out with red and white. Domes were usually painted over black, but splashers were brass-beaded.

Goods engines had the splasher beadings painted over.

1878–80 Locomotive No. 211 and some other shunting engines were painted brick-red experimentally, but the change to this livery was never carried out.

Pre 1880 Number-plates were not fixed to engines, but were painted on buffer-beams only. Some of Mr. Hurst's tender locomotives had their numbers also painted on the side of the tender tool-boxes.

Mr. Wright first introduced number-plates in the orthodox position, but it was late in his régime before all engines received them.

1883–1917 With few exceptions locomotives had been black for this period, the red banding and white lining was added at the same time as the Midland abandoned green for crimson-lake.

Pre 1888 Tender engines had in very small lettering on the tender in plain gold, "L & Y" without any full-stops. Tank locomotives had no lettering at all, but had the number-plate in the centre of the tanks.

For a short period a script monogram was carried on some tender engines, but this style was soon abandoned.

1888 Mr. Aspinal introduced the full name on tanks and tenders in gold block letters shaded with light blue. Three variations were used: (*a*) full "LANCASHIRE & YORKSHIRE" on tender engines and at first on tank types as well. (*b*) as (*a*) but arranged as a curve over the number-plate. This style was later abandoned in favour of (*c*) which consisted of straight lettering with the "&" being omitted, "LANCASHIRE" being placed to the left of the number-plate and "YORKSHIRE" to the right.

Number-plates were of cast brass with a raised edge and numbers. On the Horwich-built engines the number-plate background was black, but was red or light blue for locomotives built by outside firms. The raised edge of the plates had engraved on it "L.Y.R.Co., Makers" on the top section and "Horwich (date)" on the lower. (See Figs. 92, 93, 97 and 99, p. 280). Engines built at Miles Platting Works or by outside firms had the words "Makers" or "Horwich" omitted.

1896 Locomotives were black. The tenders and tanks of all the newest engines of the period being lined round with a thick vermilion line having a fine white line immediately inside it, and a second white line about 2 ins. inside the first. Frames and wheels were painted unlined black. Buffer-beams were red, with a black edge and white line between the red and the black. Cab interiors were painted a light umber brown, bordered with lake; the lower portion being vermilion. Number-plates were of polished brass on a black background (Figs. 97 and 98, p. 280), and the company's crest (see p. 26) appeared on the splashers or cab sides. Older locomotives were sometimes black, with two red lines only; the outer line being thicker than the inner. (See also Fig. 44, p. 114.)

Coaches were painted an umber brown in the upper panels and a dark lake in the lower,* with a black stripe and a fine white line round the windows and along the main side panels. Underframes were black, and the coach ends dark brown, with a lighter brown stripe around the outline. The door window-frames were red, and the coach numbers and lettering were in gold, with black, vermilion and white lines; but no shading. Goods stock was a dark grey with white lettering.

1899 Mr. Aspinall's 4-4-2 (No. 1400) was painted black, each boiler band being composed of parallel lines of red, white, black, white and red. Safety-valve cover was of polished brass, as was the whistle and there was a brass beading around the driving-wheel splashers. The company's crests appeared on both splashers

* It would appear from this description that the coach colours changed from umber-brown and dark lake to (40), described as medium brown and (41), described as cinnamon brown, at some time between 1896 and 1914. Though there is no definite record of this change.

on each side. The number-plate was of raised brass, the number being enclosed in a double-lined oval, around which the words "LANCASHIRE AND" appeared above, and "YORKSHIRE RAILWAY" below the number. "L & Y" was painted in golden yellow on the tender in block letters. The lining over the driving-wheel splashers, inside the brass beading was as follows: next the beading, a fine red line, then a white line, then a black line, followed by another white line; this group being followed by the black body colour.

1901 The 0–6–0 locomotive (No. 424) showed the commencement of the abolition of the small lettering on tenders. "LANCASHIRE & YORKSHIRE" in full being substituted, this being written in gold, shaded in blue.

1902 Engines of the "1400" class (Nos. 1,405–1,408) had "LANCASHIRE & YORKSHIRE" on the tanks, written in a curved line over the number-plates. (Fig. 92, p. 280.)

The locomotives with short tanks had "LANCASHIRE" above, and "YORKSHIRE" below the number-plates. (Fig. 92, p. 280.)

1902 Tank engines started to have the company's name in full ("LANCASHIRE & YORKSHIRE") in curved lines on the tank sides, with the number-plate in the centre of the tank below the name.

1903 Goods stock had " L & Y" on the sides in white letters, instead of the white solid-coloured triangle and circular badge previously used.

1905 Coach No. 1005, was built with sheet aluminium panelling and aluminium fittings. It was still in service in 1929.

1914 Coaches were brown in the upper panels and maroon* in the lower.

1914 Locomotives were black, lined with vermilion and white.

Passenger coaches were (41), described in sources as mid-brown in the upper panels and (40), described as dark purple-brown, in the lower ones. Panels were not lined out.

Wagons were grey.

1915 Coaches were (40), described as purple-brown, in the lower panels, and (41), described as cinnamon-brown, in the upper ones. Engines were black.

Crest on page 26

* See footnote on p. 89.

LONDON, BRIGHTON AND SOUTH COAST RAILWAY

SERVING practically the whole of the county of Sussex, Kent and parts of Surrey and Hampshire, the London, Brighton and South Coast Railway was formed in the year 1846 by the amalgamation of the London and Croydon Railway (opened 1835) and the London and Brighton Railway (opened 1837).

The London and Croydon Railway tried out, with some success, the atmospheric system of train propulsion in 1845, between London and West Croydon, at which station some of the original pipes have been found from time to time.

The first locomotive superintendent recorded is Mr. Statham, who was followed by John Gray (of the London and Croydon Railway), who held office between 1845 and early in 1847; from which date the successive holders of the post were as follows:—

May, 1845 Mr. Statham
May, 1845–January, 1847 John Gray
February 1, 1847–1847 S. Kirtley
1848–1869 J. Chester Craven
1869–1889 William Stroudley
1889–1904 Robert J. Billinton
1904–1911 D. Earle Marsh
1911–1922 Lawson B. Billinton

Up to 1849 Boilers of most locomotives had polished mahogany lagging, with brass banding.

Those locomotives built by Longridge (Nos. 96, 97 and 100–105), and by Wilson (Nos. 61–70); Longridge's being 0–6–0's and Wilson's 2–2–0's, had painted wooden lagging striped alternately red and green.

1850 (c) Locomotives were green with frames and splashers dull red. Brass safety-valve casings and copper tops to chimneys. Boilers were banded black with a fine white line on either side. Panels on cab side-sheets and tenders were lined with a black line with a white line outside black and a red line inside. A polished brass band passed round the front of the fire-box. Number-plates were oval with the number in raised brass figures on a vermilion ground, and an ornate design around the number in raised brass. The springs and smoke-box were black.

1850 The Sharp locomotive No. 74 (tender) was painted (6), described in sources as Brunswick green, edged with darker green. Frames were crimson, with a black edge and a vermilion line on the inside.

1852 The engine "Jenny Lind" had (6), dark green, as the main colour. Fenders, splashers and underframes were vermilion red, lined out in black and orange; the wide black being flanked with the latter colour. Hand-rails were brassed and polished, hand-rail stanchions were steel. The dome was green, as was the safety-valve casing; but the base of the dome was green lined out with black and vermilion.

The tender was green, lined out with wide black, flanked with narrow orange lines. The tender underframes were vermilion red.

All wheels were green, and all piping polished copper, including the sand-pipes. The body of the axle-driven pump was green. Axle-box flaps were bright brass, and there was a wide brass band between the boiler and the fire-box. Boiler-bands were wide black, flanked with narrow orange lines. Axle-boxes were lined orange-black-orange, with incurved corners. There was a brass beading along the top edge of the fenders. The name "JENNY LIND" appeared in raised brass serif letters against a black background in a rectangular brass-edged frame.

1858 Mahogany lagging was discontinued.

1860 *No.* 56 (2–4–0) had a copper top chimney, brass domes, red frames, splashers and sand-boxes. (6), described as green, boiler and fenders. Green bands around front and rear of fire-box, and the engine number in an oval on the fenders, the figures being yellow on a red background, and the oval being surrounded by a wreath.

No. 57 (2–4–0). Front dome was brass cased with a red base, whilst the rear dome was all polished brass. The chimney was copper-topped. The framing and splashers were red. The boiler and fenders were (6) described as green, with the engine number on the boiler in brass figures.

No. 59 (2–4–0) had a brass dome and safety-valve pillar, together with a copper-topped chimney. Frames were red, as were splashers and sand-boxes; and the boiler and fenders were green.

The engine number appeared on a red background in an oval surrounded by a wreath on the fenders.

No. 67 "Jenny Lind" had fluted domes and safety-valves, the tops of which were bright copper, the fluted portions (6), green, and the bases red. Splashers were red, edged with brass, and the sand-boxes and frames were red. There were copper bands around both front and rear of the fire-box, the boiler was mahogany and the fender green. The engine number appeared in an oval, red-background wreath on the fender sides. Boiler-bands were brass. (See also entry under 1852.)

No. 87 (Stothert and Slaughter, 2–2–2) had a black stove-pipe chimney, and a brass dome and safety-valve casing. Brass splashers. Red frames and sand-boxes. Green boiler and tender-body. The tender-frames were red, and the engine number was on a small rectangular panel mounted on the boiler.

No. 90 (2–4–0) had a copper top to chimney, and bright brass lower corners to dome, also to safety-valve casing. Red splashers with brass edging. Boiler, forward dome and fenders were green. Frames red. Engine number in brass figures on the boiler.

No. 97 (2–4–0) had a fluted dome with a brass top, green fluting, and red base. The chimney-cap was polished copper, and the fire-box dome was polished brass. Frames were red, as were the sandboxes. Splashers were brass-edged and were painted red. There were polished brass beads around both front and rear of the fire-box. The boiler and fenders were green; and the engine number appeared as in No. 59.

No. 99 (0–4–0) had a brass dome and fire-box sheathing. Chimney top was polished copper, and the boiler-bands were of polished brass. The safety-valve casing was of brass, as were the splashers. The boiler was green, and the bar-type frame, black. Sand-boxes were red, and the number-plate appeared on the boiler, and was oval in shape.

No. 109 (2–4–0) had a copper top to chimney, and brass domes. Brass-banding round front and rear of fire-box. Red splashers, frames and sand-boxes (6), described in sources as green, boiler and fenders, the engine number being placed in an oval panel in yellow figures surrounded with a wreath, on the fenders. Background of figures was red.

No. 112 (0–6–0). The forward dome was fluted, with a bright copper top, green fluting and red base. The chimney was copper-topped. Frames, sand-boxes and splashers were red, and the fire-box dome was bright brass all over. The boiler and fenders were green, and the engine number appeared in a red background oval on the fender-sides, surrounded by a wreath.

1860 Locomotives of older types had number-plates on boilers in large brass figures, which were fastened direct to the lagging, whilst later types had their numbers in yellow painted figures on a red ground, surrounded by a wreath; the whole ensemble being situated on the "fenders" (lower panel of the "cab-side"). Other engines had their numbers painted on the boiler in yellow figures on an oval red background. the oval being bordered by a dark green line. The individual liveries of several engines of the period were as follows :—

No. 7 (2–2–2) had a copper cap and bright brass dome base corners; also bright brass safety-valve covers. Splashers were red, edged with bright brass. Boiler was green, as was the forward dome and fenders. Frames and sand-boxes were red. Buffer-beams were vermilion, with "B7" thereon in large yellow figures and letters.

No. 40 (2–4–0) had a copper top to chimney. Brass dome and safety-valve column. Brass bands around fire-box. Red splashers, edged with brass. Red frames and sand-boxes. Green boiler and fenders, the engine number being in brass figures on the boiler.

No. 44 (0–6–0). Copper top to chimney. Both domes had bright copper tops, green fluted bodies and red bases. Copper bands were around front and rear of fire-box. Splashers, frames and sand-boxes were red. Boiler and fenders were green. The locomotive number appeared in brass figures on the boiler.

No. 46 (0–6–0) had a copper top to chimney. Dome and safety-valve pillars were bright copper tops and green flutings and red bases. Fire-box banding was copper. Splashers, frames and sand-boxes were red.

No. 49 (0–6–0) had a copper top to chimney. Copper top, green body and red base to dome and safety-valve pillar. Copper bands round front and rear of fire-box. Red splashers with bright brass edging. Green boiler, fenders and sand-box. Locomotive number being in yellow figures on an oval red background, surrounded by a wreath.

No. 51 (0–6–0) had a copper-topped chimney, a brass dome with a red base, and brass safety-valve column with a red base. Frames, splashers and sand-boxes were red. Brass bands around front and rear of fire-box, and "51" in large brass figures on the boiler.

No. 52 (2–4–0) had a copper-topped chimney, and a brass dome with a red base. Safety-valve pillar was brass with green base. There were brass bands round front and rear of fire-box. Frames were red and splashers green. Sand-boxes were green, as were the boiler and fenders. The number was on the boiler in brass figures.

No. 53 (2–4–0) had a copper-topped chimney, and both domes were bright brass. There were brass bands around front and rear of fire-box. Frames were red, as was the smoke-box. Splashers were red, with bright brass beading. The boiler and fenders were green, and the engine number was painted on the boiler.

Nos. 55 *and* 60 (2–4–0). Chimneys, copper-capped. Domes, brass with red bases. Safety-valve pillars, brass with red bases. Frames and smoke-boxes, red. Splashers, red, edged with a black line. Painted yellow bands round front and rear of fire-box. Boilers and fenders, green.

No. 96 (Jones and Potts, 0–6–0). Boiler, dome and fenders, green. Running-plate, red. Splashers and sand-boxes, red. Buffer-beam (front), red, with a large yellow "B" to the left of the coupling and "96" to the right. Chimney cap was bright copper. Dome (front) was bright brass. Fire-box dome was edged with bright copper, whilst safety-valve casings were brass.

1860 Bury locomotive No. 99 now (6), described in sources as standard "Brighton" green, with vermilion buffer-beams, polished brass dome, splashers and running-boards. This locomotive, an 0–4–0, was painted blue when delivered, her buffer-beams being "overlain"* with polished brass.

No. 71. This engine had a copper-topped chimney, and a brass dome and safety-valve column. There were two brass bands round the fire-box, and the boiler and fender were green. Splashers were red, edged with brass. Frames were red, as were the sand-boxes. Engine numbers were in an oval red wreath in yellow figures on the tender-sides.

* Probably "edged".

1860 Engine No. 16 had a copper-topped chimney, and the dome and safety-valve had copper tops with the flutings bright green. The bases of dome and safety-valve were vermilion. Fire-box bands were polished copper. Splashers and frames were vermilion. Boiler was green, as were the fender and sand-boxes.

Locomotives Nos. 166 and 167 had copper-topped chimneys and copper bases to the chimneys. The middle part was painted stove black.

Engines Nos. 178 and 179 had standard double-banded brass splashers, with vermilion between the brass bands.

Pre 1870 Engines were (6), described as green (passenger), and dark green (goods).

Pre 1870 Locomotives were (6), described in sources as bright green.

Pre 1870 Those locomotives which were painted were (6), described in sources as Brunswick green, lined with a broad black band having a fine white line on each side of it. The frames were crimson-lake. Domes were fluted, and the safety-valve casings were of polished brass. Chimney-caps were polished copper. The whole ensemble was of very smart appearance. No locomotives were named except a few of the first, and two 6-coupled purchased from the Manchester, Sheffield and Lincoln Railway, "Orestes" and "Europa", which were painted chocolate-brown, with brass name-plates and brass number-plates on the front of their boilers.

1870 Stroudley's new colour-scheme appeared.

The first locomotive to be painted (33), described in sources as "yellow", was No. 173, which was never named. She originally had spokes lined with white. but the practice was discontinued on account of cost. Locomotive No. 174 originally had brass beading round splashers, which was first painted over then cleaned off and polished; this finish being retained till she was broken up. (No. 174 was a 2–4–0.)

No. 174 had double brass beading round her splashers, and originally did not have a copper top to the chimney. (This also was the case with Nos. 175, 176 and 177, all of which were 2–4–0's). No. 174 had her splasher beadings altered as above by Stroudley, and had her number on rear splasher.

1870 Stroudley changed the engine colours to an ochre yellow he called "Stroudley's Improved Engine Green". Panelling was edged with (12), described as dark olive-green, and lined out with a black band having a red and white line on either side. The angle framing was a deep brown edged with black, red and yellow lines. The buffer-beams were elaborately painted and lined out.

Goods locomotives were green (dark) lined out with black bands only, but engines fitted with air brakes had a fine red line on either side of the black.

Several "E" class goods tank locomotives were engaged on passenger work, and their colour was changed to ochre, but they soon reverted to dark green. Stroudley's livery remained during J. Billinton's office, and the elaborate painting up to 1905 (*c*).

1871 Stroudley "C" class goods engines were (4), described in sources as dark olive-green, with broad black lines. The spoke shapes were continued across the counter-balance weights on the wheels by black painted lines. Guard irons, buffer-beams, buffers and sand-pipes were vermilion; the buffer-beams being bordered with a black line with a white line on each side of it.

1872–1906 Stroudley's colour-scheme for passenger locomotives was, according to the highest authorities, as follows :—

The main body colour was (33),* a deep, rich, slightly greenish-yellow; the bordering and panelling being olive-green of a dark shade, edged with a black band. On the green side of the black band was a fine red line, whilst on the yellow side was a white line.

The boiler bands were black with a red line on each edge, whilst next to the red line and on either side of each band was (4), an olive-green stripe, with a white line next to the body-colour—yellow.

The wheels were yellow, with black tyres and olive-green axle-ends, whilst the frames, sole-bars and foot-steps were painted slightly darker than (28), claret colour, edged all round with a black band, on the outer side of which was a fine yellow line, and on the inner side a fine red line.

Locomotive names were in gold transfers of plain sans-serif

* The London, Brighton and South Coast Railway locomotive colour adopted by Mr. Stroudley, known as "Scotch Green" or "Stroudley's Improved Engine Green" (32) is accurately matched to "Gladstone" in York Railway Museum. The colours of both "Boxhill" (at Farnham) and the Brighton "Works Terrier" are greener and "cooler" in hue (33), this shade being also selected by living authorities, who well remember the Stroudley livery.

letters shaded to left in bluish-green, picked out in white, and to the right in black.

Buffer-beams were claret-coloured, with a bright red panel in the centre, the panel being bordered with a black stripe lined with yellow and red. Coupling-rods were claret-coloured with their ends left bright steel.

The number-plates were of polished brass with the title of the company round the border, and the slightly-raised brass figures were on a bright blue background.

The chimneys had a brightly-polished copper cap and the cab windows were brass-beaded.

1871–1905 Locomotives were painted Stroudley "yellow" (33).

The last engine to run in "Stroudley ochre" (33) was No. 591, "Tillington", which was still doing duty as station pilot at East Croydon in 1916. She was repainted in Marsh livery in February, 1917.

1873 0–6–0 "C" class goods locomotives when fitted with air brakes were lined out with a fine red line on either side of the broad black band which ran round cab side-sheets, splashers, boilers and tanks (if any).

1874 Originally all goods locomotives fitted with air brakes were painted the standard passenger colours.

1880 Stroudley locomotive head-lamps were black, lined out with two rectangles of red lines for goods locomotives and with two rectangles of yellow lines for passenger engines. The engine number was painted in red* on the left-hand side, the numerals being of the same design as those appearing on the number-plates.

1889 Locomotive "Edward Blount", No. 189, had cab interior painted yellow (light stone) with a white inner roof. Fire-box stays were black, and the panel over the fire-door tray was olive-green. Outer cab roof white.

Fire-box lagging-plate in cab olive-green (this within the large curved edge-plate, which was yellow). Above the whistle handle the driver's name and mileage record in gold capitals and italics. Reversing wheel spokes were olive-green with a polished steel rim.

1889 The standard Stroudley buffers had two sets of bands painted round the claret-coloured sockets, each band being composed of red, yellow and red lines, with black between them. Each group of bands was two inches wide.

* Yellow according to some authorities.

1889 Stroudley livery (according to another authority): Body-colour (33), described in sources as golden yellow. (Oxford ochre, chrome yellow and white and oxide). Edging of splashers, panels, etc., was (4), described in sources as olive-green, this being separated by a 1½ in. wide black band, having on its inner side (yellow side) a thin white line, and on its outer (olive-green) side a fine red line. Boiler bands were 2 in. wide, and were black, with a fine red line on either side. On either side, again, was a 2 in. wide olive-green band, which was painted on the cleading, and separated from the yellow lines (on either side) by a fine white line. Corner lining was inverted; (see Fig. 5, p. 6.)

Number-plates were polished brass with a dark blue background to the figures and black inset waxed lettering round the border (Fig. 69, p. 209).

The angle-framing was (28), described in sources as a rich claret colour, edged on the outer side by a narrow black band, the latter having a fine yellow line on its outer edge and a thin red one next to the claret colour.

Buffer-beams (Fig. 76, p. 258), were claret, with a vermilion panel in the centre, the panel being edged with a broad black band, bearing a yellow central line flanked by a white line next to the vermilion and by a red one next to the claret. Coupling-rods were also claret-coloured, with long polished ends and eyes. Sand-pipes, guard-irons, motion-plate, insides of main-frames, cranks and eccentric rods were vermilion. Wheel-spokes and hubs were golden yellow, with the ends of the axles and tyres olive-green. All brake gear was black. The engine name was in gold block letters shaded to the left-hand with light green with fine strokes of claret and white superimposed on the light green. The letters were shadowed to the right in black (Fig. 75, p. 258).

Pre 1896 Coaches were nearly all painted a bright red-brown, (44) with yellow lines round all panels, the lettering being gold, with vermilion shading. The paint was very highly varnished. There were still a few coaches running, finished in varnished teak with gold lining.

The complete ends of all passenger brake vans were painted bright scarlet (vermilion).

Goods wagons were painted a light grey slightly lighter than (42), with white lettering, the ironwork being black. Cast-iron number-plates with raised white letters on black ground.

1896 (Oct.) Locomotives had dome casings painted "yellow", (33) safety-valve levers red, spring-balances of polished brass. The Westinghouse pump on the right-hand side was painted yellow, with banding similar to the locomotive boilers. The vacuum exhaust pipe on the right-hand side was painted yellow, as were the springs. Buffer sockets were lake-colour to match the framing.

1897 Coaches: Some coaches were painted experimentally, being finished with their upper panels white, tinged with green, and their lower panels and underframes a medium green. Striping was gold with a fine vermilion line on the side next to the green. Coach numbers, so long placed within a garter on the door were now placed on the long centre waist panels.

1897 New Stroudley 1st class coaches (6-wheel) were repainted experimentally at the end of the year with upper panels white, tinged with green, and lower portion and underframes a medium green. Lining was in gold with a fine vermilion line on the side next to the green.

1898 A new style of numbering was introduced, in which the numbers were put on the long centre panel of the coaches instead of within the garter on each door.

1899 First class coach No. 539 was experimentally painted dark green on its main panels and light green on its upper panels.

1899 Locomotives Nos. 487 ("Fishergate"), and 488 ("Oakwood") differed from previous ones in being painted standard passenger engine colours. Nos. 489 ("Bohemia") and 490 ("Boxgrove") were similarly distinguished. They appeared from the shops in their new livery No. 487 (May, 1899), No. 488 (May, 1899), Nos. 489 and 490 (June, 1899).

1900 Standard goods locomotive colour was olive-green, (4), picked out with black.

1900 (c) Vulcan goods engines were (4), described in sources as dark olive-green, lined with a fine line flanked by a fine red line on each side. Number-plates were brass with raised figures on a blue background. Lettering, and double-lined border were black (sunk). Guard-irons, buffer-beams and buffers were vermilion. Buffer-beams and sockets were lined with a black line. Cab interiors were olive-green, as also were the coupling-rods, but a three-inch length at each end of the latter was left polished steel. The hinged cab spectacle-plate windows had polished brass frames. Maker's plates were fitted on the splashers of Nos. 433–4, and on the back panel of the tenders of all the others in the "Vulcan" class; viz. Nos. 435–452 and 521–550.

Cranks and eccentric straps vermilion.

1901 Express passenger coach No. 23 (first class) was painted dark green in its lower panels, and white, lined with emerald green in its upper ones. Lining was yellow with a vermilion line separating the yellow from the dark green body colour. Coach No. 115 (first class) had upper panels of the "locomotive ochre", lined out with fine white, and lower panels of dark olive-green.

1902 A whole train of suburban coaches was painted olive-green in its lower panels, and Stroudley locomotive yellow in its upper panels; experimentally.

1903 One of the bogie suburban train sets was repainted with its upper panels the same colour (ochre) as the contemporary passenger engines, the lining being in fine white and yellow. The lower panels were dark olive-green.

1905 (c) The actual measurements of the lining on "Gladstone" now preserved in York Railway Museum* are as follows :—

Lining of cab panel (reading from foot-plate surface upwards): Olive-green (4), $3\frac{3}{4}$ ins. Vermilion (now a dark salmon-colour), $\frac{5}{32}$ in. Black, $1\frac{1}{2}$ in. White, $\frac{1}{8}$ in. These linings and borderings making, in all a "border" $5\frac{9}{16}$ in. in width. (Fig. 76, p. 258.)

Lining of underframes (reading from under surface of foot-plate downwards:) Maroon (31), 3 ins. Vermilion (now dark salmon-colour), $\frac{1}{8}$ in. Black, $\frac{7}{8}$ in. Yellow, $\frac{5}{32}$ in., this last line being located $\frac{1}{16}$ in. from the edge of the metal. These linings and borderings making in all a "border" $4\frac{3}{16}$ in. in width.

The boiler-banding consists of a black (raised) band $1\frac{1}{2}$ in. in width with a $\frac{3}{16}$ in. wide vermilion (now dark salmon-colour) line immediately next to it. A $\frac{1}{8}$ in. white line appears on each side of this assembly at a distance of $2\frac{1}{8}$ ins. This makes the overall width of the boiler bands (across the outer white lines) $6\frac{3}{8}$ ins.

The buffer-beam panelling (reading from outside to inside), consists of a vermilion (now salmon) line $\frac{3}{32}$ in. wide next to the outside maroon panel (31), this being followed by a $\frac{5}{8}$ in. wide black line, which is again immediately edged by a $\frac{3}{16}$ in. middle chrome yellow line; then another $\frac{5}{8}$ in. black, and another line of

* See note on page 97.

white $\frac{1}{8}$ in. wide. This line is immediately followed by the vermilion buffer panel. The overall width of the lining is, in all, $1\frac{11}{16}$ in. (Fig. 76, p. 258.)

Number-plates are 18 in. × 11 in. (Fig. 69, p. 209.)

Inside of cab roof, white, and the rest stone colour. The engine shed appears in abbreviated form in white block letters at the forward end of the foot-plate valance, thus: B'TON.

Brake pump cylinders are lined in vermilion and white only, with the vermilion line at the cylinder ends.

The details of the engine name letters are as follows :—

Block letters of gold, shaded with bright emerald green to left and below, and in black to right and below. The green shading being flecked with white high-lights, and the under-shading of horizontal portions of the letters being darkened with a touch of mauve or maroon. (See Fig. 75, p. 258.)

1905 (c) Goods locomotives were painted a dark olive-green, (4), there being two styles of lining in use: the older engines were lined in black, whilst the more recent "piped" goods locomotives had a fine vermilion line on each side of the broad black line already noted. Buffer-beams were red, lined round with black, and the frames and wheels were dark olive-green. Safety-valve levers were painted red, and their spring-balances, polished brass.

1905 (Nov.) Locomotive No. 486, formerly "Godalming" left the shops black, with red and white lining with "LBSCR" on her tanks.

1905 (Nov.) There was some talk of passenger locomotives being painted olive-green, and the goods and shunting engines black; but Mr. Marsh's livery was not known until December, 1905.

1905 The cost of locomotive painting was reduced, and Marsh's first scheme was (4), described in sources as a dark green colour, lined out with red and white lines; and three tender and one tank engine were thus finished. This livery was followed by a "D" tank engine being painted in (35), described as umber brown, and lined out in black bands with an orange line on one side and yellow on the other.

The engine No. 60 (a "B–4") used on the Director's inspection coach was painted umber brown, edged with a darker shade of brown, lining being a black band with a fine gold line on either side.

Tenders and tanks carried initials "LB & SCR" in gold, but

later "LBSC" was used, and yellow lining and lettering replaced the gold.

Goods engines were black, lined out in red.

All locomotives had vermilion buffer-beams, unlined, and had their numbers painted thereon in gold—which was later also changed to yellow.

Splashers of express engines carried the company's crest or initials in monogram form.

The Marsh livery lasted until grouping in 1923.

1905 (c) Locomotives were painted (33), described in sources as ochre-yellow or mustard colour (called by some a "rich, slightly greenish-yellow"), with a border round the tanks, cabs and tenders of (4), described as a dark olive-green, whilst separating these two colours and forming the panels, was a black band, with a red line on its outer side and a white one on its inner. The locomotive frames were (31), described as crimson, with black edging, and yellow and vermilion lines; the buffer-beams having a vermilion panel with a crimson border, the latter being edged with yellow lines. The wheels were of body-colour with dark olive-green tyres and red lining; whilst the underframing was painted vermilion.

The insides of the cabs were painted medium stone colour, with the name of the driver appearing between the spectacles in 1 in. block capitals. The fire-box front was lagged, the lagging-plates being painted olive-green. Number-plates were of bright brass, having the figures and lettering raised against a bright blue ground. Locomotive names were in gold with emerald green shading. Coupling-rods were painted chocolate colour. (See Figs. 69, 75 and 76, p. 279.)

1905 (c) Engine No. 453 ("E3" class, 0–6–2T), "Broadbridge", was specially painted on one side only and named thereon "Charles C. Macrae". The engine never ran in this odd livery, which was purely for photographic purposes.

1905 (Dec.) The new style for locomotives was finally settled: Express locomotives (35), described in sources as umber, lined out with two gold lines. Black number-plates and red buffer-beams, with the lettering on the latter in gold, shaded black. Passenger tank locomotives, the same as the express types, but lined out in orange. Goods engines, black—lined out with two red lines. Red number-plates, and lettering on buffer-beams in yellow, shaded red. Cab interiors (all types of locomotives) light stone.

1906 Locomotive No. 486, formerly bearing the name "Godalming", appeared without the name, and painted black, with red and white lining; LB & SCR appearing on the tank sides.

1906 Three Pullmans appeared—"Princess Patricia", "Princess Ena", and the "Duchess of Norfolk"—with their exteriors in the then new style adopted by the Company. This was umber lower panels with ivory white above with gold lining.

1906 About April of this year a number of locomotives were already repainted the new standard colour of dark madder-brown, (35), whilst at the same time, in a number of cases the names were removed.

For some of the express locomotives the dark olive-green of the goods engines seems to have been preferred. The letters "LB & SCR" were inscribed in place of the names on tank locomotives, and the crest of the company on tender-engines.

1906 (Mar.) Locomotives were being repainted a dark madder-brown (35), and a number of their names were being removed, though these had been a feature of L.B.S.C. locomotives.

Some express locomotives were the dark olive green (4) of the goods engines, the letters LB & SCR being inscribed in place of the name on tank locomotives and the company's crest replacing the names of express engines.

1906 (Dec.) The naming of engines was first abandoned and then partially resumed this year, and it seemed probable that names would be affixed to 25 engines.

1907 When locomotive No. 173 ("Cottesloe") was repainted in the Marsh livery, she retained her name.

1907 Locomotives: The driver's name was inscribed in sans-serif letters inside the cab. The word "Driver" appeared under his name in upper and lower case serif letters.

1907 The Marsh umber (35) and cream coach livery was lined out with a $\frac{3}{8}$ in. wide straw-coloured, not a varnished, line. The same width and colour of line persisted with the all-umber coaching stock.

1907 Marsh livery for locomotives: Body colour a (35), described in sources as deep umber tint, lining in plain gold for express passenger locomotive, and yellow for those doing less important duties. In lieu of names, upon each coupled wheel splasher is the company's monogram in plain block letters. As regards some of the "Gladstones", the date-plate, which was previously fixed to the leading driving-wheel splasher, was placed centrally between the two wheels on the coupling-rod cover. Another innovation of the time was that the number of the locomotive appeared in large figures on both buffer-beams.

Locomotive No. 177 was the first of the "Gladstones" to be finished in the new colours, but in this particular case the monograms were not gilded upon the wheel splashers; this practice being introduced to add to the dignity of No. 215. The date plate appeared centrally on the coupling-rod casing.

There were three exceptions to this standard livery which were all "Gladstone" class engines. No. 173 "Cottesloe", No. 184, ex-"Carew D. Gilbert", (later renamed "Stroudley"), and No. 214, which retained the name "Gladstone".

1909 Locomotive No. 643 (formerly No. 43 "Gipsy Hill") carried an oval number-plate with the numerals in raised brass block, and without outside lettering.

1909 (Dec.) The "push-pull" motor train designed by D. Earle Marsh, for working on the Epsom Downs branch, contained an 0–4–2T which was lettered "L & B" on the tank sides in 18 in. serif letters, and "627" in small sans-serif figures on the bunker-sides.

Locomotive No. 192 (0–4–2 tender) had the company's crest on the rear driving-wheel splashers and the building plate on the front ones.

1911 The colour-scheme for passenger vehicles was again changed and there were then three distinct schemes in vogue :— (*a*) (35), described in sources as plain umber, relieved with orange lines, (*b*) an improved shade of umber of almost a plum-colour, lined out with gold, and (*c*) umber (35) and white, with gold lining on a black stripe. The two latter types looked extremely well.

The coaches built in Birmingham for the company were finished in the third style noted.

1911 Goods locomotives were painted black, lined out crimson, which livery superseded the more attractive and serviceable dark olive-green of 1906.

1911 All rebuilds now had their oval brass number-plates removed as they passed through the shops, large painted numbers on the cab side-sheets being substituted.

1914 Coaches were painted (35), described in sources as a darker brown, which was a change from the older dingy red. Experiments were also made with white upper and brown-umber lower panels; also with white upper and greenish lower panels.

1914 Coaches were altered from mahogany colour to umber (lower panels) and umber-tinted upper panels, but umber colour all over was finally selected; and by the middle of 1915, all coaches were (35), described as umber.

1914 Locomotive No. 327 had the engine number in gold on the front buffer-beam, shaded black below and to the right on vermilion ground. Lining was in yellow, and letters and figures in gilt, black-shaded.

1920 (*a*) Coaches fitted with chain inter-communication which operated the electric bells in the guard's compartment and driver's cab only were distinguished by the contact-boxes at the ends of the vehicles being painted vermilion red.

(*b*) Vehicles fitted with chain communication which applied the continuous brake in addition to ringing the bells had the contact-boxes painted black. Coach-end indicator discs were red.

(*c*) On "push-pull" rail-motors the pipes at the ends of motor-fitted vehicles, trailer cars and the engine were painted in different colours as follows: Main pipe, operating Westinghouse brake-blocks, black; regulator control pipe, light blue; storage pipe, dark green; and back-pressure pipe, yellow.

(*d*) On overhead electric trains the bow-operating pipe was light blue, and the reservoir pipe dark green.

(*e*) On slip vans the pipes used in connection with the air-lock apparatus were painted white.

(*f*) On all vehicles fitted with either vacuum or Westinghouse continuous brakes, all pipes operating brake-blocks were painted black, and all those not operating brake-blocks were vermilion red.

1922 0–6–0 engine No. 540 after rebuilding was repainted in umber with yellow lining; not black. 0–6–0T engine No. 106 was also painted the same style. Many locomotives were thus treated to use up umber paint.

The locomotive "Remembrance" (No. 333), carried a bronze plaque worded: "In grateful remembrance of the 532 men of the

L.B. & S.C.Rly. who gave their lives for their Country. 1914–1919".

Prior to grouping the engine was painted for photographic purposes a special dove-grey, relieved with the old standard black bands, but lined in white. The number on the bunker, and the name on the tank-sides was in white numerals and letters, back shaded in black. The engine never appeared in the umber livery.

LONDON, BRIGHTON AND SOUTH COAST RAILWAY CREST

LONDON, CHATHAM AND DOVER RAILWAY

INCORPORATED as the East Kent Railway in 1853, and taking the name London, Chatham and Dover Railway in 1859, this railway absorbed the Kent Coast Railway (opened in 1863) in 1871. After many years of financial difficulties a working union was agreed upon in 1899, with its rival, the South Eastern Railway to form the South Eastern and Chatham Railway; as such it finally passed into the Southern Railway in 1923.

The first locomotive engineer of the line was Sir William Cubitt, who held office from 1853 until 1860, being followed successively by William Martley (1860–1874), and William Kirtley (1874–1898); when amalgamation with the South Eastern Railway took place (see p. 193).

1860 The Robert Stephenson and Co's. engines "Aeolus", 71, "Bacchus", 72, "Vulcan", 73, and "Comus", 74, were originally built for export and appeared painted yellow. They were afterwards altered to (15), green, the standard colour.

1860–65 Locomotives "Rose", "Shamrock", "Thistle", "Myrtle", "Narcissus" and "Daphne" were painted a dark green (15) and lined out in red and white. The outside frames and coupling-rods were dark red (crimson ?).

1862 Locomotive "Leopard" (2–4–0), bodywork was (15), described in sources as a dark malachite green. Boiler bands were wide black, flanked with first fine white then vermilion lines. Ring between fire-box and boiler was polished brass. Fire-box, safety-valve and dome, as well as safety-valve spring cases were polished brass. Spectacle-plate edging and glasses were brass, as was the back end of the fire-box. Fenders were green, panelled first with a vermilion line, then a black one, and a white line innermost; all with incurved corners. Piping was polished copper. Frames were (38), described as chocolate, lined red. Spring buckles were green, lined out with a white line. The upper half of outside bearings were vermilion, and coupling-rods bright steel. Wheels were green with grey tyres. Buffer-beams were (38), described in sources as chocolate, lined with red. The ends of buffer-beams were lined out with white and red. Front axle-boxes were chocolate lined out with a red panel.

Tender body was green with black lining over all rivet lines, with a square-cornered white line within. Tender inner panels were lined first with red then black, with a white line inside all. Corners of inner panels were incurved. The tender underframes were the same colour as those of the locomotive, as were the axle-boxes. Brake gear and track guards were black, and the tender tool-boxes green.

1862 Locomotive "Herald" (No. 1379, by Sharp, Stewart) had white-lined panels, blocked with black, the lining having incurved corners. There were double brass beadings round the front driving-wheel splashers, the outer bead being wide and the inner narrow. There was also a wide brass band between the fire-box and the boiler. The dome and safety-valve casing were bright brass. There was no lining below the foot-plate level, either on the engine or the tender. No number-plates were fitted on the cab sides, and the framing was painted a chocolate shade.

1862 The engine "Jackall" was decorated exactly as "Herald" and "Leopard", but had the number-plate on cab side-sheets, and a brass banding round the rear end of the fire-box. These additions were also apparent on "Constantine" (see p. 110).

1862 Locomotive "Templar" (No. 47–456, a 2–4–0 by Brassey) was similar to "Jackall", but had a polished brass band between the smoke-box and the boiler as well as between the boiler and fire-box; the rear corners of the latter being also brass-bound. The building date-plate was mounted between the driving-wheel axle-boxes.

1862 The engine "Flirt" (No. 29. Originally a 2–4–0) when rebuilt as a 4–4–0 was lined as "Herald", "Jackall" and "Templar", but also carried large oval brass number-plates with "LONDON, CHATHAM" above, and "DOVER RAILWAY CO." below the small block figures "29" in the centre. Figures and letters were raised brass.

1866 Locomotive "Jura" (0–4–2T by Nelson) had a polished metal chimney-cap fitted, and the dome and safety-valve casing were of polished brass. There were polished brass bands between both the smoke-box and boiler and the boiler and fire-box. The name-plate was rectangular in shape with a raised border and lettering, the background colour being green.

The top and bottom leaves of all springs were lined white, and splashers were bordered with brass beading. The outside frames were lined with white lines only, these being done round all apertures. The ends of the buffer-beams were panelled out with incurved corners (Fig. 4, p. 6). The date-plate was oval, with raised brass letters on a background colour similar to that of the engine body.

1866 Locomotive "Constantine" (0–6–0, by John Fowler & Co.) had a copper-topped chimney and polished brass dome and safety-valve casings. The name-plate was rectangular and was centrally placed on the boiler under the dome. The lettering was raised brass serif capitals. The maker's plate was oval, the lettering appearing thus: "ENGINEERS" in Gothic characters across the centre, with "JOHN FOWLER & CO." curved above, and "LEEDS, 1866", curved below. The plate was mounted on the foot-plate valance immediately under the dome.

There was also a Company's plate of rectangular shape mounted on the fender-sides with "LONDON, CHATHAM AND DOVER RAILWAY" in very condensed capital letters, and "SEPTEMBER, 1866" in another line below. The plate had a raised brass border with incurved corners.

The engine had wide brass bands between the smoke-box and the boiler, and between the latter and the fire-box. Boiler bands were single black lines, devoid of any flanking lining.

1873 The Martley engines "Albion", "Thanet", "Erin", "Cambria", "Mona" and "Scotia", had copper-topped chimneys and bright brass casings to the pair of spring-balance safety-valves which were placed over the fire-box.

1873 Locomotives Nos. 53–56 ("Asia", "Africa", etc.) were green, (15), with chocolate-coloured framing. Their name-plates were mounted on the boiler immediately to the rear of the smoke-box.

1873 The following engines of the "N" class, (designed by Mr. Martley)—"Alert", No. 1348, "Dawn", No. 1347, "Frolic", No. 1380, "Herald", No. 1379, "Pioneer", No. 1381, and "Vigilant", No. 1342; all by Sharp, Stewart and Co.—had their numbers written in gilt on the buffer-beams as well as on oval plates on the cab fenders; those in the latter position being added by Mr. Kirtley; who also removed the name-plates, and replaced Mr. Martley's copper chimney-caps with cast-iron ones.

1874 When William Kirtley took office, the six engines (Nos. 59–64, later Kirtley class "F") were given numbers in addition to their names ("Sondes", "Sittingbourne", "Crampton". "Lake", "Faversham", and "Chatham"), these being painted in gold on the front and rear buffer-beams. When these engines were rebuilt, the names were removed, and the numbers were placed additionally on the centre of brass plates located on the cab or tank sides; the name of the company also appearing thereon around the numerals.

1875 Engine No. 106 (0–4–4T by Neilson) had oval number-plates with raised polished brass letters and figures set on the tank sides, being accommodated between the two panels. The latter were formed within a fine white line border with squared corners (Fig. 2, p. 6). This outer line only was carried round the upper parts of the cab. Full lining was given to the bunker-sides and back, as well as to the lower sheeting of the cab. Valances and steps had the single white line, as also had the leading splashers.

A brass band was fitted between the boiler and the smoke-box, as well as brass rims to the spectacles. Dome and safety-valve casings were bright brass. Wheels, tyres and axle-ends were painted body colour and lined single white line, which, in the case of driving-wheel hubs, extended round the crank. There were single white lines round the ends of the buffer-sockets.

1875 (Aug.) Locomotives were only numbered after 1875, and Martley engines retained their names, but had additional numbers painted on their tender backs and locomotive buffer-beams.

1875 Mr. Kirtley painted all the locomotives designed by himself, black, but green was maintained for Martley locomotives until they were rebuilt some years later; and it was not until about 1885 that green engines finally disappeared.

1875 Engines were painted an art black, excepting the "Namer" tender engines (Nos. 95 and 100) which were olive-green, (12).

1877 Locomotive No. 158 (4–4–0, by Neilson and Co.) had broad black lining with a very fine white line on either side, all corners being incurved (Fig. 4, p. 6). The script "L.C.D.R." monogram appeared in the centre of the single tender-panel. The number-plate was similar to that of No. 208 (1880), and was placed on the cab side-sheets. The maker's plate was fixed to the front driving-wheel splasher.

The sand-boxes and front driving-wheel splasher were separately lined out. The top and bottom leaves of the tender-springs were white lined, as also were the ends of the buffer-beams, track guard-irons, steps, valance and locomotive head-lamps.

1880 Engine No. 174 (0–4–4T, by Kitson) had the number-plates placed centrally on the tank sides, the letters and numerals being sunk and filled with black wax in a bright brass plate; the latter being ringed with a sunken black oval line.

The main lining had incurved corners (Fig. 4, p. 6). The rear sand-box was panelled, and the front sand-box was panelled out separate to the splasher of which it was part. There was a brass band between the smoke-box and the boiler, and the condenser pipe was polished copper.

Engine No. 208 (0–4–4T, by Sharp, Stewart) had number-plate as No. 174, but with *raised* letters and numerals on a black background on tank sides. The maker's plate was also of cast brass with raised letters, and was mounted on the bunker side-sheets.

The lining round the corners of tanks, etc., had no outer blocking, as No. 174. Sand-boxes were lined *integrally* with the front splashers. There was no lining to the upper side-sheets of the cab. There was a brass band between the smoke-box and the boiler. The rear sand-box and front box were panelled with single white lining. There was also a single white line round the axle-ends.

1881 Goods engines were black, and all passenger engines green, (12) (including those rebuilt early in 1881). The first black-painted passenger engines were seen in 1882, No. 8 being the first. All rebuilds after 1882 left the shops in black livery.

1885–6 The 0–4–2T engines ("Scotchmen") were painted a lighter green than other engines; but after re-boilering by Mr. Kirtley, they left the shops in black livery.

Pre 1889 Locomotives were green, (12), with brass domes, safety-valve casings and name-plates.

1889 Martley engines, still running in their old livery, were a medium green, (15), with black bands and red and white lining. The domes and safety-valve casings were bright brass, and the chimney tops were bright copper. Underframes were brown. This colour-scheme had been standard until Mr. Kirtley's time (1875). (Martley engines were very picturesque, with brass name-plates.)

1892 Engine No. 54 (late "Asia" built by Sharp, Stewart & Co.), after being rebuilt by Mr. Kirtley was painted black with a varnished finish. Safety-valve springs were red, and their columns of polished brass. The number-plates were also brass with black backgrounds. All was black except the buffer-beams, which were vermilion with a black edging. Coupling rods were polished steel. The cab sides were lined with a wide grey line, edged outside with a fine red line, and inside with a thin yellow one. This lining also appeared round the driving-wheel splashers and sand-boxes. The tender was similarly lined in one large side panel with a gilt monogram in the centre of the panel "LC and DR". The frames were black, with a fine red line running round one inch inside the frame edges. The guard-irons, the ends of the wooden buffer-beams, the outside cranks, axle ends, tender coping and spring buckles also having the fine red lining. The engine number appeared in gold figures, shaded with black on the front buffer-beam. The front tube-plate angle-iron had a polished brass casing. Boiler-banding was 3 in. wide, and composed of a 2½ in. black band sandwiched between two ¼ in. red bands. Locomotive number on buffer-beam was in serif letters (capital "N" and small "o" with a dash beneath the latter), letters and figures 10 ins. high.

Mr. Kirtley painted new engines black with grey bands and yellow and vermilion lines.

1892 Locomotives Nos. 53–56 were painted black. (In 1900 their numbers were 512–515.)

1896 Locomotives painted black, with a wide grey band round the tanks, cabs, splashers and tenders. On the outer edge of this band was a thin vermilion line, and on its inside a fine yellow line. The buffer-beams were red, with black edging and buffer-sockets. The locomotive number was painted in gold on the buffer-beam with black shading. Frames and wheels were black, with narrow vermilion lining. Number-plates were of brass, with raised figures on a black background. The company's monogram was placed in the centre of the tank or tender-sides in gold. Both goods and passenger engines were similarly decorated.

Coaches were varnished teak, with gold lettering, shaded with red; all their underframing and ironwork being painted black.

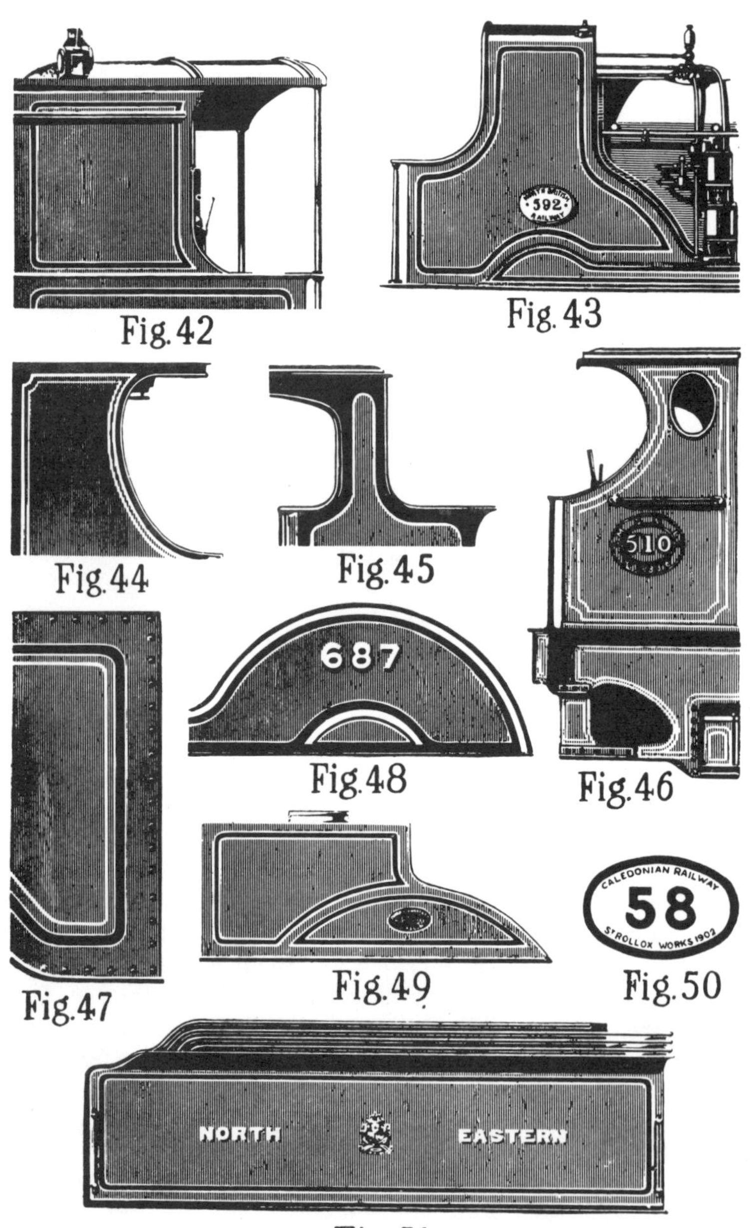

Fig. 42 Fig. 43 Fig. 44 Fig. 45 Fig. 46 Fig. 47 Fig. 48 Fig. 49 Fig. 50 Fig. 51

Goods stock was painted a dark shade of grey, with white lettering and figures.

1899 Locomotive No. 4 (built at Longhedge), a four-coupled bogie engine, had her number-plates painted red.

Immediately before amalgamation with S.E.R., express engines were black, with a broad grey band flanked on one side with a vermilion line and on the other by a yellow one. A monogram of the company's initials appeared on the tender-sides in gold.

Goods engines were also black, but were devoid of the grey band, having only vermilion lining. All buffer-beams were vermilion, the engine number appearing thereon in bold gold figures, shaded black.

LONDON, CHATHAM AND DOVER RAILWAY CREST

LONDON AND NORTH WESTERN RAILWAY

THIS important company dated from the year 1846, when the London and Birmingham Railway (p. 233), the Grand Junction Railway (which had already taken over the Liverpool and Manchester Railway), and the Manchester and Birmingham Railway were amalgamated.

In the Liverpool and Manchester Railway (p. 232), the London and North Western Railway inherited one of the oldest established railway companies in the passenger railway business, and in the London and Birmingham Railway, the first main line from London to be opened for traffic.

Robert Stephenson was the engineer of the London and Birmingham Railway, and the famous Rainhill locomotive trials in 1829 were held on the Liverpool and Manchester Railway main line, his "Rocket" achieving a maximum speed of a fraction over 24 miles per hour, thus proving the advantage of steam over horse-traction. "The Rocket" subsequently drew trains on the Liverpool and Manchester Railway and finally passed to the Midgeholme Railway, near Carlisle, where it ceased running in 1844. It was acquired by the South Kensington Museum in 1862.

The London and North Western Railway also includes some of the then most daringly-conceived engineering works ever seen on railways, and of which the Britannia Bridge over the Menai Straits, and the Runcorn High-level Bridge may be mentioned as outstanding examples. For many years, the London and North Western Railway was known as the "Premier Line" of England, a title it had every reason to be proud of.

The Railway's total trackage was over 2,000 miles, of which nearly all was owned; 207 miles being joint, 4 miles leased, and 48 miles worked by L.N.W.R. stock.

The Lancashire and Yorkshire Railway was amalgamated with the London and North Western Railway as from 1st January, 1922.

COMPONENT COMPANIES OF THE ORIGINAL LONDON AND NORTH WESTERN RAILWAY

<table>
<tr><td>Bolton and Leigh Railway (1828–45)</td><td></td><td rowspan="8">Grand Junction Railway, (1837) amalgamated with L.N.W.R. in 1846</td></tr>
<tr><td>Liverpool and Manchester Railway (1830–46)</td><td></td></tr>
<tr><td>Kenyon and Leigh Railway (1831–45)</td><td></td></tr>
<tr><td>Warrington and Newton Railway (1831–45)</td><td></td></tr>
<tr><td>Wigan Branch Railway (1832–46)</td><td rowspan="2">North Union Railway</td></tr>
<tr><td>Preston and Wigan Railway (1838–46)</td></tr>
<tr><td>Chester and Crewe Railway (1840)</td><td></td></tr>
<tr><td>Trent Valley Railway (1847)</td><td></td></tr>
<tr><td>Warwick and Leamington Railway (1844–46)</td><td></td><td rowspan="6">London and Birmingham Railway (1837) amalgamated with L.N.W.R. in 1846</td></tr>
<tr><td>Bedford Railway (1846)</td><td></td></tr>
<tr><td>Dunstable Railway (1848)</td><td></td></tr>
<tr><td>Aylesbury Railway (1839)</td><td></td></tr>
<tr><td>Rugby and Leamington Railway (1851)</td><td></td></tr>
<tr><td>West London Railway (1844) (Birmingham, Bristol and Thames Junction Railway)</td><td></td></tr>
<tr><td>Manchester and Birmingham Railway (1840)</td><td></td><td>Amalgamated with L.N.W.R. in 1846</td></tr>
</table>

RAILWAY COMPANIES ABSORBED BY L.N.W.R. (Between 1846 and 1923)

1847 Leeds, Dewsbury and Manchester Railway
Buckinghamshire Railway. (Comprised of Buckingham and Brackley Junction Railway, and Oxford and Bletchley Junction Railway)
Birmingham, Wolverhampton and Stour Valley Railway
Preston and Wyre Railway and Preston and Wyre Dock
Blackpool and Lytham Railway
Huddersfield and Manchester Railway
Shropshire Union Railway

1849 Manchester, South Junction and Altrincham Railway (Jointly worked with M.S. & L.R. [later G.C.R.])

1856 Chester and Holyhead Railway
Mold Railway (opened 1849)
Bangor and Carnarvon Railway

1859 Lancaster and Carlisle Railway
Lancaster and Preston Junction Railway
Kendal and Windermere Railway
West London Extension Railway. (jointly with G.W.R., L.S.W.R. and L.B.S.C.R.)
Warrington and Altrincham (later named Warrington and Stockport Railway)

1861 South Staffordshire Railway. (Comprised of South Staffordshire Junction Railway and Trent Valley Midland and Grand Junction Railway)
Birkenhead Railway. (Comprised of Chester and Birkenhead Railway and Birkenhead, Lancashire and Cheshire Junction Railway)

1862 Shrewsbury and Hereford Railway
Cromford and High Peak Railway
Oldham, Ashton-under-Lyne and Guide Bridge Railway
Merthyr, Tredegar and Abergavenny Railway

1863 Knighton Railway
Cannock Chase Railway

1864 St. Helens and Runcorn Gap Railway (opened 1833)
Shrewsbury and Welshpool Railway. (jointly with G.W.R.)

1865 Bedford and Cambridge Railway (opened 1862)

1866 Tenbury Railway. (jointly with G.W.R.)
Cockermouth and Workington Railway (opened 1847)
Whitehaven Junction Railway (opened 1847)
Stockport, Disley and Whaley Bridge Railway (opened 1857)
Nerquis (private) Railway

1867 Hampstead Junction Railway (opened 1860)
Preston and Longridge Railway (opened 1840)
Fleetwood, Preston and West Riding Junction Railway (opened 1850)
Vale of Clwyd Railway (opened 1858)
Nuneaton and Hinckley Railway (later named South Leicester Railway)
Conway and Llanrwst Railway (opened 1863)

1868 Central Wales Railway (opened 1862)
Central Wales Extension Railway (opened 1866)

1869 Derbyshire, Staffordshire and Worcestershire Junction Railway (name later changed to Cannock Mineral Railway)
Brynmawr and Blaenavon Railway (opened 1866)

1870 Nantlle Railway (opened 1828)
Carnarvonshire Railway (opened 1867)
Carnarvon and Llanberis Railway (opened 1869)

1871 North and South Western Junction Railway (opened 1853)

1875 Newport Pagnell Railway (opened 1867)

1876 Sirhowy Railway (originally Sirhowy Tramroad, opened 1805)
Anglesey Central Railway (opened 1866)

1877 Whitehaven, Cleator and Egremont Railway (opened 1856)

1879 Denbigh, Ruthin and Corwen Railway (opened 1862)

1881 Watford and Rickmansworth Railway (opened 1862)

1883 Lancashire Union Railway (opened 1869)

1884 Vale of Towy Railway (opened 1858) (joint by with G.W.R.)

1885 Portpatrick and Wigtownshire Joint Committee. Comprising Portpatrick Railway (opened 1861) and Wigtownshire Railway (opened 1875)

1891 Swansea and Carmarthen Railway (opened 1865). Name changed in 1873 to Central Wales and Carmarthen Junction Railway

1892 Ludlow and Clee Hill Railway (jointly with G.W.R.)

1899 Harrow and Stanmore Railway (opened 1890)

1902 Brynmawr and Western Valleys Railway (jointly with G.W.R.)

1909 East and West India Docks and Birmingham Junction Railway (opened 1850). Name changed in 1853 to North London Railway.

The chief mechanical engineers of the railway from its commencement were as follows :—

Northern Division (*Crewe*)

——1841	Buddicom
1841–1857	Francis Trevithick
1857–1862	John Ramsbottom

North Eastern Division (*Longsight, Manchester*) (*Merged into the Northern Division in* 1857)

1846–1857	John Ramsbottom

(Locomotive Superintendent, Manchester and Birmingham Railway, from 1842)

Southern Division (*Wolverton*)

1846–1852	J. Edward McConnell (formerly of Birmingham and Gloucester Railway)
	Edward Bury (Locomotive Superintendent, London and Birmingham Railway.)

Entire L.N.W.R. System (*Crewe*)

1862–1871	John Ramsbottom
1871–1903	Francis William Webb
1903–1909	George Whale
1909–1920	Charles John Bowen-Cooke
1920–1921	Capt. Hewitt Pearson Montague Beames
1922 until amalgamation	George Hughes

The locomotive superintendents of the original Liverpool and Manchester Railway were as follows:—

1831–1836	John Dixon
1836–1837	Edward Woods
1837–1840	John Melling
1840–1846	John Dewrance

(Southern Division Livery)

1846 The "chocolate" and white coach livery was adopted about this date, though Official records do not reveal a more exact date.

1849 The Southern Division 2–2–2 engine (No. 12), (Bury, Curtis and Kennedy, No. 280), had a boiler painted (6), described in sources as dark green, fender, wheels and buffer-beam ends also being this colour. Chimney and smoke-box were black. There was a brass band between the smoke-box and the boiler. The fire-box was polished copper, and the safety-valve casing brass. Boiler-bands were dark grey. Axle-ends were painted yellow, and the splashers were brass. Wheel-tyres were grey, and the feed-pipe copper.

1849 The Crampton 6–2–0 for the Southern Division, built by Bury, Curtis and Kennedy and named "Liverpool" was painted a bluish-green, (15), cylinders and splashers being also this colour. The fire-box was copper, as were the pipes from the cylinders to the smoke-box, and the pipes to the central "dome"; which latter was green. Underframes were dark grey, as were the wheels. The safety-valve casing was bright brass. Smoke-box and chimney were black.

The builder's plate on the driving-wheel splasher was brass as were the name-plates, upon which the word "LIVERPOOL" appeared in sunken letters on polished brass. The feed pipe from tender to engine was copper, and the piston-rod-driven pump was bright brass. Connecting rod big-ends were brass, as were the little-ends. The lower portion of the copper fire-box had lagging painted dark green.

1861 Locomotive No. 375, an extra large "Bloomer" designed by J. E. McConnell (and also engines Nos. 372 and 373) was painted (36), described in sources as a bright vermilion red. (See plate facing p. 65) The boiler was banded with broad black lines flanked with fine white lines. The smoke-box and fire-box rings were of polished brass, as were the dome and safety-valve casings; whilst the top of the chimney was of polished copper. The engine number was repeated in large serif cut-out brass figures on the front of the chimney.

There was a double brass beading round the driving-wheel splashers, which were fretted; the openings being lined out with a fine black line.

The cab-sides, tender-sides and back were panelled out with a thin black line and a fine white line within it, the corners being incurved. Number-plates were of brass, being oval and fastened to the fender sides, and had white figures thereon; the plates being surrounded by a fine black line.

The steps and tender-frame, together with the foot-plate valance were lined with a fine medium grey line flanked by white lines. Spring-buckles and shackles were black, but the springs themselves were painted a medium shade of grey. Axle-boxes and their tie-rods were black, and brake-blocks were medium grey (iron).

Buffer-beams and shanks were vermilion red, as were the wheels; but the axle-ends were black and the wheel-tyres grey.

Sand-pipes were polished copper, and the feed-pipe at the front-end of the boiler was bright brass. Hand-rails were of polished steel, and the sand-boxes were vermilion red; but the tool-box on the tender-top was black. The cock at the side of the smoke-box was brass, and the guard-irons (front only) were vermilion red lined with black. The injector piping was of polished copper.

This livery also applied to the small and large "Bloomers" of the same period, and serving on the Southern Division of the London and North Western Railway.

(Northern Division Livery)

1849 The 2–2–2 Allen locomotive was painted (6), described in sources as green, with main-frames a lighter shade of the same colour. Smoke-box and chimney were black. The dome was green, as was the base of the safety-valve, though the casing of the latter was polished brass. Cylinders were black, and the fire-box dark green. Splashers were dark green, but the frames, and buffer-beam ends were light green. Splashers were brass-beaded. Wheels were black. Hand-rails were covered polished brass. The front cylinder caps were iron polished bright. Axle-boxes were light green, and all piping copper. The safety-valve spring casing was bright brass, as was the connecting-rod big-end.

Pre 1860 Engine "Columbine", the first engine built at Crewe, and now in York Railway Museum, is Northern division green, (6), (though this appears very dirty). Lining is a black band flanked by red on one side and yellow on the other. There is a copper band between the fire-box and the boiler, the safety-valve column is bronze and the spring-case brass. There is a brass band round the rear of the cylinders, the drain-cocks of which are also brass. Buffer-beams are red and cylinder-front lubricators brass. The base of the safety-valve is copper, and the spectacle rims of the cab, brass.

The interior of the cab is red, and there is a copper band round the rear of the firebox. Dome in cab is brass. The oiling flaps to the tender axle-boxes are brass. The lining of the tender-panels consists of an outer border of black, followed by a ¾ in. wide grey line, then a ⅛ in. white, a 2 in. black, and a ¼ in. red; all corners being rounded.

Below frames, reading from above to below, the lining is wide red, wide black, narrow white, ¾ in. grey, then black.

1860 The engine "Lady of the Lake" No. 531 (2–2–2 tender), when built and running on the Northern Division, was painted (6), described in sources as a bluish-green. Boiler-banding was in black, as also was the colour of the smoke-box and upper half of the cylinders. Buffer-beams were red (vermilion), panelled with black; but their tops and ends were green. The plates between the buffers and the beam were black, and the shanks were green; whilst the actual end ring of the shanks was black.

The fender sides were green, but the top plates of the fender sides were vermilion red, the sanding-lever being also this colour. The dome was green. Number-plates were of cast brass with black figures, and wheels were green with black tyres. The front wheel splashers were green with black casings and heavily-lined fronts. The cylinder lubricator cocks were bright brass. The rail round the top of the cab sides as well as the vertical supporting stanchions were of bright steel. The top of the chimney was of polished brass, and the safety-valve lever of bright steel. The tender-sides and back were green, panelled out with a black outside line and a white inner, both with incurved corners. The tender-springs and axle-boxes were green, but the spring-buckles were black. Brake-shoes were black, as were the brake-hangers and track guard-irons, together with the axle-box tie-rods. The transverse brake-rodding was vermilion red (see also Fig 57, page 200).

The main-frame of the tender was green, lined out finely with black, and the rear buffer-beam was vermilion red between the guard-iron attachments, but green between the latter and the end of the beams. The buffers were painted in the same style as those on the engine. The tender water-scoop handle was painted vermilion red.

The inside of the cab front was painted vermilion red in its top half, and black below; whereas the insides of the cab sides were painted vermilion red all over.

The shape of the number-plates was rectangular, with incurved corners, and the lines of rivets down the sides of the tender horn-plates were painted black.

When first built the engine had a polished brass beading round the cab end of the fire-box, and the spectacle-plate rims and safety-valve casings were also of polished brass. The tender axle-boxes also had brass lids.

1861 The new Queen's coach was painted in dark ("Royal") claret, (29), bearing in the centre of the side panelling the Royal arms. On the side panels appeared the insignia of the Order of the Garter, the Bath, and the Thistle. The cornice of the roof was festooned with carved figures which were picked out in gold against a white background.

(United Northern and Southern Division Livery—From 1861)

1867–71 McConnel's Extra Large "Bloomers" were painted the standard Crewe (Northern Division) dark green (see p. 122).

1873 On April 17th, the first "black" L.N.W. engine appeared.

1873 The first black (50)* locomotives appeared.

1877 Mr. Webb first fitted the Company's crest on the driving wheel splashers on his second batch of "Precedents" (see Figs. 54 and 56, p. 200).

1877 Mr. Webb first adopted the practice of placing the company's crest on the locomotive driving-wheel splashers, the second batch of "Precedents" (857) being the first engines so to appear.

1878 Brass number-plates commenced to be used on locomotives, numbers being painted on in Mr. Ramsbottom's time. Mr. Webb introduced the cast-iron number-plates upon which the number was painted in yellow (Figs. 52 and 58, p. 200).

"Crewe Goods" (2–4–0's) before rebuilding were painted dead black, and were devoid of any lining or number-plates; the engine number appearing in yellow figures on the cab fenders, shaded with light blue.

1896 Passenger engines were painted black, and lined with a broad light-blue stripe with a fine white line on either side. One and a half inches away from this was a vermilion line. Boiler bands had a vermilion red line on either side.

Buffer-beams were red with black lining, and the buffers themselves were black. Number-plates were of brass, with polished figures raised on a red background. Cab interiors were painted a light nut-brown.

Goods engines were painted all black without any lining, and their buffer beams were red, edged with a black line. Their number-plates were the same as those fitted to passenger locomotives.

The coupling-rods of all engines were originally painted black, but in 1896 several engines appeared with the flutes of bright polished steel. The chimney-tops of express locomotives were of cast-iron and they were kept brightly polished.

1896 Engine No. 3212 (saddle tank) had its cab painted and lined in the same style as passenger engines.

1897 (Queen Victoria's Jubilee) Engine "Great Britain" was painted (36), described in sources as poppy red, with lining composed of a black band flanked with narrow gilt lines. The

* This colour was not absolute black (49) but a very intense blue-black.

smoke-box and underframes remained black, but the tender tool-boxes were red. (Fig. 59, p. 200).

1897 Coaches were now running in three distinct styles of livery:—

(*a*) Main-line and most stock. White (47) upper panels tinged with blue, with lower panels a (43) described as "dark chocolate" shade. On the inner edge of the panels was a yellow or gold stripe. Underframes were also a dark chocolate colour. Lettering was in gold, edged round with a fine black line.

(*b*) Suburban trains on the "Outer Circle" underground system had carriages with plain varnished wood, and were devoid of lining. The lettering was the same as that on the main-line stock.

(*c*) Workmen's trains and some branch trains were painted a dark chocolate brown all over, being without lining and lettered in medium chrome yellow.

The coaches and saloons of the West Coast Joint Stock were finished the same as those for normal main-line use, but the lettering was in gold, shaded with emerald green.

Goods stock was painted a dark slate colour, and the framing of goods brakes and covered goods stock was black. Lettering was white, and a large solid white diamond was the distinctive mark of the company.

1897 The locomotive "Queen Empress" was repainted white with gilt lettering.

1902 Locomotive "Queen Empress" carried a gold medal from the Chicago Exhibition of 1893, over the number-plate on the near-side of the engine.

1903 The "new" 20-ton all-steel coal wagons had the two white diamonds and the word "LOCO" pressed out on their sides. This raised design and lettering was then painted white.

1906 Locomotive cab roofs were painted white.

1906 Three 4–4–2T locomotives (Nos. 528, 531 and 784) appeared in July carrying a different type of number-plate upon which the date was shown; this type being introduced with these engines. The plate was carried on the bunker-sides and the company's initials appeared on the tank sides.

Motor-car vans were painted chocolate, with lining and lettering in gold (ex-Wolverhampton works):—"LNWR" and "No. (603)" appearing in two lines in the centre panel. The words "For Motor Car Traffic" appeared in three lines on each end panel of the vehicles.

1908 Goods stock was initialled in smaller letters "LNWR".

1911 The "Experiment" 4–6–2T (No. 2670) designed by Bowen-Cooke had the letters "LNWR" on the tanks in 18 in. letters, shaded to the right, below. The L.N.W.R. crest was placed on the upper cab side-sheets. (See Fig. 47, p. 114.)

1911 The 5,000th engine to be built at Crewe works was named "Coronation" and numbered 1,800. The name was surmounted by a crown with "Coronation" in raised letters, and below this was a plate reading: "The 5,000th engine built at Crewe Locomotive Works, June, 1911". The locomotive had gilt and red lining.

1912 Locomotive lining was a ¾ in. outer band of grey, edged on its inner side by an ⅛ in. yellow, then at 1½ in. further inwards, an ⅛ in. red line.

1913 "Claughton" engines (Bowen-Cooke, No. 2222, etc.) were painted black, (50), with red, cream and grey lining. Smoke-box and fire-box were unlined black, but the cab side-sheets were panelled with red and white lines. The splashers and openings in the frames were lined round in red, as were the tender-frames. Buffer-beams were vermilion red, but the buffer shanks were black. The tender-sides and rear were lined in single panels with red and white.

1914 The livery in use at this time commenced in 1873, and still continued to be materially the same, both for coaches and locomotives.

Engines were black, (50), lined out in red, with red and cream blocked yellow lines on cab side-sheets. Name-plates were of polished brass with black waxed letters, and number-plates were of cast iron with yellow figures on a red background. Buffer-shanks were black, and buffer-beams red, with a black-lined panel effect. There was no lining at the rear of the tender, and the rear buffer-beam was black.

Coaches were (43), described in sources as purple-brown, in their lower panels with (47), described as bluish-white, upper panels (see Fig. 55, p. 200).

Goods vehicles were (42), described as medium grey.

1915 Coaches were (43) "chocolate", with (47) white upper panels.

1919 Locomotive "Patriot" fitted with special name-plates (Fig. 52, p. 200).

1920 Destination boards in the London area were black, with white lettering.

1922 Engines were black, (50), lined out in red and white.

Crest on page 200 (Fig. 54)

LONDON AND SOUTH WESTERN RAILWAY

PROMOTED in 1831 as the Southampton, London and Branch Railway and Dock Company, and living the first few years of its life as the London and Southampton Railway, the London and South Western Railway adopted this title in 1839; through rail communication between London and Southampton being completed in 1840.

The London and South Western Railway acquired the Bodmin and Wadebridge Railway in 1845, but this was not physically connected with the parent system until 1895, fifty years later.

The Woking and Guildford Railway (opened in 1844) was included in 1845, the Exeter and Crediton Railway (opened in 1845) was amalgamated in 1879, the Taw Vale Railway (opened in 1848) was acquired in 1907, and the Salisbury and Yeovil (opened in 1860) in 1878.

The locomotive superintendents of the London and South Western railway were as follows :—

1835–1841	Joseph Woods	1871–1877	W. George Beattie
1841–1850	John Viret Gooch	1878–1895	William Adams
1850–1871	Joseph Hamilton Beattie	1895–1912	Dugald Drummond
		1912–1922	Robert W. Urie

1840 The coaches on the 11 a.m. train to Basingstoke (then the end of the line) were all painted chocolate, being 1st class three-compartment vehicles. The company's crest appeared on the panel of the middle door, whilst the two end doors were ornamented with red dragon's wings. (The guard's dress was a bright scarlet coat with silver buttons, and trousers of bright blue with scarlet piping.)

1850 The engine "Stromboli" was painted deep crimson-red.

1850 Locomotives were dull red (very similar to the Furness Railway locomotives immediately before grouping), with black boiler-bands, smoke-box and chimney. Splashers were brass beaded, and name-plates were brass with raised letters on a black background.

1850 (c) Locomotives were Indian red, with plain black bands, and were liberally decorated with polished brass and copper fittings.

1850 (c) Engines were Indian red with black bands and white lines. The splasher perforations were picked out with vermilion lines. There were, however, several variations to this livery. The older engines at this time had their chimney-caps painted in red, orange or pinkish-yellow to simulate cheaply the copper tops of the then modern engines. The 4–4–0 "Jumbos" (348 class) had painted domes.

1853 The engine "Milo" was painted a dull rose vermilion shade as a body-colour. The smoke-box and chimney were black, as were the axle-boxes, brake-blocks, track-guards, boiler-bands, and springs. The leading driving-wheel splashers were brass beaded, and the safety-valve springs were also brass-cased. The dome was dull rose vermilion as were the wheel spokes, counter-balance weights and outside cranks. Handrails were steel as were the safety-valve levers.

1856 (c) The varnished teak coaches of this period continued in many cases in their original livery well into the '70's. It appears from contemporary paintings that the "brown and salmon" livery of later days had appeared occasionally at a comparatively early period, when there were also two-colour coaches running with dark olive-green or brownish lower panels and greenish-yellow or very "dark-cream" upper panels. Brake vans had vermilion ends.

Pre 1859 Engines were Indian red with black banding.

1859–70 Engines were chocolate coloured and lined out in black and white. Black, white and vermilion lining was used for express engines.

1860 (c) "Herod" had a purple-painted chimney, probably for working the funeral train of a notable person.

1860 (c) The engine "Ariel" (No. 70) was (38), described in sources as chocolate, with black boiler-banding with white lining on each side of the black. The splasher edging was white-black-white. Cab side-sheets were chocolate with a black outer edge with orange, black and white lining within, and orange lining outside the panel. The slits in the driving-wheel splashers were lined out individually, white within and orange outside.

MIDLAND AND GREAT NORTHERN JOINT RAILWAY NO. 42 AS RUNNING *circa* 1891 (P. 161)

Sandboxes were lined out orange, black, white; the orange being on the outside. The name-plate was rectangular, with the letters in raised brass on a black background. Smoke-box was black, as was the chimney, the latter having a copper top. Safety-valves had brass casings. Underframes and valances were chocolate, lined out in orange and white only. Immediately under the foot-plate edge was black. Cylinders were chocolate lined out with white, black and orange, the latter colour being outside. The front sand-boxes were lined out in white only. Buffer-beams were red, lined out with white, black and white; and carried the number in gold, shaded with black to the right and below. Wheels were chocolate, and the feed-water heater pipe along the boiler was black. All injector piping was polished copper. Date-plate was oval brass, and appeared on the cab side-sheets. There were brass beadings round spectacle windows and round front of fire-box.

Early 1860 The locomotive colour was changed to (38), described in sources as chocolate, with black lagging bands, edged with white. Splasher beadings black with a fine white line on each edge. Around splasher slots was a fine white line outside which was a fine vermilion line, the space between being black. This same lining was on the panel-plate and on the rectangular panel of the cylinders. The front of the panel-plate had only a narrow black edge with a fine white line dividing it from the chocolate panel. Most of the passenger locomotives were thus lined out, but a few had white lines on both the edges of the black panel band; this slight modification also applied to goods and tank engines of the time.

Buffer-beams were vermilion, with a black edge, the latter being separated from the vermilion panel by a fine white line. The ends of buffer-beams were chocolate, edged with black, round which, on the outside was a fine vermilion line, and inside, separating the black line from the chocolate, was a fine white line. The letters "No." and the engine number were in gold, shaded with black, placed one on each side of the drawbar hook. The stiffening ring on the smoke-box door of some engines was polished, as also was the strip of brass or iron along the top edge of the cylinder casings. The domes and safety-valve casings were of cast iron, and were painted in the body-colour.

1862 The long-boilered engines Nos. 1 to 7 (the latter being *ex* S. and D.J.R. No. 14), and Nos. 8 to 15 were painted green.

1863 Locomotives dark brown. Polished brass. (Beattie 2–4–0T.) (see plate 8, facing p. 192.)

1863–78 All engines built by Beyer, Peacock & Co. between these dates, as well as the first lot of their goods locomotives (1866), had the outside of their frames painted vermilion. The inside of frames of all locomotives was also vermilion, as were the outside cranks.

1865 The later Beattie locomotives had polished brass domes and copper-topped chimneys, whilst the older ones had not. The standard colour was then chocolate brown.

1866 The first batch of Beyer Peacock engines had vermilion underframes. Their domes and safety-valve casings were normally painted over, but were often divested of their paint and brightly polished by their crews.

1868 The J. Beattie engines Nos. 95 to 100 inclusive had slight variations in their number-plates. "Plutus" (No. 98) had "98" in large brass figures instead of the number-plate. "Pegasus" and "Castor" had their original plates slightly altered. The Adams rebuilt "Stromboli" (No. 116) also had the number in large figures instead of on the name-plate. A small oval rebuilding plate appearing under the "116".

1868 All the new locomotives and many of the older ones had copper-topped chimneys and polished brass domes and safety-valve covers (which were previously present on those purchased from Beyer, Peacock & Co.). Some of the double-framed engines had the outside frames painted vermilion.

On some engines which had iron chimney-caps, the latter were painted to resemble copper—some a salmon shade, some bright red or orange.

1868 Engine "Python", No. 0100 (2–4–0 tender) had number-plates wherein the name appeared in a curved panel, the words "No. 0100" appearing above and "July, 1868" below in contiguous oval panels. The lettering was very deeply recessed on a black background. The plates were mounted on the cab side-sheets. There was a wide brass beading round the front driving-wheel splashers, and white lines round all splasher cut-outs. Splasher lining; (see Fig. 18, p. 29.)

The letters "SWR" appeared widely spaced on the tender, shaded to the left and below.

The engine "Sussex" (2–4–0 tender) had the same type of

number-plates as "Python", and also the wide brass-bead round the forward driving-wheel splashers, but the splasher frets were not lined out with white; nor was there any lettering on the tender-sides. Both engine and tender were completely devoid of all lining and panelling.

1869 Polished brass domes and safety-valve covers became more general and continued thus for some eight years.

1870 (c) W. G. Beattie altered the engine lining to bands of yellow ochre with a white edge.

1871–77 Some changes were made in locomotive styles. The body colour remained chocolate shade, but the cab-splashers and panel-plates were edged with yellow ochre, separated from the chocolate panel by a fine white line. Boiler lagging bands were yellow ochre, separated from the chocolate body colour by a fine white line on each side of the yellow ochre. Passenger engines were devoid of any polished metal-work.

1872 Newly-built passenger stock was brown, with upper panels of cream of a dark-greenish hue. Van ends were vermilion and remained so for years. Second class and first class coaches had lemon-yellow window frames.

1872–78 Engines were dark greenish-brown.

1875 The lining was changed on express engines to dark yellow edging, divided from the chocolate by a thin white line.

1875 The special locomotives of the Civil Engineering Department were painted green, whilst all Beattie engines were chocolate.

1875 (c) Engines were painted a greenish (dirty) brown, with a lining of green, red and black for passenger types, and a lining of dark green only for the goods engines.

1878 Locomotive livery was changed to umber with black bands and orange and bright green lining.

1878 Mr. Adams adopted umber instead of chocolate for locomotives, with black banding and fine orange and pea-green lines. The buffer-beams lost the previous black and white edging used by Mr. Beattie. The Beattie engines still running were either painted black or a very dark green.

1878 Mr. Adams introduced a darker and fresher-looking chocolate umber, with finer lining, but this shade was not in use very long. The colour changed in 1885 to a bright green, and remained thus until after Mr. Adams' retirement.

1878 (c) Locomotive colour was changed to umber, and the lining scheme altered. Boiler lagging bands were black, with bright green lines on either side of the black. A fine orange line was then placed at a distance of half an inch from the green lines on either side of the plain black band. The splashers had a black edge, inside which was a fine green line, with a fine orange line placed at a distance of about half an inch from the green. Buffer-beams were vermilion, but were devoid of lining, and the letters and figures thereon were block, without any shading.

1879 All the Beyer, Peacock engines (4–4–0, 4–4–2T and 0–6–0) had numbers cut out in brass block figures and mounted on the cab side-sheets. There were double brass beadings round the forward driving-wheel splashers (broad outer and narrow inner), between which the words "BEYER, PEACOCK & CO., MANCHESTER, 1879" appeared on a curved brass plate.

1885 Mr. Adams retained chocolate for his first engines (Nos. 135–146, built by Beyer, Peacock & Co.).

1885 Mr. Adams adopted a new colour-scheme for engines in which (2), generally described as pea-green, was used as a body colour with black edging and white lining for express types. He afterwards extended the new scheme to all his passenger engines as well as to rebuilt Beattie types in 1887. This colour remained unaltered until 1896 when Mr. Drummond introduced his "grass-green".

1885 Locomotive colour changed to (2), described as a light pea-green, for all passenger engines. The tanks of tank locomotives as well as their cabs and frames were edged round with a narrow black band, having a fine white line inside it. (See Fig. 45, p. 114.) Brass beading appeared round splashers. Numbers were applied as solid brass block numerals, without a plate or frame, but when engines were painted light green a brass number-plate with raised figures and letters on a vermilion background was used. (See Figs. 73 and 74, pp. 209 and 258.)

1885 Pea-green was applied to all Mr. Adams' passenger engines and also to rebuilt Beattie 4–4–0's and 2–4–0's, including the three 2–4–0's at Wadebridge.

1885 From 1885 until 1894, Mr. Adams seems to have applied his pea-green locomotive livery to goods engines as well as to passenger types. The official photograph of "G–6" (0–6–0T) No. 257, built in 1894, clearly shows her painted in the Adams "passenger" livery.

1885 All locomotives with the exception of Adams express types were painted dark green with a single bright green line and narrow edging. (See also Fig. 68. p. 209.)

1885 Pea-green with black edging and white lining began to be used for the latest express engines, all others being painted dark holly green and lined out with light green and a black edging. This latter livery afterwards became the standard for goods engines.

1885 (c) The engine "Ironsides" had a "red" chimney top (probably copper).

1887 (onwards) All Adams passenger-engines and rebuilt Beattie express types were (2), described as pea-green, with a black edging and a fine white line between these two colours. On a few rebuilt Beattie locomotives (e.g. Nos. 85, 298 and 314), oval brass number-plates were fitted, with polished raised figures on a red, sunken background. (See also under date 1885). (Fig. 67, also Fig. 68, p. 209.)

1887 Locomotive colour changed to a lighter shade of green for passenger types.

1887 Old engines and goods types (not rebuilt) were a dark green with black edging and fine pea-green lining. This remained the goods engine livery till 1923. Coaches were originally chocolate all over.

1887–90 Locomotive No. 185 (0–4–4T was temporarily named "ALEXANDRA", this appearing on the tank sides instead of the usual "LSWR" in small block letters shaded to the right and below in the usual way. The name was surmounted by a white Prince of Wales' feathers, and the company's standard monogram below. The number-plate was of the standard oval pattern and was mounted on the bunker-sides. This was done when she hauled a Royal special to Bisley. All "0–2" class engines were painted in the standard passenger livery.

1895 Engines were turned out having brass number-plates with sunken numerals and letters (see Fig. 67, p. 209), the lettering on their tenders or tanks being gold, with black shading. Buffer-beams were painted vermilion, with the locomotive number in gold.

1895 "T–6" class locomotives were lined out in a slightly different style to the previous "X–2"s, the lining being more generally taken into the extreme quirks and points of acute angles; whereas, in the "X–2" class, such corners were treated with small radius curved lines. The difference was particularly noticeable on the cab side-sheets. All these locomotives also had Adams' style of number-plates, which were mounted on the rear driving-wheel splasher-cum-cab-sides. (Fig. 67, p. 209.)

1895 The upper panels of coaches were painted light buff with dark umber brown lower panels, picked out with black and vermilion; with the lettering and numbering in gold, shaded with black, appearing in the lower panels.

1896 Locomotives Nos. 657–666 had a new type of number-plate (see above), and the style of painting was changed so that the cab, splashers, etc., were still the standard green, but were edged with lines of black and purple-brown, these colours being divided by fine white lines.

1897 Twenty-five Drummond bogie tanks (Nos. 242–256, and 667–676) appeared, of which the later engines had " LSW " on their tank sides instead of " SWR ".

1897 New Drummond goods engines (No. 687 onward) were painted dark green with black borders and bands, and a single bright green line, with "SWR" on tender sides; this being done on all locomotives as from this date. (Fig. 48, p. 114.)

1897 Drummond 0–4–4 tank locomotives of the "243" class (Nine Elms) were light green, with a chocolate-coloured and black border, the latter being edged with white lines. The letters " SWR " appeared in gold on the tank-sides, and the cab interiors were painted and grained.

1897 Coach compartment interiors had roofs of dead white, with a chocolate-coloured line and ornamental corners. 1st and 2nd class coaches boasted an embossed pattern on material.

1898 Ten new "242" class locomotives (Numbered 31–40) were lettered " LSWR " on the tank-sides, instead of the previous " SWR "

1898 The last of the "677" class engines had several new decorative features as compared with the "577" class of 1890. The company's crest appeared on the driving splasher in place of the monogram. (Fig. 70, p. 209.). The "657" class had all the alterations of the "677" class, but had no brass beading round the splashers, and a new pattern number-plate somewhat similar to the Caledonian locomotives, *i.e.* with engraved letters on solid brass, "SOUTH WESTERN RAILWAY" and number appearing on it. " SWR " in very large letters appeared on the sides of the tender.

1898 D. Drummond's 4–2–2–0 locomotive No. 720 was, for about three months, painted similar to London, Brighton and South Coast "Stroudley yellow", but later was altered to LSW green, with a chocolate-coloured border and very wide black bands having white lines on each side to form the panels. Lettering on the tenders was altered also from "LSW" to "LSWR", in gold, shaded black.

1900–05 Locomotive colours were being used which were adopted by Dugald Drummond in 1896.

Locomotive colour was a grass-green (17) made up of Cypress green—4 lbs., zinc white in oil—2 lb., lemon chrome yellow in oil—1 lb.

The bordering of the cab sides of engines as well as tender-sides was a shade of purple-brown made up of purple-brown in oil—6 lb., burnt sienna in oil—¼ lb. burnt umber in oil—¼ lb.

Lining was a simple black band edged on either side with a white line. Engine numbers and the initials "LSWR" were in gold, shaded with black.

The coaches had upper panels described in sources as "salmon-pink" (48).* This was produced by a mixture of white lead in oil—4 lb. 5 oz., burnt sienna in oil— 3oz., Venetian red in oil—2½ oz., middle chrome yellow in oil—¾ oz.

The lower panels were painted (43, but with a green tinge) with a mixture of Quaker green in oil—2 lb. 2 oz., purple-brown in oil—6 oz., orange chrome yellow ½ oz., drop black in oil—½ oz. This produced a very dark greenish-brown which appeared black except when seen in sunlight. This colour is sometimes known as "invisible" green. (See note on p. 85). Coach lining was in red and black, and the lettering was in gold, shaded in black.

1900 (c) The goods stock was painted dark umber-brown with white lettering; whilst all underframing was painted black.

* The London and South Western Railway coach at Farnham, to the upper panels of which the "salmon" colour of (48) was accurately matched, was *re*-painted when it was withdrawn from service and preserved; and it would appear that originally this somewhat odd colour was at one time lighter, tending towards the "pink" of a primer paint coat.

It has been suggested that the upper panel colouring appearing on the old Bassett-Lowke "0" gauge tin-plate coaches was more similar to the original shade. Many L. and S.W.R. specialists state that they can remember the likeness, but memory can play queer tricks with such subtle shades of colour.

However, the names of the colours of the pigments used, together with the proportions necessary to produce the "salmon" shade are given above; this being the official formula.

1901 Destination boards were white letters on a red board for Portsmouth line trains, and white letters on a blue board for boat trains. Flesh-coloured boards with gold letters were also in vogue.

1903 Locomotives were green, (17), described in sources as a "brilliant emerald". The "new" bogie 4-coach block trains departed from the usual style of livery by bearing large figures denoting the classes upon the doors.

1907 Many locomotives had their oval number-plates removed, and the number painted in large gold figures on the cab side-sheets. Milk vans were painted the light colour of the upper panels of passenger stock, and fine lined in red and black.

1910 Goods engines generally were described in sources as a very deep olive green, darker than the L.B.S.C.R. colour of goods locomotives of *circa* 1905. Locomotives were sometimes black. The lining was not very elaborate, and the older types were not lined at all.

1914 Passenger engines were light green (getting yellower towards 1923) with chocolate banding and black and white lines.

Passenger coaches were dark brown in the lower panels with the upper panels and mouldings a salmon shade of brownish-pink (up to 1916).

Ventilated meat and milk vans were painted salmon shade all over. Wagons were dark brown, this colour weathering to a terra-cotta shade.

1914 All Drummond passenger locomotives were painted green, their boilers being lined with a fine black line and fine white lines on each side; then broad chocolate-coloured lines outside the white lines. Cab spectacles were brass-beaded. There was a raised brass ring round the inspection plate on the splashers. Cab side-sheets, splashers and tender-body were green, surrounded by a chocolate border, with fine white lines, separated by a broad black line between the chocolate border and the green body colour. The locomotive number appeared in gold shaded to the right and below on vermilion buffer-beams. (See Fig. 73, p. 209.)

1914 Coaches. Buff upper panels, and maroon lower panels.

1914–18 A deterioration took place in the shade of green used for passenger engines. It took on a yellowish tinge ("sage green"), and the lining-out was considerably simplified to black bands and borders with a single white line.

1915 Electric stock was green from its inception.

1915 Coaches were walnut-colour lower panels with salmon (pale) upper panels.

1920 Coaches for the Bournemouth service were green, like the LSWR electric stock.

1921 (May) Green with yellow lining was standardized for coaches, and later for engines in Mr. Maunsel's time.

LONDON AND SOUTH WESTERN RAILWAY CREST

LONDON, TILBURY AND SOUTHEND RAILWAY

PROMOTED jointly by the Eastern Counties Railway and the London and Blackwall Railway, and opened in 1854, the London, Tilbury and Southend Railway had no locomotives of its own until 1875; engines being supplied, first by the Eastern Counties Railway, and later by the Great Eastern Railway.

The Railway was acquired by the Midland Railway in 1912, and finally passed into the London, Midland and Scottish Railway group in 1923.

Its first locomotive engineer was T. Whitelegg, who held the post from 1879 until 1910, being followed by R. H. Whitelegg in 1910, who carried on until 1918, when he went to the Glasgow and South Western Railway.

1897 Locomotives were (14), described in sources as a light green, with chocolate and red bordering. Names on tank-sides in gold letters.

1898 Locomotives were (14), described as a bright green, with tanks, bunkers and cabs bordered with a bright chocolate brown, with a fine vermilion line on the inside edges. This line ran square with the panels. Within the panels, but with its corners rounded, was a black stripe with a fine white line on either side of it. The frames were painted chocolate, with a black edge and a vermilion line; and at a small distance from the latter was a thin yellow line. Boiler barrels were green, with chocolate bands, having a thick red line to separate the chocolate colour from a black stripe edged with white, which was on each side of the chocolate-coloured band. Buffer-beams were vermilion, bordered with black, with a yellow line between; and the engine number appeared thereon in gold figures, shaded with black. The locomotive's name was also in gold, similarly shaded, on the tank sides; being written in an arc over the company's crest. Cab interiors were a chocolate brown, as were the tyres of the wheels.

The passenger rolling-stock was of varnished teak, the lettering being in gold, shaded with red.

Goods stock was painted a medium grey, with yellow lettering, shaded black. Underframes and ironwork were also black.

1899 The 0–6–0 tender engines (Nos. 49 and 50, by Sharp, Stewart) did not have names, but were in the standard colouring, with "LTSR" on the tender-sides in shaded gold serif letters. The numbers on the cab sides was in similar style, and the maker's date-plate was on the middle offside splasher.

1900 The two 0–6–0 tender engines built by Messrs. Sharp, Stewart (Nos. 49 and 50) were painted and lined in the standard livery of the period, and they originally carried L.T.S.R. (with full-stops) in large gold letters on the tenders. The engine numbers appeared in large figures on the cab side-sheets, though this was later replaced by the company's crest. Builder's date-plates were oval and were placed on the centre driving-wheel splasher. The tenders were lined out in a single panel, as were the cab side-sheets; and the forward sand-boxes were fully lined out in the style of the period. The full-stops were removed from between the letters on the tenders about the year 1905.

1900 Destination boards were white lettered on black "FENCHURCH" not "FENCHURCH ST." A London, Tilbury and Southend board was carried on the chimney of engines working over the G.E.R. lines and a white disc with a red cross by those running via Upminster cut-off from Barking to Pitsea.

1901 Cab interior of locomotive "Stepney" was light blue.

1902 Engines Nos. 3, 7, 23 and 29 were painted black for working the Whitechapel and Bow section of the District railway, after the electrification of which Nos. 23 and 29 were repainted green, the other two remaining black.

1902 Locomotives Nos. 23 and 29 were rebuilt as condensing tanks, and the tanks were painted with black japan to stand the heat when condensing, without blistering. The cab interiors on these two engines were a light blue.

1902 Engine No. 61 was specially painted for the coronation of King Edward VII and fitted with a copper-topped chimney, which was carried for some years.

Pre 1907 Engines were (14), described in sources as light green, with purple-brown borders round tanks, bunkers, etc., this being edged with vermilion. The tank and bunker-sides also had an inner panelling of black, edged with white lines. The buffer-beams were vermilion, and the engine number appeared thereon. Names were painted in a curved line on the tank sides in large serif gold letters, shaded; the Company's crest being carried immediately below the name in a central position. On engines Nos. 37 to 48 (inclusive), and Nos. 79 to 82 (inclusive) the crest was on a raised plaque, whilst all other engines had transferred crests. The maker's date-plates were lozenge-shaped and were fitted to the bunker-sides.

1907 Engine No. 39 ("Forest Gate") was the first to be painted in the lavender-grey livery that was in temporary use until 1910.

1907 Horse-boxes had the passenger's compartment lettered "GROOM'S COMPARTMENT" in golden-yellow block letters.

1909 Engine No. 53 ("Stepney Green") was painted (14), described in sources as green. Engine No. 80 ("Southend") was painted lavender, and was exhibited thus at the White City Exhibition.

1910 The engine "Thundersley", No. 80 (4–4–2T), was specially decorated for the coronation of King George V by having the tank and bunker sides lined out with gold and relieved by a blue edging and decorated gold corners; the outer bordering being crimson-lake. The chimney cap and safety-valve casing were specially nickel-plated, and the lagging bands round the boiler were polished brass. The cylinder casings were of planished steel and were decorated by a bright steel moulding with the Royal coat-of-arms in relief in the centre of the panel.

Wheel tyres,* drawgear and side chains were finished bright steel, and the bogie and trailing-wheel splashers were outlined with half-round polished brass beading, as were the brake-hangers.

The footplate edge was festooned with gilt chains, which were supported from aluminium pillars; whilst at each corner of the foot-plate were square columns which carried copper vases containing bunches of blue cornflowers.

Centrally on the front foot-plate were fixed life-size busts of the King and Queen, these being supported on white and gold fluted pedestals between which a small fountain played; the water being supplied from the side-tanks.

The smoke-box door was ornamented with wreaths of flowers and a replica of the Royal crown rested upon a purple velvet

* Some wheel tyres were painted lake colour.

cushion at the base of the chimney. Tank and bunker-sides were roped with multi-coloured artificial flowers, with a silver bell at each top corner of the tanks. On either side of the engine's name was a copper vase with flowers, resting on pedestals. Along the tank-tops was an ornamental aluminium rail and a coat-of-arms backed by flags.

The bunker was similarly treated; a life-size bust of Queen Alexandra appearing centrally at the rear. At the front and rear ends of the engine were scroll-shaped boards, the front one bearing the words "GOD BLESS THEIR MAJESTIES", and that at the rear "LONG LIVE THEIR MAJESTIES", in gold outlined letters on a white ground.

Destination boards were white, with gold letters, and code discs were made of mirror-glass.

The decoration was carried out under the personal supervision of R. H. Whitelegg.

1910 The pre-1907 livery was reverted to, as the lavender-grey used between 1907 and 1910 did not wear well. On absorption the Midland Railway Company removed the crests and also many of the engine names, and substituted the large "Midland" numerals. This livery, together with the use of the M.R. crest lasted until 1928. This livery was (28), described in sources as "Midland red", for passenger engines, with black panelling and yellow lining. Goods engines were unlined black. (Under the London, Midland & Scottish all ex-L.T.S.R. engines were painted a glossy black relieved with vermilion lining. This lining was abolished in 1939.)

1912 After absorption by the Midland a cast number-plate was fitted on the smoke-box. (*See also* 1910.)

1912 The London, Tilbury and Southend Railway was taken over by the Midland Railway. (*See also* 1910.)

1913 The stock working on to the District railway was first painted a dark green, then scarlet and brown.

1914 Ealing to Southend stock was of varnished teak, as was all other stock.

1914 (June) The stock was painted as the Midland Railway stock.

1921 Coaches were running in both varnished teak and crimson-lake.

MARYPORT AND CARLISLE RAILWAY

THIS very lucrative little railway which boasted only 42¾ route miles of track was incorporated in 1837 and opened throughout in 1845, other additions taking place until 1867.

The rolling-stock of the Maryport and Carlisle consisted (in 1922) of 28 tender engines, 5 tank engines, 77 passenger vehicles, 1,480 goods vehicles, and 73 service vehicles; but in spite of its smallness, it survived until it was amalgamated into the London, Midland and Scottish Railway in the 1923 groupings.

The earliest Locomotive Engineer was Mr. Scott who was succeeded by George Tosh (1854–1870), followed by Hugh Smellie (1870–1878) who went to the Glasgow and South Western Railway in a similar capacity in 1878. He was followed by Robert Campbell (1878–1893), William Robinson (1893–1898), William Coulthard (1898–1904) and J. B. Adamson (1904–1922).

1895 Coaches were painted to represent red teak, and some of these older vehicles lasted in this livery in local service between Bull Gill and Workington until 1912.

1897 Locomotives were green, with black bands lined on both sides with vermilion. Buffer-beams were red with gold figures. Tender lettering was in gold, shaded red. Number-plates were bright brass raised figures on a vermilion background.

Coaches were varnished teak, with gold lettering, shaded black.

1900 Locomotive colour was of a very similar shade (16) to the well-known Great Western Railway locomotive green. This was edged with black lining with a fine white line outside it and a vermilion line within. Boiler-bands were black, edged with a fine white line on each side. Foot-plate valances and steps were black, edged with a fine white line. The tank or tender sides carried the words "MARYPORT AND CARLISLE" in gold letters, shaded with two shades of green on the left and to below; being counter-shaded with black on the right.

1900 The 2–4–0 tender engines carried the letters "M & CR" on the tender panels, the company's crest on the leading splashers, and a large cast brass oval number-plate with "M & C" in sans-serif letters above the number. The 0–6–0 tank engines had the crest on the bunker-side panels, and "M & CR" forward of the oval number-plates on the tank sides. The 0–6–0 tender goods locomotives did not carry the initials of the Company on the tenders, nor was the crest used. The 0–6–0 tender engines with open splashers, has these brass-beaded.

All three types of engine had brass bases to safety-valves and copper piping to injectors and whistles. In cases where double sets of buffers were used, the whole of the double buffer-beam was painted vermilion.

1901 Coaches were natural teak colour, varnished. Locomotives were a dark green.

1905 Coaches began to be painted with upper panels a faint greenish tinge, and the lower panels were painted the same green as that used for the locomotives. The upper panels were edged with a fine green line, bordered on the inside with yellow; and a narrow yellow line also surrounded the lower panels. The initials "M AND CR" and the vehicle number, together with the class designation appeared in plain green-shaded gold block letters on the waist panels. Roofs were white and the coach ends black.

Goods stock was painted a dark grey, with "M & C" in large white letters on the left-hand side, and the number of the vehicle on the right-hand side in the same size as the figures and letters on the left side. A rectangular number-plate on the sole-bar bore the initials "M & CR" above the number in raised white letters. All ironwork was black, and the roofs of covered vans were white.

1905 Coaches changed from teak colour to green lower and white upper panels.

Pre 1906 Engines carried the abbreviated title of the company—"M & CR" (without full-stops after the characters) shaded with two shades of green to the left and below and counter shaded with black to the right hand side. The engine number-plates were oval in shape with raised brass figures and rim, the letters "M & C" in block characters appearing above the number in the centre of the oval, and the building date appeared below.

1909 Coaches were (16), described in sources as a dark green, with white upper panels. Locomotives a dark green, relieved with vermilion lining and gold letters.

Wagons were lead-coloured, with "M & C" in large white letters.

1908 Engines were green with black and red lining. Coaches were green with white upper panels, having been lately changed from varnished teak.

1913 Some of the green engines had polished brass safety-valve covers.

1915 Coaches were (16), described in sources as green, with white panels. Locomotives were painted the same green.

1916 Engines were green, of a similar shade to 1937 Great Western locomotives. Edging was black, with a white line outside and a vermilion line inside. Boiler-bands were black with a white line on each side. Foot-plate valances and steps were black, lined fine white. Tenders or tank-sides carried the full title—"MARYPORT AND CARLISLE" in gold letters, shaded with two shades of green on the left and below, and countershaded with black on the right-hand side. Coaches had their lower panels painted the same shade of green as that of the engines, and their upper panels were white, with the faintest cream tinge, these being edged with a fine green line bordered on the inside with a yellow line. A thin yellow line also surrounded the lower green panels. The initials "M & CR" and the coach number, together with the class appeared in green-shaded gold block letters on the waist panel. On guards' brake-composite coaches the initials of the company were written "M & C", with square full-stops after each character.

Engine buffer-beams were vermilion, and carried the engine's number in gold block figures shaded similarly to the rest of the lettering.

1916 Coach roofs were painted white, and their underframes and ends, black.

Goods stock was painted dark grey, and was lettered "M. & C." (with full-stops) on the left-hand panel and numbered on the right-hand panel with figures of the same size as the initials on the left. A rectangular number-plate on the sole-bar bore the initials "M. & C.R." above the wagon number in raised white characters.

The roofs of covered vans were painted white.

NORTH STAFFORDSHIRE RAILWAY 2–2–2 LOCOMOTIVE NO. 18, BUILT IN 1884 IN ORIGINAL LIVERY (P. 186)

METROPOLITAN DISTRICT RAILWAY

USUALLY called the "District" Railway, this line, with the Metropolitan Railway, formed the original "UNDERGROUND" Railways of London, the two systems being connected by joint lines. The District Railway was incorporated in 1864, and the first portion—from Kensington to Westminster—was opened in December 1868.

In 1918, P. V. McMahon was Superintendent of Power.

Up to 1871 All stock and locomotives were Metropolitan; the District engines built in that year were dull green, and continued in this livery until electrification.

1897 Enamelled iron plates were used to denote the class figures on the coaches.

1898 Steam locomotives were painted a dark olive green with black bands and vermilion lining. Domes were bright brass, and the buffer-beams red. Lettering was white, shaded with black (Fig. 20, p. 34). Carriages were either left plain teak and varnished or painted a dark shade of brown. The complete ends of brake-vans were red. Coach numbers were in gold shaded with blue.

1903 The first electric train coaches were painted a bright yellow, picked out with maroon.

1909 Train destination boards were of enamelled iron. Red and white for the "non-stop" trains, and blue and white for the "stopping" trains.

1913 The electric locomotives and cars were scarlet, with a chocolate strip at top and bottom. Roofs were a lead grey. In the steam days locomotives were olive green with brass domes. Carriages were then a red-chocolate colour.

1914 The all-steel stock was painted in the standard red and lake.

1918 Locomotives were chocolate-coloured, and coaches teak.

1923 The two steam 4–4–0 tank engines still in service in the engineering department were in the old dark olive green livery.

1926 Locomotive No. 34 was repainted black. Tanks were lined out in red and carried numbers and letters uniform in type and size with engine No. 34 on the Metropolitan (see p. 147) which was built in 1881. Originally, wrought-iron chimneys and polished brass domes were retained.

The Beyer Peacock 4–4–0T engine was purchased, which was No. 22 in the Metropolitan list, built in 1860. She was renumbered 35, and was painted a rich chocolate colour, with tanks and bunker lined out in black, with two fine white lines. The standard word "UNDERGROUND" was in the centre of the tank, below the "35". Safety-valve and dome, which were originally bright brass, were painted a chocolate colour.

METROPOLITAN DISTRICT RAILWAY CREST

METROPOLITAN RAILWAY

ORIGINALLY incorporated as the North Metropolitan Railway in 1853, the Company was re-incorporated with its later title the following year. Some of its earlier steam locomotives were designed by Mr. Gooch of the Great Western Railway, but from 1868 until 1873, Robert Harvey Burnett was the locomotive superintendent, being followed by Mr. Tomlinson (1873–1885), who was succeeded by J. J. Hanbury in 1885. In 1896, T. F. Clarke took over the locomotive department, leaving in 1903. C. Jones was appointed Chief Electrical and Locomotive Engineer in 1917.

1863 The very first engines were a dark green, being named in brass panels on the boiler immediately to the rear of the smoke-box. Numbers were carried in brass figures on the front of the chimney.

1864–85 Locomotives were bright green with a copper top to the chimneys upon which the engine number appeared in brass letters. Domes were polished brass.

1875 The locomotive "Hercules" (built by Beyer Peacock) had its name-plates on the boiler barrel immediately to the rear of the smoke-box. The date-plate was oval in shape, and appeared on the tank sides. The number of the engine appeared in brass figures on the front of the chimney.

1885-96 The locomotive colour was changed to red, which was retained until 1896–7. The engine number was painted in the middle of the side tanks in the centre of a double-lined oval, which had the words "METROPOLITAN RAILWAY" in serif capitals enclosed between the concentric ovals. (See Fig. 87, p. 280.)

1885 (?) Locomotives were painted a dull red, with black banding and stripes, with yellow lines on either side. Buffer-beams were vermilion, and the numbers on the tank sides were in yellow inside a double-lined oval, the word "METROPOLITAN" appearing between the lines of the oval. These letters and figures were shaded with black. The locomotive number was also displayed in brass figures on the front of the chimney of most engines.

At the same period the different classes were distinguished by the coaches being painted differently. Thus the first class carriages had white upper panels lined with fine red and blue lines; and second and third class were of varnished teak. Coach lettering was in gold, shaded with black—for all classes.

The few goods wagons and goods brakes were dark grey, with white lettering.

1886 During Mr. Hanbury's régime the locomotives were a uniform chocolate colour, with brass numbers on a black chimney. There was a copper top to the condenser escape pipe.

1889 The engine "Hercules" was rebuilt with very large concentric oval lined number-plates on the tank sides; both border and number was painted on. The date-plate was removed to the upper part of the cab side-sheets.

Pre 1895 Prior to 1895 steam locomotives were a dark blue-green, with the side panels marked with wide bands of a lighter shade; with white lines on the left and upper sides, and black lines on the lower and right hand sides; thus giving the effect of relief. The tops of chimneys were copper, and domes polished brass. Buffer-beams were red.

1896 Locomotives Nos. 77 and 78 had cast iron chimneys and polished brass dome covers. They were painted red with the company's name cast on the leading sand-boxes. Brass number-plates were carried on the bunker-sides, on which large figures appeared within an oval; both figures and border being raised. The tank sides were divided by lining into three panels.

1899 The "new" coaches were of varnished teak with gold stripes with four red lines on either side of the gold.

1899 The new steam stock for Verney Junction was varnished teak and gold stripes with a fine red line on each side.

1903 (Oct.) The coaches of the Ealing and South Harrow Railway (the electrified section of the Metropolitan District Railway) had rather novel liveries, the two trains of four cars each having their first coach painted a greenish yellow, the second and third with white upper panels and red lower, and the fourth coach in the train a greenish yellow, like the first. The other train was composed of one car with white upper and red lower panels, and three cars a bright red.

1906 The steam trains on the Hammersmith service were painted cream and teak colours. Lettering was in gold, shaded with blue —similar to the electric trains.

1909 Locomotive domes were painted green to match the boiler.

1910 Engines were slightly darker than Midland "red" (28). Coaches were varnished teak. Wagons were grey, with white lettering. Goods brakes had vermilion ends.

1916 Locomotives 94, 95, 96 and 97 (Lord Aberconway, etc.) had the crest on the tank sides with "METROPOLITAN" above and "RAILWAY" below in curved lines of block letters shaded below and to the left. The date-plate was on the smoke-box saddle, and a curved brass name-plate over the front driving-wheel splasher. The number-plates were on the bunker sides in rectangular frames of brass, with raised figures.

1928 Name-plates were fitted to electric locomotives, (*e.g.* No. 9, "John Milton").

1939 (Summer) Locomotive No. 8, "Sherlock Holmes", was the last to remain painted in the Metropolitan livery.

METROPOLITAN RAILWAY CREST

OTHER LONDON UNDERGROUND RAILWAYS

Central London Railway

1900 The bogie locomotives were painted an "invisible" purple-brown, and lined out in yellow.

1905 (c) The two 0–6–0T locomotives used for tunnel repairing and inspection were painted a medium shade of greenish brown (not true olive green). The lining was in red and white, the scheme being a wide black banded border having a red line on its inner edge. Two inches inside this red line was another white line with incurved corners. Buffer-beams were vermilion, edged with black, having a white line on its inner edge; this line following the buffer socket-plates. Main frames were brown outside and vermilion within, the outsides being edged with a black band and a white line on its inner edge. Axle-ends were black, outlined with white, and wheels were brown, with black tyres, a red line running round between the two colours. Lettering "C.L.R." was in gold, shaded with red to the left and below, and picked out in white. The maker's plate was oval in shape and was of polished brass; with engraved black lettering. Boiler-bands were black, with a red line on each edge (between the black and the body-colour), and a white line in the centre of the black. Dome-casing and safety-valve casing was of polished brass. Smoke-box and chimney were black. Inside of cab was brown in its upper half, and black below.

1914 Electric locomotives were chocolate. Passenger stock chocolate with white upper panels. Motor cars had the louvres at the back of the driver's compartment picked out in vermilion.

Bakerloo and Watford Extension Railway

1917 Coaches were dark lake, with white upper panels. Lettering was in gold. The stock was otherwise standard London Electric Railway stock.

City and South London Railway

The first electric locomotives were painted chocolate, but were later chocolate panelled out in deep chrome yellow. Coaches were chocolate all over.

1908 Coaches of varnished teak, the only lettering was "C. & S.L. Ry." in straw-yellow unshaded block letters, the full-stops being square. The coach numbers appeared at one end of the coach only on the left-hand side in 2½ in. straw-yellow block letters: *e.g.*, No. 10.

Great Northern, Piccadilly and Brompton Railway

1907 Coaches were "Derby" red ("Midland" red), with "GNP & B" on the centre panels of the sides in gold. Coach numbers were in gold serif figures at each end of the coaches.

Great Northern and City Railway

1906 New all-steel stock was teak-coloured, picked out with Indian red and gold.

MIDLAND RAILWAY CREST (*page 152*)

MIDLAND RAILWAY

FORMED in 1844 by the union of the Midland Counties Railway, the North Midland Railway, and the Birmingham and Derby Junction Railway, the Midland Railway did not have its own tracks into London until 1868, when St. Pancras Station was opened for traffic. Prior to this, the Midland trains had worked over the Great Northern into King's Cross for ten years, and earlier still, over the L.N.W.R. into Euston.

The Company later absorbed the following lines :—

1845 Sheffield and Rotherham Railway (1838)
Erewash Valley Railway (1847)

1846 Leicester and Swannington Railway (1832)
The original Bristol and Gloucester Railway, which in 1837 became known as the Bristol and Gloucestershire Railway, was itself composed of :—
(*a*) Gloucester and Cheltenham Railway (1810)
(*b*) Birmingham and Gloucester Railway (1840)

1848 Mansfield and Pinxton Railway (1819)

1851 Leeds and Bradford Railway (1846)

1861 Dursley and Midland Junction Railway (1856)

1863 Furness and Midland Railway
Chesterfield and Brampton Railway (1873)
Manchester, Buxton, Matlock and Midland Junction Railway (1848)
North Western Railway (The "Little North Western") (1849); which included Morecambe Railway and Harbour (1848)

1872 Halesowen and Bromsgrove Branch Railway. (Later called Halesowen Railway) (1883)

1874 Hay Railway (1816)
Hereford, Hay and Brecon Railway (1863)

Wolverhampton, Walsall and Midland Junction Railway (1879)

1875 Birmingham West Suburban Railway (1876)

1876 Tewkesbury and Malvern Railway (1862)
Wolverhampton and Walsall Railway (1872)
The amalgamated Swansea Valley Railway, Swansea Vale Railway and Palleg Railroad. (These three lines were amalgamated in 1861.)

1877 Manchester South District Railway

1878 Stonehouse and Nailsworth Railway (1867)

1881 Keighley and Worth Valley Railway (1867)

1882 Evesham and Redditch Railway (1866)
Bedford and Northampton Railway (1872)

1886 Hemel Hempstead Railway (1877)

1888 Dore and Chinley Railway (1844)

1890 Bristol Port Railway, and pier

1894 Lydney and Lydbrook Railway (1813); later Severn and Wye Railway and Canal; later (1879) Severn and Wye, and Severn Bridge Railway. (Run jointly with G.W.R.)

1897 Kettering, Thrapston and Huntingdon Railway (1866)

1899 Barnoldswick Railway (1871)

1902 Tottenham and Hampstead Railway (1868)

1912 Whitechapel and Bow Railway (1902) (L.T. & S. share)
London, Tilbury and Southend Railway (1854).

1914 Tottenham and Forest Gate Railway (1894)

The locomotive engineers of the Midland Railway were as follows :—

1844–1873	Matthew Kirtley
1873–1903	S. W. Johnson (from G.E.R.)
1903–1909	Richard Mountford Deeley
1909–1922	Sir Henry Fowler

1870 When built, and after rebuilding, the "800" class of engine carried raised brass painted numbers on the centre-line of the boiler slightly in front of the leading splasher. When built in 1876 the tenders were panelled in three, but when rebuilt, the letters "M" and "R" appeared in two panels in gold serif letters. This also applied to the "170" class of 2–4–0's.

1875 (c) Engines of the "800" class were painted green (6 or 14) with the wheels also painted the same colour, but with black tyres. Boiler bands were black, with a fine yellow line on each side. The cab sides, fenders, frames and splashers were all outlined by a narrow black border, with a fine yellow line on the inside edge. Coupling-rod cranks were painted bright vermilion, and whistle, safety-valve casing and the Salter columns on the dome were all polished brass. Handrails and coupling-rods were brightly burnished steel. The engine numbers appeared in separate brass figures, and the initials "MR" were in gold, shaded in blue and white.

1882 Two engines were painted experimentally in the crimson-lake.

1882 (6 or 14), described in sources as green (see plate facing p. 80), was abolished as a locomotive colour.

1883* The locomotive green was definitely changed to crimson at the end of this summer. Ten or a dozen engines had already been painted crimson in 1881 as a trial.

1883 The first engines to be painted in "Midland red" were Nos. 1657–1666. The series immediately preceding (Nos. 1562–1581) were green.

1884 Engines were painted a "dark red", instead of (6 or 14), bright green, on the score of economy.

1889 Exhibition engine No. 1853 (4–2–2). Safety-valve levers red. Whistles, safety-valve casings, spectacle-plate window rims (14½ ins. diam.) were polished brass. Numerals "1835" were 6½ ins. high and were polished brass (see Fig. 83, p. 258), as were the 2 in. wide beadings round the driving-wheel splashers. The driving-wheel axle-boxes and the four lubricators, were brass; as were the handles and rims of the head-lamps. The trailing wheel and tender axle-boxes' top plates were of polished steel.

The body colour was (28), described as "Midland dark red tint", with a small black border with a single fine yellow line next the dark red. This lining was placed on cab front-sheet and side-sheets, round the spectacle-plate windows, at the base of the dome, round the driving-wheel splashers, the boiler lagging bands, and round the edge of the dark red main-frames which stood above the foot-plate under the smoke-box. Also along the outside frames and

* It will be seen that there is a great diversity of opinion (both from living authorities and from all available literary sources) as to the precise date of the locomotive livery change from "green" to "crimson".

foot-steps, round the guard-irons (which were vermilion red), and round the dark red sand-boxes, the driving-wheel horn-plates, and round the other axle-boxes. Wheel tyres were painted black with one yellow line, whilst the centres of the bogie wheels were red, lined with two yellow circles, with little "Vees" at the top and bottom of the spokes. Buffer-beams and sockets were vermilion, edged with black, with a fine white line. Buffer sockets had this edging at their outer ends only. (Date-plates were as Fig. 84, p. 258.) The lettering on the buffer-beams and tender side-sheets was in gold, with blue shading to the right and below. The tender side-panels had two rectangular bands of black with a yellow stripe on either side; and the coping was also lined out in yellow.

The outside springs of the engine were dark red with a yellow stripe along the bottom and top leaf. The cab interior was grained light stone shade, edged with a broad black band separated from the light stone by a fine white line.

1896 By 1896 all engines were painted (28), described in sources as dark red, being banded with black with a yellow stripe on each side. The lining was rounded at every corner it traversed. On some tank locomotives, the black band was omitted, and the remaining yellow lines drawn with square corners. On other engines, both band and lines disappeared, and splashers, tanks and cab were singly panelled round with a black and yellow line run on the inside of the latter. Cab interiors were painted and grained a light oak colour edged with black, a white line appearing inside the black on express engines. Buffer-beams were vermilion with the letters "MR" in gold, shaded with blue. Engine numbers were of solid brass with separate figures.

1896 The letters "MR" on the tender sides were in gold, shaded blue. Domes were painted, but safety-valve covers were of polished brass.

Coaches were (28), described as a dark chocolate-red, and were panelled round in black. The inner edges of the panels were run round with a gold stripe, having a fine vermilion line on each side of it. Lettering was in gold, shaded with red, and underframes were black, with a gold stripe and a fine vermilion line.

Sleeping cars were a dark umber brown, with profuse decorations in gold and scarlet; being lettered in gold, shaded with light blue, grey and white.

1897 (Dec.) Locomotives Nos. 150, 153, 154, 155 and 204 (4–4–0's) had "M.R." on the backs of the tenders or bunkers, and a round-topped "3", instead of the older flat-topped figure ("3"). (Note difference of numeral style between Figs. 83 and 85, p. 258.)

1901 Two types of destination boards were in use; one with gold lettering on dark crimson, and the other white lettering on china-blue background.

1902 In August, the 7 ft. 6 in. single driver locomotive No. 1863 was noticed to have a coronation crown painted on the driving-wheel splashers. The engine was stationed at Liverpool at the time of observation.

1905 Engines Nos. 429 and 435 were liveried as in 1908 but had cut-out numerals on the cab sides and no number on the tender, the date-plate being mounted on the frames between the front and middle driving-wheel splashers.

Engines Nos. 666, 582 and 996 were similarly liveried, but had the letters "MR" on the tender side-panels.

1905 Up to the end of this year the engine buffer-beams had the letters "MR" on them, but after that date had only the engine number and the name of the engine's shed in small letters thus:

M NOTTN. R
453

1906 (c) There were many minor variations in engine liveries about this time, and below is a short list of individual locomotives with some details.

(*a*) Locomotives Nos. 803, 813, 823, 827, and 822 (4–4–0) had the engine numbers in cut-out brass numerals fixed to the cab side-sheets (which were square). The letters "M.R." appeared on the buffer-beams in serif letters. The front driving-wheel splashers were brass-beaded, the company's crest appearing thereon.

(*b*) Locomotive No. 806 (4–4–0) had the number in cut out numerals on the rear driving-wheel splasher, and the crest on the leading splasher. Splashers and coupling-rod splashers were brass-beaded. The safety-valve casing was also brass. The letters "MR" appeared on the tender sides.

(*c*) Engines Nos. 169 and 186 were liveried as No. 806 but had not the crest on the splashers. The engine number was painted on the tender sides. Engines Nos.

205, 1338, 1577, etc., were liveried as No. 806, but had "MR" on the buffer-beams in block letters, shaded to the left and back-shaded to the right; both in a downwards direction.

(*d*) Locomotive No. 1504 (2–4–0) was liveried as No. 806, but had "MR" in serif letters on the buffer-beam, the engine number on the rear driving-wheel splashers, the crest on the front splashers, and "MR" in serif letters on the tender sides. The safety-valve casing was brass.

(*e*) Engine No. 1579 (4–4–0) was as No. 806, but had "MR" in block letters on the buffer-beam, and the number-plate fitted to the smoke-box door.

(*f*) The "Single" engines had tenders double-lined in yellow into two panels. Numbers were in cut-out numerals on the cab sides, and the crest was on the driving-wheel splashers, which were brass-beaded. The date-plate was mounted under the smoke-box.

(*g*) Engine No. 1844 (0–6–0T) had "M 1844 R" on the tank sides, the numerals being of raised brass, and the letters, serifed. Tank, bunkers, valances, and splashers were single lined yellow; as also were the upper cab-sides. The date-plate was mounted on the bunker sides.

(This livery also applied definitely to engines Nos. 2742, 1346, 1391 and 1157.)

(*h*) Engines of class 2 (0–6–0) had the letters "MR" in serif within the two, double-lined panels on the tender, and had cut-out brass engine numbers on the cab sides. The "MR" on the buffer-beams was in block letters, and the date-plate was mounted on the middle driving-wheel splasher.

Engines of this class with single-lined, single panels on the tender had their numbers in large yellow painted figures thereon, and had the crest on the cab side-sheets in place of the number.

1906 Very large numbers on tender sides commenced to be used.

1906 Coaches began to bear the word "MIDLAND" along the top panels.

1906 Engines Nos. 2185, 2196, 2202 (rebuilt 4–4–0's) had the brass-beadings painted over black. Brass number-plates also disappeared, and a white steel plate was substituted on the smoke-box door.

1906 The small 4–4–0T engines which were formerly the property of the Eastern and Midlands Railway were used on the Hemel Hempstead Branch. The engines were painted in the yellow livery of the Eastern and Midlands Railway (*see also p.* 222), and attracted a great deal of attention on that account. The engines were coupled to one of the early Midland Railway Pullman cars to form a "motor train".

1906 The neat and legible brass engine number-plates on the cab-sides were abolished, and the small oblong plates on the smoke-box were substituted from this date.

1906 (Sept.) To distinguish the classes of coach compartments, the numbers "1" or "3" was painted on the doors instead of "first" and "third" as previously. The word "MIDLAND" in decorative block letters also appeared on a small black fascia board over the centre windows.

1907 The motor train set on the Hemel Hempstead branch was painted standard Midland colours, but the engine number "10" appeared on the side tanks of the engine as well as on the centre panels of the Pullman coach.

1907 Enamelled weight-plates were fitted at the top corners of the ends of coaches stating the unloaded weight in complete tons.

1907 Some of the goods engines were running in black livery.

1908 The older 0–6–0 tender engines with outside springs on the tender had the engine number on the tender and also on the smoke-box door. Safety-valve casings were brass, and the date-plate was on the middle driving-wheel splasher. The "MR" appeared in block letters on the buffer-beam. (Nos. 3215 and 3509) Those engines working on the L.T. & S.R. had curved plates with the word "SOUTHEND" thereon, mounted either $\frac{1}{3}$ the way up the chimney or below the smoke-box (in which latter position the plate was also curved). (*See also L.T. & S. Ry., p.* 138.)

1908 Larger class figures were used on coach doors, as well as smaller figures inside the doors.

1908 An experiment was tried by Mr. Deeley by placing the engine number on the tender sides thus: "M 64 R", in one panel, instead of the engine number only.

1910 Engines were numbered in large figures on the tender sides, also in bright steel on smoke-box doors. On the outside of the upper part of the cab sides was a small brass figure indicating the power class of the engine; "1" for the most powerful type, "2" for the next most powerful and "3" for other types. An oval number-plate on the lower part of the smoke-box door showed the shed to which the engine was attached.

1911 A saving was effected by painting goods engines black.

1912 Engines had "M.R." on the buffer-beams in gold letters. The number appeared on the tenders in gold figures, as well as in raised steel figures on the front of the smoke-box. The company's crest appeared on the rear driving-wheel splashers of "Compounds".

1913 Engines were (28), described in sources as a "brown chocolate" (crimson), with black and yellow lining. Safety-valve covers and domes were also crimson. Underframes were crimson, unlined, and the fluting of coupling-rods was black. Buffer-beams and buffer-shanks were red. The number appeared in large serif figures of gold in the single panel on the tender. The building date-plate was of polished brass on a red background, and was placed on the smoke-box saddle. The company's crest appeared on the cab side-sheets.

Locomotive number 483 when rebuilt was lined out with black bands only—no yellow lines.

1914 On main-line passenger engines the power class number appeared on the cab sides immediately to the front of the side look-out cut-away; whilst in the top right-hand corner of the lower part of the cab side-sheets a small white tablet of rectangular shape appeared upon which was written in small block letters the driver's name and the locomotive shed number. The shed number also appeared in an oval plate fitted on the lower portion of the smoke-box door.

1914 Passenger engines were (28), described in sources as crimson-lake, lined out with black and yellow. Wheels were "red" from 1873 to 1903 and black from 1903 to 1922. Yellow lining appeared on black wheel tyres only.

Coaches were crimson-lake, lined with yellow. Roofs were lead grey, and the clerestory sides crimson-lake.

1917 Goods wagons were light grey.

1918 Coaches were (28), described as crimson-lake, and engines the same colour.

Crest on page 151

MIDLAND AND GREAT NORTHERN JOINT RAILWAY

THIS important East to West "joint" railway was formed by the successive amalgamations of many East Anglian lines which originally formed the Eastern and Midlands Railway in 1883; the title Midland and Great Northern Joint Railway being taken in 1893, when the Midland and Great Northern Railways assumed joint ownership.

The Norwich and Spalding Railway, the Spalding and Bourne Railway (opened 1862), and the Lynn and Sutton Bridge Railway (opened 1861), became amalgamated as the Midland and Eastern Railway in 1866; this railway acquiring the Spalding and Sutton Bridge Railway in 1877.

By Act of 1882 the Lynn and Fakenham, the Yarmouth and North Norfolk (originally the Great Yarmouth and Stalham Light Railway), and the Yarmouth Union were amalgamated to form the Eastern and Midlands Railway.

By Act of 1883 the Eastern and Midlands Railway absorbed the Midland and Eastern and the Peterborough, Wisbech and Sutton Bridge Railways.

The locomotive superintendent *circa* 1918 was William Marriott, and the Company's works were at Melton Constable.

The Midland and Great Northern Joint Railway was not amalgamated into any of the "big four" at the 1923 grouping, but remained a separate entity, like the Somerset and Dorset Railway; being under the joint control of the L.M.S. and the L.N.E. Railways; and as such persisted down to Nationalization.

1874 Locomotive No. 13 (0–6–0 tender) had rectangular number-plates on the tank sides, with the Sharp, Stewart date-plate below. The letters "E & M Ry." appeared on the tank sides above the date-plate. All lining had incurved corners. (Fig. 4, p. 6.)

1882 Engine No. 19 (4–4–0T), had the number and lettering on the tank sides thus :—

19 M & (*crest*) G N

All panelling and number-plate as No. 1A. A brass dome and safety-valve casing were fitted, and the square cab windows were brass-beaded.

The letters being shaded to the left and below and blocked to the right and below. Tank, bunker back and sides were lined in one panel with rounded corners. There were brass bands fitted round the foot and waist of the chimney, and the safety-valve casing was polished brass. The building-plate was mounted on the bunker side. The letter "A" under the number-plate was cut out of brass.

1882 Locomotive No. 1A (0–6–0t), as rebuilt at Melton Constable had numbers and lettering arranged thus :—

M & $\frac{1}{A}$ G N

1891 Locomotives were green, with the exception of the two locomotives obtained from the London and North Western Railway which were black when delivered. Also No. 16A (the Melton Constable works engine) was black with red lining. When locomotive No. 42 (ex L.N.W.R., 2–4–0) was rebuilt, it was painted and lined in the Midland and Great Northern Joint livery, but with the earlier form of lettering (see plate facing p. 129).

1893 The form of lettering used on tank and tender sides was, successively, "Jt.M. & G.N.R." and "M. & G.N.J.R."

1894 Duplicate letters were added to the numbers of some engines, and consisted of a cut-out brass "A" placed below the number-plates.

1896 Engine colour (32), described in several sources as a light yellow-brown, slightly lighter than Mr. Stroudley's engine colour. Lining was black bands with sulphur yellow lines on each side of the black. Tenders and tanks were panelled in this way, whilst splashers and frames were edged with black, with a yellow line between the black and the yellow-brown. Wheels were light yellow-brown, with black tyres and axle-ends. Buffer-beams were signal red, with a black outer band and a sulphur-yellow line between the red panel and the black border. The initials on the tanks and tenders were in gold, shaded to the right and below with royal blue. Underframes were signal red, and the cab interiors were light yellow-brown.* Some locomotives had number-plates of brass, with raised polished figures against a signal red background, whilst others had plain solid brass figures.

Coaches were painted and grained teak, with yellow lines round the quarter-lights, doors and mouldings. Coach ends were dark brown, and the underframes were a lighter shade of green. Lettering was in gold, shaded to the right and below with signal red.

Goods stock was slate-grey with white block lettering.

1904 Engines were still painted the same "light yellow". Coaches were grained to represent mahogany with a dull crimson tint, the grain of the wood being greatly exaggerated. The vertical edges of the doors and door-frames were painted a brilliant royal blue.

Coaches were to be seen in the lake colour of the Midland Railway and the teak of the Great Northern Railway, but with the letters "M. & G.N." instead of "M.R." and "G.N.R." thereon, respectively.

Locomotives began to be painted (32), described in sources as a much brighter yellow than previously. (*i.e.* in 1896.)

1905 Engine No. 41 (4–4–2T) had lettering on the tanks "Midland & Great Northern", together with the company's crest in a design, the lettering being gold, shaded to the right and below in royal blue. Number-plates were of brass with raised and polished letters and figures on a signal-red background. These plates were retained after rebuilding.

1908 Engines were painted (32), described in sources as gamboge, being lined out with black bands with sulphur-yellow lines on either side. The works engine (No. 16A) was painted black, with vermilion lining.

1910 Locomotives had the number placed on the rear driving-wheel splashers (in the case of tender types), with the crest on the forward splasher. The building date-plate had black letters and figures on a signal red background, and was fixed to the smoke-box saddle. Buffer-beams and buffer shanks were signal red, as were the safety-valve springs and levers. The safety-valve casings were polished brass. Guard-irons were painted the gamboge body-colour, as were the sand-boxes and bogie stretcher.

* Probably light stone.

1910 The saloon coach designed by Mr. Ivatt was finished in varnished teak with gold lettering shaded with bright blue.

1915 Locomotives were described as being a golden ochre (32), and the coaches as varnished teak.

1923 At grouping, engines were painted all black and lined out in sulphur yellow, with the letters "M. & G.N." on the tender sides in "L.M.S." style of letters. The engine numbers were placed on the cab sides.

Coaches were varnished teak finish. Goods brakes were painted red oxide and lettered in mid-chrome yellow.

1925 Nov. Passenger engines were still painted "yellow", but goods types were chocolate-brown.

1928 Engines Nos. 44 and 74 (class C) were painted chocolate with yellow lining-out and lettering. The company's crest appeared on the driving-wheel splashers. 0–6–0T No. 96 was painted black, and No. 98 chocolate.

1934 A few engines were still running in their original "yellow" livery and lettering.

MIDLAND AND GREAT NORTHERN JOINT RAILWAY CREST

NORTH BRITISH RAILWAY

ORIGINALLY incorporated in 1844, for a line from Edinburgh to Berwick, which was opened in 1846, the North British Railway included the first public railway in Scotland, the Monkland and Kirkintilloch Railway, which was authorised in 1824. More than fifty originally independent companies were included in the North British Railway, of which most important are the following :—

Monkland and Kirkintilloch Railway (opened 1831)
Ballochney Railway (opened 1828)
Edinburgh and Dalkeith Railway (opened 1826)
Slamanan Railway (opened 1835)
Edinburgh and Glasgow Railway (opened 1842)
(*a*) Edinburgh and Northern Railway (opened 1847)
(*b*) Edinburgh, Leith and Granton (Newhaven) Railway
Railways (*a*) and (*b*) above were united to form the Edinburgh, Perth and Dundee Railway.
Dundee and Arbroath Railway (opened 1836)
Arbroath and Montrose Railway (opened 1860)
Montrose and Bervie Railway (opened 1860)
Border Union Railway (opened 1849)
West Highland Railway (opened 1894–1901)

Mr. Paton was the first locomotive superintendent of the North British Railway (*circa* 1856), the post then being successively filled as follows :—

1861–1867	William Hurst	1881–1903	Matthew Holmes
1867–1875	T. Wheatley	1903–1919	W. P. Reid
1875–1881	Dugald Drummond	1919–1923	W. Chalmers

Pre 1870 Engine boilers, cabs and rear splasher panel-plates were dark green, lined out with black edged with vermilion. Domes were painted black, as were chimneys. Underframes were Indian red, so were the leading splashers. Wheels were dark green, and the solid bogie-wheels of the Wheatley 4–4–0's had vermilion lines round the rims. Buffers and buffer-beams were vermilion. Number-plates had raised polished letters and figures on a black background. Coupling-rods were polished steel.

The Paton singles (ex-Edinburgh and Glasgow Railway) which later became the North British "211" class were painted green, with polished copper caps to their chimneys and polished brass safety-valve casings. Underframes were generally Indian red, but some were black.

1871 Locomotive No. 224 (Wheatley, 4–4–0) was described as being painted olive-khaki shade, which was lined with a black line flanked with red, with rounded corners. Buffer-beams were red, and the wheels were the same shade as the body, excepting the disc bogies which were lined red round the rims.

Underframes, splashers and coupling-rod splashers were (29), described in sources as Indian red. Feed-pipes were brass, as were the number-plates on the cab side-sheets. Whistle and the small fitting to the rear of the chimney were also bright brass. The sand-boxes were painted the same shade as the frames, as were the footsteps.

1873 Locomotives Nos. 476–479 and 486–493 were described as being originally painted a "dark yellow" similar to that used on the London, Brighton and South Coast Railway locomotives.

Pre 1876 During Mr. Wheatley's régime, the engines were bright green, sometimes with polished brass domes and safety-valve covers.

Coaches were varnished teak.

1885 Mr. Holmes adopted a vermilion line (omitted from the "Stroudley" type of livery introduced by Mr. Drummond) and darkened the yellow body-colour. (See Fig. 43, p. 114.)

1892 Engines of both passenger and goods classes were generally olive-green.

1897 Locomotive No. 224 (4–4–0) had the company's crest on the front driving-wheel splasher, and the rebuilding date on an oval brass plate on the front coupling-rod splasher.

1897 Locomotives were dark brown with red and yellow lining. Panel striping had a red line on outer edge and yellow on inner. Wheels and framing were the same, but the latter had a narrow black border with red lines. Buffer-beams had vermilion panels upon which was the number in gold figures, shaded with red and black. Some locomotives had vermilion coupling-rods, and some outside framed ones, vermilion cranks.

The company's crest was on driving-wheel splashers, and letters NBR on tender sides in gold with red and black shading. The number-plates were of brass with black figures and letters.

Coaches were dark lake with gold lines round the edges of panels. Lettering was in gold, shaded with red and black. The crest appeared on the lower panels. Brake ends were vermilion.

Goods wagons were grey with white lettering. Cast iron number-plates with white lettering on black groundwork. Brake vans had vermilion ends and were finished in the same style.

1900 The horse-drawn "Dandy" coach which worked between Drumburgh and Port Carlisle until 1914 (now at York) is painted with (28), body-colour claret, and lined-out in light straw ¼ in. wide. The window lights were framed out in light mahogany, which is varnished.

Lettering "N.B.R." is in gold, shaded with vermilion to the left and below, the full-stops being square-shaped. The inside is grained overall to represent dark oak.

1900 Engines were a dark yellow.

1900 The names were removed from D. Drummond's "Terrier" type 0–6–0T locomotives and "N.B.R." substituted.

1902 Engines were a distinctly yellow-brown (ochre).

1904 The letters "N.B.R." were altered to "NB", with the crest between the initials.

1905 Old 2–2–2T inspection locomotives (No. 312 in 1882, then No. 875 in 1892 and No. 1079 in 1904) were still painted the old original "North British" yellow ochre in 1905.

Pre 1911 A mixture quaker green, black and blue was used for the locomotive colour, which produced more of a greenish-khaki with a bluish tinge.

Post 1911 More blue was added to the mixture which then became a dark olive-green more like the "W.D." service green used in the 1914–18 war.

Up to 1911 Locomotives were painted (34), described in sources as a brownish olive or deep khaki colour, this being made up from a mixture of "quaker" green, blue and black.

Post 1911 More blue was added to the previous colour, thus turning it into a truer green. Lining was in black, edged outside by a narrow red line, and inside by a fine pale yellow line. Buffer-beams were green, with a red panel extending between the buffers with (*e.g.*) "No. 333" in yellow. Rear buffer-beams did not have the red panel. The letters and figures used were strongly serifed and shaded below and to the left with black.

In the case of the "Atlantics", the crest of the company was carried on the trailing splasher, and the initials "N.B.R." on the tender side-sheets in 12 in. letters; the latter being in gold, and shaded to the right and below in black, and to the left and below in red and white. Other passenger engines had the initials "N.B." in 9 in. letters on the tender or tank sides, with the company's crest between them.

Goods engines had the letters "N.B.R." in 9 in. letters, but without the crest.

1912 Goods locomotives began to be painted black, lined with two red lines.

Pre 1913 Locomotives were definitely not a brown, but (34), a brownish olive, made by a mixture of burnt umber and Brunswick blue. Whilst there was certainly a brown tinge, the effect was of an olive-green rather than a brown-green.

Pre 1913 The ends of suburban brake vans were finished in vermilion, but after that date were painted lake, like the rest of the coach. Underframes and all running gear were black, whilst roofs were white.

1913 Locomotive colours were changed to even a deeper shade by the addition of more Brunswick blue. The lining was black, with a thin red stripe outside and a yellow one inside it. Buffer-beams umber green with a vermilion panel for the number.

1913 All locomotives had their numbers painted in large figures on the tenders, between the initials "N.B.", the Reid "Atlantics" carrying the company's crest, this appearing on the trailing driving-wheel splasher. West Highland 4–4–0's and two classes of Holmes and Drummond 4–4–0's together with all unnamed 4–4–0's also carried the company's crest. Number-plates were of brass oval in shape, with the numbers in sunken black figures, surrounded by the words "NORTH BRITISH RAILWAY".

Coaches were painted lake, of a similar shade to that of the Midland Railway, and lined round the panels in gold. The waist panel carried the letters "N.B.R." in small gold block letters, shaded in red. The lower panels had the company's crest which appeared *twice* on each side of some bogie coaches. Brake vans and small 4- and 6-wheeled coaches carried but one crest on either side. The words "First" or "Third" appeared on the doors; but these words were replaced on local stock by the figures "1" and "3" in 1913.

1913 Goods stock was a medium grey, and carried the initials "N.B.", and a small quatrefoil device—which was distinctive to the company's goods stock—in white. A white crescent was also painted on the vehicles, with a figure in grey upon it (*e.g.* '07, '18, '20) denoting the year in which the vehicle was due for overhaul. Goods brakes, however, had a small "N.B.R." on their sides, instead of the larger initials "N.B." of the goods wagons, and had vermilion ends. Number-plates were oblong, with scalloped corners, and were painted black, with raised white figures and the words "NORTH BRITISH".

1913 (c) Locomotives used for passenger working changed colour from brown to (34) olive green, with large numerals on the tenders. Some engines were lined with yellow, red and black bands, but with dark Brunswick ("quaker") green outer bordering. Boiler bands were black with red and Brunswick green, and double yellow lining.

From 1913 When the train control system of operations was brought in, all locomotives had large block figures for their numbers. No. 8 was the first engine so treated.

1914 The 0–6–2T locomotives and some others had large figures on tank and tender sides (*e.g.* "858") for rendering the use of the new headboard control system easier. The numbers on the front buffer-beams appeared with the "No." to the extreme left and figures to the extreme right in serif type.

1914 Engines had olive-green (dark) buffer-shanks and border to vermilion panel on buffer-beam.

1920 (c) Locomotives painted coach crimson (28), practically identical with the L.M.S. (grouping) shade. Lining was primrose-yellow (probably fading to a straw-colour). Mouldings were in the body shade. All coach-ends were black, excepting the 4- and 6-wheeled suburban stock, on which guard's van ends were painted vermilion. The coach ends of the main-line guard's vans were black. Roofs were white, and name-boards were vermilion with letters in gilt shaded with black to the left and below.

1920 Goods stock, old "N.B." type, (later LNER), 3 ton fish-vans were painted the old "N.B." carriage lake with yellow lettering. "Scotsman" newspaper vans had lake sides, yellow writing, primrose panel lining, white roof, black underframes and ironwork. Usually 4- and 6-wheeled vans had vermilion ends, and the brake ends of such stock were also vermilion; though all other coach-ends were black. The "Scotsman" herald, which replaced the word "GUARD" was coloured as follows: main scroll, white shaded with blue at the ends. Lettering bright yellow ochre. Leaves, green—in three shades with high-lights very pale green. Thistle-heads, light magenta with white high-lights and dark purple shading. The North British Railway crest was carried on the panel of the look-out wing, below the waist.

Locomotive No. 1011 was painted black, with double straw-coloured lining on boiler-bands, splashers, cab and tender side sheeting, with a single straw-coloured line on the foot-plate edging, footsteps and tender framing. The company's initials with two full-stops, were placed on either side of large numerals on the tender sides; being in gold with vermilion shading below and to the left, and a white high-light on the vertical left side, dividing the gold and vermilion shading.

The front buffer-beam was vermilion, unlined, with "No." and "1011" on either side of the draw-bar, in gold with black shading below and to the right.

The tender carried a small cast-iron oval number-plate on its back panel, the raised figures and edging being picked out in straw-colour. The tender buffer-beams were unlined black.

Brass number-plates appeared on the cab-sides, the number having "NORTH BRITISH" above it and "RAILWAY" below; the lettering and figures being recessed and filled with black wax (Fig. 72, p. 209). A similar, but smaller plate, with "Cowlairs Works" and the date of rebuilding was fixed to each leading splasher. The coupling-rods were painted vermilion. The foregoing was the Chalmers goods locomotive livery.

Corpse vans were lake with black ironwork and light yellow lettering shaded to left and below with vermilion and white. Brown wheels with white tyres.

Yeast and refrigerator vans were painted a brown composed of equal parts of Vandyke brown and chocolate. Ironwork black, roofs white. Lettering mid-chrome yellow. Yeast vans had numbers painted on sides, and (apart from refrigerators, corpse, goods brakes, horse boxes and carriage trucks and vans) no goods or passenger stock carried numbers on their sides. The North British Railway quatrefoil (the company's distinguishing mark), was painted on all goods vehicles, whilst the tare weight figures were very tall and narrow.

The prison van (only one was built) had its sides painted standard North British lake, its ends being black. Roof and wheel tyres white. Wheel centres red-brown and black. Primrose lining to panels, edged with a very fine vermilion line on inside. Letters "N.B.R.", number, Royal cypher and crown were in medium chrome, the letters and numbers being shaded to left and below with vermilion. The jewels and ornaments in the crown were picked out in their appropriate colours. The cypher "VR" was changed to "ER" in 1901, and again to "GR" in 1911. Eventually the van became a "stores" van.

1920 Engines were a dark bronze-green (sage), and goods engines black. Coaches, crimson-lake.

1922 For a short period prior to grouping some goods engines were painted black with double red lining instead of double yellow lining.

NORTH BRITISH RAILWAY CREST

NORTH EASTERN RAILWAY

AMALGAMATED in 1863 with the North Eastern Railway was the first public railway in the world to use steam traction, the Stockton and Darlington, which was incorporated in 1821 and opened on September 27th 1825.

When originally incorporated in 1854, the North Eastern Railway had been built up in the following manner :—

1. The Newcastle and Darlington Junction Railway acquired the Great North of England Railway to become the York and Newcastle Railway
2. The York and Newcastle Railway took over the Newcastle and Berwick Railway in 1847 to become the York, Newcastle and Berwick Railway
3. The York, Newcastle and Berwick; the York and North Midland; and the Leeds Northern Railways amalgamated in 1854 to form the North Eastern Railway
4. The North Eastern Railway took over the Stockton and Darlington Railway in 1863

Other acquisitions of the North Eastern Railway included the Newcastle and Carlisle Railway (opened 1839), the Malton and Driffield Junction Railway, the Darlington and Barnard Castle Railway, the North Yorkshire and Cleveland Railway, the Stockton and Hartlepool Railway, and lastly, in 1922, the Hull and Barnsley Railway (see page 83), which was opened in 1885.

The locomotive superintendents of the North Eastern Railway were as follows:—

1854–1882	Edward Fletcher	1885–1890	T. W. Worsdell
1882–1884*	Mr. McDonnell	1890–1910	Wilson Worsdell
		1910–1923	Sir Vincent Raven

* For a few months in 1884–85, when the post was vacant, the locomotive affairs were looked after by a Locomotive Committee.

Pre 1854 Before the days when coaches were painted crimson all over, they were painted plum-colour for first and second class, and dark green for third class and brake vans.

The old York, Newcastle and Berwick Railway coaches were in these same colours, but had cream upper panels.

1854–82 (c) During Mr. Fletcher's term of office, engine boilers, cabs and splashers were grass-green. Boiler bands being dark green with a black line on either side; the entire band being between two very fine white lines. Cab, panels, driving-wheel and crank-pin splashers were edged with dark green. On the panel, and on the fire-box the two shades of green were separated by a black band having a white line on either side; whilst inside this was another white line. The cab, however, had but a single white line between the border and the panel; as also had the splashers. The coupling-rod splashers were dark green with a white line. Number-plates were of bright brass with a vermilion background (Fig. 91, p. 280). Coupling-rods (except those of Neilson engines, which were bright steel) were vermilion. Sand-rods, reversing-rods, and spring-balance levers were vermilion. Wheels were grass-green. Framing was light Indian red with fine yellow lines. Axle-boxes were black, with a fine red line. Buffer-beams were vermilion, with "No." and figures on either side of the draw-hook in white. Tender wheels were black.

Locomotives painted at York had chocolate framing edged with fine yellow lines, and the background of the number-plates were white instead of vermilion.

1864–5 The "Whitby" 4–4–0 locomotives (series 492–501) and the Fletcher 2–4–0's of the "675" class; as well as the Beyer Peacock 2–4–0's (series 686–697) had their number-plates on the cab sides in exceptionally large figures enclosed in an oval border. The Beyer, Peacock engines had a double brass beading round the leading driving-wheel splasher with the words "Beyer, Peacock & Co., Manchester—1870" between the beadings.

1865 Still earlier coaches had whitish-cream upper panels (a legacy from the old York, Newcastle and Berwick Railway).

1870 (c) Locomotive boiler-bands were wide black, flanked with fine white. Domes were painted the body colour. There were brass beadings round driving-wheel splashers, and sand-boxes were blocked and fully lined. Tenders carried N.E.R. in a single panel.

Buffer-beam ends were panelled black and white. Smoke-box stays were polished steel.

Some 2–4–0's had a brass band between the smoke-box and the boiler, as also had some of the 0–6–0's. Locomotive No. 306 had very large number-plates with bold serifed numerals, whereas the plates fitted to some of the 2–4–0's had block numerals.

1874 Locomotives were light green picked out with dark green and black bands, with vermilion and white lines. Underframes were red-brown lined out with vermilion. Smoke-box hinge-bars were sometimes polished, sometimes black. Safety-valve columns were polished brass. This livery applied to engines built at Gateshead. (see plate 1, facing page 1.)

Darlington-built engines were completely different, retaining many of the characteristics of the Stockton and Darlington locomotives from which they descended. Their colour was a slightly lighter shade of the Gateshead green, and their underframes of a much darker red-brown colour. Smoke-box hinge-bars were always polished steel. York-built engines were light green, picked out with black bands and white lines. Underframes were of a claret colour with vermilion lines. The York colour-scheme was throughout almost identical with Mr. Stirling's Doncaster practice on the Great Northern Railway.

Leeds-built engines had their safety-valve casings painted green, and smoke-boxes were painted dead black. The Leeds shops had a green colour of their own—a brilliant emerald, which was thrown into prominence by being picked out with yellow lining. Prior to 1881 underframes were painted the same green as the engine, and tenders carried "N.E." in large yellow letters on the back-plates.

Pre 1877 An unusual feature was that of painting coaches in different colours for each class, after the then Continental practice. First and second class coaches were a dark plum shade (not very different, but slightly darker than that used by the company for their coaching stock immediately prior to grouping), third class coaches and brake vans were painted a dark green. The coaching stock in the central or Darlington division, however, retained its old stained teak panelling.

Engines built at Gateshead were a light green with bands of black and dark green, lined out with white and vermilion. Darlington engines were of a lighter green, and had darker brown underframes. York locomotives were virtually the same as Great Northern ones.

Pre 1878 All "N.E." tenders had an exact replica of the engine number-plate painted on the sides, the engine plates being of brass with large figures.

Gateshead, Darlington and York each had their own design (see Figs. 102, 104, 106, p. 294), in which the figures were of different shapes and sizes. For example, Gateshead, Leeds and Darlington painted number-plates vermilion, these being reproduced on the tenders. York painted its plates the same green as the engine, but usually omitted the replica on the tender. However, after 1878 all tender numbers were omitted on York-built engines.

1879 First and second class coaches were of a dark plum-red, and third class ones a dark green. Brake vans were also dark green. Wagons were lead-grey. Darlington district coaches were stained to represent teak.

1880 (c) The Fletcher 1275, 0–6–0 tender engine (now at York Museum) was finished very similarly to the "901" class. Buffer-beams had a large, shaped plate with a serpentine lower edge situated below them, this plate being also painted vermilion-red. Beams and plates were bordered black with a white line between the border and the vermilion panel. Buffer sockets were red and were lined black and white, the lining curving round the shank-retaining bolt heads.

Wheels were painted (1), described in sources as body green, this colour being on hubs, spokes and rims. Axle ends were dark green, this being ringed round by a fine white, broad black, and fine white line, respectively. The light green hub (including its coupling-rod pin extensions) was edged with a fine white and broad black line, the white line being carried down the centre of each spoke and fanning out into a curved triangle where the spokes joined the rim of the wheel. Tyres were unpainted. Wheel lining: (see Fig. 15, p. 29.)

Coupling-rods were painted vermilion right up to their bearings, being lined with chrome yellow along their top and lower edges. Their tops and lower sides were vermilion. The yellow panel lining was reversed upon itself when the coupling-rod bearings were reached and top and bottom lining met in a single line.

The date-plate (Dübs and Co., No. 708, Glasgow Loco. works,

1874) was lozenge-shaped; lettering being in raised brass on a vermilion background.

The engine number also appeared in cut-out letters of brass on either side of the dome.

Pre 1881 Up to about 1881 all North Eastern engines had an exact replica of the number-plate painted on the sides of the tender. The engine number-plates were of brass with large figures. Gateshead, Darlington and York each had their own design for number-plates on which the figures were of completely different sizes and shapes. Gateshead, Leeds and Darlington painted their plates vermilion and reproduced them on the tenders in paint. York painted theirs the same green as that of the engines, but usually omitted the replica on the tenders, and after the year 1878, omitted repetition on all tenders.

Brass ornamental collars were often fitted by drivers round the chimney bases, from which brass stars, crowns and regimental badges were often hung. The sand-boxes were also frequently decorated with large transfer pictures of royalty and prominent statesmen by enterprising engine crews. This addition to the normal livery was brought abruptly to an end when an over-enthusiastic cleaner "blacked Mr. Gladstone's eye and indulged in several minor alterations to that right honourable Gentleman's features".

Pre 1881 Leeds engines were bright green including the frames.

Pre 1881 Before 1881 underframes of engines were painted the same green as the superstructures, and tenders carried the letters "NE" in large size yellow block letters on the tender back-plates.

1882–85 In Mr. McDonnell's time an engine brown somewhat similar to that of the Great North of Scotland Railway was used for the framings and this persisted until 1903. It was lined with red and white. Engine No. 925 was so painted when first altered. Later Mr. McDonnell adopted dark blue with black bands and fine red and white lines for framings. Cab interiors were grained light oak and under-frames were a claret colour. Number-plates were of cast iron with polished figures.

1884 Engines from the Leeds shops at Holbeck (*ex* Leeds and Thirsk Railway) generally had green domes, instead of the ordinary North Eastern brass ones. The colour of engines from the Holbeck shops was a really brilliant pure emerald green—a colour all its own, picked out with yellow lining.

1884 Mr. McDonnell (from Great Southern and Western Railway of Ireland) introduced the dark olive-green for the locomotives, picked out with red and white lines. This livery used to be well-known on the Great Southern and Western Railway of Ireland.

1885 Engines built at Darlington in 1885 had their numbers painted on the cab sides like the Tennant engines, but they were later given regular number-plates. (See Fig. 105, p. 294.)

1890 0–6–0 tender engines of the "1480" class had their numbers painted on the cab side-sheets, as also had the Tennant engines; but the "1480" were afterwards given number-plates.

1895 Engine No. 1869 was painted the later "standard" light green with black banding and white lining. The chimney top and safety-valve casing was polished brass. Buffer-beams were vermilion with a narrow black edging and a fine white line. The number appeared in gold figures shaded with black and white. The splashers were beaded with a 2 in. wide brass strip which was kept brightly polished. Number-plates had raised figures and borders on a black background. Coupling-rods had the fluting painted black. Frames, footsteps and valances were black, edged with a fine white line. On the tender appeared the words "NORTH EASTERN", with the company's crest in an oval between the two words.

Pre 1896 Engines were (7), described in sources as a light yellow-green, with a deep crimson border round the tender panels, cab sides and splashers; with an intermediate black band with a vermilion line on its outer side and a white line on its inner side. Frames were lake, with a black edge and a vermilion line.

1896 The crimson bordering on engines was discontinued, and black bands with white lines on either side substituted. The colour-scheme was simplified.

1896 Locomotives were (7), described as a light grass-green with black bands with white lines either side. Boiler cab-sides, splashers were also similarly treated (Fig. 100, p. 294). Cab interiors were painted and grained light oak colour, with the lower portions red. Buffer-beams were vermilion, with a black border and a white line. Coupling-rods were red. Number-plates were raised polished brass on a black background (Fig. 91, p. 280). Tender lettering was in gold, shaded with red, with the words "NORTH EASTERN" on either side of the company's crest on passenger engines (Figs. 51 and 96, pp. 114 and 280). Coaches were a dark lake,

SOMERSET AND DORSET JOINT RAILWAY LOCOMOTIVE NO. 17 IN THE LIVERY OF *circa* 1899 (P. 192)

with a yellow line round all the panels, and the windows having a thin vermilion line around them. The bodies and frames were decorated in the same style. Lettering was in gold, shaded with light red-brown, and the ends of all passenger brake-vans were scarlet. Old coaches still in use were painted and grained a light teak colour, with lettering in gold, shaded with red. Horse-boxes, and other coaching stock was painted lake, with yellow lining and lettering, the latter being shaded with red-brown.

Goods stock was painted grey, with black ironwork, with white lettering shaded black. Coal wagons in permanent use by the locomotive department were royal blue with white letters (as L.N.E.R.). Goods brake vans were brown, with yellow lettering and scarlet ends.

1897 The Worsdell 4–4–0's ("Q" and "Q1") had polished brass chimney tops. (Worsdell and Borries' plates, see Fig. 101, p. 294).

1899 Coaches were a pure lake colour, a really beautiful crimson, but this soon became hardly distinguishable from the Midland Railway's duller brownish red.

1900 Locomotives were (7), described in sources as light green, edged with black, a fine white line separating the two colours. Angle frames were black. Buffer-sockets and beams were vermilion, edged with black and white lines. Cab roofs were white, and their interiors grained light oak. Lettering on the tender was in gold shaded with red. Boiler-bands were black, with a fine white line on either side.

1901 0–8–0 tender-engines of class "T" all had brass-capped chimneys.

1902 Engine No. 66 (originally "Aerolite") for Mr. Worsdell's private saloon was painted in (7), described as N.E.R. green and lined out in gold. The company's crest was placed on the tank sides. The chimney-cap was of brass. (*See also entry under* 1910).

1903 Engines Nos. 1682, 1683, 1684, 1685, 1694 and 1696 were experimentally painted black, with dark and light blue lining.

1903 Class "V" engines ("Atlantics") had brass-capped chimneys, No. 649 being the first of the class to be painted green with the gold lining which was substituted for the previous white. All class "V" locomotives were subsequently finished in this way.

1903 Goods engines were rapidly assuming a black livery, with thin red lining and red coupling-rods, in addition to any brass-work.

1903 Goods stock, consisting of road vans, was grey, with white lettering shaded black.

1904 The engine No. 649 (class V) was the first of its class to be painted green, gold lining being substituted for the usual white. The "Z" class "Atlantics" had a similar livery.

1904 A darker green was adopted for goods engines, but the old bright green was retained for passenger locomotives.

1905 All passenger coaches were not painted the usual lake colour. East Coast Joint stock coaches were built to G.N.R. design, and were varnished teak; the letters "E.C.J.S." taking the place of "N.E.R.". These coaches had numbers prefixed with a cypher—"0".

1905 East Coast Joint Stock Coaches: as a partner in the East Coast Route, the North Eastern Railway took its share of joint vehicles, when they were no longer required in the East Coast service. These vehicles, although constructed to Great Northern Railway designs, and of teak, retained that finish after they had become North Eastern Railway property; the initials "E.C.J.S." giving place to "N.E.R.", a cypher appearing in front of their numbers. This showed that they had gone into the duplicate rolling-stock list of their new owners.

1906 Engines were (7), described in sources as a light yellow-green, and before 1912 goods engines were also painted this colour. Lining was black, with a fine white line on either side. The foot-plate valance, tender frames and steps were also black, lined with a thin red stripe. Buffer-beams were vermilion, and in addition to the engine number, carried an indication of the locomotive class in small white letters similar to those displayed many years later on the "Shires", "J–38's" and "J–39's" and other engines of the L.N.E.R.

Goods engines were black, lined with red. The interiors of cabs were a light green.

Goods, tank, and tender engines were lettered NER, but passenger locomotives, whether tank or tender types, carried the full "NORTH EASTERN", with the company's crest between the two words. (Fig. 96, p. 280.)

Coaches were painted lake, of a rather darker shade than that of the L.M.S. Roofs were white and underframes a dull vermilion shade. Coach ends were painted black, and the side panels were lined out in gold and fine red lines. The title "NORTH EASTERN

RAILWAY" appearing in full on the long narrow panels between the cant-rail and the windows. Coaching stock was lake—to match the carriages, and was lettered NER in yellow block letters. The sole-bars were, however, black.

Goods vehicles were a dark grey and lettered NE in white, the letters being 12 in. × 12 in., and thus much more square than the L.N.E.R. lettering. Ironwork below the lower edge of the frames was black, and above that point, grey. Goods vehicle number-plates were rectangular, with scalloped corners, and had a raised white border and centrally disposed number; the words "NORTH" and "EASTERN" appearing above and below the number.

1907 Coaches built this year had an oval white panel fixed on the exteriors of the doors, at the top of the waist, below the windows; on which was painted in large black letters "FIRST". The rest of the coach bodies were crimson-lake.

1910 (c) Engine "Aerolite", now in York museum is (1), green, with (28), claret-coloured, underframes. There is a black outside border to panels, this being followed by a white line ; both black and white having square corners. Within this is a wide band of black, which is flanked by a white line on the outside and a gold line $\frac{3}{8}$ in. wide within, all with rounded corners. The underframes are edged $\frac{3}{4}$ in. black, then a $\frac{1}{8}$ in. vermilion line.

All the motion is vermilion, and clack-boxes, lubricators and axle-boxes are bright brass. Sand-pipes are bright copper. There are brass bands between the smoke-box and the boiler, and the lubricators on the smoke-box are brass. Springs are black, with the top and bottom leaves white-lined. Spring lining: (see Fig. 19, p. 29).

Buffer-beams are end-panelled, being vermilion with a gold line and black border. Buffer fixing-plates are black lined on either side with gold, and the sockets are vermilion with a gold and a black line at their tips. The smoke-box door wheel is brass, and there is a brass cap to the chimney. The lettering on the tanks is in gold, shaded with light blue to the right and with dark blue below. The number "66" is placed in a gold-lined rectangle with rounded corners. The number on the buffer-beams is in $1\frac{1}{4}$ in. gold block letters.

Sand-box fillers are brass and the pipe between the trailing wheels copper.

The name-plates have raised brass letters on a vermilion background.

1914 Coaches were a darker lake, and the electric stock used around Newcastle was red with white upper panels.

1914 Passenger engines were (7), described in sources as bright green, lined out in black, white and gold. Goods engines were black, lined out in red. All engines had polished brass safety-valve covers, and some express types had narrow brass chimney-tops. Engines painted green normally had black underframes. The underframes of the engine "Aerolite" were, however, painted red-brown. (*See also entry under* 1910).

1915 Coaches were crimson-lake. Locomotives were (7), described as green.

1918 Goods engines were black, relieved by a thin red lining. Coupling-rods were red, and most fittings were brass. Engines Nos. 2004 and 2010 were the first to appear lined out in gold, and white on either side of a black band. Buffer-beams had yellow lining with black edging, and No. 2015 the first to have the newly-arranged crest on its tender. Engine No. 1329 was the first to have the new arms on the driving-wheel splashers. Two types of crests were used on some engines, *viz.* "round type" on the splashers, and "ornamental type" on the tenders.

(Locomotive No. 1621) Lettering on front buffer-beam was in gold block letters shaded to the right and below with light blue, the lower portions of the letters being shaded dark blue. There was a fine white line between gold and the shading. The engine class was painted thus :—(CLASS) (*hook*) (M1)—in golden chrome-yellow block letters along the lower edge of the buffer-beam.

(*a*) Engine No. 1621 in York museum has bodywork green, the boiler-bands being 1½ in. black, flanked with $\frac{3}{16}$ in. white lines. There are 2½ in. wide brass beadings round the splashers, which are panelled as the boiler-bands. All piping is copper. The foot-plate valance is black, lined with a $\frac{3}{16}$ in. red line. Steps are also similarly lined. Wheels are green, the black tyres being separated from the green by a narrow white line. Axle-ends are black, lined red.

Tender axle-boxes are lined out with red, as are the spring hangers; black being outside, then white, then the body green, then white-black-white (as the boiler bands). Within all this is the main panel. Lettering is in gold sans serif, shaded with red to the right and below with heavier black shading under the horizontal parts of the letters.

(*b*) Engine No. 910 (901 class, Fletcher). Details are shown in the plate facing page 1.

Buffer-beams had a vermilion panel with a black border, with a fine white line between. Upon this appeared the engine number in serif letters and figures, thus No. 901. Buffer fixing-plates were black. Underframes were (28), described as maroon, lined vermilion. Cab interior (top half) was grained light oak, lined white. The lower half was black lined vermilion over the inner face of the rear driving-wheel splashers. Reverse levers were vermilion. Boiler bands were wide black, flanked by fine white lines, these being again flanked with wide dark green bands, and yet again by fine white lines. The cab spectacles were square, and were brass-beaded; the front of the plate was lined to conform with the rest of the panelling. The fronts of the sand-boxes were also panelled fully. The oval brass number-plates were exceptionally large.

NORTH EASTERN RAILWAY CRESTS

NORTH LONDON RAILWAY

WITH the high-sounding name of the East and West India Docks and Birmingham Junction Railway, the North London Railway was incorporated in 1846, for the building of a line from Chalk Farm (L.N.W.R.) to the West India Docks at Blackwall. Trains were later run to Willesden, Fenchurch Street Station and Broad Street Station. The name was changed to North London Railway on 1st January, 1853.

Under an agreement entered into between the North London Railway and the London and North Western Railway, the latter company worked the former after 1st February, 1909, though the North London remained independent, and its stock and livery were unchanged materially. It finally became part of the L.N.W.R. as from 1st January, 1922.

The locomotive superintendents of the Railway were William Bridges Adams (1854–1873), J. C. Park (1873–1893), and Henry J. Pryce (1893–1908).

1855 The Sharp Stewart engine No. 17 (2–4–0) had bodywork painted (7), described as "green", with black boiler bands flanked with a fine white line on each side. There was a polished brass ring back and front of the fire-box, and the dome, safety-valve and chimney-cap were also brass. Handrails and sand-pipes were polished brass. The edging to the tank and bunker-tops was brass, and the vertical handrail stanchions steel. Spectacle-plates were edged with brass, this being followed by a wide black and a fine white line. Glasses were also brass-beaded and ringed wide black and fine white lines. The brake-wheel capstan handles were polished steel. Boiler feed-pipes were brass. Smoke-box, chimney, and sand-box top and base were black, lined out with a fine white line. The hexagonal base to the sand-box was lined heavily in black at each angle. The large oval number-plates were of brass, with the figures on a red background. Fender-sides and front and bunker-sides were wide edged with black with rounded corners and a fine white line dividing the black from the green body-colour. Inside the green panel so formed was a further panelling of white, black and white lines in that order. The bunker panelling of white, black and white lines in that order.

The engine number was painted in gold on the bunker-back, the figures and letters being shaded with emerald green to the right and below, and with black to the left and below.

Underframes were a deep shade of vermilion edged black with a deep orange line between. Splashers were double brass-beaded with black edges and deep vermilion between the brass curves. Horn plates were black edged with deep orange, and the equaliser bar was red, edged with black then orange within. Cranks were vermilion, edged with black and orange within, and the black axle-ends were lined deep crimson around the circumference. Coupling-rods were black. Front axle-boxes were edged black and lined round orange. Buffer-beams had vermilion fronts and ends, being panelled with black and an orange line between the black and vermilion. Wheels were green, with spokes and tyres lined white. Guard irons were black. Buffer shanks were red, with the ends of the shanks black. The building date-plate over the front axle-box was oval, with red letters sunk on a brass plate :—

SHARP, STEWART & CO.,
No. 196
ATLAS WORKS
1855
MANCHESTER

1868–74 The Adams 4–4–0T ("No. 1" class) was a much smarter-looking engine than those running at the beginning of this century. Chimneys had copper tops and dome-casings were of polished brass, with curved ornamental covers. The body colour of (7), described as light green, was picked out with black banding, and was lined red and white. Oval number-plates were fitted on the tank-sides, and the earlier engines also carried the number in large brass figures on the front of the chimney. The green locomotive colour was retained until 1882–3, which was some ten years after Mr. Adams left the company in 1873.

1882 (c) Black was adopted as the engine body colour in place of green.

Pre 1883 Locomotives were green, with black bands lined either side with red and white, together with much polished brass-work.

1883 Engine No. 101 was the first to appear in black livery, lined out with red. Tanks were bordered round with a light blue line and a fine white line inside, these being followed by another light blue line and a white line on either side. Inside all this was a red line.

1883 Engine numbers appeared in brass figures on the front of the chimney.

1897 Destination boards were placed just under the roof of coaches, on the upper panels.

1900 Passenger rolling-stock was of varnished teak, with gold lettering edged with black, white and red on second and third class coaches, and black, white and blue on the first class ones. In either case the lettering was edged round but not shaded. The rear buffer-beams of guards' vans were painted vermilion, the ironwork was bronzed brown. Underframes were varnished wood.

What little goods stock the company possessed was painted an extremely dark grey, almost black, and was lettered in white.

1900 The company's crest began to appear on several engines, being placed under the number-plate. The engine number was also painted on the red buffer-beams, in gold figures, shaded with black.

1901 Engines Nos. 104, 111, 115, 116, 119, 121 and 122 were painted black with fine double lining in vermilion round the tanks, bunkers, boiler, bogie-frames and tool-boxes. Buffer-beams were vermilion, as were the coupling-rods.

Locomotives running had been painted (since 1889) in a similar style to the "standard" passenger tank engines with outside cylinders, viz. black banded round the tanks and bunkers, with a broad outside band composed of pale blue and yellow lines; and a narrow vermilion line inside all.

1902 Engines were black, panelling being obtained by a wide white line and a thin red one, with a small space between them. Coupling-rods were red. Frames were black, with a white lined edge, and wheels were lined with red. Cab interiors were painted a stone colour.

1903 The "new" suburban coaching stock had oval medallions on the doors upon which were placed the company's initials ("N.L.R.") and the class number.

1907 Large brass code figures were fitted to the near side of engine chimneys to denote their route. Thus an "o" was Richmond to Broad Street. The destination was also carried on a transverse board across the centre of the smoke-box.

1915 Coaches were teak-colour. Locomotives were black.

NORTH LONDON RAILWAY CREST

NORTH STAFFORDSHIRE RAILWAY

A PURELY local line very little known outside the Midlands, the North Staffordshire Railway was of great importance in the area around Stoke-on-Trent, where it had its headquarters.

In 1846 the Potteries Railway, the Churnet Valley Railway and the Harecastle and Sandbach Railway were sanctioned; these three companies being amalgamated to form the original North Staffordshire Railway in 1847.

The railway then absorbed the Potteries, Biddulph and Congleton Railway (opened 1859), the Newcastle and Silverdale Railway (opened 1860), the Adderley Green and Bucknall Railway (opened 1894), the Sneyds Railway (opened 1860) and the Cheadle Railway (opened 1907).

Locomotive superintendents were:—

Early 1860's	W. Angus
1866 (c)	Johnson (father of "Midland" Johnson)
1870 (c)	T. W. Dodds
1876–1882	L. Clare
1882–1902	Luke Longbottom
1902–1915	John H. Adams
1915–1923	J. A. Hookham

1882 The bright green engine livery with wide black lining was altered to gamboge brown with red and yellow lining. (See plate facing p. 144.)

1885 Old locomotives were painted "Victoria" brown. Coaches had cream, then white upper panels.

Guard-irons were painted buff.

1899 Red-brown was adopted for passenger stock.

1900 Engines were (31), described in sources as a dark chocolate colour, the tender-sides being edged with black with a very pale yellow line inside; then striped round with a broad black band, with a yellow line on either side. Inside all this was a fine vermilion line. Boiler bands were black, with yellow lines on either side;

and frames, cab and splashers were similarly lined. Buffer-beams were vermilion, with a black edge and a yellow line between the two colours. The interior of cabs was vermilion with black edging. The engine number appeared on the buffer-beams in gold figures with brown shading. The company's emblem—a "Staffordshire knot"—was painted on the tender-sides in gold, with blue shading. On those engines having a brass number-plate, it was kept polished, the background to the figures being vermilion.

1900 Passenger rolling stock was a dark chocolate brown in the lower panels, as well as round the white upper panels. A gold stripe was taken round all the quarter-lights and panels, showing a very fine white line outside it. The door ventilators were striped alternate scarlet and gold, and the underframes were a chocolate-brown shade. Coach lettering was in gold, unshaded, but lined round with blue.

Goods stock was painted a deep red-brown, with the underframes and ironwork black. It was lettered with the company's initials, and the "Staffordshire knot" (a kidney-shaped device) in white.

1901 Locomotive No. 19 (a 2–4–0 tender) was rebuilt by Mr. Longbottom, and left the shops in the gamboge livery.* This style was not altered until Mr. J. H. Adams (son of the "L. & S.W.R." Adams) changed it to crimson-lake with gold lining.

1903 Oct. A new style of engine painting was adopted. Madder lake, lined with pale yellow, edged with vermilion and black. On tenders the words "NORTH STAFFORD" appeared in gold, shaded with vermilion and black; the company's crest (Fig. 88, p. 280) appearing between the two words. Engine numbers were in block brass figures on the cab sides, in lieu of being painted on the buffer-beams, as previously.

1904 Engine No. 167 (0–6–2T) was one of the first to appear in the new colour scheme of madder-lake, with pale yellow bands edged with vermilion and black. The words "NORTH STAFFORD" appeared on the tank sides in 5 in. gold letters. Between the words was the company's crest The letters were shaded in red to the right and below. On the bunker sides was the engine number in the "Staffordshire knot", the spaces in the knot forming the background to the figures; this background being buff-coloured.

* This reference to "gamboge" seems irreconcilable with other sources of information. By "gamboge" the colour of (32) or (33) would seem to be indicated.

1909 Bogie coaches appeared painted crimson-lake, lined vermilion and picked out in gold.

1914 Engines were crimson-lake, lined out in yellow, black and vermilion.

1915 Larger letters "NS" were adopted for goods stock, to bring the company's stock into line with that of the "G.E.", "G.C.", "G.W." and "G.N.".

1915 Coaches were (28), described in sources as crimson-lake. Locomotives (31), described as lake (red-brown).

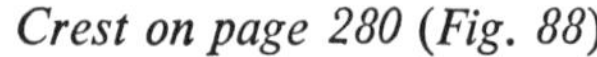
Crest on page 280 (Fig. 88)

TAFF VALE RAILWAY CREST (*page 206*)

RHYMNEY RAILWAY

INCORPORATED in the year 1854, and growing by a series of extensions up to 1895, the Rhymney Railway gave connections between various other Welsh railways with its total mileage of 50 miles. In 1876, the Rhymney Railway (jointly with the Great Western Railway) took over the Taff and Bargoed Railway, which was authorised in 1867.

In 1872, G. M. Lundie was locomotive superintendent, and in 1906, Mr. Jenkins filled this post. C. T. Hurry Riches took over in 1911 and carried on until 1922.

The Rhymney Railway was eventually amalgamated with the Great Western Railway as from 1st January, 1922.

1897 Engines were (9), described in sources as a dark green, with a black border and black panel lines with white lines on each side. Frames were chocolate, with black borders and a white line on the edge. Buffer-beams were vermilion, with a black border and a single white line between the two colours. The name of the company and the engine number appeared on a brass plate in raised letters and figures on a black background. The company's crest was placed on the sides of the bunker. Coupling-rods were left bright steel. Passenger engines had bright brass domes, and their number appeared in solid brass numerals on the back of bunkers or tenders, as well as on the front of the chimney.

Coaches were painted in two colours, with lower panels (29), described as chocolate, with pale cream (white) lines, and upper panels pale cream (white) with fine chocolate lining. Lettering and numbers were in gold, shaded with red.

Goods stock was dark red with white lettering. Goods brakes had vermilion-painted ends.

1902 Coaches were (29), described in sources as chocolate, with cream upper panels.

1904 Mr. Lundie fitted brass numbers at the foot of the chimneys, and an oblong (? oval) plate on the tank sides, giving the railway's name and engine number (Fig. 90, p. 280). The previous form, as depicted in Fig. 89, p. 280, being discontinued.

1906 Jan. The older six-wheeled coaches had their colouring changed from white and maroon to all (29), described in sources as maroon, lined with gold. Figures "1", "2" and "3" were used to designate the classes, instead of "First", "Second" and "Third", previously used.

1907 The 0–6–2T engines appearing this year had numbers on the front of their chimneys near the top in large solid brass numerals. Domes were also bright brass. Numbers also appeared on the back of the bunkers, and upon the sides of saddle-tank engines in bright brass, thus:

RHYMNEY **82** RAILWAY

Wagons were lettered "RR".

1911 Passenger tank engines Nos. 4 and 6 (P No. 5 class) were fitted with brass-capped chimneys.

1920 Coaches were (29), described in sources as dark red (maroon), with red and yellow lining.

RHYMNEY RAILWAY CREST

SOMERSET AND DORSET JOINT RAILWAY

JOINTLY leased by the Midland Railway and the London and South Western Railway, the Somerset and Dorset Railway came into being in 1862 as a result of the amalgamation of the Somerset Central Railway (first section opened 1854), and the Dorset Central Railway (first section opened 1860).

The company's title was changed to the Somerset and Dorset Joint Railway in 1875, when the Midland and the London and South Western Railways agreed to lease the line for 999 years.

The C.M.E., in 1918, was Sir Henry Fowler, of the Midland Railway.

1862 (c) Locomotive No. 11, a 2–4–0T was the only engine painted blue at the time, being nicknamed "Bluebottle". Coaches were then a chocolate shade, similar to the Midland stock.

1863 (c) The original S. and D. engines were dark green, this colour being superseded by the lighter green of the Midland in 1883. When the latter company changed its colour to crimson-lake the S. and D. followed suit, and this continued as the standard engine colour for many years, until it was replaced by dark blue.

The outside cylindered 2–4–0 tank locomotive which originally worked the Wells branch was nicknamed "Bluebottle" because she was the only engine on the line then painted blue; which later became the standard colour. The engine had a brass-cased safety-valve, and copper-topped chimney. The tanks were each divided into three panels by a black lining with concaved corners, the letters "S & DR" appearing in the leading panel, "No. 11." in the second (with full-stop), and the rectangular maker's plate in the rear panel. Fender and cab side-sheeting was also panelled out in black.

Pre 1875 Coaches were painted chocolate. 2–4–0 locomotive No. 13 had a brass dome and safety-valve casing, and a copper top to chimney. Both leading splasher and portion of rear splasher were brass-beaded, and there was a brass ring round the boiler where it joined the fire-box. "S & DR" appeared in large cut-out brass letters on the rear splasher, and No. 13 on the front splasher; all lettering being in sans-serif style.

Pre 1876 Engines were dark green, lined out in yellow. Midland colours were used in the early days of joint ownership, engines being successively blue-green and red.

1899 Engines were painted (26),* described in sources as blue; boilers, splashers, cabs and frames being this colour. Banding was black, with a yellow line on each side. Buffer-beams were vermilion, with a black edge and a yellow line separating the two colours. The letters "SDJR" appeared on the tender in gold, shaded with red of a deeper shade than that of the buffer-beams. The letters SDJR also appeared on the buffer-beams. (See plate facing p. 177.) In later years this was altered to "SD" on some locomotives. Carriages and wagons were lettered S. & D.J.R.

Passenger rolling-stock was blue of precisely the same shade as that of the locomotives, a gold stripe running round the quarter-lights and panels, with a very fine vermilion stripe outside the gold. Underframes were also blue, with a gold stripe and a fine vermilion line inside it. Lettering was in gold, with red shading. Horse-boxes were also blue, as were all other vehicles for passenger train working, but these had yellow lettering and lining.

Goods stock was painted a light grey, with white lettering and black ironwork.

1900 The 2–4–0T locomotives had polished brass domes and polished copper tops to chimneys. Piping was also polished copper.

1903 Five goods engines were painted red (as received from the makers), but were all subsequently painted the standard blue. The engines were six-coupled tender engines, and the colour was red oxide.

1915 Engines and coaches were the same blue (26).

1917 The standard colours of engines and coaches were (26), described as blue, with black and yellow lining. Goods engines Nos. 80–85 were black, and devoid of all lining.

1924 Goods engines began to be painted black, devoid of lining.

1929 The new 0–6–0T engines (class 3P–3G) were painted blue, with their numbers on the cab sides.

1930 (Jan.) It was decided to commence painting all carriage stock in standard "Southern" green (see page 329).

* (24) according to E. W. Twining.

LONDON AND SOUTH WESTERN RAILWAY LOCOMOTIVE *Locke* BUILT IN 1863 (P. 130)

SOUTH EASTERN RAILWAY

INCLUDING the Canterbury and Whitstable Railway, and the London and Greenwich Railway, opened in 1830 and 1833 respectively, the South Eastern Railway incorporated the oldest railways in the South of England.

When the London, Chatham and Dover Railway was formed in 1859, the Tonbridge direct line was constructed to get a share of the traffic to the South East and Southern coast towns.

A working union with the London, Chatham and Dover Railway took place in 1899, a committee of management being formed, and the title South Eastern and Chatham Railway being taken (p. 201).

The locomotive engineers of the South Eastern Railway from 1837 were as follows :—

1837–1845	Benjamin Cubitt	1876	A. M. Watkins
1845–1876	James I'Anson Cudworth	1876–1878	R. C. Mansell
		1878–1898	James Stirling

1842 Locomotive No. 13* (Sharp Roberts, 2–2–2), originally "Vortimer", had boiler, smoke-box, fire-box, fender, tender (over fire-door) painted (6), described in sources as a medium green,† The dome, with its square base, rear safety-valve casing, lubricator box under the dome and front safety-valve casing were polished brass. There was a polished brass ring between the fire-box and the boiler.

Springs and their hangers were black, and axle-boxes bright brass. The valve clack-box barrel was painted vermilion. Boiler-bands were black.

* Ran until 1860.

† Any precise indication of the green used for South Eastern Railway locomotives has been rendered impossible both by the absence of any definite item for matching, and by the known fact that the engines of this company were notorious for the variations of colour shade and livery. Probably Middle Brunswick Green, as (16), approximates to the average shade used.

The tender was panelled into five with black bands. Locomotive underframes were painted (29), described as Indian red, and lined round the lower edges only with a fine vermilion line.

Steps were also Indian red and lined vermilion. There was a copper-cap to the chimney upon which were mounted the figures "13" in cut-out brass, immediately under the cap.

Front buffers were painted a dull yellow (probably varnished oak). The feed-pipe from the tender-tank was polished copper, as were the sanding pipes. Handrails were left bright steel. Wheels were painted the body green, but had darker green tyres.

1842 (c) On the opening of the railway to Tonbridge, coaches were painted rich brown, the family colour of the Duke of Well ington, whose private coach had upper panels of black and lower ones of lake, with the company's crest emblazoned in and occupying the entire bottom panel of the centre door. This vehicle was known as a "Dandy" carriage, and was built in 1838 for the Croydon Railway by Jos. Wright (later Metropolitan Carriage and Wagon Works). After the death of the Duke the coach was altered and used on the Canterbury and Whitstable Railway.

At the time when the Duke of Wellington was Warden of the Cinque Ports, coaches were painted "Wellington" brown.

1844 Locomotive No. 13* was, according to another source of information, painted dark green, the boiler-banding being black. There were polished brass rings between the smoke-box, fire-box and boiler respectively; these being flanked with a black line. The smoke-box and chimney were black, the latter having a copper top and the engine number "13" in cut-out brass figures fixed to its front. The dome and safety-valve pillars, as well as the valve-spring casing were polished brass. The splashers were edged with brass, and the axle-boxes were of the same material, polished. The oil reservoir as well as the tubes leading down from it were also of polished brass. All springs and hangers were black, and the tender was panelled into five by wide black bands. The tender tool-box was also painted black.

The engine framing was unlined and of a chocolate (reddish-brown) colour. There was a polished brass beading round the spectacle-plate. Wheels were painted the same green as the body, but had black tyres.

1850 The Crampton engine (No. 85) had a dark green boiler of a

* Sharp built—ran until 1860.

similar shade (6) to that of the locomotives of the L.N.W.R. Northern Division. There was a brass ring between the fire-box and the boiler, and the dome was also of polished brass. The capuchon of the chimney was of copper, as was the top of the safety-valve; though the seating of the latter was of brass. The engine number was in cut-out figures attached to the front of the chimney which, with the smoke-box, was black.

The splashers and their frets were brass-beaded, their fronts and tops being painted a dull Venetian red. Springs were black, and the boiler bands were wide black flanked with fine white lines.

The tender was lined out with a wide black, and two fine white lines, with incurved corners. Cylinders were painted dull red, being lined out with a rectangular panel in white, with incurved corners. Underframes were dull red and buffer-beams vermilion. Buffers were varnished oak. All wheels were green, with black rims. Tender framing was red.*

Engine No. 92 (4–2–0) had the same body colour (6), boiler-banding, and tender-lining, but the fire-box was green with the safety-valve casing and spring-casing brass. The feed clack-box was brass. There was no engine number on the chimney-front, and very little decoration on the engine.

Engine No. 137 (4–2–0) was liveried the same as the foregoing locomotives, but had the number on an oval brass plate which was mounted on the boiler centre ring. Lining was as Nos. 92 and 85, but underframes were lined at the edge with white. There were large oval brass Crampton "Patent" building plates mounted on the fender sides.

1850 The scroll-end royal saloon designed by Richard Mansell was purple, picked out in crimson.

1857 to 1875 Engines of the Cudworth "118" class had polished brass domes and safety-valve casings, and very broad brass-beadings round the leading driving-wheel splashers. The numbers appeared on very small oval "Cudworth" brass plates with raised figures and lettering. The chimney-tops of most of these engines were polished copper, somewhat similar to Armstrong's Great Western pattern of 1867–74. Some of the "118" class engines

*** See E. W. Twining's article, "Model Engineer", 12th March, 1953 for additional details.**

had shorter plain chimneys of the "Fletcher" (North Eastern Railway) pattern.

1865 Engine No. 40 (a Cudworth 0–4–2T) had number-plates painted on millboard which was covered by a sheet of plate-glass and enclosed in a polished brass frame which was attached to the fender-sides. Hand-rails were polished brass, as were the dome and safety-valve spring cases. The spectacle windows were brass-beaded. The spring-equaliser bars were fully lined out.

1870–80 Coaches had upper panels of a very poor flesh tint, with a brownish hue for the lower ones, somewhat similar to pre-grouping London South Western Railway stock.

1880 (c) Stirling locomotives were dark green. The locomotive colour was changed to black, with vermilion lining.

1880 James Stirling's engines (except the "440" class which was green) were very dark brown. Coaches were a dark red-brown.

1882 (c) The upper panels as well as the lower of coaches commenced to be painted red-brown, the upper panels having been previously of a peculiar salmon tint, similar to that of the London and South Western Railway coaches.

1882–3 Engines were a "chrome green"*. Some Stirling 0–4–4T engines were painted black experimentally. The chrome green continued until the retirement of Mr. Stirling; though his last 0–4–4T was painted a slightly lighter shade of green.

Pre 1884 The upper panels of coaches were of light salmon colour, and the lower panels dark lake, or brownish hue. Their underframes were black, with yellow lining, and the lettering was of gold, with red and white shading. The ends of all suburban stock brake-vans were painted bright red, and many of the still older brake-vans were finished in dark lake with vermilion lines; but without the gold striping.

1884 Upper panels of coaches were light salmon shade and lower ones a dark lake.

1887 Engines were green, with white lining. The then new Stirling engines were black. Passenger engines were bright green, but the Cudworth 0–6–0's were painted a dark olive-green with plain black banding.

1888 The "Watkins" engines, built by Sharp, Stewart and Co. and Avonside Engine Co., respectively (Nos. 259 to 278);

* If the specific colour "chrome green" is intended, the standard pigment Chromium Sesquioxide (Cr_2O_2) is indicated.

rebuilt by Stirling between 1888 and 1891 had the Cudworth style of number-plates retained, and had treble brass-beading around their open splashers, and brass safety-valve casings. Their tenders were lined out in one long panel. The number-plates were fitted in the centre of the rear splasher, which latter constituted the lower part of the cab side-sheets.

1889 Exhibition engine No. 240, "Onward", had buffer-beams vermilion, edged with a black border and a fine white inner line. Locomotive painted black, relieved by three red lines and a yellow one; first an outer fine red line inside which were two more red lines, the three forming a narrow panel inside which was placed the yellow line. The safety-valve cover was black, but was polished brass in later years. Head lamps were painted vermilion. (See also Fig. 109, p. 294.) Main-line head-boards (14 in. sq.) were white with black corners.

1889 The first appearance of Mr. Stirling's 7 ft. 4–4–0 locomotives heralded the change from the old dark green and red-brown underframes to black, lined with red; this change being apparent on all Stirling engines. The change did not, however, affect rebuilt Cudworth locomotives, which kept their green livery when of express types. Cudworth goods engines were plain, unlined, a rather "bilious" green.

1890 (c) In an attempt to avoid painting costs, the company constructed a composite slip coach with metal framing and nickel-plated panels. However, it soon got very dirty, and the experiment was not repeated.

1893 (c) Engines again became green, but only in a few cases; though the Cudworth and Mansell engines always retained their dark olive-green livery.

1893 Locomotive No. 403 (0–4–4ST) was double-lined on the tank and bunker-side panels in red and yellow, but the bunker and tank top-flares had only a single yellow line inside a black border. The number-plates were of cast brass, with raised letters on a red background, with a raised brass rim (Figs. 107 and 108, p.294). The building date-plate was also of cast brass, with raised letters on a black background, and mounted in the centre of the bunker side-sheets. No brass bands appeared between the smoke-box and the boiler. All piping was polished brass, and the cylinders of the brake-pump were fully lined out in red and yellow.

1896 Locomotive (express) colour changed to black.

1896 Yellow lines were added to the 1880 red ones, and polished brass seatings and casings were fitted to the safety-valves.

Black was retained for goods locomotives.

1896 The "Ironclads" were always painted dark green, with black bands and white lines; and the same scheme of colouring was used for Cudworth engines. "Invisible" green* was used for goods locomotives. Coaches painted all lake, (dark).

Pre 1897 "Watkin" passenger locomotives were always painted a dark green.

Tank and goods engines were black, and were lined round the tanks and cab with an outer red line, then two red lines with a space between to form a panel; with a fine yellow line on the inside of the inner red. This yellow line did not, however, appear on all tank locomotives. The frames and wheels were black, with red lining. Carriage trucks and horse-boxes were painted a dark lake. Goods stock was light red, with white letters and black ironwork. Goods brake-vans were dark red-brown, with bright red ends; ironwork being black, and lettering white, shaded with black.

1897 The 7 ft. engines were painted green, with their tenders, cabs, and splashers bordered in black, with a fine line of red inside, then a fine yellow line, followed by a black band to produce panels. There was a red line on either side of the black band. The locomotive frames were red-brown, with a black edge and a vermilion line, with another line of white within. Wheels were green with black stripes with yellow lines on each side of the black. Buffer-beams were vermilion, edged with black and a yellow line between.

1897 The London-Hastings vestibuled coaches ("Pullmans") were painted (43), described as standard S.E.R. lake, with gold ornamental panels below the waist. "SOUTH EASTERN RAILWAY" appeared over the windows in expanded serif capital letters and "SECOND CLASS' in gold on the end panels. The company's crest was in the centre panel. All gold lettering shaded with red. Various styles of painting were used for locomotives.

1897 Coaches were a dark lake, with a wide gold stripe round the quarter-lights and drop-lights, as well as the panels; this having a fine vermilion line on its outside.

1897 All locomotives had polished brass number-plates, but the backgrounds to the figures varied, some being lake, some

* (See Hull and Barnsley Railway footnote for details of this colour.)

vermilion, and others black. Cab interiors were painted green. The Cudworth engines were painted in the same manner.

Some passenger locomotives were painted (16), described in sources as dark green, with black bands and white lines only, their framing being red-brown; with their tenders marked out in three panels. Goods locomotives were a dull olive-green, with black bands only. Some of the original tender bogie locomotives with 6 ft. driving-wheels working the North Kent line were repainted dark green in place of dull black.

Pre 1898 Before the "440" class appeared, engines had "SER" in the centre of the single-panelled tenders (*e.g.* No. 240).

1898 Bogie tanks were painted (16), described in sources as green, and lined similar to express locomotives.

Engines Nos. 440–451 (16), described as standard dark green, dark red framing and lining. Bright brass casings to safety-valves. Company's crest on the front driving splasher, and in centre of tender between the two equal-sized panels. Number-plate at rear of tender.

1899 Coaches: Suburban stock was in (43), described as standard SER colours, with gold lining on first and second class coaches, and with yellow striping and fine red lines on third and brakes. Large figures denoted the class on the doors.

1900 In coaches the graining of the upper panels was abandoned, and they began to be painted claret throughout.

SOUTH EASTERN RAILWAY CREST

SOMERSET AND DORSET RAILWAY CREST

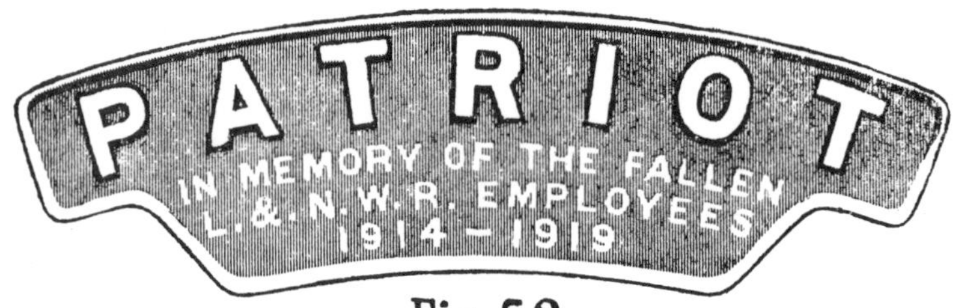

Fig. 52

Fig. 53

Fig. 54

Fig. 55

Fig. 56

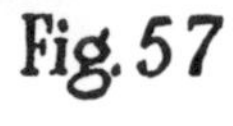

Fig. 57

Fig. 58

Fig. 59

SOUTH EASTERN AND CHATHAM RAILWAY

THIS railway was formed in 1899 for the working union of the South Eastern Railway and the London, Chatham and Dover Railway. (See pages 193 and 108.)

Harry Smith Wainwright was its first locomotive engineer (1899–1913), being followed by R. E. L. Maunsell, who occupied the post from 1913 until December 1922, and continued as Chief Mechanical Engineer of the Southern Railway until his retirement in 1937.

1899 Mr. Wainwright, of S.E. and L.C.D., experimented with a view to deciding upon colours more in keeping with the artistic taste then obtaining when compared with existing S.E.R. colours of coaching stock; and by painting S.E.R. and L.C.D. coaches the same colours, the railways of England, which continued to use a natural teak colour, lost the support of the S.E. and C.R.

The coaches then combined the leading colours of the two parent companies, and had their upper panels painted and grained teak, and the lower ones and ends crimson-lake. Crimson-lake* was also used to pick out the mouldings on the upper teak panels, and for the underframes. The upper panel mouldings were lined broad in gold, and fine lined with vermilion. All writing was in gold, with red blocking and black back-shading.

1899 Goods stock was lead-coloured, with black ironwork.

1899 (Oct.) Some 1st, 2nd and 3rd class coaches were turned out at Ashford with tops and around windows the colour of L.C. and D. coaches, but with S.E.R. colours below the waist, and lettered S.E. and C.D.R.

1899 Brass safety-valve covers to Stirling locomotives. Number-plates of raised brass, with letters on a dark crimson background.

* Probably (27) is indicated.

The Management Committee's crest appeared on the driving-wheel splashers, and the letters SE and CR in gold shaded red on the tender sides. L.C.D.R. locomotives had numbers altered by the addition of 459 (the total number of locomotives on the old S.E.R.).

United companies' painting modified. Goods stock grey with white lettering. Passenger stock had upper panels grained, with remainder the same claret as used on S.E.R. Locomotives now green, with bluish-light green bands instead of black; the fine red and yellow lines being retained.

1899 On amalgamation between the S.E.R. and L.C. and D. the locomotive number-plates were removed from tanks and placed on the bunker sides, and 459 was added to the original numbers of the L.C.D.R. engines. (The S.E.R. numbers were not altered.) The letters SE and CR were substituted on the tank sides in bold letters as engines were repainted and lined out in the "new" S.E. and C.R. style.

1899–1913 Locomotives were painted (11), described as green, with broad bands of a lighter green, flanked on one side with a yellow line and on the other with a red one. Domes, safety-valve casings, splasher beadings and chimney tops were polished brass. The letters "SE & CR" appeared on the tank or tender sides in gold letters shaded with vermilion. The number-plates were of cast brass with raised figures, on a vermilion back-ground. There was a brass cleading ring at the smoke-box end of the boiler, between it and the smoke-box. The fire-box in the cab was brass covered.

1900 Locomotives were (50), described in sources as black, with light greenish-blue striping round bunkers and tanks. Boilers had narrow red lines round the bands.

Coaches were bright lake shade, with black round the panels and gold and vermilion lining.

1900 On the "440" class of engines, in addition to the brass safety-valve casings with which the engines of united companies were fitted, and the alterations in the paint colour (from black to bluish-green with light green bands and white stripes) (LC & D locomotives were also so painted); the initials "SE & CR" in gold letters shaded red appeared on the tenders and tanks; a crest being also placed on the driving-wheel splashers of tender engines.

Most types had raised number-plates with brass figures and border on a dark crimson ground whilst some had cut-out brass figures.

Even old Cudworth locomotives were, in 1900, fitted with brass safety-valve casings as they passed through Ashford shops.

1900 All the "G" class engines (Neilson, Reid, 4–4–0) had number-plates with sunk letters on bright brass. Date-plates were on front driving-wheel splasher. There was a bright brass band between the fire-box and the boiler. The letters "SE & CR" were written on the tender-sides in the centre of a single rectangular panel with incurved corners, (Fig. 4, p. 6), shaded to the left and below.

1901 The locomotive No. 734 (4–4–0, "D" class, Wainwright) was exhibited at the Glasgow Exhibition of 1901, and was painted "Brunswick" green, (16) the splashers and cab side-sheets having a fine border of black, next to which was a very fine line of red which touched a light blue-green band. On the inner edge of this blue-green band was a fine yellow line. Boiler banding was light blue-green, flanked first with red lines, then yellow. The upper main-frames below the smoke-box were painted "Brunswick" green, being edged with black; a fine red line separating the two colours.

The dome cover was of polished brass, as was the casing of the safety-valve the springs of which were vermilion. The chimney had a copper-top. The two driving-wheel splashers were edged with a continuous brass beading, 1½ in. wide, as were the windows in the spectacle plate.

Wheels were painted green, with black tyres, around which was a fine red line. Wheel hubs were green, with a black band edging; this band having a fine red line on its inner side. Axle-ends were black. Outside framing, guard irons and steps were painted light brown, edged with black; a fine red line separating the two colours, and a fine yellow line about 1½ in. within the previous lining.

Buffer-beams were vermilion, edged with black. Buffer-sockets were lined out in black, red and yellow. Tender-coping was green, edged with black, a fine red line separating these two colours. Lettering was in gold, shaded to the left with red and white, a black shadow effect being shown on the right-hand side. The engine number was in separate brass numerals, and the crest of the "SE & CR" appeared on the leading driving-wheel splashers to balance the engine number which appeared on the rear ones. The tube-plate cover was of polished brass, as also were the surrounds of the small coupling-rod splashers. The background of the oval maker's plate was vermilion.

1903 On locomotives, the original number-plates on the tank-sides were removed to the bunker sides as the old S.E.R. engines were repainted. The letters "SE & CR" then appeared on the tanks.

1904 (c) Goods wagons were brick red, but were repainted dark grey when the South Eastern Railway amalgamated with the London, Chatham, and Dover Railway.

1904 Express locomotives had copper tops to chimneys.

1908 The new royal saloon was the usual body-colour and style, save that all the mouldings were in gold, and the royal cypher: "E v R"
VII was added on the centre panel.

1911 Standard Wainwright goods locomotives and most of the passenger engines appeared with painted domes.

1912 A new style of painting for locomotives was introduced, far less elaborate than that previously in vogue. The dark green body-colour (11) remained unchanged, as also did the light brown used for outside framing, steps and guard irons. The lining was, however, much simplified and consisted of a single fine lemon-yellow line about 1½ ins. inside the borders of cab-sides, splashers and outside framing. All bright brass and copper work was painted over, and no such ornaments were used in the future. Buffer-beams were unlined and vermilion in colour, and had the engine's number painted on in plain, unshaded yellow figures. The old "S.E. & C.R." initials on tanks and tender sides were retained.

1914 "L" class engines were all green with black bands and yellow lines, and were devoid of all polished brasswork. This was the then new standard livery for *all* engines.

1914–18 Engines were painted dark grey with white figures and coaches brown.

1915 Locomotives : green. Coaches were painted maroon.

1915 Locomotives were finished without any lining whatever; the numbers appearing in large white figures on tenders and tanks.

1916–17 All engines were finished battleship grey, with their numbers in white figures on the tank or tender. A rectangular cast plate bearing the letters "SE & CR" appeared on cab or bunker-sides instead of the engine number-plate. The number was painted on the front buffer-beam and inside the cab, as well as on the tank sides of tank engines. This war-time livery persisted until grouping in 1923.

1917 During the 1914–18 war some of the locomotives were painted black, with white lettering and very restricted lining. In other instances the lettering appeared to be of a slightly more yellow tint, and some of the tender-engines had large numerals of the "Midland" type placed between the initials "S.E.C.R."

1918 The 2–6–0 and 2–6–4T locomotives had both front and rear buffer-beams vermilion, upon which the numbers appeared in white figures and letters.

SOUTH EASTERN AND CHATHAM RAILWAY CREST

TAFF VALE RAILWAY

THE Taff Vale Railway was incorporated in 1836 and opened in 1840, the line being laid out by Brunel.

The Railway is comprised of the Llantrisant and Taff Vale Junction Railway (incorporated 1861, opened 1863, and amalgamated in 1889); the Cowbridge Railway (incorporated 1862, opened 1865, and amalgamated in 1889); the Dare Valley Railway (incorporated 1863, opened 1866, and acquired in 1889); the Rhondda Valley and Hirwain Junction Railway (incorporated 1867, opened 1878, and amalgamated in 1889); and the Treferig Valley Railway (incorporated in 1879, opened in 1883, and absorbed in 1889). Later, in 1889 and 1895, respectively, the Cardiff, Penarth and Barry Junction Railway (incorporated in 1885 and opened in 1887), and the Cowbridge and Aberthaw Railway (incorporated in 1889 and opened in 1892) were acquired by the Taff Vale Railway. In 1902, the Aberdare Railway (opened in 1846) was absorbed.

The Penarth Harbour, Dock and Railway (opened in 1865) was leased by the Taff Vale, as from 1864; and the Penarth Extension Railway (opened in 1878), from the date of its opening.

Samuel Fisher (1870) was the first locomotive superintendent. From 1873 until 1911, when he entered the service of the Rhymney Railway, C. T. Hurry Riches was the locomotive engineer of the Taff Vale Railway ; his place being taken in 1911 by J. Cameron, who occupied the post until 1922.

1864 The locomotive No. 24 (a 2–4–0 tender type designed by Mr. J. Tomlinson) was painted (7), described in sources as green, the boiler being lined with wide black bands flanked with fine white lines. Dome was green and whistle manhole green. Fire-box was green and panelled in sections with (29), described as Indian red, (early engines were painted a bluish-green) with a fine white line within, the panel corners being concave. The safety-valve spring was cased in brass. The chimney and smoke-box were black, the smoke-box being panelled out with an Indian red outer line and white inner one. The chimney base was lined round in Indian red only.

The fenders were green and panelled on their extreme outside by an Indian red line of fair thickness, this being followed by a fine black line. The corners of this outer panel were square. Within this outer panel was another panel with incurved corners formed of a fine white line and a black line within it. Inside this second panel was a third panel with an outer fine white line and an inner fine black line. Between each of these three panels the green body-colour was visible. Number-plates were oval brass with the figures on a black background.

Underframes were (37), described as Venetian red, being lined with a fine white edge then (29), described as red, within at a fair distance from the white edge. Sand-boxes were panelled front, sides and top with a white outer line and a red (29) inner line. Wheels were green, lined on the spokes and rim with white. Splashers were double beaded with brass, the lining between the brasses being black, white, red—body green—red, white, black; reading from the inside of the outer bead towards the outside of the inner bead. All piping was copper, and the injector body was black. Coupling-rods were bright steel. Steps and tender-horn-plates were black.

The tender panelling was the same as that of the fender sides. Spectacle plates and windows were edged with polished brass, and the tender filler was black. The locomotive number was repeated on the back panel of the tender by a plate of the same style as that on the locomotive. Buffer-beams were (37), described as Venetian red, being lined with (29), described as red, and double-panelled on either side of the draw-bar with a white outer and a red oxide inner line; these panels having incurved corners (Fig. 4, p. 6).

The ends of the buffer-beams were (37), described as Venetian red, panelled with Indian red within and white outside. Spring hangers and spring equalising bar were black, lined out in Venetian red within, and white outside.

On engine No. 157 the engine number was repeated in small figures on the tender, a small oval plate being attached to the tender main-frames immediately over the centre pair of wheels for the purpose.

1850 All early engines in the green livery carried names of places of local association. This applied to both the 2–4–0 and 0–6–0 types.

1862 The practice of naming engines was abandoned when locomotive construction commenced at Cardiff.

1873–80 Engines under Mr. Hurry Riches were painted red-brown.

1875 Mr. Riches' 0–6–0 tender-engines were painted (for the first batch) (38), described in sources as chocolate, with black lining, picked out with vermilion. Chimney-tops were bright brass, and the safety-valve casing of polished gunmetal. Number-plates were brass with raised figures against a sunken red background.

1878 Subsequent batches of the 1875 series of engines were finished black, with lemon yellow, white and vermilion lining. The company's crest was also transferred to the cab sides.

1880 Mr. Hurry Riches painted passenger engines red. They had polished copper-topped chimneys and polished brass safety-valve covers.

1897 Mr. Hurry Riches' 0–6–2T engines from the Vulcan Foundry were black, with red, gold and white lining. The crest appeared on the bunker sides, and the numbers in oval plates in the centre of the tank sides, the words "TAFF VALE" being above the number and "RAILWAY" below it (*e.g.* 197).

1898 Engines were black, being lined out thus: First a red line, then a broader gold or yellow line; and finally a white line. Buffer-beams were vermilion, edged round with a black border and a white line between the two colours. Number-plates were in bright brass, on the goods engines. Cab interiors were black, and dome-casings and chimney-tops of most engines were polished brass.

Passenger coaches were (39), described in sources as a dark shade of chocolate, below the waist line, this colour being carried around the upper panels, which were of a cream colour. A lemon chrome striping ran all round the edges of the panels and the quarter-lights, with a fine vermilion line dividing it from the chocolate border. Lettering was in gold, shaded with red, the company's crest appearing in the lower panels.

Passenger train stock was painted (39), described as chocolate, with yellow lettering. This style applied to carriage trucks and horse-boxes.

Goods stock was a dark rich red, with white lettering. The ends of goods brakes were vermilion, and all ironwork was painted black.

Fig.60

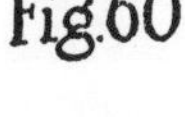

Fig.61

Fig.62

Fig.63

Fig.64

Fig.65

Fig.66

Fig.67

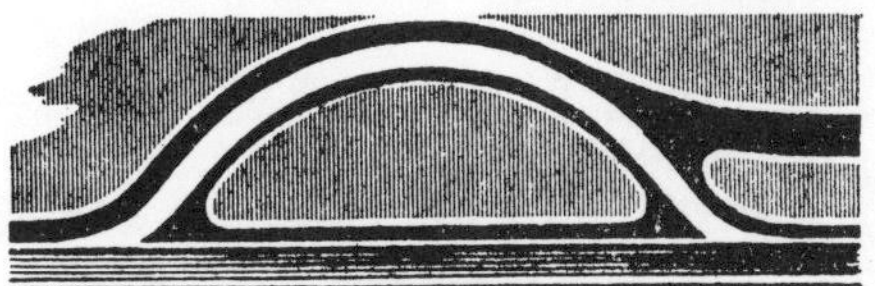

Fig.68

Fig.69

Fig.70

Fig.71

Fig.72

Fig.73

1901 Locomotive No. 170 (4–4–2T). This passenger engine was painted black, and was picked out in red and yellow. The crest of the company was placed on the bunker-side panels. Dome and safety-valve casings were of polished brass, and the chimney-top was copper. The bogie splashers were edged with brass.

Engine No. 193 (an 0–6–2T) was painted and lined as above, but did not have brass fittings, these being of polished gunmetal.

1907 Coaches were (39), described in sources as dark chocolate, with cream upper panels.

1908 0–6–2T No. 39 (Hurry Riches) was painted black. The boiler-banding consisted of a fine white line flanked by red lines. The joint-ring between the smoke-box and fire-box was of polished brass. Safety-valve casing and whistle were of brass, whilst the safety-valve spring and lever were painted vermilion red. Tank sides, bunker and upper cab side-sheets were lined out in red, with one white line within on the side-sheets and two white lines within on the tank and bunker-sides. The cab door was also lined with red and single white. The leading driving-wheel splasher was brass-edged, being lined out in red and single white; and carrying the building date-plate. The engine number appeared in the centre of the tank-sides on a brass-edged oval plate the figures and rim being raised. The plate was surrounded by a fine red line. The balance-pipe between the side and bunker tanks was painted vermilion, as were the buffer-shanks; the ends of which were black. Wheels were black with a fine red line around the rims and centre-boss. Steps and guard-irons were also lined out in red. All hand-rails and their stanchions were of polished steel. The lubricator and knuckle on the side of the smoke-box were polished brass.

1914 Engines were black, lined out in yellow, vermilion and white.

Coaches were (39), described in sources as chocolate, with white upper panels.

1914–21 Engines were painted black, with red and yellow lining. Coaches were painted chocolate in the lower panels and white (giving a primrose-yellow effect when varnished) in the upper ones. The panels were separated by two thin lines, a black at the top and a gold at the bottom.

1915 Large letters "T V" were adopted for goods stock.

Crest on page 188

MINOR RAILWAYS

AND

PREVIOUS OLDER COMPANIES

ASHOVER LIGHT RAILWAY
BIDEFORD, WESTWARD HO! AND APPLEDORE RAILWAY
BIRMINGHAM WATERWORKS (ELAN VALLEY) RAILWAY
BIRMINGHAM AND GLOUCESTER RAILWAY
BISHOP'S CASTLE RAILWAY
BODMIN AND WADEBRIDGE RAILWAY
BRISTOL AND EXETER RAILWAY
CAMPBELTOWN AND MACRIHANISH RAILWAY
CANTERBURY AND WHITSTABLE RAILWAY
CHESHIRE LINES COMMITTEE
CLEATOR AND WORKINGTON JUNCTION RAILWAY
COLNE VALLEY AND HALSTEAD RAILWAY
CORRINGHAM LIGHT RAILWAY
CORRIS RAILWAY
COWES AND NEWPORT RAILWAY
DERWENT VALLEY LIGHT RAILWAY
DOVER HARBOUR WORKS RAILWAY
EASINGWOLD RAILWAY
EAST LANCASHIRE RAILWAY
EAST AND WEST JUNCTION RAILWAY
EASTERN COUNTIES RAILWAY
EASTERN AND MIDLANDS RAILWAY
FESTINIOG RAILWAY
FRESHWATER, YARMOUTH AND NEWPORT RAILWAY
GARSTANG AND KNOTT END RAILWAY
GLASGOW AND EDINBURGH RAILWAY
GLASGOW SUBWAY
GREAT NORTH OF ENGLAND RAILWAY
HUNDRED OF MANHOOD AND SELSEY TRAMWAY
ISLE OF MAN RAILWAY

ISLE OF WIGHT CENTRAL RAILWAY
ISLE OF WIGHT RAILWAY
JERSEY EASTERN RAILWAY
JERSEY RAILWAYS AND TRAMWAYS
KENT AND EAST SUSSEX RAILWAY
LAMBOURNE VALLEY RAILWAY
LANCASHIRE, DERBYSHIRE AND EAST COAST RAILWAY
LEEDS AND SELBY RAILWAY
LEEK AND MANIFOLD VALLEY LIGHT RAILWAY
LEICESTER AND SWANNINGTON RAILWAY
LIVERPOOL AND MANCHESTER RAILWAY
LONDON AND BIRMINGHAM RAILWAY
LONDON AND BLACKWALL RAILWAY
LYNN AND FAKENHAM RAILWAY
LYNTON AND BARNSTAPLE RAILWAY
MANCHESTER AND MILFORD HAVEN RAILWAY
MANCHESTER, SHEFFIELD AND LINCOLNSHIRE RAILWAY
MANX NORTHERN RAILWAY
MAWDDWY RAILWAY
MERSEY RAILWAY
MIDLAND AND SOUTH-WESTERN JUNCTION RAILWAY
MID-SUFFOLK LIGHT RAILWAY
MILLWALL EXTENSION RAILWAY
MONMOUTHSHIRE RAILWAY (AND CANAL)
NEATH AND BRECON RAILWAY
NEWCASTLE AND CARLISLE RAILWAY
NEWCASTLE AND NORTH SHIELDS RAILWAY
NIDD VALLEY LIGHT RAILWAY
NORTH DEVON RAILWAY
NORTH MIDLAND RAILWAY
NORTH SUNDERLAND RAILWAY
NORTH WALES NARROW GAUGE RAILWAY
OXFORD, WORCESTER AND WOLVERHAMPTON RAILWAY
PETERHEAD HARBOUR RAILWAY
PORT OF LONDON AUTHORITY RAILWAYS
POTTERIES, SHREWSBURY AND NORTH WALES RAILWAY
RAVENGLASS AND ESKDALE RAILWAY
REDRUTH AND CHACEWATER
RHONDDA AND SWANSEA BAY RAILWAY
ROMNEY, HYTHE, AND DYMCHURCH RAILWAY

MINOR RAILWAYS AND PREVIOUS OLDER COMPANIES

ROYAL INDIA DOCK RAILWAY
RYE AND CAMBER TRAMWAY
ST. HELEN'S RAILWAY
SAND HUTTON RAILWAY
SHEFFIELD AND ROTHERHAM RAILWAY
SHROPSHIRE AND MONTGOMERYSHIRE RAILWAY
SHUTT END RAILWAY
SNOWDON MOUNTAIN RAILWAY
SOUTH DEVON RAILWAY
SOUTHWOLD RAILWAY
STAFFORD AND UTTOXETER RAILWAY
STANHOPE AND TYNE RAILWAY
STOCKTON AND DARLINGTON RAILWAY
STOCKTON AND HARTLEPOOL RAILWAY
STRATFORD-UPON-AVON AND MIDLAND JUNCTION RAILWAY
SUNDERLAND AND SEAHAM HARBOUR RAILWAY
SWANSEA AND MUMBLES RAILWAY
TAL-Y-LLYN RAILWAY
VALE OF NEATH RAILWAY
VALE OF RHEIDOL RAILWAY
WATERLOO AND CITY RAILWAY
WELSHPOOL AND LLANFAIR LIGHT RAILWAY
WEST LANCASHIRE RAILWAY
WEST MIDLAND RAILWAY
WESTON, CLEVEDON AND PORTISHEAD RAILWAY
WHITBY AND PICKERING RAILWAY
WHITEHAVEN, CLEATOR AND EGREMONT JUNCTION RAILWAY
WHITEHAVEN AND FURNESS JUNCTION RAILWAY
WIRRAL RAILWAY
WREXHAM, MOLD AND CONNAH'S QUAY RAILWAY
YARMOUTH AND NORTH NORFOLK RAILWAY
YORK, NEWCASTLE AND BERWICK RAILWAY
YORK AND NORTH MIDLAND RAILWAY

MINOR RAILWAYS AND PREVIOUS OLDER COMPANIES

Ashover Light Railway

1925 Locomotives: Midland Red and coaches to match, lettered in gold.
Later Locomotives: black.

Bideford, Westward Ho! and Appledore Railway

INCORPORATED in 1896, and opened from Bideford to Northam in 1901, and on to Appledore in 1908; this little railway was closed and dismantled by the Government in 1917. The locomotive and general engineer of the line was Mr. Henry Sowden.

1901 Coaches were polished teak, with interiors panelled in polished oak. Ceilings were painted pale green, and picked out in gold, with dark teak mouldings.

Birmingham Waterworks (Elan Valley) Railway

1906 On this semi-private railway the engines "Methan", "Nantgwyllt" and "Marchnant" were saddle-tanks which were painted light green panelled in dark green, edged with red and yellow lining. Cast brass number-plates appeared on their tank sides.

The coaches were a heterogeneous collection of obsolete Cambrian and Great Western stock, and they were painted a dark chocolate shade of brown; being devoid of all lining and lettering.

Birmingham and Gloucester Railway

1841 First and second class coaches were a dark buff colour picked out in black, the company's crest being emblazoned on the centre doors. There were three classes.

Bishop's Castle Railway

THIS 9¾-mile long railway was incorporated on 26th June 1861, and opened on 1st February 1866. It was later closed after a long financial struggle, reopened and worked until finally closed in 1936.

1870 The engine "Carlisle", purchased from the North Eastern Railway, was green, being lined out similarly to the engines of that company (see p. 171). The name-plate was of brass, and was fixed on the driving-wheel splashers.

1908 (Dec.) The engine "Carlisle" was painted black, after having been green, like the others in use.

1909 The locomotive "Carlisle", an 0–6–0 tender engine, was black, picked out in red and white. Another six-wheeled engine, purchased from the Great Western Railway was painted in that company's green livery, but with brown wheels; its original number-plate being removed and the bright brass dome painted over to match the boiler.

Coaches were a dark chocolate shade, and were ex-L.N.W.R. stock.

1925 Coaches were light grey all over.

1934 "Carlisle" was in the old N.E.R. livery.

Bodmin and Wadebridge Railway

THE Bodmin and Wadebridge Railway was absorbed into the London and South Western Railway in 1845.

1834 The three-compartment coaches were coloured blue and cream, their underframes being painted scarlet. Those designed for second and third class accommodation were painted blue all over.

The Bodmin and Wadebridge open third class coach in the York Railway Museum is painted black, being lined out with broad bands of light chrome yellow flanked by fine vermilion lines. The word "THIRD" which appears on the doors is in light chrome-yellow block capital letters, shaded to the right and below in vermilion.

Bristol and Exeter Railway

INCORPORATED in 1841, this railway was absorbed into the Great Western Railway in 1876.

1853–4 Engines were painted dark green, picked out with black until after the double bogie single engines appeared. Green was used on the wheels and boiler, and in all probability on the frames.

1853–4 Locomotive No. 42 carried the letters "B & ER" and No. "42" on either side of the driving axle hornplate supporting braces. The building plate was escutcheon-shaped, and was placed centrally on the fender-sides. (Locomotive No. 42 was a 4–2–4T).

1864 (up to Oct.) Coaches were painted brown all over until this date, when the directors decided that the upper panels of all classes should be painted white. When varnished this produced the familiar cream tint.

1865 The green colour was discontinued, and engines were painted black, without any relief whatever.

1874 Engines were all black, with "B & E" and the number in raised bright brass letters and figures. Engines were black—even to the chimney-tops and buffer-beams, without any lining at all. The initials of the company and the locomotive number were in raised bright brass figures and letters. Coaches: raw umber.

RHONDDA AND SWANSEA BAY RAILWAY CREST (*page 245*)

Campbeltown and Machrihanish Railway

THIS 2 ft. 3 in. gauge line of some six miles in length was incorporated in May, 1905 and opened in August, 1906; and had in 1918, four locomotives, six passenger, and two goods vehicles.

1906 Locomotive "Argyll" (0–6–2T) was painted exactly as contemporary North British Railway locomotives. Coaches had cream upper panels and olive green lower ones.

1906 Coaches were cream in upper panels and olive green in the lower.

1914 Engines were olive green, lined out with yellow, black and vermilion.

Coaches were unchanged in colours.

Canterbury and Whitstable Railway

1830 It is stated in old records that when the railway was opened on May 3rd, 1830, the "Invicta" locomotive had water-tank, boiler, cylinders, and wheels painted vermilion; whilst the smokebox, chimney, and wheel-centres were black; the dome being grey, and the steam-pipes polished copper. It is unknown whether the engine was repainted black when alterations were made to its boiler later in its life.*

Cheshire Lines Committee

At first, in 1865, the owners of the Cheshire Lines Committee consisted only of the Great Northern Railway and the Manchester, Sheffield and Lincolnshire Railway (later the Great Central), but in 1866, the Midland Railway became the third part owner; the railway being joint property of the three companies.

In 1865, 51 miles of track were vested in the Committee, viz. between Stockport, Timperley and Altrincham, 9 miles; between Stockport and Woodley, 2½ miles; between Garston and Liverpool, 4 miles; as well as the Cheshire Midland Railway (12¾ miles) and the West Cheshire (22¾ miles).

The title of the railway is misleading, as the most important part of the system was in Lancashire, where the large terminal stations at Manchester and Liverpool are situated.

The owning Companies supplied the locomotive power, the Great Central engines hauled most of the trains. In 1918 passenger rolling-stock consisted of 576 vehicles, goods stock 706, and 101 service vehicles.

1922 Immediately before grouping, the colour of the passenger stock was oak brown (varnished teak).

* She is now painted vermilion and black.

Cleator and Workington Junction Railway

INCORPORATED in 1876 and opened in 1879, this railway was partly worked by the Furness Railway. In 1918 Mr. H. Murray was the locomotive superintendent.

1912 The company had not any passenger stock.

1915 Coaches used were painted lake with white upper panels. (See Furness Railway, p. 23.)

1922 The high-sided 12–15 tons mineral wagons were painted a dark red oxide, with the "C & W" in large sans-serif letters.

Engines carried name-plates with raised brass letters which were fitted on the tank sides. Number-plates were oval brass plates on the cab side-sheets. The domes were polished brass.

Colne Valley and Halstead Railway

INCORPORATED on June 30th 1856 and opened on April 16th 1860, this little standard gauge line of 19 miles long boasted 188 vehicles and five locomotives in 1922.

The Locomotive Superintendent of the line (1922) was Mr. E. S. Hawkins, who also held the posts of General Manager, Secretary, and Engineer.

1901 Engines were black, picked out with red lining. No. 1, "Halstead", "Hedingham" and "Colne"; built by Hawthorn, Leslie and Co.

1911 Engines "Colne" and "Hedingham" were relieved with a broad red band edged on either side with white lines. The letters "CV" appeared in large gold letters on the side tanks. Coaches were varnished teak with gold striping, the company's monogram appearing in the lower panels, and "COLNE VALLEY" in large letters along the top panels.

Corringham Light Railway

WITH a length of only 2¾ miles, the Corringham Light Railway was incorporated in 1899 and opened in 1906; its chief engineer being Mr. M. J. Paley.

1905 Locomotive "Kynite" (0–4–2T) was brick red, with black bands to form panels, and fine yellow and vermilion lines inside. The name was on the tanks in gold serif letters, shaded in light blue and black to the right and below.

Corris Railway

OPENED in 1859 as the Corris, Machynlleth and River Dovey Tramroad, this railway was re-named the Corris Railway in 1863; at which time the part west of Machynlleth was abandoned. In 1883 the railway was completely re-opened to passenger service and in 1864 for goods, and continued to operate until the passenger services were cancelled in 1930. The track gauge of the line was 2 ft. 3 ins. It was finally closed and the rails removed in 1948.

1908 Passenger rolling-stock was painted chocolate shade.

Cowes and Newport Railway

SITUATED on the Isle of Wight, this line, together with the Ryde and Newport Railway (incorporated 1872), and the Isle of Wight (Newport Junction) Railway (incorporated 1868), were amalgamated to form the Isle of Wight Central Railway in 1887.

1861-80 The locomotives "Pioneer" (No. 1) and "Precursor" were painted light blue and lined out in red, with double brass-headed splashers. Engine No. 3 was painted olive green. Engine numbers were painted on the cab sides within a garter lettered "COWES & NEWPORT RAILWAY". (See also Isle of Wight Central Railway, p. 226.)

Derwent Valley Light Railway

Line authorised by Light Railway Orders of 1902 and 1907. Opened: First section (Cliff Common to Wheldrake)—October 20th, 1912; Throughout (Cliff Common to Layerthorpe, York)—July 21st, 1913. (Official opening—Saturday, July 19th, 1913).

1913 Coaches, royal (dark) blue with the Company's name in full in gilt sans-serif capitals along top panels. Goods vehicles were dark blue with "D.V.L.R." (the full points between the initials are part of the livery and always used) in white sans-serif capitals on the sides.

1927 Coaches were warm brown and wagons dark blue, all with white "D.V.L.R." in white sans-serif capitals. (This colour change took place about two years before the line was closed entirely to passenger traffic on September 1st, 1926.)

1930 (c) Other wagons purchased secondhand were run in their existing colours with "D.V.L.R." in white sans-serif capitals painted on them.

1961 (February) The *ex*-South Eastern and Chatham Railway passenger brake-van in use is painted middle green with "D.V.L.R." in white sans-serif capitals on the horizontal panels of the guard's lookouts.

This railway is one of the few which still remain outside the nationalisation scheme of British Railways. It still operates a paying freight service and is very much alive!

Dover Harbour Works Railway

1898 The Peckett tank engines were brick red, lined out in black and yellow. Chimneys had copper caps, and the domes were polished brass. The engine names were "Admiralty" and "Dover".

Easingwold Railway

THIS Railway, with a length of just over 2 miles, was incorporated on 23rd August, 1887 and opened to traffic on 27th July, 1891; and had but one engine and two passenger coaches in 1918.

1890 (c) The original locomotive was painted "Midland" red, with black and yellow lining; which was Hudswell Clarke's standard livery.

1903 Engine No. 2 was in the same livery as No. 1 (*see* 1890).

Pre 1908 Locomotives were black, with polished brass dome casings. Coaches were lake below the waist-line, and cream above.

1911 From this date up to about 1934–5, locomotive No. 2 was painted black, with red lining; the lettering being in gold at first, then yellow; in each case shaded with red. Coupling-rods, buffer-beams and shanks were vermilion, and safety-valve casings and columns polished brass.

1915 (c) The three ex-North London coaches were painted brown.

1931–42 The single ex-N.E.R. 6-wheeled 1st and 2nd class brake composite and the present ex-Cheshire Lines Committee coach were plain brown with yellow class numerals, and "E.R." on the waist-line. The North Eastern Railway coach had in full "EASINGWOLD RAILWAY". The two ex-N.E.R. 6-wheel coaches running as 4-wheelers were similarly finished. The Cawood line "Sentinel" coach was in green and cream livery; bright green below the waist and cream above.

1935–48 Locomotive No. 2 was once more painted "Midland" red livery, and was not the "dark brown" of the coaching stock. This colour was the result of "mellowing" with age.

East Lancashire Railway

Pre 1859 Engines were dark green with red-brown underframes, and polished brass or copper domes. Some engines were painted dark green throughout.

(1859 *Amalgamated with the Lancashire and Yorkshire Railway.*)

East and West Junction Railway

1908 Some Midland brake vans were lettered "EWJR" for working over the East and West Junction Railway on the 3½ miles of this Company's track on the route from Broom to London.

Locomotives were black, and dome casings were also painted black. Coaches were painted all over lake, and relieved only with a broad cream band at the waist-line.

Eastern Counties Railway

1856 to 1865 Under Robert Sinclair, the general engine colour was light green with black banding and white lining. Bufferbeams were green, and frames chocolate.

1865 to 1873 Under S. W. Johnson, the locomotive colour was changed to a darker shade of green. Three of Sinclair's engines (Nos. 51, 60 and 291) were painted chrome yellow during Johnson's time, and some of his "T-7" class 0–4–2T engines were also yellow.

1873 to 1882 Under W. Adams, the locomotives were painted black, with red lining, which remained the standard livery for all engines until the colours changed to Royal blue in 1882.

(See also Great Eastern Railway, p. 37.)

Eastern and Midlands Railway

1883 The Beyer Peacock engines Nos. 25–28 were painted (34), described in sources as chocolate colour.

1887 The engines noted above were painted green with black banding and white lining on each side of the black. The outside of the frames, springs and bogie-frames, as well as the cylinders were painted (34), described as chocolate brown, with black banding and white lining. Buffer-beams were signal red, and the engine numbers appeared in gold letters and figures shaded with black; being placed on each buffer-beam. This livery applied to the engines numbered 21 to 24 (inclusive), others were painted (34), described as middle brown, and were banded black with flanking lining of middle chrome yellow.

Festiniog Railway

ORIGINALLY incorporated in 1832 and opened in 1836, the Festiniog Railway adopted steam traction in 1863; passenger services being suspended in 1940 and complete closure taking place in 1946. With a length of 14½ miles, the railway had as its acting locomotive superintendent, in 1918, Mr. H. Hughes, Mr. R. Williams occupying the post in 1922.

The gauge of the line was 1 ft. 11½ ins.

1863 The engine "Welsh Pony" (0–4–0 tender type) was painted a green slightly darker than "Southern" green but slightly lighter than "Great Western" green, on the saddle-tank, buffer-beams, cab, dome and tank-filler; the foot-plate valances also being this colour. Frames, sand-boxes, smoke-box and chimney were black. The tender was green, with black running-gear. Brass name-plates appeared on the saddle-tank sides with letters against a black background. The cab roof was black, but was reputed to be green on another engine, "Palmerston".

1880 The bogie vans built this year were painted chocolate in the lower panels and black in the upper ones.

1940* Coaches were painted myrtle-green, with maroon window and door frames and solebars. Footboards were green, and the doors of some of the coaches bore white enamelled rectangular plates bearing the words "THIRD CLASS" in red letters, with a red rectangular border. Plates with black border and lettering were also used. The old observation-car bore the letters and number in white block characters on a black rectangular panel thus:—"F R 2"—"OBSERVATION CAR", the bodywork being painted myrtle-green.

1946* Wagons were painted oxide, with oval plates with the word "Festiniog" curved above, and "Railway" curved below the wagon number. Rectangular plates were also used with incurved corners, the letters "F.R.Co." appearing above the number (*e.g.* "117") below, both being straight-lined.

Freshwater, Yarmouth and Newport Railway

ONE of the smaller railways on the Isle of Wight, this line was incorporated in 1880 and opened for passenger traffic in 1889; with a track length of 12 miles.

1898 Locomotives were painted a bright green with vermilion coupling-rods.

1917 The saddle-tank engine (0–6–0 type) was green with red coupling-rods.

Engine No. 1 (later 1w) (by Manning, Wardle) had "F.Y. & N." in block letters on the tank sides. Coaches were varnished teak.

1922 Engines were green, with white and black lining; coaches were varnished teak; and goods vehicles grey with white lettering

Garstang and Knott End Railway

THIS small line was incorporated in 1864 and opened to traffic in December, 1870. Its rolling stock consisted in 1918 of four locomotives, eight passenger vehicles, and fifty-three goods vehicles; together with two service vans. The line was 11½ miles long.

1901 The 0–6–0 engines Nos. 1 and 2 ("Jubilee Queen" and "New Century") were painted dark red, and picked out with black, white and red lines.

1908 Engines and coaches alike were painted dark brown.

1921 Coaches were lake-coloured with chrome yellow lettering.

Glasgow and Edinburgh Railway

1870 (c) Locomotives were green, with brass domes and beadings to cab. (They were numbered in the North British Railway 233 to 239)

*From observations on stock still stored at Portmadoc in 1952.

Glasgow Subway

1935 As traffic works round the track and rolling-stock is never interchanged from one track to another, there is no need for two-side livery decorations. The station platforms are of the centre-island type, and only one side of the train is ever seen by passengers. This side is painted in scarlet vermilion and cream, and lined, but the off-side is only painted dull red. In this respect the subway rolling-stock is unique.

Great North of England Railway

1845 Early coaches carried the arms of the cities of York and Durham on their side panels.

Hundred of Manhood and Selsey Tramway

RUNNING from Chichester to Selsey, in Sussex, this 8 mile long line was incorporated on 29th April, 1896, and opened on 27th August, 1897, as "The Hundred of Manhood and Selsey Tramway", changing its name to "West Sussex Railway (Selsey Tramway Section)" in 1924. The Railway was closed in January, 1935. Its locomotive superintendent in 1918 was Colonel H. F. Stephens.

1897 The 8-wheeled coaches purchased from L.B.S.C.R. together with 6 wagons and a brake van were painted red with large white lettering. Some of the 8-wheelers were painted crimson-lake. The wagons were numbered 1 to 6 in white with "HM and STy".

The 2–4–2T locomotive "Selsey" had a copper top to chimney and brass dome. Along the valance of the foot-plate was painted "Peckett and Sons, Bristol" in block letters.

1897 Locomotive "Selsey" was blue, "Sidlesham" was green, with black boiler-bands and lining.

Coaches were crimson-lake.

1909 Engine "Selsey" was (24), lined out in vermilion. She was a 2–4–2T with a bright brass dome and an oval, brass number-plate on the bunker sides. There was a bright brass beading round the spectacles, and a copper top to the chimney. The name "Selsey" appeared on the tank sides.

Engine "Sidlesham" was a 0–6–0ST and was painted "N.E.R." (7) green, with black banding and white lines. She had a copper-topped chimney and a brass number-plate.

"Chichester" was a 0–4–2ST with a polished brass fire-box dome.

Coaches were crimson-lake, and wagons (ex-L.B.S.C.R. and G.E.R.) red oxide with white letters.

1930 Locomotive "Selsey" was blue, lined out vermilion, "Sidlesham" was green, lined out black, and the rest of the engine stock was painted vermilion. Coaches were crimson lake.

1933 Some coaches were painted green.

Isle of Man Railway

THIS railway, with a gauge of 3 ft. was incorporated in December, 1870 and opened in July, 1873 from Douglas to Peel; other sections being opened at later dates.

In February, 1904, the Manx Northern Railway was acquired; thus making up a track mileage of 46¼. The company's locomotive superintendent in 1918 was Mr. J. Bradshaw.

1902 to 1914 Locomotives were described as bright green (similar to the Great Western engines), being striped with black bands, and having a fine vermilion line inside and a white line outside. Domes were brass, and chimney tops copper.

Coaches had a livery of plum lower panels and white upper ones.

1906 Engines bright green (similar to Great Western Railway) with black bands having a fine vermilion line inside and a white line outside. Domes were polished brass and chimneys had copper caps.

Coaches were (43), "plum colour", (as London and North Western Railway coach lower panels); their upper panels were cream, (white under varnish).

1918 Engines were bright green with polished brass domes and copper tops to chimneys.

1926 Coaches were lake, with top panels over the windows white. Mouldings were picked out with fine vermilion and yellow lines. The company's crest appeared in the fourth panel from each end of the coach. There were white mouldings around the windows. The top panels contained the letters "IMR" in gold letters, and the coach number "F47", etc.

Isle of Wight Central Railway

THE Isle of Wight Central Railway was the most important line on the island, running from Cowes to Ventnor and Cowes to Ryde, *via* Newport. It was formed in 1887 by the amalgamation of the Isle of Wight (Newport Junction) Railway (incorporated in 1868), the Cowes and Newport Railway (see p. 220) (incorporated in 1859), and the Ryde and Newport Railway (incorporated in 1872). In 1913 the Newport, Godshill and St. Lawrence Railway was acquired, thus bringing the total track mileage to 35.

The locomotive superintendent in 1913 was Mr. Russell Willmott.

1890 Locomotives were dark red.

1898 Locomotives were black.

1900 Locomotives "Pioneer" and "Precursor" (ex-Cowes and Newport Railway) were repainted in the standard red of the Isle of Wight Central Railway, and their name-plates were removed. They retained their brass domes and safety-valve casings. Locomotive number 3 was painted olive green and lined out in white.

1901 Locomotives Nos. 4 and 5 ("Cowes" and "Osborne") were painted the company's red, with copper-topped chimneys and brass domes. Locomotive No. 7 (*ex*-North London Railway) ran painted black till 1887, when the Newport and Ryde Railway was taken over by the Isle of Wight Central Railway.

1902 In addition to the standard locomotive livery the name of the company began to appear in gold block letters on the tank sides thus:

ISLE OF WIGHT
CENTRAL RAILWAY

The ex-L.B.S.C.R. engine "Peckham" was the first to so appear.

Locomotive No. 1 (2–2–2T) had double brass beading round the driving-wheel splashers, the outer bead being much wider than the inner one.

The engine number was painted inside a garter on the cab side-sheets, which were double-lined into a rectangular panel with rounded corners. A brass dome casing was fitted.

1906 Engines were painted red-brown.

1907 Locomotive No. 9 (0–6–0T ex-LBSCR "Terrier") had "ISLE OF WIGHT"—"CENTRAL RAILWAY" in two lines painted on the tanks in block letters, unshaded. The figure "9" also in unshaded block appeared on the bunker sides. The chimney was copper-capped, and there were brass beadings round the spectacle-plate windows. This engine ran for some time with the "Stroudley" type of buffer-beam panelling. (See Fig. 76, p. 258.)

Coaches, standard colours relieved with cream upper panels.

1914 Engines were black, with white lining and "IWC" on the tank sides. Some were lined out in vermilion.

1922 Engines were painted black with red and white lining, with gold letters and numbers.

Coaching stock was of varnished teak and mahogany, and goods stock grey, with white lettering.

Isle of Wight Railway

INCORPORATED in July, 1860 and opened in August, 1864, this line was 15¼ miles long; running from Ventnor *via* Sandown and Brading to join the Isle of Wight Central Railway near St. John's Road Station. There was also a branch line to Bembridge. The Company's locomotive superintendent in 1918 was Mr. H. D. Tahourdin.

1898 Engines were painted crimson-lake, with polished brass domes and copper-topped chimneys.

1910 Engines were painted a much brighter red.

1914 Locomotives were a rich dark red, lined out in yellow and black; with brass name-plates. No number-plates were fitted, the seven engines constituting the total stock being named "Ryde", "Sandown", "Shanklin", "Ventnor", "Wroxall", "Brading" and "Bonchurch" in lieu of numbers.

1922 Engines were painted (28), described in sources as "Midland" red, and lined out in yellow and black.

Coaches were varnished teak, with a blue and gilt garter, with the coach number within, shaded in red and white, and goods stock was grey with white lettering.

Jersey Eastern Railway

SITUATED in the Channel Islands, this 6¼ mile long Railway was incorporated in March, 1872, and opened in August, 1873.

The line was closed in 1933.

1911–1914 Engines were (16), described in sources as a bright green, on the tanks, cabs and bunkers, being lined out with white lines either side of a black band. Inside of this lining was an emerald green band, with another fine white line. Frames were chocolate lined with black and white lines. The leading wheel-springs were painted vermilion with black and white lining. Wheel centres were vermilion with black and white circular lining. Domes and sand-boxes were green. The inside of the frames and the eccentric rods were vermilion. Name-plates were of polished brass with black letters.

Engine number-plates were of bright brass figures on a black background, and appeared in the centre of the tanks.

1923 Engines "Caesarea", "Calvados", "Mont Orgueil" and "Carteret" (0–4–2 tanks) were bright green (16) with black banding and white lines.

Coaches were natural varnished teak, and were designated by letters not numbers.

Jersey Railways and Tramways

THIS line, 7½ miles long, in the Channel Islands was opened in 1870, being incorporated under the Companies Acts, 1862 to 1880 as Jersey Railways Limited, which was reincorporated as Jersey Railways and Tramways in January 1896. Its locomotive superintendent in 1918 was Mr. George Todd.

The railway was closed for traffic in 1937.

1910 (c) Engines were a lighter shade of green, and were picked out in broad white lines and boiler-bands were polished brass. Coaches were dark green with black panel lining.

1914 Engines were a dark Brunswick or olive green, lined out in black, with a chrome line outside it and a vermilion line inside. Buffer-beams and outside cranks were vermilion. Engines Nos. 1–4 had copper tops to their chimneys and brass name-plates with raised letters on a vermilion background. Engine No. 5 had a plain chimney and its name was in serif letters on the tank sides.

1914–20 Coaches were olive green, with the exception of three Post Office cars which had vermilion outlined underframes. Two coaches were plain varnished teak.

1922 Certain coaches supplied by private firms were painted dark red or green, whilst those built in the St. Helier shops were plain varnished teak.

Some engine name- and number-plates are preserved in York

Railway Museum and others at St. Helier. They have raised, polished brass figures against a vermilion background.

Kent and East Sussex Railway

INCORPORATED as the Rother Valley Railway in 1896, and opened in 1900, the Kent and East Sussex Railway had 24 miles of track, 8 locomotives and 19 passenger vehicles in 1918; when its locomotive superintendent was Colonel H. F. Stephens. It also boasted one steam and one petrol-driven rail-car.

1905 The *ex*-London, Brighton and South Coast Railway "Terrier", No. 671 was painted blue (24) with red lining and renamed "Rolvenden", No. 5.

Engine No. 4 ("Hecate", an 0–8–0T) was also blue (24) with red lining with a polished copper-topped chimney and polished brass safety-valve casing.

1908 "Terriers" were painted dark blue (24).

1914 Locomotives were dark blue, lined out in white, black and vermilion. The engines "Tenterden", "Northiam" and "Hesperus" had polished brass domes.

Coaches were dark brown, panelled cream.

1916 Engines were black (excepting four green ones). Some coaches were brown and others grey.

1935 The "Terrier" engine (No. 3) was painted a bright apple green, and was lined out in black and white. Lettering was in chrome yellow with black shading. The running-plate (valance) was Indian red, lined white. Buffer-beams and coupling-rods were vermilion. The old London and South Western Royal saloon and two coaches running were painted a light chocolate shade and lined out and lettered in yellow, the letters being shaded and blocked in scarlet.

Lambourne Valley Railway

1898 Coaches were varnished wood with black underframes. Lettering was in gold, shaded with red and black. The company's monogram within a garter appeared on the sides of the vehicles.

Goods wagons (Nos. 1 to 12) were painted a dark brown, with large white letters. Nos. 13 to 18 were old Great Eastern wagons of a slate colour with smaller white lettering.

(Up to 1899 the Lambourne Valley Railway was worked by Great Western engines).

1902 The two engines "Eahlswith" and "Aelfred" (0–6–0Ts) were blue (25) with black bands having a fine white line at the edge and a thin vermilion line inside the panels thus formed. Number-plates were of bright brass raised letters on a scarlet background. Buffer-beams were vermilion. Safety-valve casings were bright brass, and the caps of chimneys were polished copper.

Lancashire, Derbyshire and East Coast Railway

(*For further details see Great Central Railway*)

1895 Coaches were varnished teak,* with a gold stripe round the panels and windows. Underframes were painted and grained to a lighter shade of wood-brown than the bodies. Ironwork was bronze green. Lettering was in gold, shaded in blue.

Passenger stock, such as horse-boxes, was painted a light shade of umber brown, with yellow lettering shaded with blue.

Goods stock was grey, with lettering and figures.

1897 Engines were black, and tanks and bunkers had a wide light blue line (Banding: see Fig. 1, p. 6)† to form panels, with a fine pale yellow line on each edge, then a vermilion line both inside and out at a distance of 1½ in. Boiler bands were black, with a red line on each side. The cab interiors were light buff colour. Buffer-beams were vermilion with a black edge and a fine white line inside. Buffer sockets were black, with vermilion lines. The engine number appeared on the buffer-beam in gold, shaded with blue, and the initial letters "L.D. & E.C.R." were on the tank sides in gold shaded blue. The number also appeared on the bunker sides in gold figures inside a sharp-cornered rectangular gold frame, thus imitating a brass number-plate. The maker's plate on the 0–6–2– locomotives was placed on the leading sand-box.

Coaches were a bright lake, with black banding round the panels and windows, with gold stripes edged with fine vermilion lines. Underframes were black and lettering in gold, shaded with red.

Wagons were a light grey with white lettering. Underframes and

* This reference to varnished teak stock was probably accounted for by the fact that the earliest vehicles were purchased from the Great Eastern Railway.

† References to banded corners are as in Fig. 1 throughout.

ironwork were black. Goods brakes were varnished teak-coloured wood with black ironwork and lettering; their buffer-beams being painted vermilion.

1898 Engines were black, banded (see Fig. 4, p. 6) with pale blue, edged with red and yellow lines. "L.D. & E.C.R." appeared on the tank sides in gold, shaded blue. Number-plates on the bunker sides were of oblong brass, with the figures raised on a bright red (vermilion) ground. Coupling-rods were red.

Coaches were (28), described in sources as a lighter shade of crimson lake (Midland Railway red), and class numbers were in very large figures on the lower door panels, in yellow shaded with pale blue, black and vermilion.

1900 (Early) All locomotives were black, picked out with white and chrome yellow lines.

1900 (Late) Locomotives were black, with a wide light blue edging round the bunkers and tanks, and narrow red bands round the boilers.

Coaches were bright lake red, with black bands round the panels and gold and vermilion red lining.

1901 (c) Locomotives were black, with a wide light blue band round the bunkers and tanks. The boilers had a narrow red line round the bands.

Coaches were bright crimson-lake, black round the panels with gold and vermilion lining.

1906 Engines were black, lined out with grey bands, edged with chrome yellow on the outside and vermilion on the inside. Number-plates were of bright brass on a red background, and were square-cornered rectangular in shape. The company's initials was on the tank sides in gold, shaded blue. The first light engines had not any number-plates, the numbers were painted on in gilt.

(**1907** *L.D. & E.C.Rly. taken over by the Great Central Railway.*)

Leeds and Selby Railway

1841 The coaches named "Diana", "Ceres", and "Juno" were painted yellow.

Leek and Manifold Valley Light Railway

THIS line was incorporated in March, 1899, and opened in June,

1904, being worked by the North Staffordshire Railway. It was later closed, but reopened in 1933; being finally closed and dismantled in 1934. The line was partly 2 ft. 6 in. gauge, and partly standard gauge.

In 1918, the locomotive superintendency came under Mr. J. A. Hookham, of the North Staffordshire Railway.

1904 (c) Coaches were at first painted primrose yellow, but later both engines and coaches were painted red (similar to the North Staffordshire Railway).

Leicester and Swannington Railway

Pre 1846 Engines and coaches had the crest of the Leicester and Swannington company emblazoned on their sides. It consisted of a wyvern*, which later became the crest in the Midland Railway Company's "coat-of-arms", of which company the Leicester and Swannington was the oldest portion.

Post 1846 The Leicester and Swannington crest was later removed from coach sides, and the figures "1" and "3" painted on the doors in its place.

Liverpool and Manchester Railway

1825 According to the detailed diagram now in the York Railway Museum, to whom it was supplied by Messrs. R. Stephenson and Hawthorns in March, 1929, the original livery of the "Rocket" was as follows:—

Boiler, medium chrome yellow; chimney, white; wheels, yellow, lined out black, with black rims. The maker's plate in the centre of the wheels was brass with black letters. The dome top was polished copper with a brass band between the top and the sides. The cylindrical dome at the rear of the boiler was copper. The frame projection in front of the driving-wheels was black, as was the small pipe alongside the chimney. The "Tee" pieces on the latter pipe were however of brass. The exhaust pipe was bright copper. The chimney stay-rods were white.

The cylinder cover-plates were of brass, and the steam-pipes from them of copper. The fire-box was also copper. The short pipe

* (The wyvern was the standard of the old Mercian kings.)

below the cylinders was copper. Connecting rods were bright steel, and their small-ends bronze.

The coupling between engine and tender was black, as was the filler to the water-butt and its retaining hoops. The ends of the butt were medium chrome yellow, and the body of the tender was yellow, lined out in black "as a stage-coach". Tender axle-boxes were brass and the rear coupling-hook, black. No details are given as to the colour of the cylinders. The name appeared in black letters on a brass plate.

1829 The "Rocket" was yellow, but with tender and water-butt green. The chimney and the ends of the butt were white.

1829 The "Sanspareil" had a dark green boiler, cylinders and motion-work. Wheels were yellow with black rims. Safety-valve casing was of polished brass. The tender was yellow, with black wheels and axle-guards. (See also L.N.W.R., p. 116.)

1829 At Rainhill trials the "Rocket" was yellow and black, with a white chimney. "Sanspareil" green, yellow and black. "Novelty" was blue with copper piping. "Perseverance" had red wheels. Second class coaches, blue.

1837 (c) The engine "Lion" as restored by the L.M.S. for the Sefton Park Exhibition in 1930 had the boiler-casing painted bright yellow encircled by polished brass cleading bands. The haystack fire-box was brass-cased and relieved by teak lagging strips arranged vertically at the sides. There was a polished copper cap to the chimney. A polished brass beading lined the outer and inner edges of the open-work splashers. The four-wheeled tender was painted a rich dark green (chrome green) and was lined out with black bands and red lining. The frames of both locomotive and tender were dark red-brown, and the wheels were green with black tyres.

London and Birmingham Railway

(*Edward Bury, Loco. Supt. from opening of Railway to its amalgamation with L.N.W.R.*)

1837 Mail coaches were painted Post Office red in the lower panels and black above. First class coaches were buff lower panels and black upper. Second class coaches were green lower panels and black upper.

1843 Queen Victoria's Royal coach was painted a dark crimson-lake, which was "her favourite colour". The body was relieved by scarlet and gold lining, and the upper quarterings had broad borders of white around the windows, with a gold beading and small gold ornaments in each corner. The lower quarters had ornaments with the heraldic devices of the Royal Family, and the Queen's coat-of-arms was emblazoned on the door panels. The insignia of the Order of the Garter occupied the centre of each side panel. In the centre of the roof there was a large gilded representation of the Royal crown through which ventilation of the compartment was effected. The roof was painted white and the underframes deep purple-brown.

1844 Locomotives similar to those on the South Eastern Railway (Sharp's No. 13) were not so decorated as those on that line. They had not any polished brass but were painted all over in dark green—the then standard colour of the company.

1846 Locomotives were painted green, with plain black bands. Firebox was polished copper. Side number-plates and numbers on chimney were brass. Nos. 59, 60, 91, 93, 94, 96–118 had copper-topped chimneys.

London and Blackwall Railway

1841–66 Locomotives were painted bright blue, with polished copper caps to chimneys.

London and Croydon Railway

1838 (July 16) Passenger coaches blue of shade approved by the Board.

1839 (Feb. 13) Carriages to bear the City Arms on centre panels of first-class and "L & C" on end panels. (Extract from company's minutes.)

Lynn and Fakenham Railway

1880 Goods engines were chocolate-coloured, lined out in black and yellow; this livery being adopted by the Eastern and Midlands Railway. Number-plates were placed on the tank sides of the 0–6–0T engine No. 3 ("Blakeney"), with the small oval date-plate below. (Sharp, Stewart and Co.). Cut-out numbers were carried on the front of the chimney, which was copper-capped. This general livery also applied to engines Nos. 1 and 2 ("Melton Constable" and "Reepham").

1883 Locomotives Nos. 21, 22, 23 and 24 were painted green, with black borderings and white lining. The outside of frames, springs, bogie-frames and cylinders were chocolate brown with black panelling and white lining. Buffer-beams and buffer shanks were vermilion. Engine numbers were in gold, shaded with black, and appeared on each buffer-beam.

1884 Locomotives Nos. 25, 26, 27 and 28 were painted chocolate colour and lined out in black and chrome yellow. The maker's plates occupied the centre of the tank panels and the company's initials were not used. Number-plates were oval, with raised brass numerals, being mounted on the cab side-sheets. The leading driving-wheel splasher was double brass-beaded and left bright, the name of the makers (Beyer, Peacock and Co.) appearing between the beadings, as on some L.S.W.R. locomotives.

Lynton and Barnstaple Railway

INCORPORATED in June, 1895, and opened in May, 1898, this 19-mile line was purchased by the Southern (L.S.W.R.) in 1923, and finally closed and the rails lifted after the last journey had been taken on Sunday, 29th September, 1935.

1904 Covered goods stock was light grey with white lettering and black underframes thus :

L & BR
No. 7

1914 Engines were a dark emerald green, lined out in orange and a black edging. Domes were polished brass, as were chimney tops. Name-plates were of brass, with raised figures on a vermilion background. Underframes were chocolate.

Coaches were dark brown with white upper panels.

1917 Coaches had dark red lower panels and white upper ones. The engine "Lyn" was at one time black, but was now (1917) green, with small brass name-plates. The colour of the coaches was also termed "magenta".

Manchester and Milford Haven Railway

1906 (March) Engine No. 4 ("Aberystwyth", built by Manning, Wardle in 1868), "Caeder Idris", (1896), and "Plynlimmon",

(1891), were all black, lined out in orange. They had copper-topped chimneys with bell mouths.

Coaches were a dark brown with cream upper panels, similar to Great Western coaches.

Manchester, Sheffield and Lincolnshire Railway

(*For further details see Great Central Railway*)

Pre 1885 Engines were a medium green (somewhat darker than that of later years), lined out with black bands and red and white lines. Underframes were a red-brown. Number-plates were of brass with raised figures on a dark blue background. (Fig. 46, p. 114.)

1885 The engine colour was changed to a sea-green (described as a 'bilious' shade), with the lining not so elaborate.

1885 Locomotive No. 210 (Sacré 2–2–2) had outside frames double lined round all openings. Buffer-beams were square double lined at their ends. Cab side-sheets were lined double with incurved corners (see Fig. 46, p. 114), and the axle-boxes of both front and rear wheels were doubled lined. The axle-box brace-bar was treble lined, and the front pony-wheel splashers were double lined.

1886 The sea-green was discontinued, and the original medium green restored.

1890 Locomotives were a light yellow-green.

1896 Engine No. 694 was black, with red lining, with gilt lettering shaded blue on the tank sides.

1896 Engine No. 694 and three bogie coaches were painted a silver-green on one side to get an opinion as to appearance of the colour-scheme. The M.S. & L. locomotive No. 15 was painted black with red lining and gold lettering, shaded with blue on the tank sides for work on the extension into London.

1896 Appeal was made to Parliament to change the name of the company to The Central Railway. It was agreed to retain the original green of the engines, but coaches were to be painted a very light green in upper panels with lake lower panels; with gold lining. Some locomotives and coaches were thus painted, but the decision to standardize the colours was dependent upon their being durable.

1896 Engines were painted a slightly lighter green than that used fourteen years previously. A broad black border ran round the tender-sides, tanks and splashers, this being separated from the green by a yellow line. Frames were brown, with a narrow black border, separated by a yellow line. Wheels were green, and axle-ends black, with a yellow line round the joint between the axle and the wheel-hub. Tyres were left bright. Buffer-beams were vermilion and the buffers were brown, striped round with black and yellow lines. Underframes were dark red, almost lake. The company's initials ("M.S. & L."), together with the engine number appeared on the cab and tender sides in gold, shaded red (Fig. 98, p. 280). The number on the buffer-beam was in gold, shading black, and the company's crest appeared on the driving-wheel splashers and the tank sides.

1897 (Feb.) On account of the confusion between the Cambrian Railways, Caledonian Railway, and the Central Railway (the initials CR) the directors of the Railway decided to rename the line "Great" Central Railway.

1907 Immediately before becoming the Great Central Railway the locomotives were green, with black bands and white lining.

(N.B.) Some authorities state that the locomotive lining immediately pre-Great Central was black bands and *red* and white lining.

Manx Northern Railway

THIS line was acquired by the Isle of Man Railway in 1904, and had a track gauge of 3 ft.

1899 Coaches were chocolate in the lower panels and creamy white in the upper ones.

Mawddwy Railway

INCORPORATED in July, 1865 and later closed, this line was re-opened in July, 1911; being then worked by the Cambrian Railways. The railway was of standard gauge and had a length of $6\frac{3}{4}$ miles.

The track from Cemmes Road to Dinas Mawddwy was finally removed during April and May, 1952.

1904 The engine "Disraeli" was green, and "Mawddwy" was in the black, with orange lining, of the Cambrian Railways, but with fluted copper safety-valves; this latter feature appeared on both locomotives. Coaches were very decrepit, but were painted a red-brown or red-lake colour.

1906 Locomotive "Disraeli" was green. Locomotive "Mawddwy" was in Cambrian Railways' livery (black with orange lines).

Coaches were in L.N.W.R. livery until they were broken up. Coaches Nos. 3, 4 and 6 were one time red, but were in very bad repair in 1906.

Mersey Railway

THE Mersey Railway was incorporated in 1866 and opened in February, 1886; having a length of just over 4 miles.

1902 Pre-electrification engines were painted a medium green, panelled with dark green picked out in red and dark green. Rectangular name-plates appeared on the boilers, but these were removed before electrification in 1903.

According to another source, locomotives were light Brunswick green, lined out with rounded corners in dark green, and picked out in red. At one time, they had name-plates but these were removed before 1900. Number-plates were oval brass, with the figures in large serif, and the words "MERSEY RAILWAY" above and the date below ("1892").

Midland and South-Western Junction Railway

THIS very important but lesser-known railway was formed in the year 1884 by the amalgamation of the Swindon, Marlborough and Andover Railway (incorporated in 1873), and the Swindon and Cheltenham Railway (incorporated in 1881). Until the year 1898, the Great Western Railway tracks were used between Marlborough and Wolfhall, but in 1896 the Marlborough and Grafton Railway was incorporated; and opened two years later. The following year the latter railway was amalgamated with the Midland and South-Western Junction Railway.

1884 The 4- and 6-wheeled coaches had a two-colour scheme similar to that of the Great Western Railway.

1896 Engines were painted a dark red, with black bands and yellow lines on each side. Buffer-beams were vermilion with a black edge and a yellow line between the two colours. Cab interiors were painted a light yellow-brown. Number-plates were of polished brass, with the figures raised on a vermilion background. The lettering on the tender sides was in gold, shaded with blue.

Coaches were painted in two styles at this date. Some were very similar to the Midland Railway, but of a slightly darker lake shade, with black round the panels and a gold stripe and vermilion line. Lettering was in gold, with black shading. Older carriages were lined with yellow in place of gold, and were lettered in yellow with red shading. The other style of coach livery was similar to the Great Western Railway, being brown in the lower panels and white in the upper ones. Lettering was, in this case, in gold with blue shading.

Goods stock was painted a light grey with white lettering.

1898 The coach colour scheme was changed to a lake similar to the Midland Railway colour.

1899 Red-brown (deep lake) was adopted as the standard coach colour.

1900 Engines Nos. 1–8 originally had the letters "SM & A" (Swindon, Marlborough and Andover) on the tanks, but this was later changed to "M & SWJ" 4. (The engine number being in one line with the initials.) Chimneys had polished copper tops. Dome casings were polished brass. The later 0–6–0 engines had their numbers (29, etc.) in brass figures on the cab sides and MSWJR on the tenders.

1914 Engines were "Midland" red (crimson-lake). Goods locomotives were olive green. Coaches were crimson-lake. Engines had the company's initials in copper-plate script on the tenders. Passenger engine wheels were red on express engines.

1914–18 Passenger engines were changed in colour to black, being lined out in vermilion; and coaches to lake, picked out with straw-colour and vermilion.

1915 Coaches were a crimson-lake. Locomotives were also lake or red-brown.

1922 Engines and coaches were all crimson-lake.

Mid-Suffolk Light Railway

INCORPORATED in April, 1900, and opened for goods traffic in 1904, and for passenger traffic in 1908; the Mid-Suffolk Light Railway was 19½ miles long and boasted three locomotives and 38 other vehicles. The locomotive superintendent in 1918 was W. Lindsey-Badcock.

1907 Locomotives were crimson-lake, with the initials "M.S.L.R." in gold letters on the tanks. Panels were lined out in yellow and vermilion. Chimneys were copper-topped, and brass dome and safety-valve covers were fitted.

1914 Engines were dark red with copper-topped chimneys, and polished brass domes.

Millwall Extension Railway

1880 Engines were a dark yellow (similar to Stroudley's yellow on the L.B.S.C.R.) and lined. Advertisements appeared on the sand-boxes and side tanks.

1904 Engines were brick-red with black bands. Domes and safety-valve casings were polished brass, as were the number-plates.

Monmouthshire Railway (and Canal)

1870 Locomotive No. 1304, 4–4–0T (Newport Works No. 7) had a copper-topped chimney, and a brass dome and safety-valve casing. There was a brass band between the boiler and the smoke-box. The number-plate was similar in shape and lettering to the L.N.W.R. plates of the period, but was of brass, and was fitted centrally on the tank sides. The building-plate was oval in shape with raised letters (date and company's initials), and was fixed to the bunker side-sheet.

Newcastle and Carlisle Railway

1837 The first engines were painted brown or maroon, on the N. & C. and on the Brandling Junction lines.

1841 Coaches: First class, yellow picked out with black. Second class, green picked out with white.

1841 Early coaches were named "Expedition", "Despatch" and "Transit", and carried in addition the arms of the cities of Newcastle and Carlisle emblazoned on their sides.

1843 Coaches: First class: claret picked out with black. Second class: claret picked out with white and edged with yellow. Coaches on the Brandling Junction branch were bright yellow, and some light stone colour.

1843 (c) Locomotives were Indian red, lined out in black, with much brasswork. Names were painted on the tender-sides in large letters on a vermilion red panel in addition to the usual name-plates on the boiler sides, the plates being three and a half times as large as those on the engine.

The first class carriages bore names of some of the earlier mail-coaches, such as "Despatch", and "Transit"; and one of the second class coaches bore the name "Emerald".

The first class coaches were painted light yellow, picked out in black, with a crown in the centre panel and the coats-of-arms of Newcastle and Carlisle respectively, on the two end compartment door-panels. Some first and second class carriages, built by Atkinson and Phillipson of Newcastle in 1843, were painted dull claret and black, picked out in green. and others white and claret, picked out with green. Luggage vans and horse-boxes were green.

Passenger guards were dressed in scarlet laced coats, with drab-coloured trousers and cream-coloured hats.

1850 Locomotives were red.

Newcastle and North Shields Railway

Post 1841 First class coaches altered to red, and seconds to claret.

1850 (c) Early coaches were crimson-maroon for the first class (in one solitary case a rich scarlet-claret, edged with yellow was used). Second class coaches were light stone shade, and third class ones light green.

Coaches carried names such as "Times", "Herald", "Director", "Victoria" and "British Queen"; the last two also having the Royal cypher on their panels. Some coaches had 1s. (the fare) on first-class vehicles, and 6d. on third-class ones, painted on the doors. Others had pictures of chamois on the end doors of first class coaches; gazelles, antelopes and reindeer also being used as illustrations of the names of the carriages.

Nidd Valley Light Railway

OPENED in 1907 by the Bradford (Yorkshire) Corporation in connection with the town's water supply, this Railway had a total of 13 miles of track; only 6 of which were for public use. The line was closed to passenger traffic in December, 1909, and entirely closed in 1936. During its life it had 16 locomotives, which were under the charge of Mr. J. Watson. In the year 1922, C. Mitchell was locomotive superintendent.

1906 The reboilered Metropolitan 4–4–0T (Nos. 20 and 34) became Nos. 1 and 2, and were renamed "Holdsworth" and "Milner". They had cast-iron chimneys, brass domes, but retained their Metropolitan standard red; though with a darker shade of yellow lining. The Bradford coat-of-arms appeared in the centre panel of the side tanks, on which there were three panels. The left-hand panel contained the word "BRADFORD", the centre one the engine's name, and the right-hand one the word "CORPORATION", in serif capitals. Brass number-plates (No. 1) in a double-lined oval were fitted to the bunker sides.

Coaches were red, lined out in yellow, to match the engines, the words "BRADFORD CORPORATION" appearing on the panelling.

1914 The 0–6–0T engine "Milner" was black, with a polished brass dome and a copper-topped chimney.

Coaches and wagons were variously dark red or brown.

1921 The coaches were maroon red, some bearing the initials "N.V.L.R." and others "BRADFORD CORPORATION", with the arms of that city.

Wagons were grey, with the letters "B.C." in large white letters.

North Devon Railway

INCORPORATED in 1838 as the Taw Vale Railway (the later title being adopted in 1851), the North Devon Railway was leased to the London and South-Western Railway in 1863, and finally acquired by that line in 1865.

1865 The locomotives "Creedy", "Venus", "Barum" and "Tite", were painted chocolate-brown, and lined out with yellow banding.

North Midland Railway

Early Coaches coloured "Spanish" brown, picked out in black.

1838 Coaches, yellow.

North Sunderland Railway

THIS 4 mile long railway was incorporated in June, 1892, and opened (for goods traffic) in August, 1898; and for passenger traffic four months later.

1899 Engine "Bamburgh" was a light green of a shade slightly darker than (5), described in sources as the "North Eastern" green. Coaches were (12), described as "Highland" green. The coaches were purchased from that railway.

North Wales Narrow Gauge Railway

INCORPORATED in August, 1872, and opened exactly five years later, this railway's name was changed to the Welsh Highland Railway in 1922. Branch service was suspended in 1914, and all passenger traffic ceased in 1936; goods working stopped the following year. The line was dismantled in 1941. In 1918, the locomotive superintendent was Mr. G. C. Aitchison. The gauge of the line was 1 ft. 11½ ins.

1907 Engines were a dark red in the lower panels, and a light red in the upper ones. They were lined out with fine gold lines.

1909 Engines were bright crimson-lake (as Midland coaches) with black panel bands edged with yellow lines. Cranks and counter-balance weights were vermilion, and domes, bright brass.

Coaches were in two shades of brown-red, somewhat similar to the Lancashire and Yorkshire coaches of the period.

1915 Engines were "Midland" red, lined out in black and yellow.

Coaches were very similar to those of the Lancashire and Yorkshire Railway. (See p. 90.)

1930 Welsh Highland Railway engines were red, and the coaches each a different colour.

Oxford, Worcester and Wolverhampton Railway

INCORPORATED in 1845, and opened in 1850, this railway acquired the Stratford and Moreton Railway (incorporated 1821 and opened 1826); and then was itself absorbed by the West Midland Railway in 1860, together with the Worcester and Hereford Railway (incorporated 1853 and opened 1859), and the Newport, Abergavenny and Hereford Railway (incorporated 1846 and opened 1854). The

West Midland Railway became part of the Great Western Railway system in 1863.

1860 Engine "Will Shakespeare" (No. 51—a "Jenny Lind"), was painted a blue-green on boiler, sand-boxes, tender and dome, with black, red and black lining. There was a copper top to the safety-valve pillar and a copper base, the intermediate fluting being green. There was a polished brass ring between the fire-box and the boiler, and a brass band round the centre of the fire-box. The smoke-box was black. The brass name-plates were rectangular with polished letters on a red background. Cab spectacles were brass-beaded. Buffer-beams were red. The fender and tender sides panelled black, with a red line between the green and the black. Tool-boxes were unlined green. Underframes were chocolate, lined with red. Wheel spokes were green, and axle-boxes black. A rectangular date-plate was fitted at the base of the dome.

Peterhead Harbour Railway

1900 The four locomotives were a dull olive green with polished brass domes. Name-plates were placed in the centre of the tanks. The engines were 0–6–0T class and were named "Victoria", "Prince of Wales", "Alexandra" and "Duke of York".

Port of London Authority Railways

1896 Engines were green, lined out in black. Domes and safety-valve casings were of polished copper. The locomotives were old London and North Western ones, built at Crewe.

1943 (c) Locomotives. There were four classes. The two types of 0–4–0ST were painted dark red when they were new in 1915. These are only found in the West India Docks. They are now all painted R.A.F. blue-grey, lined out in white-black-white. No. 74 is still green with polished brass dome.

The 0–6–0 tanks at Tilbury and the Royal Docks are painted royal blue and have been, since about 1920. They are unlined and have black boiler-mountings. Some have "P L A" in white shaded black (and number) whilst others have an oval cast number-plate on the tank brass with a red background. No. 70 is painted green.

Rolling stock. Open wagons (*ex* M.R. or L.N.W.R.) are red (as "Bolsovers"), with a large "P L A" in white on them. The vans were also in a similar livery. Insulated vans were painted pale chrome yellow, brake-vans were red, and flat trucks were black.

Potteries, Shrewsbury and North Wales Railway

1888 At the time the engines of this line were auctioned they were painted black, though they had previously been green. They were named "Bradford", "Powis", "Hope" and "Tanat".

Ravenglass and Eskdale Railway

INCORPORATED in May, 1873, and opened for passenger traffic in 1876 as a 3 ft. gauge line, this railway was closed in 1909. It was, however, again opened as a 1 ft. 3 in. railway in August, 1915, a standard (4 ft. 8½ in.) section being added in 1926.

1880* Engines and coaches were red.

1901 Engines were green, picked out in black and orange; and coaches were chocolate-coloured.

Post 1927 Locomotives were green and coaches red.

Redruth and Chacewater

1902 Engines "Miner" and "Smelter" were brown with red lining, with bright brass splashers over the driving-wheels. "Miner" had an oval brass plate on the bunker sides inscribed "REDRUTH & CHASEWATER RAILWAY COMPANY"—"Constructed at Devoran Works, 1869": in sunk letters. (Chasewater was spelt with an "s", at that time and not with a "c", as to-day.)

1905 "Miner" and "Spitfire" were green, with brass chimney tops and safety-valve covers. "Miner" had brass corner plates to the haystack boiler. "Smelter" was painted a very dark brown and lined out in dark red, with brass driving-wheel splashers.

Rhondda and Swansea Bay Railway

THIS Railway was incorporated in 1882 and opened in stages

*At one time the 4–4–2 and 4–6–2 locomotives were painted blue.

between 1885 and 1895, having a final length of some 31 miles. In 1918 its locomotive superintendent was Mr. R. Oliver.

1903 Engines were black, picked out with blue and vermilion. Those built by Kitson & Co. had the railway company's crest (see p. 217) on the bunker sides. All engines had number-plates on the tank sides, the number being enclosed in a double-lined oval (*e.g.* "15").

Romney, Hythe and Dymchurch Railway

1948 The locomotives do not generally conform to the royal blue and cream colour-scheme maintained throughout the line, the only exception being the petrol-driven engine, which is coloured blue and cream. The liveries of the locomotives are as follows:— No. 1, "Green Goddess", No. 5, "Hercules", No. 6, "Samson", and No. 7, "Typhoon", are malachite green. No. 2, "Northern Chief" is L.N.E.R. engine green, and No. 3, "Southern Maid", Southern engine green. No. 8, "Hurricane", is in Caledonian engine blue, No. 9, "Winston Churchill", is deep crimson with gold lining; and No. 10, "Dr. Syn", is black with white lining, brass number-plates, and white rims to driving and bogie-wheels.

Most of the saloon coaches are royal blue in the lower panels, and cream in the upper ones, with a black line between. Roofs are aluminium, and the letters "R.H. (crest) D.R." appears in gold shaded with black to the right and below along the waist; the crest consisting of a garter bearing the words "Romney, Hythe and Dymchurch Railway" around an inner scroll with the words "Multum in parvo" inscribed thereon. Some coaches have square full-stops between the letters "R.H.D.R." Buffer-beams are vermilion, as are axle-box cover-nuts and spring-buckles.

Open and semi-open coaches are all-blue with "RHDR" in white without shading. Some semi-open coaches are blue, with the windows outlined in cream, and all-blue lower panels and white upper ones, with a wide black line between them. They are lettered "R.H.D.R." in white without shading. The ends of these coaches are blue.

One of the open cars, ex-Eaton railway, still carries an oval cast-iron plaque on the sole-bar bearing the words "EATON

RAILWAY" above, and "1896" below the old number "34" in the centre.

The observation cars "Martello" and "Pluto" are liveried the same as the modern coaching stock, but have a crest consisting of a vertical oval black garter bearing on it the words "OBSERVATION CAR—R.H.D.R."—in gold thereon, with a wavy maroon scroll inside the garter with the word "Martello" in gold script capitals, or in the case of "Pluto" on a deep red scroll. Brake-pipe tops are painted vermilion.

1950 Locomotives Nos. 1–8, green; Nos. 9 and 10, brown; older coaches, brown; newer stock, green or blue.

Royal India Dock Railway

1881 The engines used on this company's lines were three ex-L.N.W.R. 2–4–0 tanks, which were painted green, with black bordering and yellow lining. The tanks were panelled-out in one, the corners of the lining being ogee in shape (see Fig. 12, p. 18). The number-plates were large cast brass ovals with raised figures; being surrounded by the letters L & IDJC. These plates were mounted slightly to the rear of the centre-line of the tank-panels.

Locomotive No. 7 ("Royal Albert Dock"), one of the above engines, had the name in large and small block capital letters, with a square full-stop at the end of the work "DOCK".

Dome and safety-valve pillar were polished copper cased. The destination-board "CUSTOM HOUSE" was dropped into clips at the foot of the chimney, being lettered in white on a blue ground. The engine number also appeared in a cut-out brass figure half-way up the chimney. The lower edge of the mainframes was lined fine yellow.

The three engines were named "Royal Albert Dock", "London & India Dock Jt. Co.", and "L & IDJC" (without full-stops).

1902 The 0–6–0T locomotive "Looe" (No. 11), ex-Liskeard and Caradon Railway was painted green with black bands with yellow lines on each side. The outside frame and steps were brown with red lining. Buffer-beams and reverse-rod were vermilion. The chimney had a copper top.

Rye and Camber Tramway

OPENED in part in 1895, and over its full length of 3 miles in 1908, the Rye and Camber Tramway had only two steam-engines, "Camber" and "Victoria", both of which were 2–4–0 tanks; traffic was later worked by a petrol locomotive.

1910 The engine "Camber" was painted light green with black banding and red lines, and "Victoria" was blue, lined out in yellow. Coaches were painted red.*

1945 The petrol locomotive was painted green.

St. Helen's Railway

(*Absorbed by L.N.W.R.*)

1864 The 2–4–2T locomotive "White Raven" was painted white. (She ran experimentally on the North London Railway, and was later converted into a tender engine at Crewe.)

Sand Hutton Railway

OPENED in 1910 with a gauge of 1 ft. 3 ins., this little line was converted to 1 ft. 6 in. gauge in 1922. It was opened for passengers in 1924, and closed in 1932. The line was 3 miles long.

1923 The locomotives and coaches were painted burnt sienna.

Sheffield and Rotherham Railway

1838 First class coaches were painted a deep yellow. Open third class coaches were painted a dark green.

Shropshire and Montgomeryshire Railway

INCORPORATED in 1909 and opened in 1911, this line had a length of 26 miles; and was operated by six locomotives and 47 vehicles. The locomotive superintendent was H. F. Stephens.

1912 Engines were olive green, and coaches variously buff or dark blue.

*Maroon according to the remains of one of them still to be seen on a farm near Rye (1952).

Shutt End Railway

1906 The engine "Dudley" was painted black, with red coupling-rods, a brass dome, and a brass top and base to the chimney.

Snowdon Mountain Railway

1940 Locomotives were black; coaches red or grey.

South Devon Railway

Pre 1876 Engines were dark green, with black panelling having a fine white line on either side. Buffer-beams and buffers were vermilion.

1876 Absorbed into the Great Western Railway.

Southwold Railway

THIS line of 3-feet gauge was incorporated in 1876 and opened in September, 1879. It had a length of 9 miles, and was closed to traffic in 1929.

1880 Engines were green.

1885 Coaches were red-brown or dark red, with black lining and lettering.

1914–16 Engines were painted royal blue with red lining, similar to those of the Great Eastern Railway.

Stafford and Uttoxeter Railway

1908 Engine "Shrewsbury and Talbot" had a copper-topped chimney and a brass cover to dome and safety-valve. It was painted green.

Stanhope and Tyne Railway

1837 Engines were painted a dark slate colour.

Stockton and Darlington Railway

1825 (c) Engine "Locomotion" had the boiler horizontally lagged with mahogany with brass boiler-bands. All piping was brass, and feed-pump and cylinder tops vermilion. Chimney was black, and the bell of polished brass. Wheels had their centres and recessed parts vermilion, whilst the spokes were polished iron. All live-steam pipe-joints were painted vermilion. The name/number-plates had letters and numeral "1" in raised brass on a black background. The tender was polished teak (or mahogany) with a black tank. The letters "S. & D.R." (with full-stops) appeared on the tender-sides in gold block letters shaded to the left and below. The tender-wheel spokes were vermilion.

1825 (c) The coach "Experiment" had chocolate-coloured lower panels and cream upper ones. The sides of the seats outside were also cream, but the fronts (above and below the footrests) were black, with a white lining round each panel. The lining of the sides of the coach body was two gold lines, a broad one outside and a thin one immediately within it. The letters "S. & D.R." (with full-stops) appeared in gold block letters across the top of the coach sides, "S. &" appearing to the left of the door and "D.R." to the right. The word "Experiment" was written across the full width of the coach side in gold, centrally with the lower chocolate panel, shaded with black to the left and below. Under-frames and ironwork, together with wheels and spokes, were black.

1825 (c) Names of coaches, e.g. "Earl Grey", "Victoria", "Albert".

1825 The first coaches were painted dark blue outside, and light stone within. Later, several all-green ones appeared.

1830 Locomotive "Globe" is shown on the original drawing as having black boiler and chimney, with side framings of blue, and black; with decorative work in green and yellow. The dome is yellow, and the wheels blue.

1831 Locomotive "Wilberforce" (0–6–0, No. 23) had a green boiler. Fender, and all above foot-plate level, green, with the exception of chimney, and piping. The chimney and wheels were black, as was the smoke-box. The name-plate carried the name and number in raised polished brass letters against a red background.

1831–37 Locomotives "Jupiter" and "North Star" had yellow boiler-lagging and wheels. Frames, smoke-boxes and chimneys were black. "Jupiter" had a light green tender.

Locomotives "Liverpool" and "Fury" both had green boilers. "Liverpool" had a Bury type fire-box which was polished copper above the level of the boiler and green below.

1837 Locomotives were green and black, with blue tenders, black hoops running round the barrel on the latter vehicles.

1837 All engine boilers began to be painted green with black boiler-banding. Wheels were black, relieved with vermilion. All ironwork, except that which was polished, was painted black. Tenders were blue, with hoops and ironwork black.

1841 Coaches were yellow.

1842 (Feb. 18th) It was decided to alter the colour of all coaches from yellow to lake.

1850 The four-wheeled coach (No. 59) now in York Museum, has bodywork (28), claret-colour, and frames slightly darker, these being lined out in medium chrome yellow. The body lining is a main wide black band, flanked by fine deep gold-yellow lines, these being again edged with wide lines of a light straw colour. All geometrical and floral decorations at the curves, where the vertical lining joins the horizontal, are done in a very deep red-orange.

Springs are lined medium chrome and black, the black broad line being flanked with fine yellow ones. The colour of the springs is that of the body.

Each end door has the words "SECOND CLASS" in golden yellow block letters, shaded with light chocolate. The centre door is lettered "FIRST CLASS", with the S. and D. crest in the lower panel. The background of the "garter" is pale blue, the lettering, in duck-egg green, and the garter edging of rope, a light brown colour. Interior seats are Venetian red, and outside foot-boards, black.

The stanchions at the end of the coach are claret, this being bordered (round all corners vertically) with black. This is followed by a deep orange line, within which the body claret shows. The central panel within all this is formed of a straw-yellow line, which encloses the central panel of body-colour. There are no red or deep chrome lines on the underframes, and the lower door panels are not lined. The footboard hangers are body claret down to the thick portion, after which they are black. Buffer-sockets are body claret, and are lined out in straw-yellow and black. The individual steps are black.

1856 The engine "Nunthorpe", No. 117 (2–4–0), had the tender double-lined into three panels, and the fenders into two; all with incurved corners. The sand-boxes were lined, as also were the splashers.

The engine number was painted on the fenders in large serif numerals, which were surrounded by a rectangular border with incurved corners. The same type of number-panel appeared in the tender centre-panel. The engine number also appeared on each side of the dome, under which the name in serif capitals on a rectangular plate appeared on the boiler. The maker's plate was rectangular with incurved corners, being fixed to the front driving-wheel splashers.

1860 The engine "Brougham" (No. 160) had the tender panelled into three with incurved corners, lining being in black and vermilion; the body-colour being green. Similar panelling appeared on the cab side-sheets. There was double brass beading round the front driving-wheel splashers, and between the bands the curved rectangular name-plate (as with "Keswick"). The number was painted in the centre of the cab side panels, and also appeared in large serif cut-out numerals on the dome sides. The tender-underframes were only single-lined red, being black.

1862 The engine "Keswick" had double-lining round both splashers and sand-boxes as well as on the tender sides, dividing the latter into three panels. Splashers were double-beaded, and the horizontal base of the openings were also brass-edged. Sand-boxes were brass-edged, as was the continuation of the splashers to the smoke-box wings.

The numerals 165 appeared in cut-out brass on the sides of the dome, and the name in raised brass serif letters and rectangular border.

1867 Engine No. 134 (an 0–6–0 Manning, Wardle) was single-lined throughout, with very wide blocking round the main panels. The tender was panelled thus into two, with incurved corners. Fender-sides and fronts were panelled separately. There was a brass band between the fire-box and the boiler as well as round the rear corner of the fire-box.

Number-plates were oval and very large, with raised brass letters on a green (body colour) background. The engine number-plate was mounted on the fender-side and the tender-plate in the centre of the tender rear-panel. Maker's plates were a long rectangular shape, and were mounted over the middle axle-box on the tender-frames. One also appeared on the square base of the fluted dome on the engine. The tender back panel lining extended round the sides to the first line of rivets.

Stockton and Hartlepool Railway

(*Absorbed by N.E.R.*)

1841 Coaches were painted yellow.

Stratford-upon-Avon and Midland Junction Railway

FORMED in the year 1908 by the amalgamation of the East and West Junction Railway (incorporated 1864 and opened 1871), the Evesham, Redditch and Stratford-upon-Avon Railway (incorporated in 1873), and the Stratford-upon Avon, Towcester and Midland Junction Railway (incorporated in 1879). The Northampton and Banbury Railway (incorporated in 1863) was acquired in 1910. Before 1908, Mr. Burke was locomotive superintendent, being followed in that year by Russell Willmott.

1910 Engines were painted black and lined out in yellow. Coaches were chocolate-coloured, with cream upper panels.

1914 Locomotives were black and coaches crimson-lake.

1915 Locomotives were crimson-lake, lined out in yellow. Underframes were black.

Coaches were crimson-lake with cream upper panels, and lined out in red and yellow.

1918 Locomotives were lake and black, lined in yellow. Coaches were crimson-lake lined out in gold and lettered "SMJ".

1922 Engines: black and lake, lined out yellow, coaches: lake, lined out in gold.

Sunderland and Seaham Harbour Railway
("Londonderry Railway")

(*Amalgamated with the North Eastern Railway in* 1900)

1899 Locomotives were green with orange lining and the letters "LR" on the tanks, together with a coronet and garter; the latter emblems being enclosed in a large oval between the "L" and the "R". The engine number appeared in very large figures within two large concentric ovals to simulate a number-plate. Coaches were painted lake, and picked out in gold.

Locomotive No. 9 (2–4–0T) had not any coronet or ovals between the "L" and the "R" on the tank sides. It also had only a single-lined oval round the large numeral on the cab sides. The maker's plate was fitted on the bunker-sides.

Locomotive No. 21 (0–4–4T) had both garter and coronet between the "L" and the "R" on the tank sides, but was without the double oval enclosure round the number-plate, which was mounted at the rear end of the tank, and had small sunk numerals on an oval brass plate.

Swansea and Mumbles Railway

THIS line was incorporated in 1874 and opened between 1878 and 1900, with a total length of 18 miles.

1892 Coaching stock was painted scarlet.

Tal-y-Llyn Railway

THIS 6⅝-mile long, 2 ft. 3 in. gauge Welsh Railway was incorporated in 1865 and opened in the same year. It is an historic railway to-day, inasmuch as it is now the oldest surviving steam-hauled, passenger-carrying narrow-gauge line in the world. It still possesses its original locomotives, "Dolgoch", No. 1 (0–4–0 well tank) and "Tal-y-Llyn", No. 2 (0–4–2 saddle tank). (No. 1 was formerly named "Pretoria".) A Tal-y-Llyn Railway Preservation Society has been formed to ensure the survival of the line as a going concern.*

1908 Both engines were painted green, and the five passenger coaches were bright red.

1912 The coaches were painted crimson-lake, picked out with black lines and vermilion edging.

Vale of Rheidol Railway

THIS railway, with a gauge of 1 ft. 11½ ins. was opened in December, 1902; being 11¾ miles in length. In the year 1913 it was amalgamated

* Full particulars of membership can be obtained from P. J. Garland, A.C.A., 36, Waterloo Street, Birmingham, 2. All railway lovers are invited to join.

with and worked by the Cambrian Railways, and from 1922 was worked by the Great Western Railway. It was closed in 1940 and reopened in 1946.

1903 The engines "Edward VII" and "Prince of Wales" had colouring somewhat similar to the "Stroudley" (L.B.S.C.R.) yellow. On the tank sides was the insignia in full colours of the "Devil's Bridge", encircled by the inscription "VALE OF RHEIDOL LIGHT RAILWAY, Incorporated in 1897". There were also oblong brass number-plates at the forward end of the tank sides.

Pre 1908 Engines were painted to the livery in vogue on the London Brighton and South Coast Railway.

1908 One of the engines was painted "bright" green.

1910 (c) Engine No. 1 ("Edward VII") was painted yellow, No. 2 ("Prince of Wales") was a medium green, and No. 3 ("Rheidol") was a deep green.

Coaches were grained wood with green underframes. All the rolling-stock was built by Midland Railway Carriage and Wagon Works.

1913 All stock was painted in Cambrian Railways' colours.

1923 Stock was painted in Great Western Railway colours.

Waterloo and City Railway

(Owned and operated by L. & S.W.R., later Southern Railway)

1897 Stock was painted similarly to L. & S.W.R. coaches, *viz.* buff upper panels and brown lower, lined with vermilion.

Welshpool and Llanfair Light Railway

OPERATING from Welshpool to Llanfair–Caereinion, in Wales, this 9 mile long, 2 ft. 6 in. gauge railway was opened in April, 1903; being worked by the Cambrian Railways. Passenger services were suspended in 1930.

1903 The two engines ("The Earl" and "The Countess"—0–6–2T) were painted in Cambrian Railways' colours: black, picked out with red and yellow. Coaches were bronze-green and white.

1923 Great Western livery was adopted.

West Lancashire Railway

(*Amalgamated with Lancashire and Yorkshire Railway in* 1897)

1897 Ten engines were originally painted (38), described in sources as a dark chocolate shade, with a black border, edged by a fine yellow line. The initials "W.L.R." were on the tanks, and the engine number on the sides and back of the bunkers in gold figures shaded with red. Ex-W.L.R. engines Nos. 3 and 4 were fitted, after purchase, with standard Lancashire and Yorkshire chimneys.

1897 Most engines retained the liveries of their previous owners or builders:

Nos. 1 and 2 (*Ex* Furness) were red (p. 25).

Nos. 3, 4, 5 and 6 were dark green (*Ex* Kitson and Liverpool, Stockport and Preston Junction Railway).

No. 7 (*Ex* Brighton goods) dark green (p. 96).

No. 8 (Beyer Peacock tank) was dark purple.

No. 9 (*Ex* Brighton passenger) was yellow (p. 98).

Nos. 10, 11 and 12 (small Kitson 4-wheeled tanks) were "Brighton" yellow (p. 98).

Nos. 49 and 50 (*Ex* Sharp Stewart) were bright blue.

West Midland Railway

(*For further details see the Oxford, Worcester and Wolverhampton Railway*)

1860 Engines of the "350" class goods had their outside cranks painted vermilion.

Weston, Clevedon and Portishead Railway

INCORPORATED in 1887, and originally opened in December, 1897, with an extension opened in August, 1907; this standard-gauge line was 14½ miles in length. Five locomotives and 30 other vehicles constituted its rolling-stock.

The locomotive superintendent was Colonel H. F. Stephens.

1899 Locomotives and coaching-stock were painted crimson-lake, lined out with vermilion and black.

Whitby and Pickering Railway

1839 Early coach names were "Lady Hilda" and "Premier".

Whitehaven, Cleator and Egremont Junction Railway

34 MILES in length, this railway was jointly owned and worked by the London and North-Western and Furness Railways concurrently. The first locomotive superintendent was Mr. Robson.

1870 (Before becoming joint property) All locomotives were painted green with red and white lining. Domes were polished brass. Buffer-beams and motion were vermilion red. This practice of painting the motion red was continued by the Furness Railway after they took over the railway in 1878.

Coaches were painted chocolate, but a few were finished in natural teak, varnished; both types having a gold stripe round the panels, and being lettered in gold, shaded brown.

Whitehaven and Furness Junction Railway

1864 Locomotives were dark Brunswick green with little or no lining out. They boasted much polished brass with a band of this metal between boiler and fire-box. Number-plates were rectangular and carried the name with the number appearing above it in a square extension piece.

Wigtownshire Railway

IN 1875, the Locomotive Superintendent was Thomas Wheatley.

1875 The locomotive "Albert" was painted black and was lined out in vermilion.

Wirral Railway

THE Hoylake and Birkenhead Railway was formed in 1881 by the amalgamation of the Hoylake Railway (incorporated in 1863) and the Hoylake and Birkenhead Rail and Tramway (incorporated in 1872). The Hoylake and Birkenhead Railway, the Seacombe, Hoylake and Deeside Railway (incorporated 1891), and the Wirral Railway (incorporated in 1883) were consolidated into the Wirral Railway in 1891.

Fig.74

Fig.75

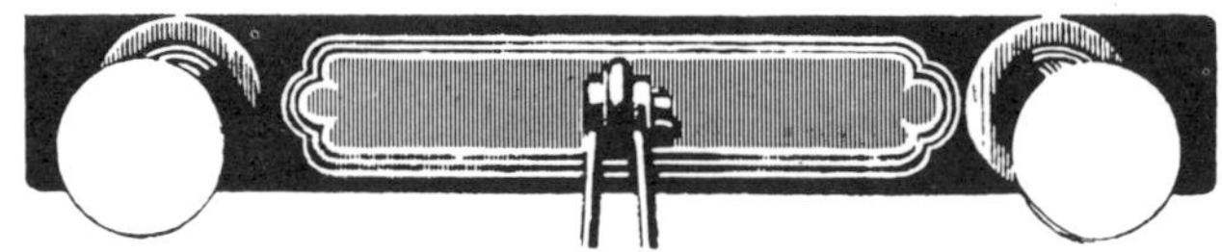

Fig. 76

Fig.77

Fig.78

Fig.79

Fig.80

Fig.81

Fig.82

Fig.83

Fig.85

Fig.84

Fig.86

1899 Engines were black, with tanks and bunkers lined with white, yellow and vermilion. The frames were black, with a red line only, as also were the outside of the cabs. Cab interiors were bright green on some locomotives and bright red on others. Coupling-rods were sometimes painted red and sometimes lake, with black edging and vermilion lining. Number-plates were raised polished brass with a scarlet background.

Coaches were generally a dark lake colour, and the name of the company appeared in a garter which surrounded a bugle. They were lined with fine yellow and vermilion lines; with plain yellow letters and figures. Some of the stock was, however, painted a warm medium brown shade, with chocolate round the panels and quarter-lights, and a vermilion line dividing the two colours. These coaches were lettered in yellow, and shaded in black and chocolate. The ends of the trains were painted scarlet.

Goods stock was painted a light French grey with white lettering and black ironwork.

1914 Coaches were a dark chocolate shade.

1915 Coaches were a rich chocolate shade, and the engines black.

1915 Locomotive number-plates were of a long oval shape with "WIRRAL RAILWAY CO." above the "No. 3", and the date in very small numerals below; all being within an oval raised brass border. The insignia of the company was (on locomotive No. 3) mounted on the forward portion of the upper cab side-sheeting, the building plate (Beyer, Peacock and Co.) being placed on the bunker sides.

Wrexham, Mold and Connah's Quay Railway

THIS railway was incorporated in 1860, and never served all the points named in its title; passengers for Mold being conveyed from Hope by the London and North Western Railway. The railway was finally absorbed by the Great Central Railway on January 1st, 1905.

1873 (c) The engine "Chancellor", at the opening of the line for goods traffic was painted green. One or two of the other early locomotives were maroon, with the letters "WM & CQ" in gilt on the tank sides.

Coaches were yellow, lined out in red. Some purchased from the L.N.W.R. retained this company's colour-scheme till they were shabby, when they were painted chocolate-colour all over.

1900 Coaches were similar to L.N.W.R. stock.

1901 Engines were Indian red. picked out with black and a fine amber-coloured line. Side tanks had "WM & CQ" and number painted, but saddle-tank engines had brass number-plates only. Insides of the frames and motion were painted a crushed-strawberry shade. Cab interiors were a cream, slightly darkened with yellow.

1902 Engines Nos. 9 and 16 were painted black, and picked out with Indian red and amber; this livery being a reversal of the 1901 practice. These two experimental liveries, and black, continued from 1902. Buffer-beams were black, not vermilion.

1908 Brymbo branch trains were still composed of the original company's stock and consisted of a saddle-tank painted Indian red and a number of old L.N.W.R. coaches, some of which retained the original white upper panels, whilst others were painted chocolate all over.

Yarmouth and North Norfolk Railway

1880 The old engine, No. 10 (a 4–4–0 outside-cylindered type built by Messrs. Hudswell, Clarke & Co.), was painted deep chrome yellow, with a polished brass dome, safety-valve casing and spectacle-plate window beading. (This engine eventually worked on the Melbourne, Ripley and Winkworth branch of the Midland Railway in 1906.)

York, Newcastle and Berwick Railway

1843 Guard's uniforms were bright green, the same colour as that used on the engines.

York and North Midland Railway

1841 All coaches were painted dark green. Early coaches carried the arms of York city on their side panels.

IRISH RAILWAYS

BELFAST AND COUNTY DOWN RAILWAY
CORK AND BANDON RAILWAY
CORK, BANDON AND SOUTH COAST RAILWAY
CORK, BLACKROCK AND PASSAGE RAILWAY
CORK AND MACROOM DIRECT RAILWAY
COUNTY DONEGAL RAILWAYS JOINT COMMITTEE
DUBLIN AND BLESSINGTON STEAM TRAMWAY
DUBLIN AND KINGSTOWN RAILWAY
DUBLIN AND SOUTH-EASTERN RAILWAY
GIANT'S CAUSEWAY, PORTRUSH AND BUSH VALLEY TRAMWAY
GREAT NORTHERN RAILWAY (IRELAND)
GREAT SOUTHERN AND WESTERN RAILWAY
LISTOWEL AND BALLYBUNION RAILWAY
LONDONDERRY AND LOUGH SWILLY RAILWAY
MIDLAND GREAT WESTERN RAILWAY
THE NORTHERN COUNTIES COMMITTEE
TIMOLEAGUE AND COURTSMACSHERRY RAILWAY
TRALEE AND DINGLE LIGHT RAILWAY
WATERFORD AND CENTRAL IRELAND RAILWAY
WATERFORD, LIMERICK AND WESTERN RAILWAY
WATERFORD AND TRAMORE RAILWAY
WEST AND SOUTH CLARE LIGHT RAILWAY
WEST CORK RAILWAY
IRISH TRANSPORT COMPANY (CORAS IOMPAIR ÉIREANN)

IRISH RAILWAYS

Belfast and County Down Railway

INCORPORATED in 1846, this railway acquired the Belfast, Holywood and Bangor Railway (incorporated in 1860) in 1884; and by subsequent extensions ultimately increased its route mileage to over 80. The locomotive superintendent of the railway in 1918 was R. G. Miller; in 1921, J. L. Crosthwait.

1906 Engines were dark green, lined out in white (see Figs. 77 and 79, p. 258).

1914 Coaches were maroon.

1914 Engines were dark green, lined out with white, black and vermilion. Coaches were (27), described in sources as maroon, lined out in gold. Wagons were lead grey.

1915 Coaches were maroon.

1918 Locomotives were painted a dark green and lined out in white.

Coaches were maroon, lined out in gold.

Wagons were a dull lead grey colour.

1920 (c) A red line was added to locomotive liveries, and coaches were changed to crimson, lined out in yellow.

1922 Engines were dark green, lined out white and red.

Coaches were crimson (28), lined out yellow.

1933 Engines were painted dark green.

Coaches were crimson-lake, lined out in yellow.

Cork, Bandon and South Coast Railway

ORIGINALLY incorporated as the Cork and Bandon Railway in 1845, the Cork, Bandon and South Coast line grew by acquisitions and amalgamations until it owned over 65 route miles of track, and leased or worked a further 28 miles. The West Cork Railway (opened in 1866) and the Baltimore Railway (opened in 1893) are part of the system; the Cork and Kinsale Junction Railway (amalgamated 1880), the Ilen Valley Railway (amalgamated in 1909), and the Cork, Kinsale and West Cork Railway (amalgamated in 1880) were later acquisitions.

The locomotive superintendent of the C.B. & S.C.R. in 1921 was J. W. Johnstone.

1914 Engines and coaches were painted in various shades of olive-green, (12), with yellow lining. Engines had polished brass domes and some had copper-topped chimneys. The upper panels of some of the coaches were of a lighter shade of green.

1915 Coaches were green and engines green.

1921 Engines and coaches were olive-green, lined out in yellow.

Cork, Blackrock and Passage Railway

This was originally a 3 ft. gauge line, some 16 miles in length, which was incorporated in 1846 and opened in 1850. Its four locomotives were superintended by Mr. J. Inman.

1900 Locomotives Nos. 1, 2 and 3 were light green, with black bands and yellow lining. Domes were polished brass. Old coaches were dark green with yellow lettering. On conversion to 3 ft. gauge, locomotives Nos. 4, 5, 6 and 7 were painted black, lined out with vermilion and white.

Cork and Macroom Direct Railway

Incorporated in August, 1861, and opened in May, 1866, the Cork and Macroom Direct Railway had a track length of just over 24 miles. The line had five locomotives which, in 1933, were under the care of M. J. Reen. In 1918, W. Gadd, was the locomotive superintendent.

1903 Engines were light green, picked out with yellow and black.

Cork and Bandon Railway

(*For details see Cork, Bandon and South Coast Railway*)

1880 (c) Engines were painted olive-green.

County Donegal Railways Joint Committee

Owned by the Midland Railway of England and Great Northern

Railway of Ireland, this Joint Committee operated some 91 miles of track with joint stock. The Committee commenced working in May, 1906.

1906 Coaches were brown, with white upper panels.

1912 Engines were indigo blue, slightly darker than (24), with red and yellow lining, thus: red, yellow, red, the tanks being single-panelled. Names were on a rectangular brass plate in the centre of the tank panels with raised letters on a black background. The company's crest appeared on the bunker sides and the number on a rectangular brass plate on the upper part of the cab side-sheets. The date-plate on engine "Ballyshannon No. 21", was triangular in shape, and was mounted on the side of the smoke-box. The underframes were indigo blue and lined in red only, and the buffer-beams were vermilion, edged with indigo; and were devoid of numbers. Safety-valve casings were brass, and the boiler bands red–yellow–red.

1914 Engines were black, lined out with vermilion.
Coaches were all brown.

1922 Engines were black, lined out in red. Coaches were chocolate lined out in red. Goods wagons were black.

1933 Engines were painted black, lined out in red. Coaches were maroon and goods stock black.

1951 Engines, geranium red.

Dublin and Blessington Steam Tramway

OPENED in 1888 after incorporation the previous year, this 15½ mile line was operated in 1918 by four engines together with 62 other rolling-stock vehicles. The locomotive chief at that date was Mr. F. C. Doyle.

1916 Engines and trailer cars were dark green, lined out in gold.
Wagon stock was a medium grey.

Dublin and Kingstown Railway

INCORPORATED in 1831 and opened in 1834, this railway was later amalgamated with the Dublin and South-Eastern Railway, which was formerly known as the Dublin, Wicklow and Wexford Railway from 1860 to 1906, and as the Waterford, Wexford, Wicklow and Dublin Railway as originally incorporated in 1846.

1851 The 2–2–2T engine built by Forrester & Co., of Liverpool, had the boiler and fire-box of copper, and the dome, safety-valve casing-top and feed-pipes of brass. The top of the chimney was copper with a brass ring immediately below the copper part. The exhaust pipes were copper.

Frames, fenders, bunkers were green (6), panelled with a broad black edging with a fine white line between the black and the green. The foot-plate valance was green, edged with a broad white line. The turned-out top of the bunker was edged with a broad black band with a fine white line between it and the body green. Hand-rails were polished steel. The spectacle-plate edge and windows were brass-beaded, the beading being followed by a broad black line, then a fine white one, within.

The safety-valve spring covers inside the cab were polished brass. Buffer-beams were of polished oak, and the buffer-shanks were black. Steps were painted black, and the cylinder casings were polished steel. Splasher covers were brass, and their fretted fronts green. Springs and the reversing-rod were of polished steel. The smoke-box was black.

The name-plate was rectangular with the word "ALEXANDRA" raised and of polished brass on a black background. Injector feeds were brass, and the safety-valve balance levers steel. The number-plate was brass with the figures in vermilion and the oval border in the same colour (vermilion).

1852 The 2–2–2 Locomotive "Jupiter" was painted royal blue for hauling the State train when Queen Victoria and Prince Albert visited Dublin.

Dublin and South-Eastern Railway

INCORPORATED in 1846 as the Waterford, Wexford, Wicklow and Dublin Railway, this railway's title was changed in 1860 to the Dublin, Wicklow and Wexford Railway, and again altered in 1907 to its present title. It was 133 miles in total length, and, in 1918, its stock of 65 locomotives were under the care of Mr. G. H. Wild.

In 1862, the locomotive superintendent was S. W. Haughton, in 1884, William Wakefield, and in 1897, T. B. Grierson.

1907 Locomotives were painted black, with yellow-edged red bands.

Lettering was in gold, shaded red and blue. Numbers were painted on the back end of tenders in yellow figures, shaded red and blue.

1914 Coaches were dark red.

1914 Engines were black, lined out in red and gold.
Coaches were crimson-lake, lined out in gold.

1915 Coaches were red-brown. Engines were black.

1921 Engines were black picked out in red and gold. Coaches were crimson-lake lined out in gold. (See Fig. 78, p. 258.)

Giant's Causeway, Portrush and Bush Valley Tramway

INCORPORATED in 1880 and opened in January, 1883 under the title of the Giant's Causeway Tramway, this line was steam-operated until the following September, when electricity was introduced as a motive-power.

The electrification was commenced within a month of the opening of the first electric railway in these Islands—Magnus Volk's Brighton Electric Railway, in August, 1883. These two events were the turning point in railway electric traction.

The Giant's Causeway, Portrush and Bush Valley Tramway, as it was known after its electrification, can also claim to have been the first electric railway in the world to be run on current generated by water-power.

1933 The steam locomotives used ("Dunluce Castle", No. 3 and "Boroimhe", No. 4) were painted green, with oval brass number-plates and name-plates. The warning bells on these engines were of polished brass.
Coaching-stock was painted cream, with medium brown panelling.

Great Northern Railway (Ireland)

IN the year 1875 the Dublin and Drogheda Railway (incorporated in 1836 and opened in 1844), and the Dublin and Belfast Junction Railway (incorporated in 1845 and opened in 1846), were amalgamated in 1875 to form the Northern of Ireland Railway which became in 1876, after other amalgamations, the G.N.R.(I). The Dublin and Drogheda and the Ulster Railways were among the oldest railways in Ireland, the latter railway being incorporated in May, 1836, and opened in 1839.

In the year 1918, the fleet of 204 locomotives was under the supervision of Mr. G. T. Glover.

1885–92 Locomotive livery was changed from (8), described in sources as a green (very similar in shade to that of the Great Northern of England), to black, then finally to a shade of blue almost identical with the immediately pre-grouping Caledonian Railway locomotive shade (see p. 17).

1892 Mr. Parke's rail motor car built in 1892 was finished in varnished teak with lettering and numbers in gold.

1899 Engines were dark green. Main line coaches were oak-coloured and those of branch lines purple-brown.

1899 Engines were green, lined out with black and white.

1900 Engine colours were changed to (16), described in sources as Brunswick green, relieved with white lining. Underframes were dark red, picked out with black and red.

Coaches were a rich crimson-lake, with broad bands of gold, fine-lined in blue.

Locomotives of the Ulster Section were bright red, picked out with broad black bands and fine vermilion lines; but those of other sections were green, picked out with black and white lines.

Coaches of the Ulster section were white in the upper panels and chocolate in the lower; but those of other sections were crimson-lake, picked out with black and white lines.

1907 Locomotives were green, lined out in black and white.

Coaches were varnished teak and wagons dark grey.

1913 Engine No. 174 "Carrantuohill" was green.

1913 Engines were green, with black bands and white lining. Underframes were chocolate, lined with red. Bogie splashers were chocolate lined red. Buffer sockets were chocolate. Wheels were green, and axle-ends lined white. The names were on curved brass plates in black letters, and the company's crest (Fig. 82, p. 258), appeared under the name-plate on the leading driving-wheel splashers. The date-plate was fixed below the crest. The engine number was in block gold on the cab side-sheets, shaded with red. "GNR" was on the tender in gold, shaded with red. Boiler mountings were green.

1914 Engines were (8), described in sources as green, lined out in black and white—or yellow. Number-plates were of brass with raised polished figures on a vermilion background. Goods engines were black, lined out in red.

Coaches were either varnished mahogany or oak.

1914–18 The engine colour was changed to black, lined out in vermilion.

1917 Engine No. 174 was black, lined out in red. Coaches were varnished mahogany, as were vans.

1922 Engines black, lined red. Coaches, varnished mahogany.

1928 Locomotives were unlined black, with the engine number in gold on the cab sides and on vermilion buffer-beams. It appeared on the latter place, however, without "No.". Tenders were lettered "GREAT NORTHERN", but did not carry the engine number. Maker's plates were painted vermilion and appeared on both engine and tender. Tank engines were lettered "GREAT NORTHERN" on the side tanks, the number appearing on the bunker, as well as on both buffer-beams. The above was the passenger engine livery.

1933 The engines "Falcon" (No. 84) and "Kestrel" (No. 87) appeared painted in (23), described in sources as a brilliant azure blue, with black and white lining. Underframes of both engines and tenders were vermilion, with a black edging and a fine white line. The company's crest was on each driving-wheel splasher, below the name-plate.

1933 Engines were painted black, lined red.
Coaches were varnished mahogany.

1937 Engines of the G.N.R.(I) were (23), described in sources as bright blue, boiler-bands being black; all other flat surfaces were also edged with the latter colour, with a fine white line everywhere separating the black from the blue. Foot-plate angles and step-plates were deep red, edged with black and fine-lined with white up to 1937, and in that year frames, cylinders and wheels began to be painted blue.

Great Southern and Western Railway

THE largest railway in Ireland, the Great Southern and Western was incorporated in 1844 for a line from Dublin to Cashel, afterwards to Cork. It owned nearly 1,000 miles of track and leased or worked a further 156 miles. The 321 locomotives it owned in 1918 were under the care of three district superintendents, the Chief Mechanical Engineer of the Company being E. A. Watson.

The G.S. & W.R. was gradually built up as follows:—

Dublin and Cork Railway (incorporated in 1844)

Cork and Limerick Direct Railway (incorporated 1860, amalgamated in 1871)

Cork and Youghal Railway (amalgamated in 1866)
Irish South-Eastern Railway (incorporated in 1863)
Killarney Junction Railway (incorporated in 1854, amalgamated in 1860)
Clara and Banagher Railway (vested in 1895)
Headford and Kenmare Railway (opened in 1849)
Kanturk and Newmarket Railway (purchased in 1892)
Killorglin Railway (opened 1885)
North Wall Extension Railway (opened in 1877)
Sallins and Baltinglass Railway (opened in 1885)
Tullow Extension (opened in 1886)
Fishguard and Rosslare Railways (opened 1906)
Waterford and Central Ireland Railway (amalgamated in 1900; see p. 276)
Mitchelstown and Fermoy Railway (purchased in 1900)
Limerick and Kerry Railway (vested in 1902)
Rathkeale and Newcastle Junction Railway (vested in 1902)
Ballywilliam and Palace East Railway (leased in perpetuity in 1902)
Waterford, Limerick and Western Railway (1901, see p. 277)

1882 Mr. J. A. F. Aspinall's (Class 52) 4–4–0's had their number-plates made of white-metal, which took a silvery polish. The cab roofs were panelled in oak (wood), and the inside of the side-sheets were painted white, picked out with crimson lining. Up to 1882 number-plates were made of cast-iron (Fig. 81, p. 258.)

1890 The engines of class "64" (2–4–0's) had their open-work splashers picked out with yellow and crimson on a dark green body colour which was the standard engine colour up to 1901.

1890 The 2–4–0 locomotives (built 1875) were painted dark green with the open-work driving-wheel splashers picked out in yellow and crimson. Dark green body colour was standard up to 1901. Number-plates were of cast-iron, raised.

1892–1901 Coaches were a dark purple lake, lined out with yellow and vermilion. Numbers and lettering was in gold, shaded with red.

Wagons were generally black with white letters. Ballast wagons were red oxide. Ironwork in both cases was black.

1898 Engines were a medium green, with black panel stripes which were bordered on each side with a light green line, inside which was a fine vermilion line. Boiler bands were black, with a fine red, and then light green line on each side. Frames were a dark red-brown, with a narrow black border, having a fine green line on its inner edge and a vermilion line inside it. Buffer-beams were red with black borders, with black buffer sockets and yellow numerals shaded with blue. Number-plates were bright cast-iron letters on a black ground. The interior of the cabs was painted a light straw colour.

1900 The corridor stock built this year for main line use was painted Indian red. The top quarters and waist-panels only were cream, lined out in yellow.

1900 Locomotives were olive-green.

Coaches dark chocolate (November) red and cream.

Coaches had cream upper panels.

1901 Engine colour was (pre-1901) olive-green, but the new colour (1901) was black.

1904 The rail motor car of this period was crimson-lake in the lower panels and cream and white in the upper panels. Lining was carried out in gold and vermilion. The engine end of the car was black, picked out with red and white lining.

1907 Engines were black, lined out in red and yellow. Wagons were grey.

Coaches had lake lower and cream upper panels.

1914 Engines were black, lined out in red and white.

Coaches were purple-lake, lined out in yellow and red.

1915 Coaches were a purple-brown. Engines were black.

1916 The Watson 4–6–0 engine No. 400 had safety-valve casing and both whistles bright brass. Wheel hubs were lined red and white. The number was in unshaded gold numerals thus: No. 400 (serif figures) on vermilion buffer-beams. There was no lettering on the tender. The number appeared on a rectangular plate of brass, the figures being on a golden brown background.

1922 Engine No. 500 had black as the body colour, lined out in panels with a fine outer vermilion line, a middle fine white line, and another fine vermilion line at a distance from the white. Corners were incurved.

Valances, main-frames, and axle-boxes were all lined as above with incurved corners.

Axle-ends were lined out with a wide red line and a fine white one. Boiler bands consisted of a black line flanked by a narrow white and a broad vermilion line on either side. Safety-valve tops were brass, and number-plates were bright steel with raised figures on a black background.

The outside of the cab roof was white, and its interior and inside wings were white, lined out in crimson, with inturned corners and corner decoration; the lining only being present on the interior side-wings. The white was bordered with wide tan-brown, and the lower third of the cab was black. The number on the buffer-beam was in gold serif letters shaded to the right below in pale blue, and to the left and below in black and white.

1933 Engines were black, with very large serif number-plates (*e.g.* No. 670).

Listowel and Ballybunion Railway

This unique mono-rail line of some 10 miles in length was incorporated in April, 1886, and opened in March, 1888. Its locomotive superintendent in 1918 was John Fisher.

1900 Engines were dark green. Coaches were a medium brown.

1904 Locomotive No. 3 had brass beadings to the cab fenders and a large rectangular brass plate on the off-side of the "tender". This was lettered:

LARTIGUE
SINGLE-RAIL SYSTEM.
PATENT

The engine number-plate was circular, with raised numbers and letters, the letters L.B.R. appearing in block between two concentric circles (see Fig. 80, p. 258; in which the letters L.B.R. appeared in the white annular space).

Londonderry and Lough Swilly Railway

Opened in 1863, this Railway includes the Letterkenny and Burtonport Extension Railway (opened in 1903). In 1918 the locomotive superintendent was E. Maslin; in 1921, W. Napier.

1899 Engines were a bright green, picked out with black and white lining. Dome covers were brass on the engine " T. Mackey ".

Coaches were almost an exact copy of London and South Western Railway coaches of the period.

1924–33 Engines were painted black with vermilion lining-out.

1949 Engines, dark green, lined black, white and vermilion.

1950 Engines, black. Coaches, grey.

Caledonian Locomotive No. 468 (*p.* 11)

G.N.R. 3rd Class Coach, 1901 (*p.* 46)

N.B.R. Locomotive No. 602, 1912 (*p.* 167)

East Coast Kitchen Carriage No. 199, c. 1900 (*p.* 46)

G.N.R. Locomotive Coal Wagon, 1903 (*p.* 47)

G.E.R. Bogie 1st-3rd Compo., 1907 (*p.* 43)

G.E.R. Locomotive No. 606 Kitson, 1881-2 (*p.* 39)

G.C.R. Horse Box, 1903 (*p.* 33)

G.E.R. 9-ton Refrigerator Van, 1898 (*p.* 41)

G.N.R. Ivatt Locomotive No. 251 in G.N.R. Livery (*p.* 46)

G.E.R. 10-ton Covered Van, c. 1888 (*p.* 41)

Midland Great Western Railway

ORIGINALLY incorporated in 1845 for a line from Dublin to Mullingar, this Railway also acquired the Dublin and Meath Railway (incorporated 1858 and amalgamated in 1888); the Navan and Kingscourt Railway (incorporated 1865 and amalgamated in 1888); the Great Northern and Western Railway (incorporated 1857 and amalgamated in 1890); and the Sligo and Ballaghadereen Railway (incorporated 1863 and amalgamated in 1877).

The locomotive superintendents were:—

Robert Ramage	*circa* 1870
Martin Atock	*circa* 1890
Mr. Cusack	*circa* 1900
W. H. Morton	*circa* 1918

1899 When Mr. Atock was succeeded by Mr. Cusack the colour of the engines, which was green, was changed to Royal blue (23).

1899 Coaches which were brown became Royal blue (23) like the engines.

1900 Engine No. 37 ("Wolf Dog") replaced a former locomotive of the same name, and was painted dark blue, picked out with yellow lines; instead of the previous green.

1901 The exhibition dining-car was painted a dark blue, in the lower panels and cream in the upper ones, with black bordering and gold lining.

1902 Engines were Royal blue*, with black panelling picked out with gold or yellow. There were bright brass beadings around the combined splashers, and a vermilion background to number-plates which had raised polished brass figures. Safety-valve casings were brass. Wheel-bosses were blue, lined out yellow. The letters M.G.W.R. appeared on the tender sides in sans-serif capitals with full-stops between the letters in gold, shaded with black.

Coaches of the new stock built by Mr. E. Cusack at Broadstone works, had Royal blue bottom panels and white top panels, being picked out with royal blue and gold. This colour-scheme was also carried out on locomotives.

Pre 1903 Engines were green, lined out with black and white.

* An actual panel of this company shows the blue to be more of an azure than a "Royal" (24) blue.

1903 A trial was made of Royal blue for engines and coaches, this colour being lined out in black and yellow for locomotives, and with white upper panels for coaches.

1906–7 The Royal blue was abandoned owing to the bad weather-resisting qualities of the colour.

1907 Engine colour reverted to green.

1907 Coach colour reverted to brown.

1912 Coaches had white upper panels and blue lower.

1912 Engines were a dark green, with black bands and white lines. The names appeared in small curved brass plates over the leading splashers, the letters being on a vermilion background. The number-plates were oval-shaped, and of brass, with the raised numerals on a vermilion background. Boiler mountings were painted dark green on locomotive No. 129.

1914 Nearly all goods engines were black, and the change of colour had spread to passenger engine livery. Engine "Mercuric" (a big 4–4–0 of the "Celtic" class) was in unlined black, with brass name and number-plates with raised letters on a red background. The letters M.G.W.R. appeared on the tender sides in unshaded gold. The engine "Connemara" also had a similar livery, but "St. Patrick" was painted a dull black with simplified lining. Two 2–4–0's also appeared in the new black livery.

1914 Engines were emerald green, lined out with black. Number-plates were of brass with raised figures on a vermilion background.
Coaches were brown, lined out in gold.

1914 Coaches were dark brown.

1915 Coaches were dark brown. Engines were green.

The Northern Counties Committee (L.M.S.)

PRIOR to 1st July, 1903 and from 15th May, 1860, the N.C.C. was known as the Belfast and Northern Counties Railway, which was an amalgamation of several Irish Railways. The Belfast and Ballymena, which was the original company was incorporated in July, 1845, and opened in April, 1848; and other minor companies later absorbed included the following: Ballymena, Ballymoney, Coleraine and Portrush Railway (opened 1855 and amalgamated in 1861); Londonderry and Coleraine Railway (opened 1852–3 and amalgamated in 1871): Ballymena, Cushendall and Redbay Railway (opened 1875–76 and amalgamated in 1884); Balymena and Lanne Railway (opened 1877–78 and amalgamated in 1889); Carrickfergus and Larne Railway (opened 1862 and amalgamated in 1890); Draperstown Railway (opened 1883 and amalgamated in 1895); Derry Central Railway (opened 1880 and amalgamated in 1901); Limavady and Dungiven Railway (opened 1883 and amalgamated in 1907); and the Portstewart Tramway (opened 1882 and amalgamated in 1897). The Londonderry and Strabane section of the narrow gauge Donegal Railway (14½ miles) was also acquired in 1906.

The Belfast and Northern Counties was taken over by the Midland Railway of England in 1903 and its name changed to The Northern Counties Committee.

1865 (c) Older engines had polished brass dome casings.

Coaches were dark lake, lined out with vermilion and gold.

1899 Coaches were dark lake with monogram B.N.C. in script letters.

1906 Engines were dark "invisible"* green, lined out in yellow, blue and vermilion. There were brass beadings to splashers on the 4–4–0's of the time. Underframes were chocolate, and bufferbeams red. Safety-valve casings were of polished brass, as were the name-plates which appeared under the splasher beadings. The engine numbers were on brass plates in raised figures against a vermilion background; the plates being fixed to the cab side-sheets.

Coaches were finished in varnished teak.

1907 Wagons, lead grey. Coaches, lake.

1914 Engines were painted an "invisible" green. They were lined out in yellow, blue and vermilion.

1926 On the Northern Counties Committee (Ireland), the passenger and goods engines were painted in crimson lake. They were not lined, and carried the letters "N.C.C." in serif characters on tenders or tanks. Brass rectangular number-plates were affixed to the cab or bunker sides.

Timoleague and Courtmacsherry Railway

1901 Engine "Argadeen" (Hunslet Engine Co.) was black. Maker's

* See footnote on page 85.

plate was cast brass with raised letters against a vermilion background.

1903 The 2–6–0T engine "Argadeen" was painted black, with a rectangular name-plate (on which were raised brass letters on a vermilion ground) located centrally on the tank side.

Tralee and Dingle Light Railway

This line was incorporated in June, 1884, and opened for traffic in March, 1891. It had a length of 39 miles, and its locomotive superintendent, in 1918, was T. German.

1903 Engines were black, with chocolate, yellow and red lining. Rectangular brass number-plates were placed in the centre of the tank sides, the number appearing thus: No. 7.

1905 Coaches were purple-brown, picked out with yellow and red lining.

Waterford and Central Ireland Railway

This railway was taken over by the Great Southern and Western Railway in 1900.

1899 Engines were dark green, with black bands and a light green line with another red inner line on the cab and tender. Frames were brown, with a black border and red edge-line.

Coaches were a dark lake with vermilion lines and gold lettering shaded with red and black.

Wagons were a dark slate colour and lettered in white. Running-gear was black.

1902 After being taken over by the G.S. & W. engines were dark green with black bands lined out in light green. The cabs, tenders, etc., had an additional inner red line. Underframes were brown with a black border and fine vermilion line. The engine number appeared in gold on the locomotive buffer-beams, and also on the tender rear panel.

Coaches were a dark lake with vermilion lining, and gold lettering with red and black shading.

Wagons were a dark slate colour, darker than (42), with white lettering. Wagons being repainted Standard G. & S.W. style.

Waterford, Limerick and Western Railway

THIS line became amalgamated with the Great Southern and Western Railway in 1901.*

1887 (c) Engines were almost identical in colour with those of the Midland Railway. Some had brass domes, like Great Western engines.

1896 Engines by Kitson & Co. (Robinson 4–4–0's) were painted "Midland" locomotive red (28), with black bands and gold stripes. The company's crest appeared under the engine name on the splashers, and on the tender sides. Chimneys had a copper top, and there was a brass bead round the driving-wheel splashers.

1899 Engines crimson-lake (28), lined out with red and yellow. Goods engines were black.

1900 Engines had copper-topped chimneys, and were crimson-lake (28), lined red and yellow. The number-plates were removed when the engines were taken over by the Great Southern and Western, and painted the latter's standard black.

Goods engines were ivory-black, with red and white lining.

1900 The 0–4–0ST (Sharp, Stewart and Co.) was painted red-brown with black bands and yellow stripes.

Pre 1901 Passenger engines and coaches were crimson-lake (28) lined out in gold. Goods engines black with red lining.

1901 At the time of amalgamation with the G.S. & W., passenger locomotives were painted crimson-lake (28) with red and yellow lining, and goods engines ivory-black with red and white lines.

1901 After 1901 brass domes and chimney tops were painted over and the engine names removed (*e.g.* the 1894 Dübs 2–4–0's).

1903 After amalgamation with the G.S. & W. the copper-topped chimneys were replaced by cast-iron ones.

West and South Clare Light Railway

1909 The locomotive No. 11 ("Kilkee") was painted black (49), with red and white lining; the broad red line being flanked by fine white ones. Number-plates were upright, rectangular in shape, the letters W.C.R.–11–1908 appearing in block characters in three lines. The name-plate was also of brass with raised letters on a red background.

* J. G. Robinson, Locomotive Superintendent (*c*) 1896.

West Cork Railway

(For details see Cork, Bandon and South Coast Railway)

Post 1866 Before amalgamation with C.B. & S.C.R. in 1879, engines were olive-green (12), lined out black and vermilion.

Waterford and Tramore Railway

INCORPORATED in 1851 and opened in 1853, this railway had a track-length of only 7¼ miles, which was worked in 1918 by four locomotives and 33 other vehicles; its locomotive superintendent at that time being E. G. Johnson.

1900 (c) Engines were green, lined with red and black.

Coaches were—third class, maroon (27); first class, Royal blue (24), with yellow lining.

1900 Engines were light green with black bands lined with vermilion. Underframes were brown. Engine numbers were in brass figures on the cab side-sheets. Dome casings were of polished brass, and chimneys copper-topped.

Coaches: First class were dark blue (24), with white lining, with lettering in yellow shaded with red. Third class coaches were dark red (27), with black lining and lettering in yellow, shaded with red,

Goods wagons were grey (27), with white lettering and black ironwork.

1900 Locomotives were light green, picked out with fine red lines. Boiler lagging bands were bright brass. The domes on engines Nos. 1, 2 and 3 were originally polished brass.

1913 Engines were light green with banding of black and lining of vermilion. Underframes were middle brown and chimneys were copper-topped. Domes and number-plates were polished brass.

The first class coaches were dark blue (24), lined out with white, and the third class ones dark red (27), lined out with black. Lettering in both cases was in yellow, shaded black.

Goods vehicles were painted lead grey, darker than (42), with white lettering.

Irish Transport Company
(C.I.E.)

1947 Great Southern locomotive black was retained, the only change being the removal of the cast number-plates and the substitution on cab and tank sides of painted yellow numerals. The "670" class of 0–6–2T have these numerals, but of a larger size and plainer style

The totem of the C.I.E. is stencilled on goods stock in light green appearing twice on each side of each wagon on the second plank from the top. The totem is 5 ins. deep by 10 to 12 ins. long. Tare weights and wagon numbers are also in green. Wagon body-colour is slate grey (42).

1948 (July) Engines light green, lined out black and white. Buffer-beams, and motion-plates, vermilion. No. 502 (a mixed traffic 4–6–0) being the first engine to appear in the new livery, followed by Nos. 61 and 405. The same colours were also adopted for the new diesel shunting engine No. 1001.

1951 Leading passenger engines, bluish-green similar to (15), lined out in black and white.

Fig. 87

Fig. 88

Fig. 89

Fig. 90

Fig. 91

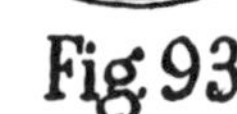

Fig. 93

Fig. 92

Fig. 94

Fig 95

Fig. 96

Fig 97

Fig. 98

Fig 99

PULLMAN CARS

1874 British Pullman cars (the first) were assembled at Derby from American parts.

1876 Pullman "Castilea" was decorated in American period style —very ornate and lavish. Name was in an oval framed scroll, and panels were lined and decorated in gold leaf on a dark mahogany-brown ground.

1879 The 1st Dining car ("Pullman Hotel Car") was named "Prince of Wales".

1890 Old Pullman cars were mahogany brown, decorated with gold leaf.

1890 The Pullman cars which were built to replace the American-built cars were painted bronze-green (4) and were picked out with gold lining and scroll-work. Their names were placed in oval panels in the centre of the waist. Roofs were rose-coloured when newly-painted. Bogies and underframes were dark brown, picked out in chrome yellow. Cars liveried in this style were running in the "Brighton Limited".

1906 Cars were painted umber brown (35) with cream (45) upper panels. The umber strip along the top under the carline is a recent innovation.

1906 The Pullmans "Princess Ena", "Princess Patricia", and "Duchess of Norfolk" were finished in a new style, with lower panelling umber and upper panelling ivory white; being lined out in gold.

1908 The umber and cream livery was adopted by the Pullman Company when they built the stock for the "Southern Belle". The umber (35) was identical with that chosen by Mr. Marsh a short time earlier for London, Brighton and South Coast coaching stock.

1910 S.E.C.R. Pullmans "Corunna", "Florence", "Savona", "Valmeia", "Clementina" and "Sorrento" were a crimson lake (28) colour, lined out in gold. Roofs were white and underframes black. The word "PULLMAN" appeared along the cant-rail in expanded serif capital letters. The names were placed in the centre panels, below the waist-line.

1914 (c) The lower panels of L.B.S.C.R. Pullman cars were painted raw umber (35) of the same shade as that of the L.B.S.C.R. Marsh locomotives. The upper panels were of a cream (45) shade when freshly painted, which varied very considerably with age and the condition of the varnish coats. Lining was in gilt.

N.B.—This livery has persisted down to the present time (1952), the lettering "PULLMAN" being in gold, shaded to the left with white, and to the left and below in deep crimson—on freshly-painted stock.

S.E.C.R. Pullmans were dark red (28), which was later adopted for the two cars on the "METRO" extension line.

1923 The Pullmans built for the Caledonian Railway "Lady Nairne", "Bonnie Jean" and "Maid of Morven", were painted in the standard Pullman colours—umber and cream, lined out in gold.*

1927 The S.E. & C. Pullman car "Carmen", up to its destruction in the Sevenoaks accident in the August of this year, ran in the maroon livery (28) which was adopted by the South Eastern and Chatham Railway for a short time for its passenger coaching stock. (See p. 204.)

1928 The Pullman cars running on the "Queen of Scots" were painted in the normal umber and cream livery (*e.g.* "Sheila" and "Geraldine".)

1939 Two Pullmans in (28) lake colouring, "Mayflower" and "Galatea" still remained in service on the Metropolitan section of London Transport.

A few old Pullman cars were rebuilt as kitchen and pantry cars for the service of meals on excursion trains, and were painted umber (35) all over, with white roofs.

1941 Pullman cars were first painted umber (35) all over as a war-time livery. Some however were laid up and painted grey. (See Fig. 103, p. 294, for Pullman Car Company crest.)

1948 (c) Matchboarded sides were covered with metal-sheeting.

* See also L.M.S. reference 1923, p. 298.

PART II

GROUP LIVERIES

1923 — 1948

GREAT WESTERN RAILWAY

Consisting of

GREAT WESTERN RAILWAY
ALEXANDRA (NEWPORT AND SOUTH WALES) DOCKS AND RAILWAYS
BARRY
CAMBRIAN RAILWAYS
CARDIFF
RHYMNEY
TAFF VALE

And the following:

Subsidiary Companies

(I) Independently Worked
 (1) Brecon and Merthyr Tydfil Junction
 (2) Burry Port and Gwendreath Valley
 (3) Cleobury Mortimer and Ditton Priors
 (4) Llanelly and Mynydd Mawr
 (5) Midland and South Western Junction
 (6) Neath and Brecon

(II) Semi-independent lines worked by G.W.R. but having separate rolling-stock
 (7) Port Talbot Railway and Docks
 (8) Rhondda and Swansea Bay

(III) Non-working Companies
 (A) *Originally leased to or worked by G.W.R.*
 (9) Didcot, Newbury and Southampton
 (10) Exeter
 (11) Forest of Dean Central
 (12) Gwendreath Valley
 (13) Lampeter, Aberayon and New Quay Light
 (14) Liskeard and Looe
 (15) Princetown
 (16) Ross and Monmouth
 (17) Teign Valley
 (18) West Somerset
 (B) *Originally leased to and worked by the Taff Vale Railway*
 (19) Penarth Extension
 (20) Penarth Harbour, Dock and Railway

(C) *Originally leased to or worked by the Cambrian Railways*

(21) Maeddwy

(22) Van

(23) Welshpool and Llanfair Light

(24) Wrexham and Ellesmere

(D) *Originally leased to or worked by the Port Talbot Railway and Docks*

(25) South Wales Mineral

(E) *Originally leased to or worked by the Barry Railway*

(26) Vale of Glamorgan

Joint Railways

(I) Joint with L.M.S.R.

(1) Birkenhead

(2) Brecon and Merthyr and London and North Western Joint

(3) Brynmawr and Western Valleys

(4) Clee Hill

(5) Clifton Extension

(6) Great Western and Great Central

(7) Halesowen

(8) Nantybwch and Rhymney

(9) Severn and Wye

(10) Shrewsbury and Hereford

(11) Tenbury

(12) West London

(13) Wrexham and Minera

(II) Joint with L.M.S.R. and Southern

(14) West London Extension

(III) Joint with Southern Railway

(15) Easton and Church Hope

(16) Weymouth and Portland

(IV) Joint with Metropolitan Railway

(17) Hammersmith and City

(V) Joint with Great Southern and Western Railway of Ireland

(18) Fishguard and Rosslare Railways and Harbours

(VI) Railways comprised after grouping, wholly in the Great Western

(19) Quaker's Yard and Merthyr

(20) Taff—Bargoed

GREAT WESTERN RAILWAY

THE Great Western Railway as an amalgamated unit was the only group to retain its original title, and no outstanding changes were made in the colour-schemes of either the locomotives or rolling-stock; though there were some minor changes made in their superficial liveries during the first few years of the Company's new formation.

CHIEF MECHANICAL ENGINEERS

Charles B. Collett	1921–1941
Frederick William Hawksworth	1941 until Nationalisation

1923 The old standard coach colours of chocolate (46) and cream, were reintroduced, and it was decided to revert to copper-topped chimneys and brass-cased safety-valves. History, of 21 years earlier, thus repeated itself.

1923 The steel-panelled stock newly-built was lined out in imitation panelling.

1923 Auto-train engines were painted at Swindon in chocolate shade.

1923 (Nov.) Engine No. 4073 ("Caerphilly Castle") was the first to be turned out after the 1914–18 war with full lining and with polished fittings. Other engines of the "2900" and "3000" classes soon followed suit as they passed through the shops.

1925 Engines taken from Welsh and other lines were fitted with number-plates bearing the name of the previous owning railway round the lower rim, and the letters G.W.R. round the upper rim above the engine number.

1926 The old crest was replaced by the crest minus the garter, on engines and tenders.

1926 Coaches ceased to be lined as they had been, and only black and yellow lines were placed between the brown (46) lower and cream upper panels. Later this was altered to black and gold and black lines.

1927 Cream (45) and brown (46) coach livery was introduced, devoid of panelling.

1928 Several engines had their buffer-beams painted a lighter shade of vermilion.

1928 Coaches fitted with oil axle-boxes had them painted pale blue, (23).

1928 Engine No. 6000 ("King George V") was fitted with a special bronze bell on the front buffer-beam, in front of the inside cylinder covers; also with two bronze medals on the cab sides. The bell bears the inscription—"Presented to the Locomotive King George V"—"by the"—"Baltimore and Ohio Railroad"—"in commemoration of its"—"Centenary Celebrations"—"Sept. 24–Oct. 15, 1927" The cab-side medals are circular and are framed in brass, glass-covered cases. The first shows the obverse side and the second the reverse. The obverse shows a modern Baltimore and Ohio railroad train, around which is the inscription "100 years, safety, speed, strength." The reverse shows the locomotive "Tom Thumb", with the inscription "The Baltimore and Ohio Railroad Company, 1827–1927."

1928 All lining for main-line passenger stock was abolished, only a gold band with a black line to separate the gold from the cream upper panels remained. The mantle and garter were also removed from the crest, the crests being placed above the shields. The G.W.R. appeared in serif widely-spaced letters, and the prefix "No." was removed from the coach numbers.

1928 The basic coach livery introduced remained in use until 1942 with minor variations.

1929 The first two "Riviera" trains were painted normally, but the "Torbays" were double-lined into a number of panels along the waist. The third and fourth "Riviera" trains were finished in the latter style. Double lining became standard for 63 ft. "wide" stock, but the sleeping cars were an exception to the rule.

1930 Exterior of coaches remained chocolate shade (46) and cream upper panels, but with gold lining and chrome-plated door-handles and slam-locks. Large lettering, "FIRST" and "THIRD" appeared on carriage doors. Roof destination boards were improved by additional lining of their lettering.

1930 Locomotive class was indicated by a coloured disc (red, blue, or yellow) painted on the cab sides, the colour being according to the axle-loading.

L. & S.W.R. Sleeping Saloon No. 42 (*p.* 136)

L. & S.W.R. Inspector's Saloon (*p.* 131)

L. & S.W.R. Bogie 3rd Coach No. 513 (*p.* 136)

S.E. & C.R. Locomotive "Onward", No. 240 (*p.* 201)

Dublin & Kingstown Railway Locomotive, 1851 (*p.* 266)

Metropolitan Locomotive No. 94 (*p.* 149)
Colne Valley & Halstead Railway Locomotive No. 5, 1908 (*p.* 219)
L.S.W.R. Tank Locomotive No. 68 (*p.* 135)
S.E.R. Locomotive "Spey", 1866 (*p.* 195)

1930 "No smoking" labels were affixed to the inside window-glasses of all non-smoking compartments. Red letters on a cream background were used, these being bordered by a red triangle with 5½ in. sides, mounted with its apex uppermost.

1933 The practice of marking the word "THIRD" on coach doors was discontinued, though the word "FIRST" remained. On the inside of doors the figure "3" was also removed, excepting on the City trains. The large-lettered "THIRD CLASS" of sleeping cars and dining cars remained.

1933 The Diesel railcars were painted chocolate (46) and cream (cream above the waist), and carried the company's crest at the front and rear of the vehicle.

1934 A "show" train belonging to the Gramophone Company Ltd., of Hayes, Middlesex, toured the country. It was composed of old Great Western stock and was painted cream and orange, with several large representations of the well-known dog listening to "His Master's Voice".

1934 A system of numbering long-distance expresses was instituted for the immediate identification at any point on route of certain trains. It was carried out by a system of numbers composed of black and white figures 16 ins. high, carried in a 3 ft. long frame on the front of the engine's smoke-box. A three-figure number was allocated to each train, the left-hand figure denoting the starting-place of the train, and the other two figures identifying the train itself. Expresses from Paddington were numbered 100–199, from Shrewsbury 200–299, from Wolverhampton and Birmingham 300–399, from Bristol 400–499, from Exeter 500–599, from Plymouth 600–699, and from South Wales 700–799. The number of each train ended with either "0" or "5", the intervening numbers (1, 2, 3, 4, 6, 7, 8 and 9) being reserved for trains which were run in more than one part. Specials, and certain boat trains, carried "0" in the left-hand slot.

1934 (Sept.) The circular monogram "G.W.R." began to be used on locomotive tenders, the first two engines to be so decorated being No. 4019 ("Knight Templar") and No. 4074 ("Caldicot Castle").

1935 The word "THIRD" was restored to all vestibuled coaches, and parcels, newspaper, luggage and stores vans began to be painted solid brown, unlined. Generally the wooden-bodied types carried the crest and the steel-panelled types the circular totem. The Ocean Mail and postal vans retained the two colours together with special lettering; being double-lined in some cases. Buffet cars had a gap left for the cream-coloured panel containing the words "BUFFET CAR".

The "Centenary" stock, of new design, and commemorating 100 years of the Great Western Railway, was in normal chocolate and cream, and, as well as the buffet cars, it also had continuous lining from end to end of the vehicles, and the "super saloons" were similarly lined and had totems on each side of the name panel. Buffet cars ceased to be double-lined.

Single class restaurant cars were lettered "THIRD CLASS—— G.W.R.——RESTAURANT CAR" the crest appearing beneath the initials and "THIRD CLASS" and "RESTAURANT CAR" spaced out between the crest and the coach numbers at the ends of the vehicle. Two-class cars were lettered "THIRD CLASS——G.W.R. RESTAURANT CAR——FIRST CLASS" these three groups being centred equidistantly. The "G.W.R." was not, however, placed over the crest but preceded the words "RESTAURANT CAR".

One of the 70 ft. end-kitchen restaurant cars had no class lettering, but the words "RESTAURANT CAR" appeared twice, placed over crests widely spaced apart.

1936 All engines were painted (19), described in sources as green, but the orange and black lining-out was omitted on secondary and goods classes. Wheels and underframes were black. Safety-valve casings were polished brass and chimney tops were polished copper. The engine number was on brass plates with raised figures on the cab side-sheets. The initials G.W.R. appeared as a circular gold and black monogram on the tender or tanks.

Coaches were chocolate (46) in the lower panels and cream above, with horizontal dividing lining of black and yellow.

Luggage and Parcel vans were painted all over chocolate.

1936 Blue axle-boxes appeared on some express passenger coaching stock.

1936 The details of the livery of the "Riviera" passenger stock were as follows: The lower panels were 2 ft. 1 in. wide and were painted brown (46). The waist panels were 9¾ in. deep across the lining which was composed of a ¾ in. wide black line at top and bottom with a ¾ in. wide gold line within it. The colour of the waist panel was brown. Above this, up to the ¾ in. black line below the gutter was painted cream.

The coach numbers appearing in the waist panels at the ends of the vehicles were in 2 in. serif characters, the initial letters of "class", "guard" and "luggage" were also this size. The words "RESTAURANT CAR", "SLEEPING CAR", etc., were in 3 in. capital letters.

1937 "King" class engines had standard green splashers, and also had one black lining stripe between the orange lines. Below the foot-plate everything was black, except that the step-plates and cylinders were picked out with orange lines. The front bogie axle-boxes were polished brass.

1938 The lower gold and black lines between the waist panel and lower half of the coaches were abandoned on ordinary stock.

1938 Shunting trucks were painted dark grey, darker than (42), and were lettered "GW" in black letters on the sole-bars and with the name of the yard to which they were attached in large and small capitals on the tool-box. Hand-rails were painted white, as were the brake levers.

1942 With the exception of "Castles" and "Kings", all engines appeared in black livery, devoid of all lining. Some had the letters "G.W.R." in plain block capital letters and others in standard "Swindon" lettering.

Engines of the "King" and "Castle" classes were painted (19), described in sources as green and black, but were without lining, and their tenders carried the 1926 crests between the letters "G" and "W".

1942 Coach roofs were often painted dark brown, and the coaches themselves all over a reddish-brown. The special saloons and Diesel rail-cars remained in cream and white livery, as did the stock trains which had previously made up the "Riviera"; though these actual trains became relegated to other more important services. The "Riviera" of those days was thus very seldom composed of its original cream and chocolate stock.

1942 Ambulance car No. 9579 was painted brown, lined yellow, with small red crosses on white discs between the doors and the end windows.

1942 Coaches reverted to brown, with one orange line only and gold lettering in the case of wood-bodied stock, and one gold line for a time on steel-panelled coaches. The "Centenary trains" and super-saloons remained with cream upper panels, but did not see much service.

In July a new train was placed in "Riviera" service which was painted brown with an orange line, and which was decorated with the old-style (transfer) crest, with "G.W.R." above.

Later in the year all repainted stock and absorbed stock were devoid of all lining.

1943 All coach lettering was now in one size of bold block characters of gold, unshaded but with a fine black line around each character. The crest also appeared with an orange continuous waist-line. The letters "G.W.R" appeared, but with only two full-stops.

1943 Since this date the coach livery has been brown and cream for all principal corridor types, with a single gold line along the waist, shaded black, with the crest and lined-out lettering. Some of the brown and cream coaches (*e.g.* the "Centenary" stock) continued to use the older shaded lettering, and the "Centenary" renewed the double lining. All non-corridor, clerestory, and absorbed coaching stock was still in brown with one orange line and lined-out lettering.

Luggage, newspaper and parcels vans were unlined brown with the monogram, with lined-out lettering, and other vans are painted similarly.

1943 Crests were restored to many tenders of both green and black engines, being flanked by the letters "G.W.". The full "G.W.R." reappeared on many tank engines.

1943 Coach roofs began to be painted black, and a bronze-coloured line was painted along the waist.

Covered wagons and containers (excepting insulated and ventilated meat wagons and containers) were painted dark brick-red.

Open wagons were painted dark red, but only on the left-hand bottom quarter board, where the standard wagon lettering was displayed in a reduced size.

1943 (Sept.) A return was gradually made to the two-colour coach livery.

1943 (Nov.) The crest was being restored to some coaches and the G.W.R. totem was being replaced by the letters "GWR" in its original size and positions.

1945 Locomotive lining re-appeared with the "County" class, and was later carried into effect on other express types. All other classes continued in the unlined green upper works and black underframe style until January, 1948.

1946 The new coaches had "GREAT WESTERN" on each side of the crest.

1947 The 8-ton, 8-wheeled side-gangway clerestory brake vans for postal service were painted brown and lettered "10-10 P.M. POSTAL"—"PADDINGTON"—"TO" "PENZANCE", in 4 in. chrome yellow block characters. This livery being carried for several years after nationalisation.

Fig.100

Fig.101

Fig.102

Fig.103

Fig.104

Fig.105

Fig.108

Fig.106

Fig.107

Fig.109

LONDON, MIDLAND AND SCOTTISH RAILWAY

Consisting of

LONDON AND NORTH WESTERN

MIDLAND

LANCASHIRE AND YORKSHIRE (*amalgamated with the L.N.W.R.* 1922)

NORTH STAFFORDSHIRE

FURNESS

CALEDONIAN

GLASGOW AND SOUTH WESTERN

HIGHLAND

MARYPORT AND CARLISLE

And the following:

Subsidiary Companies

(I) Independently worked lines
- (1) Cleator and Workington Junction (partly worked by Furness Railway)
- (2) Knott End
- (3) North London
- (4) Stratford-upon-Avon and Midland Junction
- (5) Wirral

(II) Independent lines for which rolling-stock was provided by other companies
- (6) Cockermouth, Keswick and Penrith (L.N.W.R. and N.E.R.)

(III) Non-working companies

(A) *Originally leased to or worked by the L.N.W.R.*
- (7) Charnwood Forest
- (8) Dearne Valley
- (9) Harborne
- (10) Mold and Denbigh Junction
- (11) Shropshire Union Railways and Canal. (Part jointly leased with G.W.R.)

(B) *Originally leased or worked by the Midland Railway*
- (12) Tottenham and Forest Gate
- (13) Yorkshire Dales (Skipton and Grassington)

(C) *Originally leased to or worked by the Caledonian Railway*
- (14) Arbroath and Forfar
- (15) Brechin and Edzell District
- (16) Callander and Oban
- (17) Dundee and Newtyle

(18) Killin Railway
(19) Lanarkshire and Ayrshire
(20) Solway Junction

(D) *Originally leased to or worked by the Highland Railway*
(21) Dornoch Light
(22) Wick and Lybster Light

(E) *Originally leased to or worked by the North Staffordshire Railway*
(23) Leek and Manifold.

(F) *Originally leased to or worked by several component companies*
(24) North and South Junction
(25) Portpatrick and Wigtownshire

Joint Railways

(I) Joint with L.N.E.R.
(1) Axholme Joint
(2) Cheshire Lines Committee (one-third share)
(3) Dumbarton and Balloch
(4) Great Central and Midland Joint
(5) Great Central, Hull and Barnsley and Midland Joint (one-third share)
(6) Great Central and North Staffordshire
(7) Great Northern and London and North Western
(8) Halifax and Ovenden
(9) Halifax High Level
(10) Manchester, South Junction and Altrincham (joint arrangement)
(11) Methley
(12) Midland and Great Northern Joint
(13) Norfolk and Suffolk Joint Committee. (Great Eastern and Midland and Great Northern Joint)
(14) Oldham, Ashton and Guide Bridge
(15) Otley and Ilkley
(16) Perth General Station (two-thirds share)
(17) Prince's Dock, Glasgow
(18) South Yorkshire Joint (two-fifths share)
(19) Swinton and Knottingley
(20) Tottenham and Hampstead

(II) Joint with Great Western Railway

(21) Birkenhead
(22) Brecon and Merthyr, and London and North Western Joint
(23) Brynmawr and Western Valleys
(24) Clee Hill
(25) Clifton Extension
(26) Halesowen
(27) Nantybwch and Rhymney
(28) Quaker's Yard and Merthyr
(29) Severn and Wye
(30) Shrewsbury and Hereford
(31) Taff-Bargoed
(32) Tenbury
(33) Vale of Towy (owned by L.N.W.R. but leased jointly)
(34) West London
(35) Wrexham and Minera

(III) Joint with Southern Railway
(36) Somerset and Dorset

(IV) Joint with Great Western and Southern Railways
(37) West London Extension (quarter share)

(V) Joint with Metropolitan District Railway
(38) Whitechapel and Bow

(VI) Railways comprised after grouping, wholly in the L.M.S.
(39) Ashby and Nuneaton
(40) Carlisle Citadel Station (Committee)
(41) Enderby
(42) Furness and Midland
(43) Glasgow, Barrhead and Kilmarnock Joint
(44) Glasgow and Paisley
(45) Lancashire Union
(46) Whitehaven, Cleator and Egremont
(47) North Union
(48) Preston and Longridge
(49) Preston and Wyre

Irish lines under L.M.S.R.

(1) Dundalk, Newry and Greenore
(2) Northern Counties Committee's lines
(3) Joint Midland and Great Northern of Ireland

LONDON, MIDLAND AND SCOTTISH RAILWAY

THIS group adopted a new form of organization, more on the lines of American railroads, with a special officer for all Scotch affairs. The general colours of both locomotives and passenger rolling-stock were very similar to those used on the Midland railway immediately before grouping, though there were many minor alterations of lining and lettering made during the late "twenties".

CHIEF MECHANICAL ENGINEERS

George Hughes	1923–1925
Sir Henry Fowler	1925–1931
E. J. H. Lemon (Sir Ernest Lemon)	1931–1932
Sir William Stanier	1932–1944
Charles E. Fairburn	1944–1946
H. G. Ivatt	1946 until Nationalisation

1923 The 4–4–2T engines running on the London, Tilbury, and Southend section (Nos. 2110–2117) had plates fitted which were inscribed "MIDLAND RAILWAY, REBUILT, DERBY, 1923". They also had the Midland Railway crest on their tank sides alongside the number. Nos. 2118 and 2119, however, had "L.M.S." on their bunkers over the date-plates.

1923 Engine No. 1427 appeared with the letters "L.M. & S.R." on the tender side-sheets.

1923 (June) No official information had yet been issued as to the livery styles to be adopted by the L.M.S., and ex-L.N.W. engines were leaving the shops in the old L.N.W. colours.

1923 (Oct.) It was decided by the L.M.S. to adopt the old Midland style as standard on engine liveries. This was (28), described in sources as crimson (dark red), with black panels and yellow lining. The first engines to be so treated were "Claughton", a 4–4–0

4-cylindered Horwich-built engine, and an Aspinall 4–4–0. In the latter case the letters L.M.S. appeared in very small serif characters on the rear driving-wheel splasher, and the number (70163) in serif figures on the tender side-panels.

Goods engines painted black, the line of livery demarcation between them and passenger types being drawn according to the class of work they ordinarily carried out.

Late 1923 Furness engines were at first repainted with their numbers in small yellow figures on the tender-sides and L.M.S. in small letters on the cab-sheets. They did not carry their number in raised figures on a smoke-box plate.

1924 The new official livery for engines was (28), described in sources as crimson-lake, bodywork with only one boiler-band in lining, viz. that between smoke-box and boiler-barrel. The cab side-sheets and spectacle-plate, foot-plate valances and tender were lined out in black and yellow. The letters "L.M.S." appeared in small serif characters on the cab side-sheets, and the engine number in the old Midland Railway style of serif figures on the tender. Cylinders were painted crimson-lake and were not lined. Step-plates and tender-underframes were inlined crimson-lake also. Buffer-beams were vermilion, outlined in yellow and wheels were black. The engine number also appeared in polished steel figures on the front of the smoke-box.

1924 The old "Watford" electric stock was repainted crimson-lake (28).

1924 Passenger engines were seen painted black, and goods engines painted crimson-lake.

1924 The new 4–6–4T engines appeared painted black, without any lining whatever, the number (*e.g.* 1113) appearing in chrome yellow on the tank sides, and the L.M.S. crest on the bunker sides.

1924 The first engine to appear in Scotland in the new passenger livery was 4–4–0 No. 14338, which had the L.M.S. crest on the rear driving-wheel splasher. Engine No. 15151 (0–4–4T was painted in the lake livery, contrary to the later ruling.

None of the passenger engines which bore the new colours had the "L.M.S." on the rear splasher, but the crest. Several engines appeared in all-black livery with "L.M.S." on a vermilion background on the cab side-sheets. Black seemed to have been temporarily adopted for mixed traffic as well as goods engines.

1924 A yellow "X" was painted on the end of certain passenger vehicles to indicate that they were prohibited by loading-gauge considerations from travelling over certain sections of the Midland section and also over the Maryport and Carlisle line. A yellow triangle indicated a similar restriction over the London, Tilbury and Southend and certain other sections. (*See also entry for* 1926.)

1925 The engine "Prince of Wales" came out of the shops in the new group colours, but never had her name-plates refixed.

Some engines were still appearing in black livery, presumably to reduce costs.

The ex-M.R. engine No. 765 bore the new L.M.S. crest, but the Kirtley 2–4–0 (No. 76) was repainted minus the crest.

1925 The new L.M.S. style of livery for goods engines was unlined black, with the letters "L.M.S." on a vermilion background panel. Some engines of the Midland class 4 appeared thus with the number in large yellow figures rimmed with gilt, on the tender-sides.

1925 The old Furness engine "Coppernob" was installed at Barrow station.

1926 On the Highland section a large vermilion painted board bearing the words "ENGINE FOLLOWING" was carried by the last vehicle of a train which was to be followed by a "special" train. Previously this indication was carried on the front buffer-beam of the engine of the train, and consisted of a large red canvas disc; the last vehicle displaying a similar disc with the words "UP" or "DOWN" thereon in white letters.

1926 Chrome yellow crosses and diamonds were placed on the ends of coaches to indicate that their running over certain sections of the line was prohibited by their size.

1926 Mr. Stroudley's "Lochgorm" was still at work, and carried her name together with full Highland railway green (12) livery.

1926 At this time there could be seen on the Highland section old coaches of the Midland Railway, the London and North Western Railway, the Caledonian Railway, the Lancashire and Yorkshire Railway, and the Furness Railway which had not yet been repainted in L.M.S. livery. Old North British Joint Stock coaches were also to be seen in their old livery.

1926 Furness engines were again repainted with their numbers in gold figures, with "L.M.S." on a red background on the cab-sheets, and their numbers repeated in raised figures on a smoke-box number-plate.

1927 The Fowler compound 3-cylinder engine No. 1112 was devoid of all boiler-banding, carried the L.M.S. crest on the cab sides, and building plates on the front driving-wheel splashers. The engine number appeared in large "Midland" style figures on the tender.

1927 The first 25 Fowler 0–6–0 engines (*e.g.* No. 4357) had "L.M.S." in gold on a red panel on the cab sides, and the number in gold, in the "Midland" style on the tender.

1927 As far as the L.N.W. coaching stock was concerned, comparatively few were to be seen in the old livery. There was one notable exception which survived until the second war—the former L.N.W. Royal train, which, at the express wish of the late King George V, retained the original L.N.W. livery.

1928 Many engines were running lettered and numbered in temporary styles, instead of being finished in accordance with the practice introduced after grouping. A new practice was officially adopted this year which was, in detail, as follows:—

First class passenger tender-engines ("Royal Scots" Standard Compounds, "Claughtons", "Prince of Wales" class, and Hughes four-cylindered 4–6–0's) were to be crimson-lake (28), but were to carry engine numbers on the cab sides, and the letters "L.M.S." to be prominently displayed on the tender-sides in place of the previous large engine numbers. This same method of display was to apply to all other types of engines, passenger and goods, but passenger types (other than those already cited) were to be painted black and relieved by vermilion lining. Goods engines were to be black, as heretofore. The practice on tank type engines was to put the number on the bunker and "L.M.S." on the tank-sides.

1928 Ex-Lancashire and Yorkshire 2–4–2T engines and 0–6–2T No. 6886 appeared in the crimson-lake livery. Some ex-L.N.W. tank engines still retained their pre-grouping black livery, but with the number on the smoke-box and in small chrome yellow figures on the tank sides (*e.g.* No. 7789).

1928 The two "Claughtons" (Nos. 5986 and 6024) left Crewe shops without the large tender figures, and with the number painted on the cab side-sheets. The letters "L.M.S." appeared on the tender sides. "Claughtons" Nos. 6024 and 5947 appeared painted in crimson-lake (28).

The painting of the engine number in large figures on the cab sides and the large "L.M.S." on tenders constituted a new standard practice.

1928 The 2–6–0 locomotive No. 13036 was liveried in the 1928 "new" style, but was painted in crimson-lake instead of black. Black passenger engines were relieved by a thin vermilion lining similar to that on freight and tank engines on the L.N.E.R.

1928 "Royal Scot" class engine No. 6145 ("Condor") had a crimson background to her name-plate. All other locomotives had black backgrounds to their plates.

1928 The vitreous enamelled steel brake-vans were devoid of all lining, and were numbered only at the extreme ends of the waist panel, which had L.M.S. in its centre in gold letters, shaded black.

1928 By November this year engine numbers had been removed from tenders, and had been placed on the cab sides, whether the engine had been repainted or not. The engine numbers also appeared in small figures on the back panel of tenders.

There was considerable diversity of sizes in the numerals used, as no standard transfers were yet available.

The practice of putting boiler dates on rebuilding plates of Midland division engines was discontinued. Original "built" plates were substituted in cases where the engine class was unaltered.

1929 The Fowler 0–6–0 dock shunters (Nos. 11270–11279) had the lettering L.M.S. as well as their number painted on the tank sides. The building date-plate was placed on the bunker-sides.

1929 Locomotive history was perpetuated by the addition of raised brass plates, fitted below the name-plates, bearing imprints of one or other of the very early engines. These plates were fitted to "Royal Scot" class engines Nos. 6125–6149.

Badges of the various regiments concerned were also fitted to "Royal Scot" engines Nos. 6101–6124 (*e.g.* No. 6118, "Royal Welch Fusilier").

1929 The ex-Midland engine No. 673 was preserved at Derby, and was repainted in old Midland Railway livery, with the M.R. crest; and was given the Number 118.

1931 The ex-Caledonian Railway engine No. 1081 was still running in its Caledonian livery, with original number-plates.

1931 Practically all the Liverpool-Southport electric stock had been repainted in L.M.S. colours—crimson-lake (28) and gold.

1933 Some of the earlier types of Lancashire and Yorkshire coaches were still to be seen running in their old colours—brown and chocolate. (See pages 89-90.)

1933 On the "Scotch" Pullman Restaurant cars, and on the observation car "Maid of Morven", the word "PULLMAN" was painted out when they were purchased by the L.M.S. on the expiry of the Pullman Company's contract.

1933 The L.M.S. "Royal Train" still perpetuated the old London and North Western coach colour-scheme (see p. 125). No other L.M.S. vehicles remained which were not painted in L.M.S. crimson livery, excepting the President of the Company's saloon, which was L.M.S. lake (28) up to the waist-line and cream above it.

1933 The "Royal Scot" locomotive went to America with a special train of standard L.M.S. stock. The engine returned carrying a bell, and with a special name-plate with the driver's, fireman's and fitters' names, commemorating the number of miles run on the American continent. "Royal Scot", No. 6100, had a special tender built for the visit, larger than the standard L.M.S. tender. There was a special panel lined out at the footplate end.

1934 The "Scottish" Pullman cars purchased from the Pullman Company began to be painted in crimson-lake (28) livery, with the words "DINING CAR" on the lower panels.

1934 The 2–4–0 engine No. 155 was working the officers' saloon at Crewe, and bore the words "ENGINEER SOUTH WALES" on her leading driving-wheel splasher in raised brass characters against a vermilion background.

1934 "Royal Scots," "Baby Scots", "Claughtons", Stanier 3-cylinder 4–6–0's, Horwich 4–6–0's, and the "Compound" 4–4–0's were painted crimson-lake. All other 4–4–0's and 4–6–0's were black and unlined, but those which were not destined for breaking-up were, in 1935, lined in red and given gold lettering.

1935 The first of the L.M.S. "Jubilee" class, named "Silver Jubilee" to honour King George V, was in a livery of black and chrome. The boiler bands, lettering, numerals, and various other fittings including the dome were chromium-plated.

1936 The standard body colouring of express engines was crimson-lake (28), with black wheels. Lettering was in gold, shaded in black.

Goods engines were painted black and lined in red. Lettering and numbers were in gold, shaded in red. Coaches were crimson-lake, lined out in chrome yellow and black. Lettering was in chrome yellow, but in gold on special vehicles, which also carried the L.M.S. crest.

1936 Wagons began to be painted dark brown (as on the old Great Northern Railway) instead of the previous grey.

1937 (c) Engines of the "Princess Elizabeth" class as well as other express passenger types were painted deep crimson (28) (as old Midland Railway) above the foot-plate angle, but only the extreme ends of the boiler lagging were lined black and picked out in yellow; all intermediate boiler-bands being of the same colour as the engine body—crimson. All other lining was in black, picked out in yellow, but wheels and outside frames were black. Step-plates, cylinders and the outside frames of the tenders, together with their springs and axle-boxes were crimson, edged with black and lined yellow.

1937 Engines of the "Coronation" class departed from the standard crimson livery, the engines, tenders, and the whole of the train they hauled were Royal blue (24). There was no lining on the engines, but instead the solid colour was relieved with silver-painted bands which were carried horizontally along the whole length of the train, commencing with a curved "Vee" at the front of the engine. The initials L.M.S. on the tender as well as the numerals on the cab were in chromium plate. The wheels of the locomotive were painted blue with polished rims.

1937 Wagons were lettered in three lines, *i.e.* company's initials, number of wagon, and the wagon capacity in tons, the latter being abbreviated to "T". All lettering was in small black characters, and appeared at the lower left-hand corner of the wagon sides. The tare weight was shown at the right-hand end of the sole-bars. The body colour was dark red-brown.

1938 Engines Nos. 6225–6229 were coloured crimson with gold flash lining and all lettering and figures in block characters.

Engines Nos. 6230–6234 were also crimson and single-lined on tenders, cab, foot-plate valances, step sheets, and splashers; but were devoid of boiler-band lining. Lettering and figures were in serif characters. Buffer-beams were vermilion, panelled.

1939 The first five engines of the "Princess" "Coronation" class were painted blue with silver bands along both engine and tender. (Engines Nos. 6220–6224.)

The second five were, however, streamlined and painted crimson with similar gold stripes. (Engines Nos. 6225–6229.)

M.R. 1st-3rd Brake Composite Coach in M.R. Livery (*p.* 155)

G.C.R. Composite Coach, *c.* 1904 (*p.* 33)

L.N.W.R. Corridor Coach No. 2555 (*p.* 126)

L.N.W.R. Locomotive No. 2665, 1910 (*p.* 126)

M.R. 10-ton Open Wagon (*p.* 159)

C.L.C. Composite Coach, 1904 (*p.* 218)

G.W.R. Composite Clerestory Coach No. 1481 (*p.* 66)

Engines Nos. 6230–6234 were painted crimson-lake but were not streamlined.

1939 It was officially decided to paint "Pacifics" Nos. 6220–6224 in the standard lake with gold decoration, and red lining.

1939 The change from blue and silver to L.M.S. red and gold for the "Coronation Scot" coincided with the visit of that train to America in 1939. It was never put into service in this country, but ran a trial run on the L.M.S. main line before being shipped for tour and exhibition. About 1942 the engine, which was named "Coronation", but which in reality was "Duchess of Hamilton", (she had changed name-plates with the original "Coronation"), was brought back to this country to ease the motive power situation.

1940 After preserving its original London and North Western livery for 17 years since the grouping took place, the L.M.S. Royal train was painted in the standard lake livery.

The Duke of Sutherland's private saloon was still to be seen in the L.N.W. colours.

1942 Early in the year horizontal lining only of chrome yellow became standard on new and repainted coaches, but later in the year the austerity painting abolished even this line, which was beneath the windows.

1945 An old G.N. of S. wagon (No. 3455) still existed in original livery at Glasgow.

1946 No "Pacific" engine at this time had retained its original colours, whether blue with white lining; red, with gold striping; or standard red. At different times during and after the war all engines were painted the war-time black.

1946 Engine No. 5573 ("Newfoundland") appeared in April painted a dark blue-green with maroon, almost black, edging and chrome yellow lining. The power classification was placed below the engine number on the cab sides.

1946 The new Royal coaches were painted in the standard livery.

1946 Pacific engine No. 6234 ("Duchess of Abercorn") was experimentally painted dark blue and lined with 2 in. wide maroon bands.

1946 For the past year there had been observable many different styles of painting and lettering on engines. This was considered to indicate that the authorities were giving a good trial to alternative suggestions before deciding upon a final post-war livery.

1946 (Sept.) A decision was announced as to the standardisation of engine and rolling-stock liveries:—"All engines to be black, with the exception of express passenger types, viz. 'Pacifics', 'Royal Scots', 'Patriots' and 'Jubilees', and will be unlined. The classes named to be painted black and lined out in maroon and straw colour. Carriage stock is to be maroon." (Instead of the shade often described as "Midland red".)

LONDON, MIDLAND AND SCOTTISH RAILWAY CREST

LONDON AND NORTH EASTERN RAILWAY

Consisting of

NORTH EASTERN
GREAT CENTRAL
GREAT EASTERN
GREAT NORTHERN
HULL AND BARNSLEY (*amalgamated with N.E.R. in* 1922)
NORTH BRITISH
GREAT NORTH OF SCOTLAND

And the following:

Subsidiary Companies

(I) Independently operated lines
- (1) Colne Valley and Halstead
- (2) East and West Yorkshire Union
- (3) Mid-Suffolk Light

(II) Non-working Companies

(A) *Originally leased to or worked by North Eastern Railway*
- (4) Brackenhill Light
- (5) Forcett
- (6) Great North of England
- (7) Clarence and Hartlepool Junction

(B) *Originally leased to or worked by the Great Central Railway*
- (8) Humber Commercial Railway and Dock
- (9) Mansfield
- (10) North Lindsey Light
- (11) Seaforth and Sefton Junction
- (12) Sheffield District

(C) *Originally leased to or worked by the Great Eastern Railway*
- (13) London and Blackwall

(D) *Originally leased to or worked by the Great Northern Railway*
- (14) East Lincolnshire
- (15) Horncastle
- (16) Nottingham and Grantham
- (17) Nottingham Suburban
- (18) Stamford and Essendine

(E) *Originally leased to or worked by the North British Railway*

(19) Edinburgh and Bathgate
(20) Forth and Clyde Junction
(21) Gifford and Garvald
(22) Kilsyth and Bonnybridge. (joint with Caledonian Railway)
(23) Lauder Light
(24) Newburgh and North Fife

(F) *Originally leased to or worked by the Hull and Barnsley Railway*

(25) South Yorkshire Junction.

(G) *Originally leased to or worked by several companies*

(26) Nottingham Joint Station (Committee)
(27) West Riding Railway (Committee)

Joint Railways

(I) Joint with L.M.S.R.

(1) Axholme Joint
(2) Cheshire Lines Committee (two-thirds share)
(3) Dumbarton and Balloch
(4) Dundee and Arbroath (including Carmyllie Light Railway)
(5) Great Central and Midland Joint
(6) Great Central, Hull and Barnsley and Midland Joint (two-thirds share)
(7) Great Central and North Staffordshire Joint
(8) Great Northern and London and North Western
(9) Halifax and Ovenden
(10) Halifax High Level
(11) Manchester, South Junction and Altrincham
(12) Methley (two-thirds share)
(13) Midland and Great Northern Joint
(14) Norfolk and Suffolk Joint Committee (Great Eastern and Midland and Great Northern Joint)
(15) Oldham, Ashton and Guide Bridge
(16) Otley and Ilkley
(17) Perth General Station (one-third share)
(18) Prince's Dock, Glasgow (one-third share)
(19) South Yorkshire Joint (three-fifths share)

(20) Swinton and Knottingley
(21) Tottenham and Hampstead

(II) Joint with Great Western Railway
(22) Great Western and Great Central Joint

(III) Jointly leased or worked with several companies
(23) East London (one-sixth share with Southern Railway, three-sixths share, with Metropolitan and Metropolitan District)

(IV) Railways comprised after grouping wholly in the L.N.E.R.
(24) Great Northern and Great Eastern Joint
(25) Hull and Barnsley and Great Central

LONDON & NORTH EASTERN RAILWAY COAT-OF-ARMS (*page 310*)

LONDON AND NORTH EASTERN RAILWAY

THE London and North Eastern Railway system was originally divided into four areas: Southern, North-Eastern, Southern Scottish, and North Scottish; but later the two Scottish regions were fused into one. Broadly, the colour-scheme of the locomotives of the group followed that of the old North Eastern Railway, whilst that of the passenger rolling-stock was similar to that of the Great Northern Railway.

CHIEF MECHANICAL ENGINEERS

H. Nigel Gresley (later Sir Nigel Gresley)	1923–1941
Edward Thompson	1941–1946
A. H. Peppercorn	1946 until Nationalisation

1923 On February 22nd nine engines were exhibited at Marylebone Station in various liveries with a view to choosing the final scheme of decoration for L.N.E.R. locomotives. They were as follows:—

No. 1534 (ex-G.E.) was painted in bright green with black bands and white lines, with chocolate framing with a fine yellow line above the foot-plate and a black line below. The motion was painted vermilion. On the tender "L. & N.E.R." appeared in 6 in. gold letters with full-stops between each character, and the engine number in 12 in. letters below.

No. 876 (ex-N.B.) "Waverley" in the same style as No. 1534.

No. 874 (ex-N.B., "Dunedin") in North British dark brown livery, but with tender-lettering as on No. 1534.

Nos. 1472 (ex-G.N.R.) and 2207 (ex-N.E.R.) were in the new style of livery.

No. 2169 (ex-N.E.R.) was in the old N.E. style but with number and lettering on the tender as on No. 1534.

Nos. 449 (ex-G.C.R.) and 3 (ex-G.C.R.) were in the new style livery.

No. 503 (ex-G.C.R.) was in the old G.C. style but with L.N.E. lettering and numbering.

1923 The L.N.E.R. company's arms, as authorised by the College of Arms are technically described as follows:—

"Argent on a Cross Gules between in the first and fourth quarters a Griffin segreant Sable in the second a Rose of the second leaved and slipped proper and in the third quarter a Thistle also leaved and slipped proper the Castle of Edinburgh proper between Lions passant guardant Or. And for the crest On a Wreath of the Colours Issuant from Clouds of Steam the figure of Mercury Proper."*

1923 The locomotive "Flying Scotsman", when exhibited at Wembley Exhibition, had the L.N.E.R. coat-of-arms on the cab-sheets. This was not a regular livery, but was done for exhibition purposes only.

1923 (Aug.) Engines Nos. 2169 (ex-N.E.), 1418 and 484 (ex-G.N.), 874 "Dunedin", (ex-N.B.) and 503 "Somme", and 451 (ex-G.C.) were running in their old companies colours, but with L.N.E.R. surmounting the large original numbers on their tender side-sheets. Ex-G.C. tank engine No. 1131 was also similarly liveried.

1923 A few tank and small tender-engines had at first been (5), described in sources as green, on various sections of the L.N.E.R., but the standard practice later became so that all engines with driving-wheels under 6 ft. in diameter were painted black, and that all actual express engines were green.†

Passenger stock was in the old Great Northern teak but lettered L.N.E.R. with letters affixed to show to which section they were originally attached.

Horse-boxes were painted chocolate brown, with the letters N.E.

1923 (Nov.) Ex-Great Eastern 0–6–0 tank engine No. 191 was probably the only Great Eastern engine still running in the old blue livery.

1923 On engine No. 1447 the "L.N.E.R." was in very small letters, and a small number-plate was fitted on the cab sides. A large date-plate (1908) appeared on the front driving-wheel splasher.

* See footnote on page 32.

† "Glen" class engines were painted green, although their driving-wheels were smaller than 6 ft. in diameter.

1923 No. 2368 (ex-N.E.R.) was painted black with red lining.
No. 1182 (ex-G.C.R.) was painted in the standard L.N.E.R. livery, but No. 474 (ex-G.C.R.) was liveried in black with a broad vermilion line edged with a fine white line.

1923 "Atlantic" type engines ex-N.E., G.N., and N.B. retained the standard L.N.E.R. green livery until 1939.

1923 Great Central engines of the " B–5", "B–6", "B–7", "B–8" and "B–9" classes were painted black, with red lining, but the lining was continued about 1940.

1923 When Great Central engines were first painted in the L.N.E.R. style, they had their original numbers raised by 5,000 and the suffix "C" added to the new number. Ex-Great Eastern locomotives appeared with the suffix "E", ex-Great Northern engines with the suffix "N", and North British locomotives, "B". Coaches were renumbered, the prefix "1" being added to East Coast Joint stock vehicles, "2" to ex-North Eastern, "3" to ex-North British, "4" to ex-Great Northern, "5" to ex-Great Central, "6" to ex-Great Eastern and "7" to ex-Great North of Scotland.

1923 Great Central "D–9" class engines continued to be painted standard L.N.E.R. green until 1928. Engines of the "Director" class were painted standard L.N.E.R. green (15).

1923 Engine No. 191 was still painted blue (late 1923).

1923 (c) The later engines of the "A–5" class were painted (15), described in sources as green, not black, which latter colour was the standard for L.N.E.R. tank types. The engines were, however, lettered in the standard L.N.E.R. style of the time. For some years after grouping, after they had been repainted glossy black, they continued to have a white line additionally to the standard red one, and continued thus until 1939.

1924 (Jan.) The green head-discs on the L.N.E.R. were changed to blue to avoid confusion of green headlamps at night, the latter also being changed to blue.

1924 The L.N.E.R. renumbering scheme came into operation. North Eastern engines remained as before, but Great Northern ones were advanced in number by 3,000, Great Eastern by 7,000, Great Central by 5,000 and North British by 9,000.

1924 Engine No. 4737 (ex-G.N. 0–6–2T) was painted all black, with vermilion lining, which was the standard style. Engines Nos. 9153, 9734, 9428, were renumbered without being repainted in the new colours, but 9504 and 9062 were renumbered and painted,

No. 9504 in L.N.E.R. green and No. 9062 in L.N.E.R. black. Two ex-G.E.R. "Clauds" (Nos. 8792 and 8797) reappeared painted grey, whereas Nos. 8790 and 8893 were in green (15).

1924 Several engines which had the 9000 added to their original number were still appearing in the old North British livery. (e.g. "Hazeldean", No. 9878).

1924 Ex-G.C. locomotives of the "0–4" class were painted standard L.N.E.R. green, and continued thus until 1939.

1924 Late in this year the old Great Eastern 2–4–0 engine No. 427 still bore traces of her original blue livery with red lining-out.

1925 The ex-G.C. engine "Valour" was repainted in the new green, and her name-plates were retained, whilst the "Director" class locomotives were being named in old North British style with gold letters on the driving-wheel splashers (e.g. 6378 "Bailie Macwheeble").

1925 Goods brake vans were painted brown and lettered "N.E." in white block characters.

1925 The name-plates were regrettably removed from the old G.C.R. Memorial engine, "Valour".

1926 The company designation and coach numbers were reversed in position on some of the 3rd class suburban stock (e.g. coach number 3327); the number being at the left-hand end of the coach and "L.N.E.R." at the right.

1928 The fifty new Sentinel-Cammell railcars were officially to be painted in two distinctive colour-schemes (*a*) vermilion and cream and (*b*) green and cream; in both cases the cream to occupy the upper panels. They were to be named after famous road coaches of olden days.

1928 The practice of placing the engine numbers in transfer form on the cab sides was returned to during this year.

1928 Certain of the old M. and N.B. (Midland clerestory) coaches were absorbed and were repainted in L.N.E.R. standard "teak" colour.

1928 Great Central "Director" class locomotives were painted black with red lining, and continued thus until 1939–40.

1928 Great Central "Atlantic" engines were painted black.

1928 Some tank engines (e.g. No. 2680) appeared with "L.N.E.R. 2680" in two lines on the tanks, and a very small number-plate on the bunker.

1928 (Aug.) It was officially announced that all passenger engines with the exception of "Pacifics", "Atlantics" and "Shires", were to be painted black with vermilion lining-out; this livery replacing the green previously in use. Goods engines were to be black, but devoid of the red lining.

1928–34 Teak coaches were lettered with a gold "L.N.E.R." and class number (as "3") in large figures. Coach numbers were in small serif characters, as was the designation "GUARD", etc.

1929 Ex-Hull and Barnsley engine No. 130 (0–6–0) had the crest which denoted that the engine had seen service overseas in the 1914–18 war. This decoration had a bursting grenade above and three blue chevrons below. Several North Eastern engines of the 0–8–0 type also had this badge.

1929 Later engines of the "Shire" class carried numbers on their cab side-sheets and L.N.E.R. only on the tender. This style was later used for all tender types.

1929 The new railcar trailer cars were painted green and cream to match the railcars themselves.

1929 The engine "Aerolite" was repainted for preservation in York Railway Museum.

1929 Some engines (e.g. No. 9881) had number-plates on their rear driving-wheel splashers.

1930 (c) "Atlantic" type engines had framings a deep chocolate red (as old G.N.R.) edged with black, picked out with white lines.

1930 For at least six years after this date "K–3" engines were lined similarly to the' 'P–1's", but had L.N.E.R. only on the tender, shaded to the right and below, and the engine number (*e.g.* 1125) in large figures on the cab sides. Date-plates were fixed on the smoke-box sides, and were painted black.

1931 The ex-N.E. Raven 4–4–4T engines, when rebuilt, carried the letters L.N.E.R. in small block letters with the number (*e.g.* 2162) below on the tank sides. Date-plates were carried on the bunker sides.

1931 "J–38" engines had their numbers unshaded on the cab sides and "L.N.E.R." unshaded on their tenders. Engine number (1434) appeared in small shaded figures on the front buffer-beam, the words "Class—J–38" being painted in black underneath the number along the lower edge of the beam.

1933 The Gresley "Pacifics" were painted green (5) and their boilers banded throughout. Foot-plate valances were lined, but there was no lining below the frames. Wheels had their tyres lined white, and there was a white ring round the hubs. Axle-ends were black. Date-plates were oval brass, and were fixed on the sides of the smoke-box. The engine numbers were in gold characters, shaded below and to the right, being placed on the cab sides. The letters "L.N.E.R." appeared in the same style on the tender sides. The cabs were unlined, but the tender was lined black, flanked with white with rounded corners, and a white outer line between the body green and the black outer panel. Cylinders were unlined (*e.g.* engine No. 2751).

1933 The engine "Claud Hamilton" as rebuilt was lined, but was devoid of brass beadings. The date-plate was placed on the front driving-wheel splashers, and a standard L.N.E.R. name-plate was fitted with raised brass letters on a red background. The tender was treble lined and the boiler banded. There was no lining on the cab.

1933 The lower panels of tourist trains were painted engine green.

1934 (Jan.) There was some talk of Royal ("G.E.R.") blue being used as the locomotive colour.

1934 Green was used as an engine body-colour only on "Pacifics", "Sandringhams", "Shires", "Hunts", G.N., N.E. and N.B. "Atlantics" (*not* G.C. "Atlantics"), "Sir Sam Fay" class, and on the "Super-Clauds" used for Royal train working. The selection seemed to have been made in such a way that a proportion of each of the bigger express engines from each of the constituent companies should be painted green.

1934 Engines permitted to work over the Frölich rail-brakes at Whitemoor (March) marshalling yard, had a small vermilion-coloured diamond painted over the engine number.

1934 Boards inscribed "L.N.E.R. —— TRAIN —— FOLLOWING" were placed on the last coach of trains which were to be followed by a second portion of the same train, or by a "special".

1934 The engine "Sir Sam Fay" (No. 5423) was decorated by Neasden shed staff with a "sun", "star", and "crescent" on the smoke-box door as a token of pride in the engine. No. 6024 had a "star" painted in the same position.

1934 The original camping coaches (old G.C.R.) were painted L.N.E.R. green all over and lettered "LNER — CAMPING — 25" (*e.g.*) They were six-wheeled stock with wooden headstocks.

1935 "Silver Link" (No. 2509) was finished in metallic aluminium throughout. Cab windows were brass-beaded, and lettering was chrome yellow, shaded to the right and below. "SILVER LINK" appeared in block letters on the boiler casing.

The coach bodies on the "Silver Jubilee" express which was first hauled by "Silver Link" on September 27th, 1935, were covered with aluminium-faced rexine of a silver-grey colour. Stainless steel letters were fixed to the rear vestibule-shield "THE—SILVER—JUBILEE".

1936 The standard passenger express engine livery was green, lined out in black and white. Underframes were black, lined out in red. Lettering and numbers were in gold, with red, white and black shading. Other passenger engines were black, lined red. Lettering and numbers were in chrome yellow with red and brown shading.

Goods engines were all black, without lining. Lettering and numbers were in chrome yellow, shaded in red and brown.

Coaches were finished in varnished teak with gold lettering shaded red and black. Lining was in red and yellow.

Tourist trains were engine green up to the waist, and cream above. Roofs were white.

1936 "P–1" class engines (*e.g.* No. 2393) ran with unlined tenders, the letters "L.N.E.R." appearing thereon above the engine number in gold characters shaded to the right and below. The boilers were banded with double red lines, and very small oval brass number-plates were fitted on the cab sides. The date-plates were placed on the smoke-box sides.

1936 The five A–4 "Pacifics" built for the "Coronation" service were painted "garter blue", with stainless steel lettering, numbering and fittings. Wheels were dark crimson red.

The coach bodies of the "Coronation" trains were painted garter blue up to the waist-line and Marlborough blue above, again with stainless steel lettering, mouldings and exterior fittings.

1936 Coaching stock built by Cravens (Nos. 711–712 *e.g.*) was lined similarly to the L.N.E.R., but with the letters "C.L.C." (Cheshire Lines Committee) in lieu of L.N.E.R.

1936 Camping coaches were painted green lower panels and cream upper ones, and were lettered *e.g.* "LNER — CC27".

1936 Touring camping coaches (old G.C.R. "Baldwin" stock) were painted (5), described in sources as green, and cream, and were lettered "TOURING CAMPING COACH — CC66" in shaded block letters. The carline was painted green, and end vestibule door panels were cream.

1936 Many buffet cars and some dining cars were painted green and cream to match in with special trains of excursion vehicles painted in those colours.

1937 (c) Standard passenger engines of the L.N.E.R. were painted in the old Great Northern green with black banding and white lining, this scheme appearing on the boiler, cab, splashers and tender tanks. Wheel centres and spokes were green, but everything else below the foot-plate was black, including the outside framing to the trailing wheels of "Pacifics" and their tender underframes.

1937 The engine "City of London" (No. 2870) had the boiler-casing lined with black and white bands, with a black "flash" from the chimney-fairing to the front buffer-beam, thence backward over the driving-wheels to the lower part of the cab. The tender was painted and lined-out normally.

1937 L.N.E.R. locomotive No. 5427 had the number-plates removed, these being remounted on "Sandringham" No. 2870, which was streamlined for hauling the luxury G.E.R. "East Anglian" train.

1937 The stock used on the "West Riding" Limited was decorated similarly to the "Coronation" stock which carried the name of the train on the rear shield. Other streamlined trains carried the name of the train on the vestibule-covers at the rear end of the last coach. The words "WEST RIDING LIMITED" appeared on the coaches in cut-out stainless steel letters.

Rubber streamlining between the coaches was painted to match coach-sides.

The "East Anglian" ran with varnished teak coaches.

1937 The Tourist trains (*e.g.* coaches Nos. 45000, 45001, 45002, and buffet car No. 49511) were green and cream unlined. Lettering was in chrome yellow, and coaches were individually lettered "A to D" in large yellow block characters.

1937 Engineering department rolling stock was painted medium dark blue (23), which colour tended to get lighter as the varnish wore off the paint.

1937 Both of the brake-vans on the Kelvedon and Tollesbury light railway section were lettered "N.E.", and were named "Kelvedon" and "Tollesbury" respectively on their sides.

1938 The "B–17" engines were painted and lined in the same style as that used on the 1933 "Pacifics".

1938 Engines began to appear with "N.E." only on tenders and tanks, shaded and blocked. Very small number-plates were also fitted on the bunkers of tank locomotives.

The "9000" class were treated in this fashion.

1938 The "A–4" engines "Mallard" (No. 4468) and "Sir Nigel Gresley" (No. 4498) were decorated in the same way as the later "Coronations", but polished brass was used instead of stainless steel and the lettering and figures were transfer-applied. The date-plate was fixed to the cab sides and the engine number appeared on the front buffer-beam.

1938 The occasion of the introduction of new trains for the "Flying Scotsman" was marked by the running of Patrick Stirling's famous 8 ft. single engine, which was brought out of York Railway Museum for the purpose. A period train of 6-wheeled coaches was also repainted in the old East Coast Joint Stock livery (see p. 46), complete with crests on the door panels. Engine and train made a special trip from Kings Cross to Stevenage.

1938 Three sets of old North London 4-wheeled coaches were still running in their pre-grouping colours with the N.L.R. crest, but with L.M.S. numbering.

1938 Some of the "J-39's" on the Eastern section appeared with vermilion coupling-rods. They were built at Darlington, and that was the style for those works.

1939 Engines of the V-2 ("Green Arrow") class were treated as the 1933 "Pacifics" (see p. 315), but had their date-plates fitted under the engine number (*e.g.* No. 4471) on the cab sides. There was very little variation between the years 1931 and 1939 as regards express passenger engine liveries. On engine No. 4844 the name-plates were fitted on the middle driving-wheel splashers, whereas on "Green Arrow" itself (No. 4471) the plates were rectangular and were fitted on the sides of the smoke-box.

1939 During the war years nearly all locomotives were painted unlined black, and were devoid of all embellishments. L.N.E.R. engines were lettered "N.E." only.

1940 The decision was officially made to abolish the "3" on the outside of doors of third class coaches, and to leave only the "1".

1941 "S–4" class engines (*e.g.* No. 2798) had tanks panelled with a broad black outer line and a fine white line within it. Smoke-box was black, the boiler banded with black, flanked white. Cylinders were lined.

1941 "A–4" engine "William Whitelaw" (No. 4462) was unlined in respect of the boiler, but had a fine white line around the black "flash" on both sides of the body.

1941 Tyneside electric stock was repainted with dark blue lower panels and "Quaker grey" upper ones. It had previously been painted scarlet vermilion in lower panels and cream in the upper ones.

1942 Class "A–1" engines were being converted into class "A–3", and at the same time they were repainted in the unlined black livery which thus became the standard for all engines on the L.N.E.R.

1942 "J–38's" were liveried as in 1931, but had the company's initials and the engine number on the tender, as well as a small oval brass number-plate fitted on the cab side-sheets.

1942 "J–39's" appeared with a small "L.N.E.R." on the tender, surmounting the engine number (*e.g.* 1448), all being shaded. Small number-plates were fitted to the cab sides. The number in very small figures also appeared on the left end of the front buffer-beam, with the class ("J–39") at the right hand end.

1942 The "A–4" class engine, No. 4496, "Golden Shuttle", as well as other "Coronation" engines had the number on the cab side-sheets in thin block figures of cut-out polished stainless steel. The letters "L.N.E.R." also cut from stainless steel, were affixed widely-spaced on the tender-sides. There were polished steel beadings around the cab windows, and the date-plates were fixed below the number on the cab sides. The engine's name appeared on a long raised rectangular polished steel plate fixed to the side of the smoke-box. In the case of engines bearing the name of a Dominion or country, the appropriate coat-of-arms or badge appeared on a raised plaque in lieu of the date-plate on the cab sides. The engine number and the class ("A–4") appeared on the front buffer-beam.

1942 "Coronation Pacific" No. 4489 carried a whistle of the type used in South Africa. The engine's name was "Union of South Africa". "Coronation Pacific" ("Dominion of Canada") carried a bell in front of her chimney.

1942 (c) Streamlined "B–17's" carried the letters "N.E." only, in shaded gold characters on the tender, and the number on the cab sides. They were unlined. The "B–1" engine "Springbok" (No. 8301) was similarly liveried.

1943 The new "Q–1" class engines were painted black, unlined. They had the number on the tank sides in shaded block characters. The letters "L.N.E.R." were placed on a cigar-shaped totem of brass with raised characters on a vermilion background. These plates were fixed to the bunker sides. On the front buffer-beam appeared "No."——"5058" and below this "CLASS"——"Q–1".

1945 The first L–1 class engines (2–6–4 tanks) appeared in the peace-time livery of green.

1945 The first streamlined "Pacific" to be repainted in pre-war garter blue appeared. The engine was No. 4496, "Golden Shuttle", re-named "Dwight D. Eisenhower". Engine No. 4470 "Great Northern", was repainted experimentally in Royal blue (24), and was lined out in vermilion.

1945 Post-war corridor stock (*e.g.* Nos. 1531, 1347, etc.) were unpanelled steel, lettered in gold "N.E." at one end and No. 1531 (*e.g.*) at the other in serif characters. Brake third corridor No. 152 was lettered LNER but was unlined.

1945 The first of the "L–1" class of 2–6–4T engines was painted in the old peace-time green livery, and gave rise to the hope that some of the principal types of engine would be restored to pre-war brightness.

1946 L.N.E.R. locomotive No. 2871 (rebuilt from class "B–17" into a 2-cylindered class "B–2") was renamed "Royal Sovereign" and renumbered 1671. She was painted green for working Royal trains between King's Cross and Sandringham. The engine "Claud Hamilton" (No. 8783) was also painted green.

1946 The engine "Silver Link" was renumbered 14 and painted blue with chromium plated lettering.

1946 Engine No. 9904 (0–8–4T) ran without the company's initials, only "9904" in yellow block characters appearing on the tank sides.

1946 Straight-sided coaches were unlined and lettered as 1945 stock (*e.g.* No. 7590).

1946 The engine "Great Northern" (No. 4472) was painted in Royal blue (24), lined out in red, as an experiment.

1946 (Sept.) It was announced that the whole of the engine stock of 6,400 locomotives would be painted either green or blue. The streamlined "Pacifics" were to be painted "garter" blue

G.C.R. Locomotive No. 508 in G.C.R. Livery (*p.* 33)

S. & D.J.R. 1st-3rd 4-wheeled coach No. 12 (*p.* 192)

Liverpool and Manchester Railway Coach, 1830 (*p.* 232)

G.W.R. 21-ft. Horse Box, 1920 (*p.* 71)

L.B. & S.C.R. Locomotive No. 421 In Marsh Livery (*p.* 104)

G.E.R. 12-ton Open Steel Framed Wagon, 1903 (*p.* 42)

Old L.B. & S.C.R. Guard's Brake (*p.* 81)

Old L.B. & S.C.R. Flat Wagon (*p.* 81)

S.E. & C.R. Royal Saloon No. 1R, *c.* 1911 (*p.* 204)

Bodmin and Wadebridge 2nd Class Coach (*p.* 217)

and all the others, green, of precisely the same shade and style of livery as that used by the former Great Northern Railway. Even the lining was to be the same. This scheme was never carried into effect.

1946–7 At times small block letters and larger block figures unlined appeared on tanks, with a small number-plate on the bunkers (*e.g.* "V–3", No. 7684).

1946–7 Small lettering and large figures were used on tank engines (*e.g.* No. 1525).

1947 "J–50's" appeared in black, unlined. "N.E." (only) with the engine number (*e.g.* No. 3231) below, on the tank sides in shaded and blocked characters. A very small number-plate was placed on the bunker sides. Engine No. 620 was painted green with single-lined body and steps. "L.N.E.R." with number below was on the tanks, with the date-plate at the front end of the latter. A very small number-plate was fitted to the bunker sides.

1947 Ex-W.D. 2–8–0's had their engine numbers in unshaded small block figures on the cab sides (77170). Others (*e.g.* No. 73777) also had "W.D." in chrome yellow block letters on the tender.

1947 London Outer Suburban coaching stock was devoid of lining, neither was it panelled (*e.g.* Nos. 90322 and 80323). Most of the Marylebone suburban twin sets had brown-painted buffer sockets. The new sleeping cars were teak finished, and were devoid of both lining and panelling.

Early 1948 The Gresley "Pacific" engine No. 1470 ("Great Northern") was repainted in the old Great Eastern style, but was later (as No. 113) again repainted in the standard L.N.E. apple-green livery. Large letters on tenders and large numbers on cab-sides were used on passenger engines.

Coat-of-arms on page 309

SOUTHERN RAILWAY

Consisting of

LONDON AND SOUTH WESTERN
LONDON, BRIGHTON AND SOUTH COAST
SOUTH EASTERN
LONDON, CHATHAM AND DOVER } SOUTH EASTERN AND CHATHAM RAILWAY COMPANIES' MANAGING COMMITTEE

And the following:

Subsidiary Companies

(I) Independently operated lines
- (1) Freshwater, Yarmouth and Newport (Isle of Wight)
- (2) Isle of Wight
- (3) Isle of Wight Central
- (4) Bere Alston and Callington section of the Plymouth, Devonport and South Western Junction Railway

(II) Non-working companies

(A) *Originally leased to or worked by the L.S.W.R.*
- (5) Bridgewater
- (6) Lee-on-Solent
- (7) North Cornwall
- (8) Plymouth and Dartmoor. ($2\frac{1}{4}$-mile portion)
- (9) Plymouth, Devonport and South Western Junction (excepting Bere Alston and Callington (No. 4, above))
- (10) Sidmouth

(B) *Originally leased to or worked by the L.B.S.C.R.*
- (11) Brighton and Dyke
- (12) Hayling

(C) *Originally leased to or worked by the South Eastern or London, Chatham and Dover Railways*
- (13) London and Greenwich
- (14) Mid-Kent

Joint Railways

(I) Railways comprised after grouping, wholly in the Southern Railway
- (1) Croydon and Oxted
- (2) Dover and Deal
- (3) Epsom and Leatherhead
- (4) Tooting, Merton and Wimbledon
- (5) Woodside and South Croydon

(II) Joint with other companies

(6) East London. (three shares with L.N.E.R. Metropolitan one share and Metropolitan District, one share)

(7) Easton and Church Hope. (joint with Great Western Railway)

(8) Somerset and Dorset. (joint with L.M.S.R.)

(9) West London Extension. (2 shares, with Great Western and L.M.S.R. one share each)

(10) Weymouth and Portland. (joint with Great Western Railway)

(III) Absorbed by London and South Western Railway

(11) Lynton and Barnstaple. (not covered by the Railways Act, (1921))

SOUTHERN RAILWAY

THE organisation of this group consisted of a Board of Directors, a Chairman, and a "headquarters" system consisting of a General Manager and other officers, assisted by Divisional officers in assigned districts. The colour eventually selected for passenger locomotives approximated to that used by the London and South Western constituent of the group immediately before amalgamation, but the green used for passenger rolling-stock struck quite a novel note in the South of England.

CHIEF MECHANICAL ENGINEERS

R. E. L. Maunsell	1923–1937
Oliver Vaughan Bulleid	1937 until Nationalisation

1923 Corridor boat stock was painted olive-green, relieved by chrome yellow lining. The class number was on the end vestibule doors and carriage numbers appeared near the entrance doors. "SOUTHERN RAILWAY" in gold was in the centre of the top panel.

Late 1923 Maunsell's "River" class engine (No. 790), built in 1917, was running unnamed and with its number in large block figures on the tank sides; in pre-group livery.

The body-colour of coaches was (21), described in sources as olive-green, lined with a ½ in. black line inside the panels and a ⅛ in. chrome yellow line outside the black. Steel stock was lined above and below the waist-line, but wooden-bodied stock was lined above only.

1923 (Dec.) No official statement had yet been issued as to colours or liveries, but a number of vehicles were running lettered Southern Railway and painted green.

1924 The ex-S.E. & C.R. engine No. 685 was the second to be painted in the foregoing new style.

Ex-S.E. & C.R. coaches repainted in green carried a block letter "A" on their ends to distinguish them as old S.E. stock. The numerals "1" and "3" were no longer used on the doors to distinguish classes, but "First" and "Third".

In June the Waterloo and City rolling-stock was repainted green and lettered "Southern Railway".

On the Isle of Wight the engine "Ventnor" was painted the standard green and numbered "15W", and was the first to be liveried in this style. It was followed by the Isle of Wight Central engine (No. 8) "8W", and the Freshwater and Newport engine No. 2 (2W). Island coaches were to be seen in the new colours, and some of the wagons were lettered "S.R.".

By February no official decision as to livery had been reached, but, notwithstanding, some vehicles were painted green and lettered Southern Railway. In some quarters it was considered highly probable that Marsh umber might be adopted as the standard engine colour.

1924 At some time between March and June it was officially decided to paint all passenger locomotives the old L.S.W. sage-green (Urie) (21), with large gilt numerals on the tanks or tenders, and the single word "SOUTHERN" above the number. Lining was to be in mid-chrome yellow. No number-plates were fitted on the cab sides, and those already in place were removed, but the engine number appeared inside the cab, and also on the buffer-beams.

Goods engines were painted black.

The first engine on the old L.S.W.R. to appear in the new style was No. 94.

1924 Engines on the Southern Railway (Eastern Section) had the letter "A" placed above their numbers, and 1,000 was added to their original number.

1924 The 0–6–0 tank engine "Boxhill" was painted black and renumbered 380S.

1925 The ex-L.B.S.C. engine No. 70 ran for some months with her name "Devonshire" revealed on the left-hand side only.

Engine No. 542 was running in (21), described in sources as standard Southern dark green livery.

Isle of Wight locomotives were renumbered in date of building order.

Stroudley 0–6–0 tank engine No. 136 was the last L.B.S.C. locomotive to bear number-plates, these being removed this year.

The Southern Railway announced that their express engines were to be named. The name-plates were of brass with raised polished letters on a dark green background, *e.g.* "King Arthur". Below the name the words "King Arthur Class" appeared upon a slight extension to the name-plate.

The engine colour for passenger types was the same as that introduced by Mr. Urie in 1913–14.

Engine No. 326 (formerly "Bessborough" on the L.B.S.C.) was painted in the new Southern style, but with her number-plate affixed to the back panel of the bunker.

1925 The standard coach livery as appearing on the Waterloo-Bournemouth service was officially stated as "green", relieved with black and yellow lining.

1925 The first grouping style of livery included the word "SOUTHERN" in compressed serif capitals, underneath which was a small letter ("A", "B", or "E" according to the pre-grouping section), and beneath this again the engine number in block characters.

The ex-L.B.S.C. engine "Remembrance" (No. 333) had her name in block letters on the tank sides, and "SOUTHERN", "B", and the engine number in three lines on the bunker sides. The memoriam plate was left in its original place below the name on the tank side. Engine No. 325 (previously "Abergavenny", L.B.S.C.), however, had the three-line lettering arrangement on the tank sides, the bunker sides being left blank.

The rebuilt Drummond 4–4–0 express engines (*e.g.* No. 338) retained their original brass number-plates on the cab sides in addition to the normal three-line lettering on the tender which was the standard position for it. All tender engine types with very few exceptions were rendered devoid of cab side-sheet number-plates.

The Maunsell "River" class engines were quite an exception to normal livery in that the word "SOUTHERN" was placed on the tank sides above the large brass plate carrying the engine's name (e.g. "RIVER AVON"). The "A", above the number, which was in very large block numerals, was placed on the bunker sides.

At this time the old L.B.S.C. "Atlantics" had not been named, though naming was officially contemplated.

1925 (June) The painting of passenger engines was changed to a darker and bluer shade of green similar to the coaches. The standard coach lining was black and yellow (*e.g.* the new Bournemouth stock).

1926 There was a partial return to the practice of placing brass number-plates on the engine cab sides (*e.g.* "Lord Hawke"; E 860 was thus fitted in 1930).

1926 The engine "Lord Nelson" was lined out with a single chrome yellow line, and all beading round cab windows was polished brass.

1926 Engine No. 734, an 0–4–0 saddle-tank late of the L.S.W., was the only engine from that section to retain her name-plate ("Clausentum"). Her number-plate was carried low down on the framing.

Several ex-L.B.S.C. engines retained their old brown livery, but had standard Southern numbers painted on their cab sheets. Some, however, had old type "Brighton" figures reinstated, but upon the tender, under the initials "L.B.S.C."; the engine itself carrying only plates (*e.g.* Nos. 59, 191, 423, and 49). The background colour of name-plates at this time on the Brighton section of the Southern Railway was vermilion, and one or two "Atlantics" (*e.g.* No. 422) as well as No. 329 ("Stephenson") were similarly treated. Engine No. 333 ("Remembrance") was the only Southern locomotive which preserved the old "Brighton style" of painted name on tanks.

1928 The new dining-cars were painted "green", relieved with fine orange and black lines.

1928 The 4-wheeled General Utility vans built at this time were painted olive-green, with pale green interiors.

1929 Many repainted steam and electric coaches appeared in a very dark green shade.

Engine No. B612 (0–4–2T) still retained its copper-topped chimney.

Engines of the "496" and "823" classes were painted passenger engine green.

Isle of Wight engines passing through the Ryde shops were fitted with red background number-plates on the back of their bunkers. This applied to engines Nos. 1, 2, 3, 13, 19, 20, 22, 23, 24, 28 and 32. In some cases the number-plate was bordered with a thick black and a thin white line to harmonise with the name-plate borders.

"D–1" tank No. B249 was the only engine of the old Brighton Railway which remained in Brighton livery.

1931 Ex-S.E. & C.R. engine No. 353s was awaiting scrap at Ashford, but was still in her pre-group colours.

1932 Inspection engine and saloon (No. 58S) was painted Brunswick green, for both the engine and car. It was lettered "S.R." on the tank sides in chrome yellow block characters of the same shape, size and style as that formerly used by the London and South Western Railway. The engine carried three round white headboards with vermilion rims—one at each extremity of the buffer-beam and one in front of the chimney.

1934 The last "B–1" class engine carried the L.B.S.C. number (B172) until she was broken up this year.

1934 Coaches commenced to be fitted with small raised circular plates at their ends, bearing the numbers "0" to "6"; the figures indicating the group of lines over which the particular vehicle could work.

1934 The engine "Hecate" (No. 949) was repainted dark green, including the name-plates, which were thereby rendered almost invisible.

1936 The passenger locomotive colour was Brunswick green, lined out with black and white. Number-plates were of brass, on which the characters stood out against a vermilion background.

Goods engines were painted black, lined out in pale green.

Coaches were Brunswick green, lined out in orange and black (orange outside the panels). Lettering was in gold with black shading.

1936 Passenger luggage vans ("General Utility" vans) were painted standard green with black underframes, running-gear, and brake-wheels. Solebars were also black. Lettering was in mid-chrome yellow block characters.

1937 Camping coaches were painted olive green with the words "CAMPING COACH" in 9 in. chrome yellow block letters in the lower panels. The words "SOUTHERN RAILWAY" appeared in standard style over the quarter-lights.

1937 (c) The standard livery for Southern locomotives was a middle green rather inclining to olive shade above the foot-plate, edging being black and lining white. All below the foot-plate was black, with the exception of the wheels, cylinders and step-plates, which were green.

1938 (July) The buffet cars built for the Portsmouth service were the first Southern Railway vehicles to be painted in (14), described in sources as Malachite green. They were unlined and bore the words "BUFFET CAR" along the top of the waist. (*e.g.* No. 12519).

1938 (July) Coach body colour was changed to (14), described as malachite green (specification No. 912). Black and chrome lining remaining as in 1923.

1938 (August) Malachite green began to be used for express engines.

1938 (August) (14), described as the new standard malachite green, livery was fully introduced on the trains built for the 12.30 and 4.30 down Waterloo–Bournemouth service, and for the 5.37 and 7.42 up trains between those stations. Numerals replaced words to denote class distinctions on the doors.

Six "School" class engines (No. 928, "Stowe", 929, "Malvern", 930, "Radley", etc.) were specially painted in malachite green (14) to match the trains. The word "SOUTHERN" appeared on the tender sides in larger letters, and the engine numbers were painted on the cab side-sheets.

1939 No final official decision had yet been reached in reference to changes in livery. Much stock had been painted in malachite green, and the changes in the style of lettering and numbers became almost standard practice.

On tender engines the number was transferred from the tender to the cab sides, being represented there in smaller figures. The word "SOUTHERN" in block, outlined letters remained on the tender.

Coaches had the word "SOUTHERN" below the windows instead of above them as previously, and all lining was omitted.

1939 (Dec.) Certain engines and coaching stock appeared painted in the old olive-green shade, devoid of all lining. Engines appeared with "SOUTHERN" on tanks or tenders in Gill-sans lettering, with a gold line round each letter. The engine number was shown in plain block figures on the cab of tender engines or on the bunker of tank types. Engine numbers ceased to be painted on the back of tenders or bunkers as they had been previously.

Coaches had the word "SOUTHERN", in the same style as that used on the engines, placed in the centre of the coach immediately below the windows, in the position that it had previously occupied in the case of corridor coaches with large windows carried right up to the eaves. This positioning was used instead of the words "SOUTHERN RAILWAY" being placed above the windows.

Class distinctions were indicated by numerals placed at the same level as the word "SOUTHERN", instead of being on the lower part of the doors (suburban stock), or shown in words ("FIRST" or "THIRD") (main-line stock).

This description of the livery as it was in December, 1939, must not be taken as referring to any new official standard style, as it had quite recently been announced that the question of standard colours and livery styles was still in abeyance. The liveries described are of miscellaneous stock as running at this date.

1940 The "Lord Nelson" class engine No. 852 was painted in olive-green, as was "Schools" class No. 927. They were the first engines of their class to be so painted at the time, and the light green livery appeared to be in abeyance.

Some of the 0–6–2 tank engines (Nos. 2399, 2497, 2562), and class "I–1x" No. 2602 were repainted unlined green with the engine number on the bunker and "SOUTHERN" on the tanks. Engine No. 2109 ("E–2") was, however, repainted black, with 6 in. numerals on the bunker sides.

Engine No. 2520 (4–4–2T) was painted in a lighter shade of green, and the only classes which were olive-green were "Schools", "Lord Nelsons", "N–15x", "N–15", "H–1", "H–2" and "H–15". The three last classes were, however, unlined. All these engines carried their numbers on the front buffer-beam only, instead of on both buffer-beams.

Engine No. 2255 (B255) was the first of its class (D–1) to be painted in the new style of lettering and without lining. It was never numbered as 2255 in the old style.

1940 The word "SOUTHERN", together with the engine number, began to appear in unshaded gold lettering and black shaded numerals on engines which were painted either green or black.

1941 The (14) livery, described in sources as green, was abandoned, for all but 150 of the 1,800 steam engines, the remainder being painted black. A new style of block lettering was evolved which retained on the black engines some of the previous malachite green in the form of shading which made the gold-coloured lettering stand out and thus offset somewhat the lack of lustre so noticeable with the gold-leaf previously used. No lining was used. The same style of block lettering was adopted for the remaining green engines, but with black shading and gold-coloured highlights.

A new standard style of block letters and figures were adopted for use on engines, coaches, and all other rolling-stock.

1941 Engines began to be painted black, and lettering to be shaded in malachite green, shot with yellow.

1941 Engine No. 21C3 ("Royal Mail") had the word "SOUTHERN" on the tender in a new style of shaded lettering. Horizontal lines of chrome yellow extended the whole length of engine and tender. The engine number appeared in chrome-yellow block characters above the front buffer-beam. A flat (annular) ring bearing the word "SOUTHERN" against a red background, was fitted centrally in front of the smoke-box. Special name-plates (different for each engine) consisted of a flat circular plate with "wings" on either side. The words "Merchant Navy Class" appeared on the wings, and around the circular portion the name of the shipping line (*e.g.* "Royal Mail"). In the centre of the circle was placed the house flag of the appropriate shipping company in full colours.

1941 The war-time engine livery was unlined black with gold lettering shaded green.

1943 There was at this time a bewildering variety of shades of green observable on coaches. Apart from the original olive, there was included a very bright light green, as well as a darker and yellower shade; both varieties being seen lined and unlined. The word "SOUTHERN" appeared at various different levels on the coach sides. Even newly-painted stock was seen at Hove (evidently fresh from the shops) carrying such variations.

1944 (c) The ½ in. black line was omitted from the 1923 livery.

1944 A chrome yellow solid triangle was painted on the buffer-beams of some ex-L.B.S.C.R. engines to indicate that they had been altered to conform with the standard Southern Railway composite loading-gauge. They were thus permitted to run over sections which were prohibited to engines not so altered and marked.

1945 "West Country" engines appeared in almost exactly the same general livery as that used on the "Merchant Navy class", but they had the name of West country towns in raised brass lettering on a folded stretch of brass ribbon over the appropriate shield of the town concerned. Below the shield was another narrower ribbon bearing the words "West Country Class".

1946 The white squares painted on coaches to indicate that the vehicle conformed to A.R.P. lighting regulations were still to be seen on many vehicles.

1946 (c) The chrome yellow line was omitted, thus leaving the malachite green devoid of all lining. This livery continued up to nationalization.

1948 (early) Ashford-built 8-wheeled General Utility vans were in green livery, numbered in gold block figures shaded black. Lettering was in golden yellow. These vehicles mostly remained in this livery, even after being repainted, as late as April, 1951.

SOUTHERN RAILWAY

LONDON PASSENGER TRANSPORT BOARD

FORMED April 13th, 1933, by the amalgamation of the

METROPOLITAN RAILWAY
METROPOLITAN DISTRICT RAILWAY ("DISTRICT" RAILWAY)
CENTRAL LONDON RAILWAY
BAKERLOO AND WATFORD EXTENSION RAILWAY
CITY AND SOUTH LONDON RAILWAY
GREAT NORTHERN AND CITY RAILWAY
GREAT NORTHERN, PICCADILLY AND BROMPTON RAILWAY

1933 Engines were a rich red (darker than "Midland" lake) and were lined with thick black, edged with chrome yellow. The engine number was in raised brass figures placed on the tanks or bunkers with the engine class number below it. The engine number and class were also placed on the back of the bunker in large chrome yellow characters. The word "METROPOLITAN" appeared on the tanks in chrome block letters above the number. At one time the company's crest was placed on the tanks in lieu of the number encircled by the words "METROPOLITAN RAILWAY" in chrome yellow. Buffer-beams were painted vermilion, and were devoid of lettering.

1933 Reconstructed cars carried large yellow boards with "CIRCLE" thereon in black letters.

1934 (late) The 1933 style was replaced by "INNER CIRCLE" in white letters on a blue background. Some stock had a circular target painted vermilion, behind the words; but this was only in the nature of an experiment.

The words "LONDON TRANSPORT" was painted in full on the tanks of ex-Metropolitan engines, and later in the year engine numbers appeared in large figures on the bunker back panels.

1938 "UNDERGROUND" new trains were finished a bright red, with cream verticals between the windows. Lettering was in gold, and roofs medium grey. Solebars and underframes were black. Each door carried a white label "Please keep clear of the doors". The grey rubber push-buttons for door-opening have a raised orange-yellow surround lettered in black "Press to open". Over the driver's door the words "NO ENTRANCE" appears in black.

Destination boards are in white on black, and besides these another board carried the word "BAKERLOO" in white on a black ground and "PICCADILLY" in black on a yellow ground.

1938 As an experiment for two months, trains on the Harrow and Watford service of the Bakerloo line had a broad blue stripe along their upper panels, the red and buff standard colouring remaining. They were known as "Blue" trains in contradistinction to the "Red" ones which terminated at Queen's Park.

1943 The bronze name-plates on Metropolitan electric locomotives were removed for scrap metal. One still remains out of the twenty in the L.P.T.B. Museum. In place of the plates the standard London Transport lettering was displayed in gold against a vermilion background on a board attached to the locomotive side. The liveries of the engines were also changed from crimson-lake with a gold lining to London Transport "service" grey with a vermilion line between the roof and the body. The engine number (1 to 20) was carried on a large vermilion-coloured disc at each end of the engine. Buffer-beams were vermilion and underframes black.

APPENDIX A

Classified List of Pre-group Locomotive Colour Plates which have been published in the "Railway Magazine" and the " Locomotive Magazine"

N.B.—The figures in the first column give the engine number, and those in the second the volume in which the plate appears. "L" *refers to the* "Locomotive Magazine", *and* "R" *to the* "Railway Magazine".

BELFAST AND NORTHERN COUNTIES

No. 62	R 10/11
No. 70	R 40

CALEDONIAN RAILWAY

No. 50	R 13
No. 664	R 24
No. 766	R 5
No. 769	L 3
No. 903	R 21
No. 918	R 20
Express Train	R 30

CAMBRIAN RAILWAYS

No. 81	R 8

COUNTY DONEGAL RAILWAY

No. 21	L 18

FURNESS RAILWAY

No. 96	R 25
"Coppernob"	R 20
Express (*circa* 1850)	L 15
Express Train	L 15

GLASGOW AND SOUTH WESTERN RAILWAY

No. 74	R 9
No. 241	R 20
No. 265	R 16
No. 384	R 15
4–6–0 locomotive	R 32
Express Train	R 29
Express Train	R 35

GREAT CENTRAL RAILWAY

No. 81	R 5
No. 192	R 15
No. 258	R 19
No. 434	R 35
No. 1090	R 24
No. 1113	R 23
Express train	R 25
Express train	R 27
Express train	R 29
Express train	R 30
Express train	R 35

GREAT EASTERN RAILWAY

No. 10	L 4
No. 284 (Sinclair)	L 7
No. 789	R 14
No. 1245	R 32
No. 1500	L 18
No. 1501	R 33
No. 1520	R 41
No. 1870	L 7
No. 1900	R 8
Express train	R 28
Express train	R 30
Express train	R 35
Ambulance train	L 21

GREAT NORTHERN RAILWAY

No. 1	R 10/11
No. 1 and train at Highgate Station	L 22
No. 190	R 22
No. 251	R 16

"Jubilee" locomotive L 4
"Experiment" locomotive R 41
Express train R 31
Express train R 30
Express train R 29
Express train R 34

LONDON AND SOUTH WESTERN RAILWAY

No. 70 ("Aerial") L 18
No. 310 L 7
No. 330 R 18
No. 335 R 22
No. 343 R 13
No. 395 R 15
No. 706 R 5
Express trains (two) R 28
Express train R 27
Express train R 29
Express train R 34

LANCASHIRE AND YORKSHIRE RAILWAY

No. 816 R 20
No. 1400 R 5
No. 1421 R 21
No. 1510 R 25
Express train R 27
Express train R 34
Express train L 17

LONDON, TILBURY AND SOUTHEND RAILWAY

No. 39 R 26, L 13 and L 14

MIDLAND RAILWAY

No. 116 L 3
No. 117 R 6
No. 386 R 28
No. 483 R 33
No. 999 R 21
No. 2000 (tank) R 24
No. 2601 R 8
No. 2632 R 13
Locomotive R 13
Locomotive R 19
Train and station R 17
Express train R 30
Express train R 34
Express train L 11

MIDLAND AND GREAT NORTHERN JOINT RAILWAY

No. 53 R 28
4-4-0 locomotive

MIDLAND AND GREAT WESTERN RAILWAY (I)

No. 7 R 25
No. 6 R 41
Express train R 31

NORTH BRITISH RAILWAY

No. 317 R 14
No. 411 R 42
No. 729 R 8
No. 868 R 20
No. 884 R 22
No. 898 L 15
No. 899 R 26
Express train R 30 and R 34

NORTH EASTERN RAILWAY

"R" class loco. R 21
No. 1237 R 24
No. 649 R 15
No. 695 L 14 and R 25
No. 717 L 18
No. 730 L 12
No. 733 R 32
No. 2001 R 6
No. 2111 R 9
No. 2015 R 6
No. 1352 R 26
No. 2212 R 45
Express train R 40

NORTH STAFFORDSHIRE RAILWAY

No. 8 (as 2-4-0t) L 18
No. 8 (as 4-4-2t) L 18
No. 9 R 21
No. 39 R 8
No. 114 R 40
Locomotive R 14

South Eastern and Chatham Railway

No. 490	R 15
No. 504	R 21
No. 516	R 23
No. 735	L6 and R 9
No. 764	R 35
Express train	R 29
Express train	R 32

Somerset and Dorset Joint Railway

No. 89	R 34

Taff Vale Railway

No. 39	R 25

APPENDIX B

List of British Railway Locomotives and Vehicles preserved by the British Transport Commission and other bodies

1813 Wylam Colliery locomotive "Wylam Dilly"
1813 Wylam Colliery locomotive "Puffing Billy"
1822 Hetton Colliery locomotive (0–4–0)
1825 Stockton & Darlington Railway locomotive "Locomotion" (0–4–0)
1829 Shutt End Railway locomotive "Agenoria"
1829 Liverpool & Manchester Railway locomotive "Rocket"
1829 Locomotive "Sans Pareil"
1829 Locomotive "Rocket" (replica)
1829 Locomotive "Novelty" (replica)
1830 Canterbury & Whitstable Railway locomotive "Invicta"
1830 Killingworth Colliery locomotive
1834 Bodmin & Wadebridge Railway composite coach
1834 Bodmin & Wadebridge Railway second-class coach
1834 Bodmin & Wadebridge Railway open third-class coach
1837 G.W.R. locomotive "North Star" (replica) (2–2–2)
1838 Liverpool & Manchester Railway locomotive, "Lion" (0–4–2)
1840 Stockton & Darlington Railway locomotive tender No. 18
1842 London & Birmingham Railway: Queen Adelaide's royal coach
1845 Stockton & Darlington Railway locomotive No. 25 "Derwent" (0–6–0)
1845 Grand Junction Railway locomotive No. 45, "Columbine" (2–2–2)
1845*c* Stockton & Darlington Railway chaldron wagon
1845 Stockton & Darlington Railway composite coach
1846 Stockton & Darlington Railway composite coach (No. 31)
1846 Furness Railway locomotive No. 3 "Coppernob" (0–4–0)
1847 L. & N.W.R. locomotive No. 173 "Cornwall" (2–2–2)
1850*c* Eastern Counties Railway carriage
1850*c* South Hetton Colliery chaldron wagon No. 1155
1850 Forcett Railway coach
1857 Wantage Tramway locomotive No. 5 "Shannon" (0–4–0WT)
1860*c* N.E.R. third-class coach
1861 North British Railway dandy-coach
1865 L.N.W.R. narrow-gauge locomotive "Pet" (0–4–0T)
1865 L.N.W.R. locomotive No. 1439 (0–4–0T)
1866 Metropolitan Railway "A" class locomotive No. 23 (4–4–0T)
1866 Midland Railway locomotive "Class 1" No. 158A (2–4–0)
1868 South Devon Railway locomotive (broad-gauge) "Tiny" (0–4–0)

1869 N.E.R. locomotive No. 66 "Aerolite"
1869 L.N.W.R. royal saloon (Queen Victoria)
1870 G.N.R. locomotive Stirling No. 1 (4–2–2)
1870 Seaham Harbour chaldron wagon
1872 North London Railway directors' saloon No. 1032
1872 Metropolitan Railway tram locomotive No. 807 (0–4–0)
1874 Furzebrook Tramway locomotive "Secundus"
1874 Bauxite No. 2 locomotive
1874 N.E.R. locomotive No. 1275 (0–6–0)
1875 N.E.R. locomotive "901" class No. 910 (2–4–0)
1880 L.B. & S.C.R. locomotive No. 82 "Boxhill" (0–6–0T)
1882 L.B. & S.C.R. locomotive No. 214 "Gladstone" (0–4–2)
1883 Portstewart Railway tram engine No. 3
1885 N.E.R. locomotive "1463" class (2–4–0)
1885 West Coast Joint Stock P.O. sorting van No. 186
1885 Midland Railway, 6-wheeled composite coach
1885 Mersey Railway locomotive "Cecil Raikes" (0–6–4T)
1886 Caledonian Railway locomotive No. 123 (4–2–2)
1889 Lancashire & Yorkshire Railway locomotive "K–2" class No. 1008 (2–4–2T)
1889 City & South London Railway electric locomotive No. 1
1890 City & South London railway coach
1892 L.N.W.R. locomotive "President" class No. 790 "Hardwicke" (2–4–0)
1893 N.E.R. locomotive "M–1" class No. 1621 (4–4–0)
1893 L. & S.W.R. locomotive "T–3" class No. 563 (4–4–0)
1893 Shropshire & Montgomery Railway locomotive "Gazelle" (0–4–2T)
1894 Highland Railway locomotive No. 103 (4–6–0)
1894 G.E.R. locomotive "T–26" class No. 490 (2–4–0)
1895 Duke of Sutherland's locomotive "Dunrobin"
1897 G.W.R. locomotive "2301" class No. 2516 (0–6–0)
1898 G.N.R. locomotive No. 990, "Henry Oakley" (4–4–2)
1898 Highland Railway locomotive "Ben Alder" No. 2 (4–4–0)
1898 East Coast Joint Stock third-class saloon
1899 Midland Railway locomotive "115" class No. 118 (4–2–2)
1899 Duke of Sutherland's private saloon
1900 L.N.W.R. royal dining-saloon No. 65
1901 Belfast & County Down Railway locomotive
1901 S.E. & C.R. locomotive "D" class No. 737 (4–4–0)
1902 G.N.R. locomotive "C–1" class No. 251 (4–4–2)
1902 Midland Railway locomotive "Class 4" No. 1000 (4–4–0)
1903 L.N.W.R. King Edward's royal saloon
1903 L.N.W.R. Queen Alexandra's royal saloon
1903 L.S.W.R. coach No. 6474
1903 G.W.R. locomotive No. 3717, "City of Truro" (4–4–0)

1904 G.E.R. "P–57" class, No. 87 (0–6–0)

1906 Larne Aluminium Works locomotive

1907 G.W.R. locomotive "Star" class No. 4003, "Lode Star" (4–6–0)

1909 London, Tilbury & Southend Railway locomotive No. 80, "Thundersley" (4–4–2T)

1910 War Department locomotive "Woolmer"

1913 North British Railway locomotive "Glen" class No. 256 "Glen Douglas" (4–4–0)

1914 Midland & Glasgow and South Western Joint Railways, dining-car No. 3463

1914 Pullman car "Topaz"

1919 G.C.R. "11F" class No. 506 "Butler Henderson" (4–4–0)

1920 Great North of Scotland Railway locomotive "F" class No. 49, "Gordon Highlander" (4–4–0)

1923 G.W.R. Castle Class No. 4073 "Caerphilly Castle" (4–6–0)

1934 G.W.R. diesel railcar No. 4

1947 G.W.R. "94xx" class No. 9400 (0–6–0T)

APPENDIX C

Initials borne by Pre-Group Rolling Stock and Wagon-Sheets *circa* 1896

Barry Railway

Coaching stock lettered "Barry Coy", wagons lettered "Barry Coy". Wagon sheets were initialled Barry Coy., with three red bars at right-angles.

Belfast and County Down Railway

Coaching stock, wagons, and wagon sheets were lettered "B.C.D.R."; the sheets being devoid of any other distinguishing marks.

Belfast and Northern Counties Railway

Coaching stock, goods stock, and wagon sheets were lettered "B.N.C.R."; sheets being devoid of any other distinguishing marks.

Brecon and Merthyr Railway

Coaching stock and goods stock were lettered "B. & M.R.", wagon sheets being initialled "Brecon and Merthyr Railway" across the centre, and "B. & M." with the number on each corner.

Caledonian Railway

Coaching stock, goods stock and wagon sheets were lettered "C.R.", the sheets being also marked with a blue "X".

Cambrian Railways

Coaching stock, goods stock, and wagon sheets bore the word "CAMBRIAN", the sheets being also marked with a blue and red "X" with a Prince of Wales' Feathers on each side of it.

Cheshire Lines Committee

Coaching stock was lettered either "CHESHIRE LINES" or "C.L.C". Wagons had the words "CHESHIRE LINES" on the sides, and C.L.C. on the sole-bars. Wagon sheets had a wavy white line round their borders.

Colne Valley and Halstead Railway

Coaching stock, goods stock, and wagon sheets were lettered "C.V.R.", and the sheets carried no other special markings.

Cork, Bandon, and South Coast Railway

Coaching stock and goods stock were lettered "C.B.S.C.R."

Dublin, Wicklow and Wexford Railway

Coaching stock, goods stock, and wagon sheets bore the letters "D.W.W.R."

East and West Junction Railway

Coaching stock, goods stock, and wagon sheets bore the letters "E. & W.J.R."

Furness Railway

Coaching stock was lettered "F.R.", wagons "FURNESS", and wagon sheets "F.R.C."

Garstang and Knott End Railway

Coaching stock was lettered "GARSTANG AND KNOTT END RAILWAY", goods stock, "G. & K.E.R.", and wagon sheets as the goods stock.

Glasgow and South Western Railway

Coaching stock was lettered either "G. & S.W.R." or "M.S.J.S." Wagons and their sheets bore the initials "G. & S.W."

Great Eastern Railway

Coaching stock goods stock, and wagon sheets bore the initials "G.E.R.", the sheets carrying the company's crest and a 1½ in. wide red stripe from corner to corner.

Great North of Scotland Railway

Coaching stock was initialled either "G.N.S." or "G.N.S.R." Goods stock carried the full name—"GREAT NORTH OF SCOTLAND RAILWAY". Wagon sheets were lettered "G.N.S.R."

Great Northern Railway

Coaches were lettered "G.N.R.", and wagons either "G. NORTHERN R." or simply "G.N." Wagon sheets had the words "GREAT NORTHERN RAILWAY" and the sheet number at each side. "G.N.R." and the number also appeared at each end, and "G.N.R." on the back. The sheets carried blue and white stripes from corner to corner.

Great Northern Railway (Ireland)

Coaches, wagons and sheets were lettered "G.N.R.", the sheets also being distinguished by red and blue stripes crossed diagonally.

Great Southern and Western Railway

Coaches, wagons, and sheets were lettered "G.S. & W.R.", the sheets also being distinguished by a single red stripe from corner to corner.

Great Western Railway

Coaches, wagons, and wagon sheets were initialled "G.W.R.", the sheets also bearing a white stripe at right-angles, and the company's crest at each end.

Gwendreath Valleys Railway

Wagons bore the initials "G.V.R."

Highland Railway

Coaching stock bore initials "H.R.", and wagons the word "HIGHLAND". Wagon sheets were lettered "H.R."

Hull, Barnsley, and West Riding Junction Railway and Dock (Hull and Barnsley Railway)

Coaching stock was either lettered "H.B. & W.R." or "HULL, BARNSLEY, AND WEST RIDING JUNCTION RAILWAY"—in full. Wagons were initialled either "H. & B.R." or "H.B. & W.R.J.R. & D. Co." Sheets bore the initials "H. & B.R.", and were further distinguished by a red and white crossed stripe.

Lancashire and Yorkshire Railway

Coaches were lettered "L.Y.R.", as were the wagon sheets. Wagons, however carried the full name: "LANCASHIRE & YORKSHIRE". Wagon sheets carried the full name of the company, together with the word "MANCHESTER" and red and white stripes.

London, Brighton and South Coast Railway

Coaches, wagons, and wagon sheets bore the initials "L.B. & S.C." Sheets were devoid of any further distinguishing marks.

London, Chatham and Dover Railway

Coaches, wagons, and wagon sheets bore the initials "L.C. & D.R." Sheets were devoid of any other distinguishing marks.

London and North Western Railway

Coaching stock was lettered "L. & N.W.R.", whilst wagons and their sheets were initialled "L. & N.W." Wagon sheets were distinguished by a red cross.

London and South Western Railway

Coaching stock carried the name in full, and wagons were initialled either "L. & S.W.R." or "L.S.W.R." No distinguishing marks were made on the wagon sheets, which either bore the letters "L. & S.W.R. Co." or "L.S.W.R."

London, Tilbury and Southend Railway

Coaches, wagons, and wagon sheets carried the initials "L.T. & S.R.", the sheets being further distinguished by a blue stripe across from corner to corner.

Manchester and Milford Railway

Coaching stock and wagons bore the letters "M. & M.R.", whilst wagon sheets were inscribed "MANCHESTER AND MILFORD RAILWAY".

Manchester, Sheffield and Lincolnshire Railway

Coaches, wagons, and sheets were lettered "M.S. & L."; the sheets being further distinguished by a five-pointed yellow star and red and yellow stripes.

Manchester, South Junction and Altrincham Railway

Coaching stock was lettered "M.S.J. & A.R." Wagons carried the full name of the company, and wagon sheets were lettered "M.S.J. & A. Ry."

Maryport and Carlisle Railway

Coaches, wagons and sheets were lettered simply "M. & C."

Metropolitan Railway

Coaches were lettered "METROPOLITAN RAILWAY". Wagons "METROPOLITAN" on each side, and "Met. W Rly." on the sole-bars. Sheets had "METROPOLITAN W RAILWAY" in the centre of the sheet, with "Met. Rly." and the sheet number in each corner. Corners were painted red.

Metropolitan District Railway

Coaches were marked "DISTRICT RAILWAY" and wagons "D.R."

Midland Railway

Coaches and wagon sheets were lettered "M.R.", and wagons, "M.R. MIDLAND RAILWAY". Wagon sheets were further distinguished by a yellow border with a white Maltese Cross at each end of the sheet.

Midland and Great Northern Joint (Committee) Railway

Coaching stock was initialled "Jt. M. & G.N.", whilst some wagons were similarly lettered. Other wagons were still running lettered "EASTERN AND MIDLANDS RAILWAY". This also applied to the wagon sheets, some of which were lettered "Jt. M. & G.N." and others "EASTERN AND MIDLANDS RAILWAY". Later sheets also carried a diagonal white cross and white cornering.

Midland and South Western Junction Railway

Coaches were marked "MIDLAND & SOUTH WESTERN JUNCTION" and "M. & S.W. Jc. R." Some older passenger stock was initialled "S.M. & A.R." Some wagons were marked "M. & S.W. Jc. R.", and others "S.M. & A.R., their sheets showing the same variations of inscription.

Midland Great Western Railway

Coaches, wagons, and sheets bore the initials "M.G.W.R."

Neath and Brecon Railway

Coaches were lettered "N. & B.R." Some wagons bore "N. & B.R." and others "NEATH AND BRECON".

North British Railway

Coaches, wagons and wagon sheets bore the letters "N.B.R." Wagons and their sheets also bore a white quatrefoil on a black ground as a distinguishing mark.

North Eastern Railway

Coaches, wagons and wagon sheets were lettered "N.E.R.", the sheets being further distinguished by a white cross at each corner of the sheet, on the back.

North London Railway

Coaching stock and wagons were initialled "N.L.R." (The company possessed no wagon sheets.) First class coaches bore the full name of the company on its crest.

North Staffordshire Railway

Coaching stock, goods stock, and wagon sheets bore the letters "N.S.R.", the wagon sheets being further distinguished by a "Staffordshire" ("True lovers") knot, and the name of the sheet contractors.

Pembroke and Tenby Railway

Coaches and wagons were initialled "P. & T.R.", whilst wagon sheets carried the full name of the company.

Portpatrick and Wigstownshire Joint Railways

Coaching stock and goods stock bore the letters "P.P. & W."

Rhondda and Swansea Bay Railway

Coaching stock, goods stock, and wagon sheets bore the initials "R. & S.B.R."

Rhymney Railway

Coaching stock was lettered "R.R.", wagons, "RHYMNEY" and wagon sheets either "R.R. Co.—RHYMNEY RAILWAY"; also carrying two white bars across, from corner to corner.

Somerset and Dorset Joint Railway

Coaches, wagons and sheets were lettered "S. & D.J.R."

South Eastern Railway

Coaching stock and goods stock was initialled "S.E.R." Wagon sheets were characteristically marked with a red double cross with the letters "S.E.R." and the sheet number displayed around the cross, thus:—

Taff Vale Railway

Coaches and wagons were marked "T.V.R., and wagon sheets bore the same letters with the sheet number at each side and end. There were also red and green stripes on each sheet, from corner to corner.

Waterford and Central Ireland Railway

Coaching stock, goods stock, and wagon sheets bore the initials "W. & C.I.R."

Waterford, Limerick and Western Railway

Some coaches were lettered "W.L.R." and others "W.L. & W." Some wagons were initialled "W.L.R." and others "W.L. & W."; whilst the majority were further distinguished with a small white Maltese cross. Wagon sheets were lettered to coincide with the wagons, either "W.L.R." or "W.L. & W."

Waterford, Dungarvan and Lismore Railway

Coaching stock and goods stock were lettered "W.D.L.R."

West Lancashire Railway

Coaches, wagons and sheets were initialled "W.L.R.", and the sheets were further distinguished by two white triangles of solid colour placed either side of the sheets number, the bases of the triangles being next to the number.

Wirral Railway

Coaching and goods stock, as well as wagon sheets were initialled "W.R."

Wrexham, Mold, and Connah's Quay Railway

Coaching stock, goods stock, and wagon sheets were lettered "W.M & C.Q.R."; the sheets being further distinguished by a chrome yellow right-angled cross.

APPENDIX D

Linings and Diagrams (*vide* Figs. 1-109)

FIG.

1 Banded Corner Lining.
2 Squared Corner Lining.
3 Rounded Corner Lining.
4 Incurved Corner Lining.
5 Inverted Corner Lining.
6* Recessed Corner Lining.
7* Outside Greek Fret.
8* Inside Greek Fret.
9* Inverted Loop.
10* Inverted Band.
11* Square Incurved Band.
12 Inset Rounded Band ("Ogee").
13* Square Panel and Outside Fret.
14 Shading and Highlights on letter.
15 Wheel Lining.
16 Letter shading and Blocking.
17 Boiler banding and lining.
18 Splasher and pierced footplate lining.
19 Spring and spring-hanger lining.
20 District Railway locomotive. Portion of tank panel, showing number and style of lettering.
21 Great Northern Railway Stirling "single" locomotive, showing numbering.
22 Barry locomotive number-plate.
23 Building plate on Great Northern Stirling "single" locomotive.
24 Great Eastern Railway locomotive number-plate with compressed numerals.
25 Great Eastern Railway locomotive number-plate with normal numerals—on rebuilds.
26 Great Eastern Railway locomotive number-plate on "Claude Hamilton".
27 Great Eastern Railway locomotive name-plate on "Claude Hamilton".
28 Name-plates of Great Western Railway locomotive "North Star".
29 & 30 Name-plates and crests on Great Western Railway locomotives "Armstrong" and "Agamemnon."

* These types of corner lining, although known (c. 1902) to have existed, cannot be traced in surviving records of locomotive lining schemes. They were, however, not necessarily confined to any one class of locomotive or to any particular railway, but, in the days of hand-painting, were used at the painter's discretion.

31 Great Western Railway locomotive number-plate.
32 Cab side-sheet and number-plate from Great Western locomotive "Edgcumbe".
33 Lettering on bronze axle-box cover of Great Western locomotive.
34 Number-plate from Great Western locomotive "Great Bear".
35 Portion of name-plate from Great Western locomotive "Lord of the Isles", showing style of lettering.
36 Name-plate and date-plate, Great Western locomotive "Great Bear".
37 Great Western locomotive number-plate showing style of figures.
38 Great Western monogram as used on tender of locomotive "Great Bear".
39 Great Western locomotive name-plate, showing how short names were accommodated thereon.
40 Great Western locomotive name-plate, showing style of lettering.
41 Great Western Railway crest.
42 Highland Railway "Jones" goods locomotive No. 111, showing cab side-sheet lining details.
43 North British Railway "Holmes" locomotive No. 592, showing cab side-sheet lining details.
44 Lancashire and Yorkshire "Aspinall" 4–4–2 locomotive, showing cab side-sheet lining details.
45 London and South Western Railway locomotive lining details on cab side and bunker of Adams 0–4–4T.
46 Manchester Sheffield and Lincolnshire Railway locomotive cab side lining and numbering.
47 London and North Western locomotive No. 2798, showing cab side-sheet lining details.
48 London and South Western Railway locomotive splasher lining.
49 Highland Railway "Jones" goods locomotive showing details of splasher and sandbox lining, also Sharpe Stewart building plate.
50 Caledonian Railway locomotive number-plate.
51 North Eastern Railway tender lettering, lining, and crest.
52 Name-plate from London and North Western locomotive "Patriot".
53 London and North Western Railway standard "Webb" locomotive number-plate.
54 London and North Western Railway crest.
55 Portion of London and North Western coach, showing style of lining and lettering.
56 Name-plate from London and North Western locomotive, showing disposition of crest.
57 Name-plate from London and North Western locomotive "Pandora".
58 London and North Western locomotive number-plate, showing style of numerals.
59 Portion of splasher from London and North Western locomotive "Greater Britain", showing coupling-rod splasher lining.
60 Caledonian Railway locomotive number-plate.
61 Highland Railway locomotive name lettering, showing style.

62 Highland Railway "Stroudley" type locomotive number-plates.
63 Great North of Scotland Railway locomotive number-plate.
64 Great North of Scotland builders' plate on locomotive No. 77.
65 Highland Railway locomotive number-plates, showing style of figures.
66 & 67 London and South Western Railway "Nine Elms" locomotive number-plates.
68 London and South Western Railway coupling-rod splasher, showing lining. (Engine No. 687).
69 London, Brighton and South Coast Railway locomotive cab side-sheets and number-plate, showing special corners of lining.
70 London and South Western monogram, as on locomotive No. 580.
71 London and South Western "Neilson" locomotive building plate.
72 North British Railway locomotive number-plate, showing block numerals.
73 London and South Western Railway "Adams" locomotive number-plate, without company's title or building dates.
74 London and South Western Railway. Unshaded style of locomotive numbering.
75 London, Brighton and South Coast Railway, Locomotive name lettering and shading on splasher.
76 London, Brighton and South Coast Railway. Locomotive buffer-beam, showing elaborate lining and shading.
77 Name-plate and splasher of Belfast and County Down Railway locomotive "Parkmount".
78 Lettering and number-plate of Dublin, Wicklow and Wexford Railway locomotive.
79 Number-plate of Belfast and County Down Railway locomotive "Parkmount".
80 Listowel and Ballybunion Railway locomotive number-plate.
81 Great Southern and Western Railway (Ireland) locomotive number-plate.
82 Great Northern Railway (Ireland) crest.
83 Midland Railway. Style of locomotive numbering.
84 Midland Railway. Derby locomotive building plate.
85 Midland Railway. Another style of locomotive numbering.
86 Furness Railway crest.
87 Metropolitan Railway. Painted locomotive number and style of tank lining.
88 North Staffordshire Railway crest.
89 Rhymney Railway. Locomotive tank lining (*c.* 1910).
90 Rhymney Railway. Locomotive tank lining (*c.* 1908).
91 North Eastern Railway locomotive number-plate.
92 & 93 Lancashire and Yorkshire Railway locomotive number-plates.
94 & 95 Great Central Railway locomotive number-plates.
96 North Eastern Railway tender lettering and crest.
97 Lancashire and Yorkshire locomotive plates.
98 Manchester, Sheffield and Lincolnshire Railway locomotive numbers.

99 Lancashire and Yorkshire locomotive plates.
100 North Eastern Railway locomotive cab lining scheme and number-plates.
101 North Eastern Railway "Worsdell and Borries Patent" plate on locomotives.
102 North Eastern Railway Gateshead-built locomotive number-plate.
103 Pullman Car Company crest.
104 & 106 Two styles (block and serif) of Great Northern Railway locomotive number-plates.
105 Great Northern Railway locomotive builders' plate, (1885).
107 & 109 South Eastern Railway locomotive plates.
108 South Eastern Railway "Neilson" number-plate (1891).